Hotel America

Hotel America

Scenes in the Lobby of the Fin-de-Siècle

◆

LEWIS H. LAPHAM

VERSO

London • New York

For Joan

First published by Verso 1995
© Lewis H. Lapham 1995
All rights reserved

Verso
UK: 6 Meard Street, London W1V 3HR
USA: 180 Varick Street, New York NY 10014–4606

Verso is the imprint of New Left Books

ISBN 1–85984–952–0
ISBN 1–85984–062–0 (pbk)

British Library Cataloguing in Publication Data
A catalogue record for this book is available from the British Library

Library of Congress Cataloging-in-Publication Data
Lapham, Lewis H.
Hotel America : scenes in the lobby of the fin-de-siècle / Lewis H. Lapham
p.   cm.
Includes index.
ISBN 1–85984–952–0. — ISBN 1–85984–062–0 (pbk.)
1. United States — Politics and government — 1989 – 1993.
2. United States — Politics and government — 1993 – I. Title.
E881.L37 1995
973.92—dc20   95–21592 CIP

Typeset by Keystroke, Jacaranda Lodge, Wolverhampton
Printed and bound in Great Britain by Biddles Ltd,
Guildford and King's Lynn

Contents

SOCIETY

CULTURE

CONTENTS

Introduction

The essays collected in this book describe the several states of confusion visited upon the protectors of the American commonwealth by the abrupt disappearance of the Cold War. The unforeseen collapse of the Berlin Wall in December 1989, which was as much of a surprise to the Central Intelligence Agency as it was to the editors of the *New York Review of Books*, nullified the the *raison d'état* that for nearly fifty years had supplied nine American presidencies with boundless wealth and certain virtue, but the geopoliticians were slow to take the point. The spectacle of the jubilant German crowds dancing under the arches of the Brandenburg Gate was followed by what seemed like a series of always fortunate events—in Prague and Warsaw and the Persian Gulf as well as in Moscow—and the curators of the nation's best opinion (history professors, newspaper columnists, senior statesmen) abandoned themselves to a prolonged and triumphant hymn of praise. Marx was dead, western civilization was saved and what was left to do but make a joyful noise unto the Lord. The more ecstatic prophets of the red, white and blue millennium announced "the end of history" or proclaimed a "new world order," and it wasn't until the late summer of 1991, when the economy had stumbled into severe recession and the gilding had worn thin on the victory in Kuwait, that people began to wonder what they were going to do without the Russians.

The more closely they considered the question, the more clearly the country's ruling and explaining classes understood that the Cold War had furnished the dark blackcloth against which they were accustomed to project the bright images of American innocence and goodness of heart.

The military and foreign policy establishments in Washington had relied on the evil Soviet empire (a.k.a. the Land of Mordor) as the enemy of first resort—as necessary to the American gross national product as General Motors and Iowa corn, as fundamental to the idea of American freedom as the Constitution and the Fourth of July. The constant fear of nuclear annihilation had sustained the constant demand for more weapons and more binding laws, and the obvious failures of Soviet Communism served as cautionary tales proving the perfection of American capitalism. To anybody tactless enough to ask why the government set up surveillance of its own citizens, or why so many Americans were hungry or in jail, the answer invariably turned on the retort: "Yes, but think how much worse things would be in Russia."

But without the Russians, on what new pedestals were we to erect the statutes of America's preeminence in the world, and to whom could we assign the part of the bestial apparition in the alien snow? Tear down the operatic stage set of the Cold War (and with it the cover story for acts of official deceit that otherwise might have been seen as undemocratic or criminal) and what then becomes of the national security state dependent upon the guarantee of permanent war? Remove the menace of a world-encircling Communist conspiracy, and under what set of standing orders do we contain not only the approach of foreign armies but also the outbreak of domestic discontent?

The unfamiliar questions reawakened the American people to the uses of the political imagination. Once free of the atmosphere of incessant crisis and no longer listening to the weekly announcements of imminent doom, they remembered their right to self-government. By and large, they didn't like what they could see of the country's political affairs, and no matter how different their lists of specific grievance—the non-payment of the Pentagon's promised "peace-dividend," the continuing failure of the schools, the rising rates of crime and immigration—they found themselves in perfect agreement on three points of general principle:

1. Over the course of the last forty-odd years something had gone seriously wrong with the American dream. The last time anybody looked —in 1945 before the long march through the labyrinth of the Cold War—the United States was the wonder of an admiring world. Different people cherished different aspects of the happy memory, but everyone was certain that long ago and once-upon-a-time America was the great, good place still visible in the movies starring Gary Cooper or Myrna Loy.

2. Whether composed of Democrats or Republicans, the federal government at Washington was as incompetent as it was corrupt—a parliament of fools befuddled by imbecile social theory, complacently squandering the national treasures on uselsss luxuries and idle toys.

3. It was no longer true that everybody was as equal as everybody else. Owing in large part to the diligence of the Reagan administration, the United States by 1989 had so arranged its financial affairs that 10 percent of the population held at least 70 percent of the nation's wealth, and 5 percent of the population owned all of the nation's capital assets. What was once a democracy apparently had become an oligarchy.

The three propositions were easily divisible into the subsets of further complaint—about multiculturalism, school prayer, junk television—and by the autumn of 1991 (at about the time that the Senate Judiciary Committee confirmed Judge Clarence Thomas's appointment to the Supreme Court) much of what passed for the public conversation in the United States turned on the question, who and what is American? Prior to the collapse of the Berlin Wall, the answer had seemed self-evident. Americans weren't Communists. Americans were the freest and happiest people ever to walk the face of the earth, generous to a fault, always fair and open-minded and on their way to a bright future. Two years later, nobody was sure of any of the old axioms, and the future was beginning to look a good deal less sunny than it was pictured in the travel advertisements.

By the winter of 1992 the comforting certainties of the Cold War were sorely missed, and during that year's election campaigns most of the country's politicians were hard-pressed to define what they meant by the word democracy. Democracy for whom? For the corporations that hired the high-priced lobbyists or the citizens who paid the tax bills? The general feeling of disgust with Washington found its loudest and most vivid expression in the populist harangues of H. Ross Perot, who lost the election but tuned the instrument of American politics to what soon became its distinctive note of resentment. Although briefly interrupted by the rise and fall of President Bill Clinton's image in the public opinion polls, the storm of words has continued unabated and unresolved for the last three and one-half years, amplified by the chorus of scornful voices calling in their objections to the talk radio shows, carried forward through the 1994 congressional elections by the furious recriminations of Newt Gingrich, now the Speaker of the House of Representatives, already projected into next year's presidential elections by the scolding presence of

Pat Buchanan and Senator Phil Gramm, both of them promoting their candidacies for the Republican nomination on the promise to recall the American people—if necessary by exceedingly harsh disciplinary measures—to their rightful state of prosperity and grace.

The polemic is angry but at the same time wistful. Like Rush Limbaugh's legion of self-styled "ditto-heads," the politicians talk about the glories of Walt Disney's American past, and instead of raising questions that might prove relevant to the next century (the ones about the biological sciences and the communications technologies, about America's changed place in the world and its urgent need of a revised plan for sharing the nation's wealth) they dwell on the questions of conduct and deportment once dear to the hearts of nineteenth-century churchmen. Instead of asking why the country assigns more money to the building of prisons than it does to the building of schools, the keepers of the nation's conscience complain about the scenes of violence at the movies and deplore the sexual conduct of fourteen-year-old welfare mothers. On the campaign hustings they pose for the television cameras in the attitudes of exemplary self-righteousness, showing themselves off as the kind of people who know what it means to meet a payroll or break a horse, who stand on their own feet and chop their own wood. When in need of an easy laugh or a bracing round of applause, they make fun of their less fortunate fellow citizens. Senator Gramm, as alert as a prizewinning dog to the scent and spirit of the times, already has advanced a particularly hard line against both the extravagant distribution of food stamps ("We're the only nation in the world where all our poor people are fat") and the coddling of old people with expensive medical treatments ("Most people don't have the luxury of living to be eighty years old, so it's hard for me to feel sorry for them").

Listening to the campaign speeches, I think of the sentimental revivals geared to the Broadway musical comedy crowd and to the nostalgic remembrance of an America that was once as rich as it was safe, Gary Cooper's America, an America famous for its apple cider and happy endings. Similarly elegiac longings show up in the Sunday newspaper editorials regretting the loss of civic virtue, or in the journal articles wondering what happened to the study of great books, and if so much of what now goes by the name of political argument borrows the liturgical vocabulary better suited to a church, it's because the argument has less to do with the reconfiguring of the American government than it does with the reformation of the American character.

For the last six years the angriest debates in Congress and the news media have taken as their texts the condition of the country's morals rather than the condition of its rivers, jails, schools and roads. The same questions find expression in the muffled euphemisms for gender, race and social class as well as in the blunt explosions of mail and truck bombs. Nearly always they can be traced back to the disappearance of the Cold War. In the absence of the Communist conspiracy and the Russian antagonist on the totalitarian steppe, who is the protagonist on the freedom-loving prairie? What kind of people do we wish to become, and how do we know an American when we see one?

The questions remain unanswered because, for the time being and preferably for as long as possible, we would rather not fill out the printed forms. Too definite an answer might limit our options and subtract from the sum of our contradictions. Possibly it's true that chastity is a lost American art, and certainly it's true that not many high school students know the names of Homer and Michelangelo and Robert E. Lee, but it's also true that we lead the world in the consumption of cocaine as well as in the manufacture of pornographic film and the construction of gambling casinos, and maybe we're not as anxious to repent (at least not yet) as the evangelical Republicans on Capitol Hill would have us believe. The substitution of the questions of individual character for the ones about the nature and purpose of our collective enterprise—an enterprise that might encompass the hopes of the poor as well as the interests of the rich —allows us to find fault with the world at hand (never a difficult trick) and so postpone, perhaps indefinitely, the task of imagining the world as it might become. In the meantime, while waiting for divine revelation or a run of luck, we vote presidents and moralists in and out of office as if they were transient vaudeville acts, and we go on conceiving of the American commonwealth as a resort hotel deserving of respect in the exact degree to which it satisfies the whims of its patrons and meets the public expectation of convenience and style at a bargain price.

The essays in this book, most of them sketches and observations rather than sermons or suggestions for reform, describe the period of adjournment between the winter of 1989 and the spring of 1995 in which the American explaining classes were casting around for a national folk tale to take the place of the Cold War, and the American electorate, suspicious of all things political, was wondering what it was exactly that a government, any government, was supposed to do. The essays often take a comic turn because so many of the rebukes and admonishments sound like the complaints to the hotel management about the rudeness of the staff and the quality of the other guests. Where is the family entertainment and why does the management permit obscene dancing in the lounge? Who are those awful people seated under the windows in the dining room and why can't the chamber maids speak English?

In a society still rich enough to afford a politics expressed as a Puritan inspection of souls and made to the measure of *The Larry King Show*, the eminent guests pass through the lobby on their way to one of 10,000 conferences about risk-free environments or the meaning of the deficit. While waiting for something really important to turn up (a new revolution in Russia, say, or a race riot in northeast Washington) they come and go talking of Thomas Jefferson and the Internet, admiring one another's moral poses, dismayed by the rumors of war and second-hand smoke, wondering whether it might not be possible to put the whole of the country, or at least the continental forty-eight states, behind bars or under glass.

GOVERNMENT

TAX AND SPEND What all elected politicians do for a living. An occupation, like nursing or carpentry, not an ideological program.

BUDGET REFORM Noble cause.

CONGRESSIONAL DEBATE Ritual performances meant to sustain the belief in democracy.

GRIDLOCK A comfort presented as an affliction.

THE AMERICAN PEOPLE Admired and excessively praised as an abstraction but distrusted when encountered in person. Too many of them cling to the superstition that their money is their own.

PRESIDENCY (THE) Awesome office.

Democracy in America?

The spirit of liberty is the spirit
which is not too sure it is right.
— JUDGE LEARNED HAND

*O*ver the course of the last eighteen months, no American
politician worth his weight in patriotic sentiment has missed
a chance to congratulate one of the lesser nations of the earth
on its imitation of the American democracy. The tone of the compliment
is invariably condescending. The politician presents himself as the smiling
host who welcomes into the clean and well-lighted rooms of "the
American way of life" the ragged and less fortunate guests, who—sadly
and through no fault of their own—have wandered for so many years
in ideological darkness.

The orators haven't lacked edifying proofs and instances. First, the
Chinese students in Tiananmen Square, holding aloft a replica of the Statue
of Liberty against the armies of repression. Next, the German crowds
dancing on the ruin of the Berlin Wall; then, the apprentice democrats
triumphant in Budapest and Warsaw and Prague; then, Gorbachev in
Washington, amiably recanting the Communist heresy to his new friend
in the White House. And always the Americans, saying, in effect, "You see,
we were right all along; we were right and you were wrong, and if you
know what's good for you, you will go forth and prosper in a bright new
world under the light of an American moon."

At the end of last summer Ronald Reagan was in Berlin, conducting a
seminar for the East Germans on the theory and practice of democracy;

9

John Sununu, the White House chief of staff, was in Moscow, showing the hierarchs in the Kremlin how to organize the paperwork of a democratic government; a synod of American journalists had gone off to Budapest to teach their Hungarian colleagues how to draft a First Amendment; in Washington the chief correspondent of the *New York Times* was celebrating the crisis in the Persian Gulf as great and glorious proof that the United States had regained its status as the world's first and foremost superpower, that all the dreary talk about American bankruptcy and decline was just so much sniveling, trendy rot.

I listen to the speeches and read the bulletins in the newspapers, and I marvel at my own capacity for the willing suspensions of disbelief. Humming along with the self-congratulatory cant on *Nightline* and *Face the Nation* or beating four-quarter time with the jingoists' chorus in *Newsweek*, I forget for the moment that we're talking about a country (the United States of America, a.k.a. "the light of hope and reason in a dark and discordant world") in which the spirit of democracy is fast becoming as defunct as the late Buffalo Bill. About a country in which most of the population doesn't take the trouble to vote and would gladly sell its constitutional birthright for a Florida condominium or another twenty days on the corporate expense account. About a country in which the president wages war after consultation with four or five privy councilors and doesn't inform either the Congress or the electorate (a.k.a. "the freest, happiest and most enlightened people on earth") until the armada has sailed.

Although I know that Jefferson once said that it is never permissible "to despair of the commonwealth," I think it is possible that the American experiment with democracy may have run its course. Not because of the malevolence or cunning of a foreign power (the Russians, the Japanese, the Colombian drug lords, Saddam Hussein), but because a majority of Americans apparently have come to think of democracy as a matter of consensus and parades, as if it were somehow easy, quiet, orderly and safe. I keep running across people who speak fondly about what they imagine to be the comforts of autocracy, who long for the assurances of the proverbial man on the white horse likely to do something hard and puritanical about the moral relativism that has made a mess of the cities, the schools and primetime television.

If the American system of government at present seems so patently at odds with its constitutional hopes and purposes, it is not because the practice of democracy no longer serves the interests of the presiding oligarchy (which it never did) but because the promise of democracy no longer inspires or exalts the citizenry lucky enough to have been born under its star. It isn't so much that liberty stands at bay but, rather, that it has fallen into disuse, regarded as insufficient by both its enemies and its nominal friends. What is the use of free expression to people so frightened of the future that they prefer the comforts of the authoritative lie? Why insist on the guarantee of so many superfluous civil liberties when everybody already has enough trouble with the interest rates and foreign cars, with too much crime in the streets, too many Mexicans crossing the border and never enough money to pay the bills? Why bother with the tiresome chore of self-government when the decisions of state can be assigned to the functionaries in Washington, who, if they can be trusted with nothing else, at least have the wit to pretend that they are infallible? President Bush struck the expected pose of omniscience in the course of the 1988 election campaign when he refused to answer a rude question about an American naval blunder in the Persian Gulf (the shooting down of an Iranian airliner) on the ground that he would "never apologize for the United States of America. I don't care what the facts are."

As recently as 1980 I knew a good many people who took a passionate interest in politics, who felt keenly what one of them described as "the ancient republican hostility" to the rule of the self-serving few. They knew the names of their elected representatives, and they were as well-informed on the topics of the day as any government spokesman paid to edit the news. By the end of the decade most of them had abandoned their political enthusiasm as if it were a youthful folly they no longer could afford—like hang gliding or writing neosymbolist verse.

Much of the reason for the shift in attitude I attribute to the exemplary cynicism of the Reagan administration. Here was a government obsequious in its devotion to the purposes of a selfish oligarchy, a regime that cared nothing for the law and prospered for eight years by virtue of its willingness to cheat and steal and lie. And yet, despite its gross and frequent abuses of power, the country made no complaint. The Democratic party (the nominal party of opposition) uttered not the slightest squeak of an objection. Except for a few journals of small circulation, neither did the media.

During the early years of the administration, even people who recognized the shoddiness of Reagan's motives thought that the country could stand a little encouragement—some gaudy tinsel and loud advertising, a lot of parades and a steady supply of easy profits. The country had heard enough of Jimmy Carter's sermons, and it was sick of listening to prophecies of the American future that could be easily confused with a coroner's report. In return for the illusion that the United States was still first in the world's rankings, the country indulged Reagan in his claptrap economic and geopolitical theories. For a few years it didn't seem to matter that the Laffer curve and the Strategic Defense Initiative had been imported from the land of Oz. What difference did it make as long as the Japanese were willing to lend money and Rambo was victorious in the movies?

But it turned out that the lies did make a difference—the lies and the Reagan administration's relentless grasping of illegal and autocratic privilege. Congress offered itself for sale to the highest bidder, and the political action committees bought so many politicians of both denominations that it was no longer possible to tell the difference between a Republican and a Democrat: both sides of the aisle owed their allegiance to the same sponsors. Nor was it possible to distinguish between the executive and the legislative functions of government. Any doubts on this score were dissolved in the midden of the Iran-Contra deals. President Reagan and his aides-de-camp on the National Security Council sold weapons to a terrorist regime in Iran in order to finance a terrorist revolt in Nicaragua. The scheme obliged them to make a mockery of the Constitution, dishonor their oaths of office and seize for themselves the powers of despotism. They did so without a qualm, and the subsequent congressional investigation absolved them of their crimes and confirmed them in their contempt for the law and the American people. The principal conspirators were allowed to depart with no more than a reprimand.

It was this series of events—so obviously and complacently corrupt throughout the whole course of the narrative—that proved even more damaging to the American polity than the reconfiguration of the economy. Justified by a timid Congress and excused by a compliant media, the Reagan administration reduced the Constitution to a sheaf of commercial paper no more or less worthless than a promissory note signed by Donald Trump or a financial prospectus offering shares in the Wedtech Corporation.

The defeat might be easier to bear if the politicians would quit mouthing the word "democracy." If they were to say instead, "Yes, we are a great nation because we obey the rule of the expedient lie" or, "Yes, believe in our power because we have gerrymandered our politics to serve the interests of wealth," I might find it easier to wave the flag and swell the unison of complacent applause.

But not "democracy." Maybe "plutocracy," or "oligarchy," or even "state capitalism," but not, please God, "a free nation under law" or, as a professor of government put it in an address to a crowd of newly naturalized citizens of Monticello, the "moral and political reasoning [that] is the republic's unique and priceless heritage."

What "moral and political reasoning"? Between which voices of conscience, and where would the heritage be exhibited to public view? On network television? In the United States Senate? In a high school auditorium in Detroit?

Saddam Hussein's invasion of Kuwait presented a fairly prominent occasion for a display of America's moral and political reasoning, but it was a spectacle that nobody wanted to see or hear. The national choir of newspaper columnists banged their cymbals and drums, shouting for the head of the monster of Baghdad. Loudly and without a single exception, the 535 members of Congress declared themselves loyal to the great American truth that had descended into the Arabian desert with the 82nd Airborne Division. The television networks introduced a parade of generals, all of them explicating the texts of glorious war. The few individuals who publicly questioned the wisdom of the president's policy instantly found themselves classified as subversives, spoilsports, ingrates and sore thumbs.

The judgement is one with which I am familiar, probably because my own remarks on the state of American politics often have been attacked by more or less the same gang of adjectives. With respect to the argument in progress, I can imagine the rejoinder pronounced by a self-satisfied gentleman in his middle forties, a reader of *Time* magazine and a friend of the American Enterprise Institute. He wears a three-piece suit and speaks slowly and patiently, as if to a foreigner or a prospective suicide. Having done well by the system, he begins by reminding me that I, too, have done well by the system and should show a decent respect for the blessings of property. His voice is as smug as his faith in the American political revelation ("not perfect, of course, but the best system on offer in an imperfect world"). His argument resolves into categorical statements, usually four, presented as facets of a flawless truth. As follows:

1. The American government is formed by the rule of the ballot box. What other country trusts its destiny to so many free elections?

The statement is true to the extent that it describes a ritual, not a function, of government. Early last spring the Times Mirror Center for the People and the Press conducted a survey of the political attitudes prevailing among a random sampling of citizens between the ages of eighteen and twenty-nine. To nobody's surprise the survey discovered a generation that "knows less, cares less, votes less and is less critical of its leaders and institutions than young people in the past." The available statistics support the impression of widespread political apathy. In this month's election it is expected that as many as 120 million Americans (two-thirds of the eligible electorate) will not bother to vote.

The numbers suggest that maybe the people who don't vote have good and sufficient reasons for their abstentions. Vote for what and for whom? For a program of false promises and empty platitudes? For ambitious office-seekers distinguished chiefly by their talents for raising money? For a few rich men (that is, the sixty or seventy senators possessing assets well in excess of $1 million) who can afford to buy a public office as if it were a beach house or a rubber duck?

Since the revision of the campaign finance laws in the late 1970s, most of the candidates don't even take the trouble to court the good opinion of the voters. They speak instead to the PACs, to the lobbyists who can fix the money for campaigns costing as much as $350,000 (for the House of Representatives) and $4 million (for the Senate). The rising cost of political ambition ensures the rising rate of incumbency (47 percent of the present United States Congress were in office in 1980, as opposed to 4 percent of the Supreme Soviet). The sponsors back the safe bets and receive the assurance of safe opinions. (As of last 30 June, the incumbent senators up for reelection this month had collected $83.1 million for their campaigns, as opposed to $25.9 million raised on behalf of the insurgents.)

A democracy supposedly derives its strength and character from the diversity of its many voices, but the politicians in the Capitol speak with only one voice, which is the voice of the oligarchy that buys the airline tickets and the television images. Among the company of legislators in Washington or Albany or Sacramento I look in vain for a representation of my own interests or opinions, and I never hear the voice of the scientist, the writer, the athlete, the teacher, the plumber, the police officer, the farmer, the merchant. I hear instead the voice of only one kind of functionary: a full-time politician, nearly always a lawyer, who spends at least 80 percent of his time raising campaign funds and construes his function as that of a freight-forwarding agent redistributing the national income into venues convenient to his owners and friends.

Maybe it still can be said that the United States is a representative government in the theatrical sense of the word, but if I want to observe the workings of democracy I would be better advised to follow the debate in the Czech Parliament or the Soviet Congress of People's Deputies. The newly enfranchised politicians in Eastern Europe write their own speeches and delight in the passion for words that allows them to seize and shape the course of a new history and a new world. Unlike American voters, voters in the Soviet Union (repeat, the Soviet Union, Russia, the USSR, the "Evil Empire," the Communist prison) enjoy the right to express the full range of their opinions at the polls. Instead of marking the ballot for a favored candidate, the Soviet voter crosses off the names of the politicians whom he has reason to distrust or despise. He can vote against all the candidates, even an incumbent standing unopposed. Because a Soviet politician must receive an absolute majority, the election isn't valid unless more than half of the electorate votes, which means that in Moscow or Leningrad the citizens can vote for "none of the above," and by doing so they can do what the voters in New York or Los Angeles cannot do— throw the thieves into the street.

2. Democratic government is self-government, and in America the state is owned and operated by the citizens.

I admire the sentiment, and I am willing to believe that in the good old days before most of what was worth knowing about the mechanics of government disappeared under the seals of classified information, it was still conceivable that the business of the state could be conducted by amateurs. In the early years of the twentieth century it was still possible for anybody passing by the White House to walk through the front door and expect a few words with the president. It's true that the promise of democracy is synonymous with the idea of the citizen. The enterprise requires the collaboration of everybody present, and it fails (or evolves into something else) unless enough people perceive their government as subject rather than object, as animate organism rather than automatic vending machine.

Such an antique or anthropomorphic understanding of politics no longer satisfies the demand for omnipotence or the wish to believe in kings or queens or fairy tales. Ask almost anybody in any street about the nature of American government, and he or she will describe it as something that belongs to somebody else, as a them, not an us. Only advanced students of political science remember how a caucus works, or what is written in the Constitution, or who paves the roads. The active presence of the citizen gives way to the passive absence of the consumer, and citizenship devolves into a function of economics. Every two or four or six years the politicians ask the voters whether they recognize themselves as better or worse off than they were the last time anybody asked. The question is only and always about money, never about the spirit of the laws or the cherished ideals that embody the history of the people. The commercial definition of democracy prompts the politicians to conceive of and advertise the republic as if it were a resort hotel. They promise the voters the rights and comforts owed to them by virtue of their status as America's guests. The subsidiary arguments amount to little more than complaints about the number, quality and cost of the available services. The government (a.k.a. the hotel management) preserves its measure of trust in the exact degree that it satisfies the whims of its patrons and meets the public expectation of convenience and style at a fair price. A debased electorate asks of the state what the rich ask of their servants—that is, "comfort us," "tell us what to do." The wish to be cared for replaces the will to act.

3. The American democracy guarantees the freedom of its people and the honesty of its government with a system of checks and balances; the division or separation of powers prevents the government from indulging the pleasures of despotism; the two-party system ensures the enactment of just laws vigorously debated and openly arrived at.

It was precisely this principle that the Iran-Contra deals (the trading of weapons for hostages as well as the subsequent reprieves and exonerations) proved null and void. President Reagan usurped the prerogatives of Congress and Congress made no objection. President Bush exercised the same option with respect to the expedition in the Persian Gulf, and again Congress made no objection, not even when it was discovered that Saudi Arabia had offered to hire the CIA to arrange the overthrow of Saddam Hussein. For the last forty years it has been the practice of the American government to wage a war at the will and discretion of the foreign-policy apparat in Washington—without reference to the wishes or opinions of the broad mass of the American people.

Dean Acheson, secretary of state in the Truman administration, understood as long ago as 1947 that if the government wished to do as it pleased, then it would be necessary to come up with a phrase, slogan or article of faith that could serve as a pretext for arbitrary decisions. He hit upon the word "nonpartisan." Knowing that the American people might balk at the adventure of the Cold War if they thought that the subject was open to discussion, he explained to his confederates in the State Department that a militant American foreign policy had to be presented as a "nonpartisan issue," that any and all domestic political quarreling about the country's purposes "stopped at the water's edge."

"If we can make them believe that," Acheson said, "we're off to the races."

Among the promoters of the national security state the theory of "nonpartisanship" was accorded the weight of biblical revelation, and for the next two generations it proved invaluable to a succession of presidents bent on waging declared and undeclared wars in Korea, Vietnam, Guatemala, Grenada, Panama, Cambodia, Lebanon, Nicaragua and the Persian Gulf. President John F. Kennedy elaborated the theory into a doctrine not unlike the divine right of kings. At a press conference in May 1962, Kennedy said, with sublime arrogance: "Most of us are conditioned for many years to have a political viewpoint—Republican or Democratic, liberal, conservative or moderate. The fact of the matter is that most of the problems . . . that we now face are technical problems, are administrative problems. They are very sophisticated judgements, which do not lend themselves to the great sort of passionate movements which have stirred this country so often in the past. [They] deal with questions which are now beyond the comprehension of most men."

To President Bush the word "nonpartisan" is the alpha and omega of government by administrative decree: a word for all seasons; a word that avoids the embarrassment of forthright political argument; a word with which to send the troops to Saudi Arabia, postpone decisions on the budget, diffuse the blame for the savings and loan swindle. The White House staff takes pride in the techniques of what its operatives refer to as "conflict-avoidance." Speaking to a writer for *The New Republic* in August, one of Bush's senior press agents said, "We don't do [political] fighting in this administration. We do bipartisan compromising."

But in a democracy everything is partisan. Democratic politics is about nothing else except being partisan. The American dialectic assumes argument not only as the normal but as the necessary condition of its continued existence. The structure of the idea resembles a suspension bridge rather than a pyramid or a mosque. Its strength depends on the balance struck between countervailing forces, and the idea collapses unless the stresses oppose one another with equal weight, unless enough people have enough courage to sustain the argument between rich and poor, the government and the governed, city and suburb, presidency and Congress, capital and labor, matter and mind. It is precisely these arguments (that is, the very stuff and marrow of democracy) that the word "nonpartisan" seeks to annul.

With reference to domestic political arguments, the word "consensus" serves the same purpose as the word "nonpartisan" does in the realm of foreign affairs: it is another sleight of hand that makes possible the perpetual avoidance of any question that might excite the democratic passions of a free people bent on governing themselves. The trick is to say as little as possible in a language so bland that the speaker no longer can be accused of harboring an unpleasant opinion. Adhere firmly to the safe cause and the popular sentiment. Talk about the flag or drugs or crime (never about race or class or justice) and follow the yellow brick road to the wonderful land of "consensus." In place of honest argument among consenting adults the politicians substitute a lullaby for frightened children: the pretense that conflict doesn't really exist, that we have achieved the blessed state in which (because we are all American and therefore content) we no longer need politics. The mere mention of the word "politics" brings with it the odor of something low and rotten and mean.

Confronted with genuinely stubborn and irreconcilable differences (about revising the schedule of Social Security payments, say, or closing down a specific number of the nation's military bases), the politicians assign the difficulty to the law courts, or to a special prosecutor or to a presidential commission. In line with its habitual cowardice, Congress this past September dispatched a few of its most pettifogging members to Andrews Air Force Base, where, behind closed doors, it was hoped that they might construct the façade of an agreement on the budget.

For the better part of two hundred years it was the particular genius of the American democracy to compromise its differences within the context of an open debate. For the most part (with the tragic exception of the Civil War), the society managed to assimilate and smooth out the edges of its antagonisms and by so doing to hold in check the violence bent on its destruction. The success of the enterprise derived from the rancor of the nation's loud-mouthed politics—on the willingness of its citizens and their elected representatives to defend their interests, argue their cases, and say what they meant. But if the politicians keep silent, and if the citizenry no longer cares to engage in what it regards as the distasteful business of debate, then the American dialectic cannot attain a synthesis or resolution. The democratic initiative passes to the demagogues in the streets, and the society falls prey to the ravening minorities in league with the extremists of all denominations who claim alliance with the higher consciousness and the absolute truth. The eloquence of Daniel Webster or Henry Clay degenerates into the muttering of Al Sharpton or David Duke.

The deliberate imprecision of the Constitution (sufficiently vague and spacious to allow the hope of a deal) gives way to rigid enumerations of privileges and rights. A democracy in sound working order presupposes a ground of tolerance, in Judge Learned Hand's phrase, "the spirit which is not too sure that it is right." I might think that the other fellow is wrong, but I do not think that he is therefore wicked. A democracy in decay acquires the pale and deadly cast of theocracy. Not only is the other fellow wrong (about abortion, obscenity or the flag); he is also, by definition, an agent of the Antichrist.

4. The Constitution presents the American people with as great a gift of civil liberties as ever has been granted by any government in the history of the world.

But liberty, like the habit of telling the truth, withers and decays unless it's put to use, and for the last ten years it seems as if the majority of Americans would rather not suffer the embarrassment of making a scene (in a public place) about so small a trifle as a civil right. With scarcely a murmur of objection, they fill out the official forms, answer the questions, submit to the compulsory urine or blood tests and furnish information to the government, the insurance companies and the police.

The Bush administration cries up a war on drugs, and the public responds with a zeal for coercion that would have gladdened the hearts of the Puritan judges presiding over the Salem witch trials. Of the respondents questioned by an ABC/*Washington Post* poll in September 1989, 55 percent supported mandatory drug testing for all Americans, 52 percent were willing to have their homes searched and 83 percent favored reporting suspected drug users to the police, even if the suspects happened to be members of their own families. Politicians of both parties meet with sustained applause when they demand longer jail sentences and harsher laws as well as the right to invade almost everybody's privacy; to search, without a warrant, almost anybody's automobile or boat; to bend the rules of evidence, hire police spies and attach, again without a warrant, the wires of electronic surveillance. Within the last five years the Supreme Court has granted increasingly autocratic powers to the police—permission (without probable cause) to stop, detain and question a traveler passing through the nation's airports in whom the police can see a resemblance to a drug dealer; permission (again without probable cause) to search barns, stop motorists, inspect bank records and tap phones.

The same Times Mirror survey that discovered a general indifference toward all things political also discovered that most of the respondents didn't care whether a fair percentage of the nation's politicians proved to be scoundrels and liars. Such was the nature of their task, and it was thought unfair to place on the political authorities the additional and excessive burden of too many harsh or pointed questions. "Let them," said one of the poor dupes of a respondent, "authoritate."

Democracy is never easy to define. The meaning of the word changes with the vagaries of time, place and circumstance. The American democracy in 1990 is not what it was in 1890; democracy in France is not what it is in England or Norway or the United States. What remains more or less constant is a temperament or spirit of mind rather than a code of laws, a set of immutable virtues or a table of bureaucratic organization. The temperament is skeptical and contentious, and if democracy means anything at all (if it isn't what Gore Vidal called "the great American nonsense word" or what H. L. Mencken regarded as a synonym for the collective fear and prejudice of an ignorant mob) it means the freedom of thought and the perpetual expansion of the discovery that the world is not oneself. Freedom of thought brings the society the unwelcome news that it is in trouble. But because all societies, like all individuals, are always in trouble, the news doesn't cause them to perish. They die instead from the fear of thought—from the paralysis that accompanies the wish to make time stand still and punish the insolence of an Arab who makes a nuclear bomb or sells gasoline for more than twenty-five dollars a barrel.

Democracy allies itself with change and proceeds on the assumption that nobody knows enough, that nothing is final, that the old order (whether of men or institutions) will be carried offstage every twenty years. The multiplicity of its voices and forms assumes a ceaseless making and remaking of laws and customs as well as equations and matinee idols. Democratic government is a purpose held in common, and if it can be understood as a field of temporary coalitions among people of different interests, skills and generations, then everybody has need of everybody else. To the extent that democracy gives its citizens a chance to chase their own dreams, it gives itself the chance not only of discovering its multiple glories and triumphs but also of surviving its multiple follies and crimes.

November 1990

Notebooks

ANNUS MIRABILIS

The essential matter of history is not what happened
but what people thought or said about it.
—FREDERIC MAITLAND

On the day that the holes appeared in the Berlin Wall I was
surprised by a sudden lightness of spirit that was as inchoate as
it was unexpected. Together with the crowds dancing under the
arches of the Brandenburg Gate, I was content to revel in the feeling of
exaltation and the conviction that somehow, as of that moment and for
reasons still opaque, the world had been unalterably transformed.

For most of the first day and the better part of the second, I didn't
question either the emotion or the jumbled sequence of hastily formed ideas
supporting the weight of a historical certainty. It was enough to read the
papers, to marvel at the images drifting across the surface of the television
news, to rejoice in a newly awakened sense of boundless possibility.

By the afternoon of the third day, nearly two million people had passed
from East to West Berlin, and I began to assemble a list of random notes
and observations. Because I hadn't thought myself capable of being so
forcibly moved by so distant an event, I was curious to know how and why
I had arrived at so uncharacteristic a state of optimism. My cheerfulness
had nothing to do with the European future, which I expect to be anything but easy or democratic or safe, or with the prospect of a reunified
Germany, which I believe to be a consummation best avoided. Were I
charged with the task of redrawing the map of Europe, I unhesitatingly
would return the Germanies to the boundaries of 1837, dividing them

safely into the kingdoms of Saxony, Bavaria, Prussia, Baden, Hannover, Schleswig-Holstein, Würtemberg and Mecklenburg.

What delighted me was the feeling of a lucky escape from the jail of the past. The holes in the Berlin Wall informed me that the First World War was at last ended, that both Hitler and Stalin were dead, that the twentieth century had run its ignoble, blood-stained course. No longer would I read the works of Brecht or Orwell or Joyce in quite the same way that I read them as recently as last week. Nor would I look in the same way at the paintings of Picasso and Paul Klee, at the architecture of the Bauhaus, at the films of Fritz Lang or at the art deco lamps in the lobby of the Royalton Hotel. It wasn't that the Holocaust had been lost to memory, or that Estragon wasn't still waiting for Godot, but rather that a habit of thought and a manner of speaking suddenly had receded into the past tense.

The shift in the line of sight is undoubtedly a function of my age. In 1945 I was ten years old, and although Hitler presumably had died in a bunker near the Potsdamer Platz and the world, once again, supposedly had been made safe for democracy, I wasn't old enough to be weaned from the belief in a state of permanent war. By the time I was twelve, Stalin had been assigned Hitler's role as the archvillain of the century, and the managers of the international political theater resumed advertising continuous performances of the familiar crusade under the posters of the Cold War. For the next forty years I found myself looking at a Wagnerian stage set, backlit and gray, engineered for atonal sound effects and storms of Russian snow.

At American universities in the 1950s the curators of the best-selling truths insisted on the great modernist principle of dehumanization—history reduced to a game of checkers played by anonymous socioeconomic forces, diplomacy translated into the problems of logistics, philosophy presented as a set of variations on a theme for solo and alienated violin. All the authorities bore witness to the unhappy news that in the twentieth century the womb of time had spawned ill-omened and monstrous births. The professors of literature taught the canon of modernism, and from Pound and Eliot I learned that the age had gone bad in the teeth, that the torrents of the poetic imagination had evaporated in a desert of dry stone. The custodians of the history of art told the same pallid story—the richness of nineteenth-century form wrecked on the shoals of cubism, the once-adventurous figure of the artist changed into a frightened rabbit hiding in the thickets of increasingly impenetrable symbolism.

Scored for the brass ensemble of the mass media, the thesis of despair sustained the grimly operatic melodrama of the Cold War. Against the suspicions and reinforced police powers of the modern state, no mere individual dared entertain the romantic hope of a life of one's own. Because the state held the monopoly not only on the nuclear fire but also on all the instruments of credit, only Princeton sophomores could be pardoned for failing to profess allegiance to the doctrine of Mutual Assured Destruction.

If as a child watching World War II newsreels I concluded that most of the trouble in the world was the fault of Nazi Germany, by the time I reached the age of forty I was inclined to think that the fault could more properly be assigned to imperial Germany, to Kaiser Wilhelm and his preposterous military uniforms, to Moltke and Bismarck and Nietzsche, to the idiot confusion of the summer of 1914 and to the failed peace treaty signed five years later at Versailles.

Similarly, whenever I questioned the tenets of modernism, whether with a political or aesthetic motive (or simply because I couldn't bear Woody Allen's amateur cynicism or Philip Johnson's architectural imitations of Albert Speer), I invariably found myself forced back on what had been said and thought in Vienna or Berlin during the first two decades of the twentieth century. No matter where I picked up the lines of inquiry—with a character in a novel by Le Carré, with a newspaper explanation of America's Soviet policy, with a progression of minor chords in one of Stephen Sondheim's musicals—I soon found myself (if in Berlin) at the Hotel Adlon or the Café Josty or (if in Vienna) at the cafés Landtmann or Central in the company of the century's Ur-texts, that is, with Gropius, Kraus, Freud, Ernst, Brecht, Einstein, Reinhardt, Von Braun, Schwitters, Canetti, Hesse, Hindemith, Heisenberg and Goebbels. The voices of the German wars sounded in concert with the voices of the modern cultural imperium.

If the breach in the Berlin Wall marked the end of the war set in motion by the kaiser's generals in August of 1914, so also it opened the prospect of a new horizon of thought and feeling. As of 9 November 1989, I could imagine the possibility of an aesthetic in no way beholden to Kafka's cockroach or Reichsmarschall Göring's passion for emeralds.

Watching the crowds pressing against the lighted shop-windows on the Kurfürstendamm, it occurred to me that the Wall had crumbled as easily as if it were made of sand, and I was prompted to laugh at the vanity of statesmen who imagine that they control events with the solemnity of children running electric trains. As recently as last June I attended one of those conferences in Washington at which the synod of policymakers admires the beauty of its own wisdom. The conference took up the question of the NATO alliance, with specific reference to next season's planting of nuclear weapons in German soil, and a procession of self-important gentlemen took their turns at the microphone to say that the world would never change. They adduced as reasons for their certainty their suburban faith in a status quo beyond the reach of mortal men. No matter what anybody did or said, nothing could be done because history followed upon the play of historical abstraction, and it refused to recognize anything so hopelessly behind the times as an individual's will, courage or imagination.

But Mikhail Gorbachev had made nonsense of the Marxist theory of history. Working my way eastward in space and backward in time from the crowds in the Kü'damm, I couldn't help but come to Gorbachev's willingness to stake his own safety (not to mention the destiny of nations) on what amounted to a throw of the dice. I know that it's customary to say that Gorbachev sought an end to the Cold War because he was frightened by the militant visage of American resolve—by America's willingness to spend $300 million a day for weapons and the fierce iconography of President Reagan's fantastic Star Wars. But I suspect that Gorbachev wasn't in the least frightened, that Reagan's bluster inclined him to precisely the opposite conclusion, that is, that the Americans were merely posturing, that they had no wish to make trouble and that they preferred to fight a war only if it engaged an enemy no more dreadful than Libya, lasted no longer than three days and could be fitted into the script of a heroic mini-series made for primetime television.

Impressed by America's weakness instead of its strength, and knowing that the Soviet Union scarcely could afford its military pretensions (to say nothing of its hope for a satisfactory civilian economy), Gorbachev in 1985 made so bold as to strike the stage set of the Cold War. Within the remarkably small space of four years Poland dismissed its Communist regime, Hungary declared itself a republic and the Berlin Wall was broken up into souvenirs.

If one individual could accomplish so much, then what remains of the theory of the puny anonym, of the system inevitably triumphant, of the man in the gray flannel suit, of society's victim and the hapless fool lost in the lonely crowd?

If so much can be done against such long odds in police states well versed in the arts of repression, then how much more might be done under governments nominally democratic? If they can do that there, then what can we not do here? Who is to say that the American political system cannot be redeemed, or the schools reformed or the balance of justice redressed? I look at the television footage of an East German child staring at a chocolate cake and for the first time in ten years I wonder why I haven't written an essay saying that the barometer of change is rising toward the promise of the new.

The old idea of a frontier suggested something solid and heavy—a wall, a barricade, a fence, a pile of stones. Frontiers were meant to preserve the past, to hold in check the movements of peoples and the passage of time. But, given the systems of modern communication, who can defend a border or define a sphere of influence? Foreign habits of thought pass as easily between cultures as do the labels on Japanese watches and Mexican T-shirts. The frontier dissolves into the lightness of air and the world is full of holes.

The traditional practice of foreign policy assumes the presence of a world in which it is easy to tell who or what is, in fact, foreign. The old portfolio of theories doesn't fit the new set of facts. The weight of mass immigration joined with the velocity of modern communications yields a new equation of human energy. It is an equation that presents the rulers of large and supposedly sovereign states with a hard problem in political mechanics. If nothing is foreign, and nobody is an alien, then on what principle does the state design such a thing as a foreign policy?

January 1990

DÉJÀ VU

Others may fear what the morrow may bring, but I am
afraid of what happened yesterday.
—OLD ARAB SAYING

*I*f everything else hadn't been so well and elaborately staged, I don't think I would have been so disappointed by the omission of the scene with the horse. The American government clearly had gone to no small trouble to make the invasion of Panama a memorable photo opportunity, and on the fourth or fifth day, after the army had quelled what was left of the armed resistance, I began to hope that President Bush might make a cameo appearance in the streets of Panama City. I imagined him on a white horse, waving a slouch hat like the one Teddy Roosevelt wore in Cuba during the splendid little Spanish-American War. The prospect didn't seem to me too farfetched, because so much else about the invasion resembled a gallery of dioramas meant to replicate selected scenes from the nation's military history: parachute drops in the manner of World War II, helicopter sorties suggestive not only of Vietnam but also of the movie *Apocalypse Now*, a $1 million bounty on the head of a *bandito* reminiscent of the old American West. Given the budget assigned to the production, I thought it possible that the army might have brought the horse on the same cargo plane that brought the T-shirts printed with the slogan "Operation Just Cause."

Maybe the president's theatrical advisers thought that he didn't cut a fine enough figure on horseback or, more probably, they didn't schedule the scene with the horse because nobody could be certain of the exact moment at which Mr Bush might be called upon to ride in triumph up Ancon Hill. The promoters of the event could anticipate a prompt victory over the Panamanian army, but then they had to confront the logistics of Christmas. What if Mr Bush had already been scheduled to light the tree on the White House lawn or hand out dolls in an orphanage? I can appreciate the difficulties, and I know that the staging of an invasion is just as complicated as the staging of the Rose Bowl Parade or the Miss America Pageant, but, even so, I missed the horse.

It's a small criticism and perhaps overly technical, but if Mr Bush wishes to reenact the glorious American past, his staff should aspire to the standards of accuracy achieved by the Civil War enthusiasts who organize the annual restoration of the Battle of Gettysburg.

It was, of course, President Teddy Roosevelt's policy that Mr Bush chose to resurrect, and Roosevelt, accompanied by a troop of Rough Riders, entered Panama City on horseback soon after he seized the Canal Zone in 1903 on behalf of what he called "the interests of collective civilization." Like Mr Bush, Roosevelt had little feeling or sympathy for anything so absurd as Panamanian sovereignty. To Roosevelt, the Latin American nations were "those wretched republics [that] cause me a great deal of trouble," and he regarded most Latin American politicians as "wicked and inefficient types" whom the United States was obliged to correct and chastise for their "chronic wrongdoing."

To Roosevelt, the great game of gunboat diplomacy was both adventure and Sunday school sermon, a chance to play with the toys of war and a chance to preach the lessons of free enterprise and Christian virtue. He

conceived of foreign policy as a missionary enterprise, and his biblical reading of geopolitics set the course of American diplomacy in the twentieth
century. In Washington the gentry acquired the habit of looking upon the
Latin American republics as the servants' quarters of the Western
Hemisphere and the Latin American peoples as the household help.

Every so often one or another of the "wicked and inefficient types" forgets
his place, becomes insolent or presumes too much, consorts with Communists or steals the family silver. On such occasions, the United States
invariably sends the marines. Because hardly anybody in Washington
has ever thought of the Latin American republics as sovereign states, it
seldom occurs to anybody that the Central Americans might possess the
right to do anything other than what they're told to do.

The traditional bias was reflected in the American media's indifference
to details of the damage inflicted on Panama during last December's
invasion. About the American casualties the media were precise (23 killed,
324 wounded), but about the Panamanian casualties they were as vague
as a Park Avenue hostess talking about the rumors of drug killings in
Harlem. Some reporters put the number of Panamanian casualties at
300 dead and 1,000 wounded; other reporters guessed that maybe 1,000
were dead and 3,000 wounded; but nobody took the trouble to assemble
accurate figures. What difference did it make? Who counted the number
of Mexicans dead at Tampico?

Nor were the Panamanians allowed to install their new president or
mete out their own justice to General Manuel Noriega. The Americans
installed their hired puppet, Guillermo Endara, in a ceremony hastily
convened at an American military base and applauded by a claque of
dignitaries recruited from the 82nd Airborne Division. Noriega was taken
to Miami in chains, as if he were one of the hunting trophies that Roosevelt
so furiously collected for the Museum of Natural History in New York
City.

In the aftermath of the invasion, I met a number of earnest people who
worried about the niceties of the law. They pointed out that the invasion
violated the UN Charter of 1945, the Rio Pact of 1947, the Bogotá
Charter of 1948 and the Panama Canal treaties signed in 1904 and 1977.
Their concern was touching, and again I was reminded of Roosevelt and
his attorney general, Philander C. Knox. Only once, and then briefly and
in passing, did Roosevelt inquire about the legal precedents for his seizure
of the Canal Zone. "Oh, Mr President," Knox said, "do not let so great an
achievement suffer from any taint of legality."

A few years later, in the summer of 1914, Justice Felix Frankfurter, then a young lawyer in what was still known as the War Department, formulated the operative principle when he was asked to research the question of whether President Woodrow Wilson's invasion of Mexico constituted an act of war. President Wilson wished "to teach the Latin Americans to elect good men," and to that end he sent several thousand American troops to Veracruz to depose a ruler who had been judged unacceptable by the consensus of high-minded opinion in Washington. Frankfurter explained that he didn't need to look up any laws. "It's an act of war against a great power," he said. "It's not an act of war against a small power."

The two sentences admirably state the precedent that has governed American policy in Central America for a hundred years, justifying, among other punitive expeditions, the invasion of Nicaragua (1926), the overthrow of the democratically elected government in Guatemala (1954), the attempt to defeat Castro at the Bay of Pigs (1961), the intervention in the Dominican Republic (1965), the overthrow of the democratically elected government of El Salvador (1979), the invasion of Grenada (1983), the arming of the Nicaraguan Contras (1981–1989) and the mining of the harbor at Managua (1984).

No American government, of course, admits to so bald a use of force. The doctrines of American exceptionalism forbid American politicians to see any contradiction between what they practice and what they preach. America is always and everywhere innocent, a country so favored by fortune that its cause is always just. In deference to the presiding orthodoxy, Mr Bush offered a number of noble motives for last December's invasion. None of them can pass honest examination, but I think them worth rebutting in some detail if for no other reason than to indicate the contempt implicit in their shoddiness. Had the Panamanians been deemed important enough to warrant first-class sophistry drawn up by a first-class lawyer, the United States might have taken the trouble to manufacture pretexts of a slightly higher grade.

Safeguarding American lives

A pretext that allows the United States government to send troops to any city in the world, not only to Lima or Bogotá but also to Detroit and East Los Angeles. The planning of the invasion quite clearly had been in progress for several weeks, and the killing of a single American soldier at a military checkpoint on the Saturday preceding the Wednesday on which the paratroops arrived from points west and north merely served as an incident of convenience. One or more American soldiers die in some sort of incident every month at one or another of our military outposts somewhere in the world, and of the American citizens resident in Panama, few were confronted with imminent peril. The United States at all times maintains a garrison of 12,000 troops in Panama, a force equal in strength to the entire Panamanian army and fully capable of defending American nationals against any assault.

To protect the Panama Canal

From whom? General Noriega never threatened to destroy the Canal, possibly for the very good reason that the tolls charged to ships passing through the Canal provide Panama with its principal source of revenue. The treaty signed by President Carter in 1977 granted Panama eventual jurisdiction over the Canal, and unless the United States wishes to declare the treaty null and void, the Panamanians retain the right to operate the Canal in whatever manner they deem fit.

The American Congress verified the treaty because it had been persuaded that the Canal had lost its value as a strategic American interest. The interest was real enough when the Canal opened for business in 1914. The Canal allowed American naval vessels an easy transit between the Pacific and Atlantic oceans, and in the early years of the century, before the building of the interstate highway system, the Canal carried much of the commerce between the east and the west coasts of the United States. By 1950 most of the dry cargo moved by railroad or truck, and the navy's newest ships, like the larger oil tankers, were too big to pass through the locks at Miraflores.

To restore to Panama the principle and practice of democracy

A reason so specious that it could be mistaken for satire. The fiction of a free and independent Panama bears analogy to the fiction of a free and independent South Vietnam. Throughout the twentieth century the United States has intervened at will in Panamanian political affairs, sustaining the corrupt oligarchies that governed the country in the 1920s and 1930s, casting out a democratically elected government in 1941, destroying another democratically elected government in 1969, funding the military despotism practiced over a period of twenty years by generals Omar Torrijos and Manuel Noriega. What Washington has always wanted in Panama is not a democratic government but a gamekeeper who could be trusted to manage the rabbits.

Interdicting the drug trade

A fine phrase, but as futile as the Bush administration's hope of burning all the cocoa plants in Peru. Panama City lost much of its importance to the drug trade in 1988, after the United States imposed sanctions on the Panamanian economy and restricted the credit available to the Panamanian banks. Because the banks could no longer act as clearing-houses for money acquired under questionable circumstances, the South American drug cartels moved their business out of town.

The rescue of the brave and oppressed Panamanian people

Another doubtful proposition. The Panamanians have never been known for their idealism, their political courage or their passionate love of liberty. Panama is a nation of middlemen who thrive on tolls, offshore banking, percentages, pieces of the action and flags of convenience. So profound is the Panamanian allegiance to the doctrine of the bottom line that the whole of Panama City could be confused with a duty-free shop. Panamanian politics traditionally have avoided the difficulties of issues or beliefs; they have been centered instead on rich and charismatic individuals who govern by means of patronage and bribery. Throughout the country's history, few Panamanian politicians (no matter what the form of their nominal rhetoric) have left high office without having amassed fortunes large enough to assure the comfort of their retirement in Miami or Paris.

Not being the kind of people to make their own revolutions, the Panamanians gratefully received the deliverance arranged for them by the United States, and they were only too happy to wear the T-shirts advertising "Operation Just Cause." Within an hour of swearing himself into office, the new Panamanian president reminded his new American friends that he was hard-pressed for money. The good citizens of Panama City responded to the promise of freedom not by lighting candles (as was done in Prague) or by defying a column of tanks (as was done in Beijing), but by looting the nearest store. Jubilant Panamanians, their arms filled with stolen TV sets and microwave ovens, greeted American soldiers in the ruined streets with loud cries of "Viva Bush."

The capture of the devil incarnate

The Bush administration made a point of insisting that the capture of General Manuel Noriega was, in and of itself, sufficient reason for the invasion. Never in the history of mankind had so terrible a villain preyed upon the peace of nations. The American news media obligingly elaborated the line of official propaganda with testimonials to Noriega's monstrous depravity—a man who practiced voodoo, molested teenage girls, kept a mistress, indulged his bestial appetite for drink, pornography and cocaine, adorned his walls with portraits of Hitler, took sadistic pleasure in acts of torture and murder. On CBS News, Dan Rather placed the general "at the top of the list of the world's drug thieves and scums." The nomination was seconded by ABC and NBC, as well as by all of the country's major newspapers and newsmagazines. When Noriega first eluded his captors, the *New York Post* asked, in 200-point type on its front page, "Where's the rat?"

The image doesn't quite fit all the facts. As a young army officer, Noriega was recruited by the CIA in 1967, and for the better part of twenty years, despite his heavy drinking and sexual peculiarities, he performed faithful service to his employers in return for fees that eventually were raised to $200,000 per annum. He became acquainted with President Bush in the 1970s, when Bush was director of the CIA; and in the 1980s, after he had acceded to power with the enthusiastic endorsement of Washington, Noriega allowed the Americans to make use of Panama as an intelligence and weapons base for the war against the Sandinista government in Nicaragua.

Judged by the standards of violence applicable elsewhere in Central America, Noriega's behavior appears to have been almost benign. Between 1983 and 1989 the political killings in Panama numbered no more than twenty; other regimes sponsored by the United States achieved far more savage effects—as many as 40,000 civilians killed by an American-trained army in El Salvador since 1979, 100,000 civilians killed in Guatemala since 1978, an unknown number of civilians killed in Nicaragua since 1980 by the American-owned force of Contras.

Nor does Noriega pass muster as an especially greedy or accomplished thief. The most extravagant estimates of his net worth as yet published in the American news media list his assets at $23 million held in Caribbean or European banks. The sum dwindles into a pittance when compared with the sums stolen by Ferdinand Marcos and the Shah of Iran, both clients of the United States who were far less zealous in their collaboration with the CIA than was General Noriega. Nor do the general's profits seem excessive when compared with the cost overruns charged to the Pentagon by American defense contractors or with the sums stolen by Republican bankers from S&L associations.

The lack of a strategic or economic purpose for the invasion of Panama (that is, the absence of any national interest other than Mr Bush's vanity and spite) in no way compromised its success as a patriotic entertainment. No American politician and, to the best of my knowledge, nobody in the American news media thought to ask why the United States, the most heavily armed nation-state in the known world, should take pride in occupying a country so pitiably weak as to be all but helpless.

Mr Bush's invasion of Panama coincided with the revolution in Rumania, and the contrast between the two sets of footage made plain the degree to which the American media have come to function as a government information service. The news from Bucharest looked like news; the news from Panama City looked like a commercial. In Rumania the cameras followed the fighting in the streets, but in Panama the American audience saw nothing but cheering crowds and Pentagon public-relations officers. The American military declared the scene of the fighting off-limits to the American press. Journalists asking to see the army's own game films were told to file a request under the Freedom of Information Act.

As an advertisement for Mr Bush, the invasion of Panama satisfied all but the most demanding requirements set by the promoters of the event. Mr Bush dutifully allied himself with the myth of the triumphant American past, with a nineteenth-century America still defended by Teddy Roosevelt and two oceans, with Ronald Reagan's postcard optimism, with John Wayne under the cottonwood trees at the head of the canyon, hopelessly outnumbered by Apaches and rustlers and Mexican bandits, standing his ground as the steadfast symbol of the American belief that with a shy smile, enough ammunition and a few kind words to the sheriff, time can be made to stand still. Like Roosevelt and Reagan and Wayne, President Bush promised to defend the sanctity of myth against the heresy of fact. If the effect was a little false, not quite up to the standards of big-time Hollywood epic, it was because Bush forgot what Roosevelt and Reagan and Wayne never forgot: no matter what the producer says, or how much the director complains, always bring the horse.

March 1990

LINES IN THE SAND

Perhaps in time the so-called Dark Ages will be
thought of as including our own.
—GEORG CHRISTOPH LICHTENBERG

During the last weekend in July, four days before Saddam Hussein's armies sacked Kuwait, I attended a university conference given over to the divination of the future. The topics in hand were the triumph of capitalism, the political geography of the post-Cold War world and the end of history. The mood was genial, almost elegiac. None of the invited theorists could imagine the arrival of any urgent news. Between seminars they wandered across the quiet, quadrangular lawns admiring the weather and regretting the loss of the ideological sound and fury that had provided so many of them with academic tenure or a corner office in one of the Washington defense ministries. For the most part, they contented themselves with jocular gossip about the failures of communism, which were recent and many and obvious.

About the map coordinates of the future they weren't quite as specific as the advance notices might have led their audiences to expect. Certainly the world would be different now that Marxism-Leninism had vanished from the earth, but just how different nobody was prepared to say. Under persistent questioning from the back rows the consensus of prophetic opinion agreed to only two general observations:

1. Narrative and incident no longer counted for much in the telling of the human story. No mere individual could stand against the global tide of the macroeconomic data base.

2. Because all the intellectual disputes had been so satisfactorily resolved, the future was bound to be somewhat dull and monochromatic.

The millennium presented itself as a problem in hotel and restaurant management, not as an occasion for genius or melodrama.

A summary of the conference's findings failed to reach Baghdad before the early morning of 2 August, and the Iraqi tanks moved south into Kuwait unaware of their historical irrelevance. Within a matter of hours they had deconstructed the whole of the academic text, and before noon a feeling akin to panic seized the financial markets in Europe and Japan as well as in the United States. A despot unknown to the editors of *People* magazine had rearranged the geography in the Arab world, and by nightfall the network television correspondents were mourning the absence of the Cold War fairy tale about the American cowboy and the Russian bear. Tom Brokaw informed the NBC audience that the world was "a dangerous place," and among those of his viewers who didn't live in New York City (where four children had been killed by random gunfire in the preceding two weeks) the bulletin presumably was received with gasps of astonishment.

Broadcasting from Amman, Jordan (against the backdrop of a minaret), Dan Rather on CBS also noticed that Hussein wasn't in the least like the Russians. He was not the same sort of familiar and metaphorical enemy who could be relied upon to practice a postmodernist diplomacy of gesture and countergesture. To Hussein tank divisions were still real (instruments of power rather than images of power), and apparently he meant to steal the money and the oil—not because he wished to prove a point of ideological pride but because he was hardpressed to feed his army and his ambition. The media portrayed him as a bandit escaped from a B-movie or a lunatic asylum, as treacherous as he was violent, willing to wage war for the old Roman or nineteenth-century reasons—for the gold and the silk or the women and the slaves.

Confronted with so primitive a theory of events, American policy descended almost at once into the same pit. Like Hussein, Bush sent for the army. Hussein wanted control of the price of Arabian oil and the politics of the Middle East. So did the United States. Just as Hussein imagined himself forced into desperate circumstances (a bankrupt economy, an unhappy populace and four recent attempts at assassination), Americans imagined themselves forced to the edge of an abyss, threatened with the loss of what Bush subsequently proclaimed to be "our jobs, our way of life, our own freedom . . . " Hussein summoned a jihad against the perfidy of Christendom. Bush organized a crusade against the infidel East.

By 7 August, less than a week after Iraqi troops occupied Kuwait, the United States had mustered the largest military parade to be sent overseas since the Vietnam War. President Bush did his best to dress up the motive in the language of conscience and virtue. Explaining the national purpose to the American people, he said that the time had come for the United States "to stand up for what's right and condemn what's wrong, all in the cause of peace." His manner was that of a sincere and boyish scoutmaster, trying not to use too many big words, his earnest smile meant to convey an impression of goodness. A villain had arisen in the desert, a villain guilty of an "outrageous and brutal act of aggression," and the villain had to be punished. "America," the president said, "has never wavered when her purpose is driven by principle." He ended his speech by inviting his fellow countrymen to pray.

But pray for whom or for what? For a lower interest rate or the guarantee of unlimited gasoline at $1.17 a gallon? For the king of Saudi Arabia or the emir of Kuwait, both of them feudal monarchs renowned for their cowardice and greed? For the belief that all the oil in Arabia is somehow "our" oil? For the lost art of falconry and the practice of beheading a woman taken in the act of adultery?

On the day that he ordered advance elements of the 101st and 82nd Airborne Divisions into the Nefud Desert, Mr Bush announced that he had "drawn a line in the sand." The phrase resounded with the bravado of schoolboy romance (possibly because lines in the sand have a way of being all too easily blurred or blown away), and when I understood what it meant, I knew why history had not yet come to an end and why capitalism hadn't yet achieved (and probably never would achieve) the laurels of its presumed triumph.

The line Mr Bush so boldly drew in so empty a desert was the line between profit and loss. To the capitalist sensibility, the geopolitics of money transcend the boundaries of sovereign states. The world divides, unevenly but along only one axis, between the nation of the rich and the nation of the poor. The frontiers run not only between Kuwait and Iraq but also between east and west Los Angeles; between black and white, north and south, surfeit and famine; between the first-class cabin of a Boeing 747 en route to London and the roof of a fourth-class train on the way to Calcutta. The Upper East Side of Manhattan belongs to the same polity as the seventh arrondissement in Paris; the yachts moored off Cannes or the Costa Brava sail under the flags of the same admiralty that posts squadrons off Newport and Palm Beach. The American or Japanese plutocrat traveling between the Beau Rivage in Lausanne and the Ritz Hotel in Madrid crosses not into another country but into another province within the kingdom of wealth. His credit furnishes him with a lingua franca translated as readily into deutsche marks as into rials or yen or francs, buying more or less the same food in the same class of restaurants, the same amusements and the same conversation, the same politicians, dinner companions, newspaper columnists and accordion music. The realm of money assumes the ecumenical place once occupied by the Catholic Church, and within this favored estate everybody obeys the same laws and pays homage to the same princes.

If the analogy has any truth in it, then the post-Cold War world begins to look like medieval Europe. The possessing classes are safely at ease behind the barbican of a high interest rate, assured of their salvation by the idols of a radiant technology, content among computers and fax machines and megatrends and cellular phones. On the other side of the walls, in the desolate slums of the Third, Fifth and Sixteenth worlds, the nomadic mass of the heathen poor, otherwise known (in French policy journals) as "the terminally impoverished," tear at one another for bones.

But at what cost, and for how long, can the kingdom of wealth protect its comfort and preserve its cynicism? With what weapons and against how many enemies? Let George Bush draw a few more lines in the sand (along the border between Mexico and California, between Kennebunkport, Maine and downtown Detroit), and who will pay for the ammunition?

Just as the breaking down of the Berlin Wall symbolized the failure of communism to make good on its promise of paradise regained, the American military presence in the Persian Gulf symbolizes capitalism's failure to redeem the same promise. If capitalism can sustain itself only by main force against increasingly hopeless odds, then how does it embody an intellectual or a spiritual triumph? Who explains the loveliness of the free market to the crowd in the streets of Rio de Janeiro?

The mechanics of the free market armed Saddam Hussein with the means to a murderous end. France sold aircraft to Iraq; the Soviet Union sold tanks and rifles; the Italians sold the equipment with which to manufacture weapons-grade plutonium; the Americans supplied food subsidies and export loan guarantees (in 1983); and the West Germans provided the poison gas.

Two days after the Iraqi army seized Kuwait, I found myself seated at lunch with an independent oil-well operator from Midland, Texas. West Texas intermediate crude oil had moved from $22 to $25 a barrel, and after buying the table still another bottle of champagne, the gentleman from Texas read aloud to the assembled company the telegram he sent that morning, only partly in jest, to Saddam Hussein: "Warm congratulations on your well-earned victory. Every good wish for your continued success."

The joke was funny because its logic was unanswerable. The capitalist ethic is rooted in the doctrine of the bottom line and the sanctity of the expedient price. Like communism, capitalism is a materialist and utopian faith; also like communism, it has shown itself empty of a moral imperative or a spiritual meaning. To the questions likely to be asked by the next century, the sayings of the late Malcolm Forbes will seem as useless as the maxims of Lenin.

October 1990

BRAVE NEW WORLD

Saints should always be judged guilty until they are
proved innocent.
—GEORGE ORWELL

During the autumn advertising campaign meant to sell the American public on the prospect of war in Iraq, President Bush dressed up his gunboat diplomacy in the slogans of conscience and the costume of what he was pleased to call "the new world order." First and foremost, he had it in mind to prove to the lesser nations of the earth that any misbehavior on their part (any sacking of cities or setting of commodity prices without express, written permission from Washington) would be promptly and severely punished. Never, he said, would Saddam Hussein be allowed to receive any reward, profit, acclaim, benefit or honor for his trespass in the desert. No, sir, by no means, under no circumstances, not while the United States still had soldiers and bombs to send eastward out of Eden.

The president's righteousness waxed increasingly militant as the merely political or commercial reasons for war proved inadequate to the occasion. When the expedient arguments failed (the ones about the price of oil, the preservation of American jobs and the American way of life, the protection of Israel, the likelihood of nuclear war), Mr Bush shifted his flag to the higher ground of the moral argument, the one about the American obligation to enforce the laws of God. Behold, he said, the villainy of Saddam Hussein, an evil man committing acts of "naked aggression" in what was once the innocent paradise of Kuwait. Know, O doubting world, that America stands willing to make the crooked straight and the rough places plain.

By October the president had tuned his rhetoric to the pitch of intransigent virtue announced by Saddam Hussein. Saddam was talking about "rivers of blood," about the will of Allah and a holy war against the foreign infidel. Mr Bush was saying that "no price is too heavy to pay" to defend the standards of Christian behavior in a world already too densely populated with thugs. In late November, in an interview on CNN and still summoning the faithful to a twelfth-century crusade, Mr Bush looked firmly into the television camera and asked what I'm afraid he thought was a shrewd and high-principled question: "When you rape, pillage and plunder a neighbor, should you then ask the world, 'Hey, give me a little face'?"

The answer, regrettably, is yes. Of course you ask the world for a little face, not only for a little face but for as much face as can be had at the going rates. Why else did three American presidents persist in the devastation of Vietnam, at the price of 57,000 American dead, if not for the sake of what they defined as "America's credibility," "America's honor," "America's image in the world"? Why else did Mr Bush invade Panama if not to prove that America's military prowess deserved the compliment of the world's fear and applause? Why else have we sent 400,000 troops to the Persian Gulf if not to outbid Saddam Hussein in the display of aggression?

I write these lines on 17 January, the second day of Operation Desert Storm. Why else did Mr Bush give the order to attack Iraq if not to ask of the world, "Hey, give me a little face"?

The phrasing of the president's question proclaimed his allegiance to the old world order, the one governed by force and the show of force. The autumn's diplomatic maneuvers made it clear that the White House meant to restore what used to be called the "Pax Americana."

Between August and January the United States paid handsome bribes for the votes of the Security Council at the United Nations but otherwise listened as inattentively to the counsel of its nominal allies as George Will might listen to the political views of the wine steward in an Argentine restaurant in Santa Monica. The alliance put together in the Persian Gulf, with whichever kings or kingdoms happened to be free on waivers from OPEC or the Arab League, might as easily have been arranged by the late John Foster Dulles.

Careless of the costs, knowing little or nothing of the languages, history or cultural traditions of the Middle East, confident that the war with Iraq would be won in a matter of weeks if not within hours or days, the makers of American policy assumed (as did Saddam Hussein) that their own moral equations somehow were synonymous with the laws of nature and the will of God.

In opposition to the incessant moralisms broadcast from the White House, a fair number of people in Washington, both in Congress and in the national media, offered tentative sketches of a world order that might not have been so easily understood by Saladin or Godfrey of Bouillon. They argued for patience, for the efficacy of economic sanctions, for an army under the command of the United Nations, for a coalition comprised of more or less equal interests, for the use of as little force as possible and then only as a defensive measure. They questioned the American capacity to balance the world on the scale of American justice or in the ledger of American commerce. From whom did we think we could borrow the money to pay for the imperial legions? Upon conquering the wicked city of Baghdad, whom did we hope to appoint to the office of proconsul?

The voices of doubt and restraint were lost in the din of the marching bands. Nobody in the Bush administration made the slightest attempt to imagine a future that didn't look exactly like the past. Nobody wished to understand the historical origins of Iraq's grievances, which have more to do with the British and Ottoman empires than with the United States. Nobody wished to restrain the predatory oil pricing that suits our own convenience. Nobody said anything about taking down the expensive military arsenals that we have so profitably sold to so many aspiring despots. Nor did anybody say much of anything about a decent settlement of the Arab-Israeli dispute, about alternative fuels and the management of the world's energy resources, about redistributing the wealth of the Middle East in some way that might promote the chance of peace.

By trying to preserve the illusion of a balance of power along the lines set forth by Lord Palmerston or Kaiser Wilhelm, Mr Bush and his nostalgic friends in Congress and the Pentagon seek to comfort themselves with the cheerful news that they live in an orderly and coherent world, or at least in a world in which order and coherence remain within the range of the heaviest artillery.

The old world order assumes a distinction between naked and fully clothed aggression. On Sunday afternoons in Mozambique and Guatemala, law-abiding families vanish as abruptly from sight as did the law-abiding citizens of Kuwait, but they leave so quietly and so often that they offer no affront to the harmony of nations. Through the autumn ad campaign crying up the prospect of war with Iraq, the Bush administration made little mention of the thirty-three other wars currently in progress in the world. Nor did our media think to make the point that our own society assumes a norm of violence that would frighten all but the most remorseless Arab. No other modern nation, whether capitalist or socialist or Christian or Muslim, shares the American tolerance for crime. The indexes of murder and theft in the United States (that is, aggression dressed in old sneakers as well as by Brooks Brothers and Bijan) dwarf the comparative statistics in England, Libya, France, Germany and Iran. As with the old game of power politics, the rich man's aggression provokes less censure than the poor man's aggression, which suggests that Saddam's fault can be found not only with his tank captains but also with his tailor.

But the idea of a balance of power implies the existence of reasonably long-term interests and alliances, and in a world subject to sudden techno-logical revolutions as well as to the bewildering movements of peoples, currencies, markets, oil spills and fervent nationalisms, who can be sure that anything will remain the same from one week to the next? So many forces and allegiances have been let loose in the world, and the major powers find so many ways in which to combine and recombine that even so subtle a statesman as Metternich would have been hard-pressed to change last year's enemies into next year's friends. What would have become of his certainties about Germany or Russia or the Polish frontier?

The fear of an ambiguous future in the aftermath of the Cold War gives rise to the wish for simplifications and a safe return to the past. Often on seeing Mr Bush threaten Saddam with the scourge of war, I thought that he might be trying to substitute a lesser fear for a greater one, as if he would rather confront Iraq, no matter how despotic or heavily armed, than confront a world dissolved into anarchy, a world in which any terrorist with a crackpot dream of heaven can stuff an atomic weapon into an old suitcase and hold for ransom the life of New York or Washington.

Americans tend to think of foreign affairs in terms of sporting events that allow for unambiguous results. Either the team wins or it loses; the game is over within a reasonable period of time, and everybody can go back to doing something else. Much to everyone's regret, and regardless of the outcome of this winter's war in the Gulf, the events of the next twenty years seem likely to make nonsense of the sporting analogies. Too many powers can make their anger known to the world (if not at conference tables, then by means of an assassination or the poisoning of a reservoir), and the chains of causation have become much longer and more democratic than those conceived of by the Congress of Vienna.

If tomorrow morning at ten o'clock Iraq renounced its belief in Allah and withdrew its armies from Kuwait, the crisis in the world would not resolve itself into a finale by Busby Berkeley and the chorus line at the American Enterprise Institute. If it isn't the Iraqis, then it will be the Syrians; if not the Syrians, then the Brazilians or the Lithuanians or the South Africans.

The pervasive intuitions of dread give rise to a confusion of feeling that makes it difficult to interpret such phrases as "the national interest" or to guess whether the voices prophesying war mean to signal an advance or a retreat. The presentiment of a terrible looming just over the horizon of the news seeps through the voices of people pleading for surcease and disengagement, who argue that the United States has wasted enough blood and treasure in the ill-conceived crusades of the past thirty years, that the country should retire to the fastnesses of its coasts and leave the rest of the world to its murdering corruption.

But where is it safe to hide? Odysseus could return from his wanderings to Ithaca, but the modern world doesn't provide the refuge of home islands. Who is not hostage to the interconnectedness of the AIDS virus and the radioactive wind?

Within the world's military headquarters I'm sure that innumerable officers have drawn contingency plans for all kinds of wars—wars against revolutions, proxy wars, diplomatic wars, wars in Yugoslavia and Korea, wars for oil and bauxite and grain, wars fought with conventional weapons, amphibious wars, air wars, ground wars, nuclear wars. But how large will these wars become and how many people might have to be killed before the bugles sound the retreat?

Nobody likes to discuss this question in public (as witness the recent silence in Congress about our probable casualties in the Persian Gulf) because it has become difficult to find either a sufficiently high-minded principle or an inescapable material interest on behalf of which 250 million people might think it glorious to sacrifice their children.

The vagueness is traditional. In August 1914 none of the Allied or Central powers could explain its reasons for going off to the First World War. Four years later, after 10 million soldiers had died in the trenches, the governments in question still could not give a plausible reason for the killing. The best that anybody could do was to say that the war had been fought to end all wars, that its purpose had been to establish a "new world order" immune to the disease of power politics.

March 1991

HARD TIMES

The art of taxation consists in so plucking the goose as
to get the most feathers with the least hissing.
—ASCRIBED TO COLBERT

The proofs of recession had been so unmistakable for so many months that I had thought President Bush might wish to say something pertinent on the topic in his State of the Union address. He spoke on 29 January, and January had been an especially grim month along the whole line of the economic front. The Bank of New England failed on 6 January, at a cost to the government of $2.3 billion; on 7 January the Defense Department canceled a $52 billion weapons contract, obliging two defense contractors (McDonnell Douglas and General Dynamics) to lay off 10,000 workers in St. Louis and Fort Worth; over the course of the next two weeks the unemployment rate reached 6 percent; Eastern Airlines collapsed and Pan American World Airways filed for protection under the bankruptcy laws; numerous major corporations, among them Occidental Petroleum and Manufacturers Hanover, halved the dividend paid to stockholders; the governors of twenty-eight states declared what one of them called "financial martial law" and preached what another of them called "the gospels of austerity" (that is, more taxes and fewer public services); the big automobile companies reported heavy losses and the consumer-confidence index receded to its lowest ebb since the Great Depression.

Together with the news of general and institutional failure, the media supplied a fund of grim anecdotes that measured the winter's defeats in the specific instances of individual suffering and panic: people losing jobs, houses, their definitions of self; a woman in Iowa too frightened to go into a store because she couldn't afford to buy anything; a former owner of a marketing company in California glad of the chance to clean toilets; two high school students in North Carolina who had given up the hope of college; and a woman in Massachusetts saying, "It's scary; it's like unemployed people are coming out of the sky, there are so many of them."

The casualty reports apparently didn't make much of an impression on President Bush. Buoyed by the applause of the Congress on the evening of 29 January, the president talked mostly about his beloved war in Iraq and his exciting collection of planes and boats in the Persian Gulf. He took up the question of the nation's troubled economic affairs with an air of faint distaste, as if any extended discussion about money was somehow beneath the dignity of a gentleman. About a third of the way into his speech he descended to the topic by means of a transition from the patriotic heights of sententious moralism: "We are resolute and resourceful," he said. "If we can selflessly confront evil for the sake of good in a land so far away, then surely we can make this land all that it should be."

For the next fifteen minutes Mr Bush read through the list of catchwords that his speechwriters deemed appropriate to the occasion—"hard work of freedom," "shining purpose," "thousand points of light," "next American century," "economic expansion temporarily interrupted," "what America is all about," and so on. He dutifully performed the ritual of polite phrases, and at one point he even went so far as to try to express a feeling of heart-felt concern. Blinking earnestly in the light, his voice reaching for the note of tremulous sincerity, he said: "I know, tonight, in some regions of our country, people are in genuine economic distress. And I hear them."

The effect was embarrassing. It was obvious that Mr Bush didn't hear anybody who wasn't talking to him about the sport of war in "a land so far away." His attempt at genuine emotion proved as unctuous and vacant as the sentiment sent to an unknown nephew on a Hallmark card. His failure was one of the imagination, what his handlers in the 1988 election campaign recognized as his difficulty with "the vision thing." His words were empty because he couldn't see through the veil of abstraction (deficit, interest rate, percentage of unemployed, loans defaulted) to the scenes of human suffering implicit in the numbers. He didn't know—quite literally—what he was talking about.

Given Mr Bush's temperament and the nature of his experience, his lack of sympathy is by no means surprising. Listening to him speak, I remembered that he was a rich man, accustomed from birth to the attitudes of mind associated with the habits of privilege and wealth. Rich people find it almost impossible to imagine the existence of anybody unlike themselves. Their indifference follows from their inability to take seriously other people's desires, and they constantly ask themselves the peevish questions, "Who *are* all those other people out there, and what in Heaven's name do they *want*?" The self becomes so inextricably identified with money that the rich man imagines that only his attachment to it gives it meaning, substance and virtue. Money has no discernible reality in the hands of lesser mortals because lesser mortals have no decent use for it. The philosophers of the reactionary Right dress up this congenital selfishness with the argument that although money is good for the rich it is bad for the poor. The rich know how to ward off the corrosive evil of government subsidy and inherited stock portfolios. Similar temptations placed in the way of the poor (such as welfare payments, student loans or food stamps) invariably corrupt their morals and destroy their sense of self-worth.

Because the rich object to the very thought of other people also becoming rich—crowding the golf courses, commanding tables at the better restaurants, taking up too much of the available light, space, air, and publicity—nothing comforts them so much as reading the obituary notices of their peers, or the reports of ruin and catastrophe visited, like moral judgements, on the lower classes. From the point of view of people with money in hand, an economic recession is always extremely good news.

As long ago as last December the secretary of the treasury, Nicholas Brady, a friend of Mr Bush's and himself a rich man, put the matter as plainly as possible in answer to a journalist's question about the state of the deteriorating economy: "I don't think it's the end of the world," he said, "even if we have a recession. We'll pull back out of it again. No big deal."

No big deal for Mr Brady, who rests comfortably on an expensive fortune, and certainly not the end of the world for Mr Brady's fellow members of the Links Club and the Essex County Hunt, who welcome the bracing atmosphere of bankruptcy and debt as a sign that soon they will have the chance to buy property at gratifyingly distressed prices. The business principle is as simple as the looting of Kuwait. Students of human unhappiness as different from one another as J. P. Morgan and Voltaire understood that the comfort of the rich requires an abundant supply of the poor. Without the goads and spurs of poverty, who would clean the toilets in California or carry the golf clubs at Burning Tree or enlist in President Bush's armies?

Although the mathematics of recession remain constant—the rich get richer, the poor get poorer—the tone of the accompanying sophism reflects the balance of power between the possessing and the nonpossessing classes. If it is thought that the poor offer a clear and present danger to the moral perfection of the status quo, the rich give some thought to their choice of words. During the recession of 1982 the managers of the national finance took as much care with their rhetoric as with their raids on the Treasury. If the Bush administration no longer feels obliged to maintain anything other than the minimum appearance of polite concern, it is because the rigged financial markets of the Reagan administration called into being what can be fairly described as an American *rentier* class.

Between 1978 and 1987 American families belonging to the poorest 20 percent of the population became 8 percent poorer; during the same period of time American families within the richest 20 percent of the population became 13 percent richer. The disparity between rich and poor was most glaringly apparent at the extreme points of measurement. The income received by the upper 1 percent of American families improved by 49.8 percent in the years between 1977 and 1988; simultaneously, and by no means accidentally, the income received by families in the lowliest 1 percent of the population declined by 14.8 percent. Somewhere toward the middle of the decade of the 1980s, for the first time in the nation's history, the income that the American people earned from capital (that is, from rents, dividends and interest) equaled the sum earned as wages.

The people who profited so handsomely from the miracle of the junk-bond markets and the wonders of deregulation meant to keep what they had, and the election of President Bush ratified the division of the spoils. The company of the blessed (citizens of newfound leisure enjoying the view from the society's box seats) may not represent an impressive percentage of the population (probably no more than 5 percent), but when counted as an absolute number (ten or twelve million timid and self-interested individuals) they comprise a formidable political faction. By and large they are the people who manage the government, operate the media and the banks, control the universities and the advertising images, print the money and write the laws. Not all of them, of course, have had the sense to recognize their own interests, and I assume that a good many of them failed to heed the advice of their accountants last summer and so neglected to buy heavily in the bond markets. Some others among them undoubtedly found themselves on the wrong side of the corporate ledger when it came time for the company chairman to write the awful memo-randum about how the company had no choice (given the need to "restore America's competitive spirit in the world") but to let go entire battalions of its middle management.

Even so, and no matter what accidents might befall as much as a third of the membership, the possessing classes stand to profit from the recession. Assured of their prerogatives, and knowing that their interests will be flatteringly portrayed in the press, the possessing classes can count on the full faith and backing of President Bush. By the end of January they understood that the phrase "thousand points of light" referred to the fireworks displays in Kuwait and Iraq. If they had any further doubts about the president's distrust of the American poor, they had only to study the bias embedded in the budget that he presented to the Congress on 4 February. Like the State of the Union address, the budget offered no concessions to charity: no public works; no nonsense about social safety nets. Richard Darman, the budget director, complained, becomingly, about so much money (the wretched entitlements) still being wasted on the greedy poor, and he recommended a subtraction of $46.6 billion over the next five years from the line items that fall under Medicare, farm price supports and schools. With the projection of a $318 billion deficit for the next fiscal year (a sum certain to prove grossly understated), everybody holding cash or its equivalents could look forward both to a near-term fall in property prices and a long-term rise of the interest rates.

Even if the Bush administration wished to correct the economic imbalances in the country, I doubt that it possesses the means to do so. The government's fiscal and monetary policies appear to work against one another, and the interests of the domestic economy seem almost directly opposed to the interests of the international economy. Nor can anybody expect much help from the Congress, which endorses (unanimously and by acclamation) whatever expedient purpose serves its own nonpartisan vanity and cowardice.

Like the president, the Congress obeys the rule of money, and the successful politician learns, as do the merely rich, that in order to preserve the coldness of heart necessary to the maintenance of a safe fortune or a public image he must alienate himself from anything so subversive as an honest thought or a magnanimous act. He can buy a place for himself in the midst of events (the front row at the Los Angeles Coliseum, say, or a seat in the United States Senate), but if he knows what's good for his career (and President Bush always has known, as unerringly as a blind pig on the scent of a white truffle) then he will listen to the advice of the family lawyers (or the National Security Council, or the Federal Reserve Board, or the Joint Chiefs of Staff) who warn him against the folly of generous feeling. The rich have very little talent for loving anybody other than themselves. It's possible to love one's dog, or one's dress, or one's duck-shooting hat (maybe even one's air force or one's Ferragamo shoes), but a human being presents a problem of a far more difficult order of magnitude.

In his State of the Union address Mr Bush spoke more touchingly about the distress of the nation's banks than he did about the suffering of his fellow citizens. The priority of his concern reminded me of a press conference last summer at which a government bank examiner was trying to explain why it was going to cost yet another $2 billion to make good the debts of yet another savings bank. The man was impatient and annoyed. For some days he had been looking for trace elements of liquidity in the desert of the balance sheet, and he was in no mood to comment on the loss of jobs likely to result from so spectacular a fraud. In answer to what he thought was a stupid question, he said, in an irritated tone of voice, "Excuse me, I only represent banks, not people."

From the point of view of the season subscribers in the box seats, the recession presents itself as spectacle—something seen on television, a kind of downmarket sitcom that allows the audience to laugh about the beggars pawing through the garbage in the streets, about the 37 million Americans who cannot afford the price of health insurance, about the grammar schools abandoned to the drug trade, about all those homeless people lying around on the sidewalks. If we find the jokes depressing, we can always switch the channel to the scenes of glorious war in Iraq. The brightly smiling newscasters will assure us, once again, that we are doing the right and noble thing, that we have become, just as President Bush promised, a kinder, gentler nation.

April 1991

TYROMANCY

The deterioration of every government begins with the
decay of the principles on which it was founded.
—MONTESQUIEU

T he Supreme Court ruled in May that people who accept government money must say what the government wishes them to say. The ruling followed from the Court's interpretation of *Rust* v. *Sullivan* and forbade mention of the word "abortion" in any of the 4,500 clinics that receive federal funds and provide advice and care to as many as 4 million women in the United States, many of them frightened and most of them poor. The Court imposed its fiat by the narrow majority of 5–4, and it relied on a line of reasoning (supplied by Chief Justice William Rehnquist) that defined speech as a function of congressional subsidy. Because the government doesn't choose to fund the practice of abortion, then the government cannot talk about the practice of abortion. Speech becomes a privilege instead of a right.

Any reader who thinks that I exaggerate the arrogance of Justice Rehnquist's argument has only to read the two or three clumsy sentences with which he grinds the First Amendment into the pulp of sophism. As follows:

> The government can, without violating the Constitution, selectively fund a program to encourage certain activities it believes to be in the public interest, without at the same time funding an alternate program which seeks to deal with the problem in another way. In so doing, the government has not discriminated on the basis of viewpoint; it has merely chosen to fund one activity to the exclusion of the other. . . .

The chief justice makes the word "fund" a synonym for the word "viewpoint," and the reasoning is as autocratic as the reasoning that sustains the government's theory of "classified information." The four justices who joined Rehnquist's opinion (Justices Souter, Scalia, Kennedy and White) presumably also share his inclination to recognize only those truths that appear in court with an acceptable financial statement. If the viewpoint is funded, it may be discussed; if the viewpoint is not funded, it cannot be introduced in polite company. A clinic retains permission to talk about abortion only on condition that it does so in a separate building under the disguise of a separate program that receives none of its funding from the federal government.

The Court's ruling is consistent with the squinting and repressive attitude of mind with which the government over the last decade has sought to dilute or eliminate as many civil liberties as could be brought up on charges of sedition. The expansion of the state's police powers (in the universities and regulatory agencies as well as the jails) has swelled its desire to impose on the American people the habits of obedience. Reading the announcements issued in Washington (whether by the Supreme Court, the White House or the Pentagon), I hear the voice of an ascendant ruling class that sometimes confuses itself with the French nobility during the reign of Louis XIV and at other times with the Soviet Politburo during the early years of the Cold War. Royal prerogative and ideological doctrine take precedence over undignified behavior and plain fact.

Justice Rehnquist and his associates apparently choose to ignore what they regard as the contemptible rabble they occasionally notice—in passing and at a distance—in the dingier precincts of Washington, DC. The Court's ruling upholds regulations appended by an administrative bureaucrat in 1988 to the Public Health Service Act passed by Congress in 1970. Like the ruling, the regulations make no attempt to imagine the lives of the women condemned to bear the burden of the government's moralism. The women who apply for help in the clinics under Rehnquist's jurisdiction cannot afford to go to Paris to buy perfume and the newest lines in contraception. Few of them can afford the price of medical insurance, much less the cost of their own physician. Many of them cannot read a fifth-grade grammar. Of those among them who find themselves pregnant at the age of fifteen or sixteen, almost none possess the resources (emotional, financial or social) to raise and educate the children born at the government's command.

The Supreme Court holds all such evidence circumstantial and irrelevant. Compassion is the vice of liberals; knowledge is weakness, and any deviation from the party line subverts the New American World Order. Any doctor receiving any fraction of federal money must never utter the word "abortion"; if the patient mentions the word, the doctor must say, solemnly and by rote (in the voice of a prison guard), "This clinic does not consider abortion to be an appropriate method of family planning." Instead of affirming a principle for the sake of its people, the government sacrifices its people to a principle as unforgiving as an Aztec bird god.

Among the justices who dissented from the majority opinion, Justice Harry A. Blackmun most forcibly stated the objections to what he construed as the negation of the constitutional right to free speech. As follows:

> Until today the court never has upheld a viewpoint-based suppression of speech simply because that suppression was a condition upon the acceptance of public funds. Whatever may be the government's power to condition the receipt of its largesse upon the relinquishment of constitutional rights, it surely does not extend to a condition that suppresses the recipient's cherished freedom of speech based solely upon the content or viewpoint of that speech. . . .

Maybe Blackmun is persuasive because he writes in English (as opposed to the bureaucratic jargon assembled by Rehnquist), but I find his arguments convincing, and so I'm left to marvel at the damage a society can inflict on itself once it chooses to live in the land of wish and dream.

The United States derives its strength from the willingness of its citizens to ask questions and say what they mean. Democracy isn't supposed to be easy. It assumes conflict not only as the normal but also as the necessary condition of existence, and it allies itself with the freedom of mind and the continuing process of change. The demand for autocracy—for more laws, more rules, more regulations, more police, more prisons—speaks to the wish to make time stand still and denies, as if by totalitarian diktat or royal decree, the first of the principles on which the United States was founded.

Under the title *The March of Folly* the late Barbara Tuchman in 1984 published a set of instructive essays addressed to what she called the "surpassing wooden-headedness" exhibited by various states bent on the destruction not only of their own best interests but also of their existence. She classified the practice of misgovernment under four headings:

1. *Tyranny or Repression* (examples so numerous as to require no citation);

2. *Excessive Ambition* (the Spanish Armada, Germany's twice-attempted conquest of Europe, and so on);

3. *Incompetence or Decadence* (the late Roman Empire, the last Romanovs, and so on);

4. *Folly or Perversity.* Under the fourth heading Tuchman took as her four texts Troy's welcoming of the Greek wooden horse; the misrule of six successive Renaissance popes who, by virtue of their spendthrift tastes for luxury and murder, incited the Protestant Revolt and Reformation; Britain's loss of North America in the late eighteenth century; and the American defeat in Vietnam, promoted by four presidents who comforted themselves with a succession of preposterous lies. In each instance Tuchman presents the portrait of a ruling class that no longer knows the difference between what is true and what it chooses to say is true.

Pope Sixtus IV (a.k.a. Francesco della Rovere) stages a banquet so elaborate that it invites comparison with the licentiousness of ancient Rome; Pope Alexander VI (a.k.a. Roderigo Borgia) makes a resplendent show of both his mistresses and his cavalry squadrons. It never occurs to either prince that somebody might notice his estrangement from Christian doctrine. The British House of Lords in the 1770s chooses to see the American colonists as a contemptible rabble, and General Thomas Clarke, aide-de-camp to King George III, boasts in the presence of Benjamin Franklin that "with a thousand Grenadiers he would undertake to go from one end of America to the other and geld all the males, partly by force and partly with a little coaxing." President Johnson evokes the laughter of the White House claque by referring to Vietnam as "that raggedy-ass little fourth-rate country."

The Supreme Court decision in the matter of *Rust* v. *Sullivan* satisfies Tuchman's criteria for an act of folly because it insists that the desire of a petulant ruling class is synonymous with judgement and reason and that words can be made to stand as surrogates for things. Rehnquist speaks for a majority, not only of the Court but also of the Washington oligarchy, when he rules that the American experiment has gone far enough and that the republic no longer can tolerate the risk implicit in the freedom of speech and the freedom of thought.

Henceforth, says Rehnquist, the truth is a function of dogma. The government will pay to hear only what it wants to hear. Any statement that fails to conform to the prerecorded political or religious announcement isn't welcome at the White House dance.

John Adams noticed precisely the same habit of mind in London in the years prior to the Revolutionary War. The ministers of the Crown were so disdainful of the American cause that they never troubled to send a representative, much less one of their own august company, to the far shore of the Atlantic Ocean to so much as glance at the cities of Boston or New York. "The pride and vanity of that nation [Britain] is a disease," said Adams. "It is a delirium; it has been flattered and inflamed so long by themselves and others that it perverts everything."

Given the Supreme Court's current theory of the universe, I expect that we can look forward to further distinctions between funded and unfunded speech. Extended to the schools, Rehnquist's interpretation of *Rust* v. *Sullivan* can be made to inform the curriculum with whatever truths the government finds most flattering to its own image of itself. If a doctor can be forbidden to mention abortion, surely a teacher can be forbidden to mention Lincoln or Ho Chi Minh or the planet Uranus. If the government can discuss only what it has agreed to fund, then any institution taking money from the government (the National Weather Service, say, or the National Institutes of Health) would be bound to keep silent about any and all events that lack the authority of a congressional appropriation. A flood washes through the Mississippi Delta, but no federal official can acknowledge its arrival. The bubonic plague kills 12,000 people in East Los Angeles, but no federal official can say that the epidemic is anything other than a slander put about by the tabloid press or the Democratic party.

Let reason and desire become one and the same, and the possible stupidities become as infinite as the number of the fixed stars. Isidore of Seville affirmed that menstrual blood was a fluid dispensed by the Devil and that the merest touch of it caused blossoms to fade, grasses to wither, iron to rust and brass to turn black. In colonial America, anyone caught eating mince pie was suspected of royalist sympathies. The host of beetles that ravaged the vineyard of St Julian were commanded to appear in King's Court, and when they neglected the summons, a lawyer was appointed to speak on their behalf. The art of tyromancy divines the future in the coagulation of cheese.

The delirium of vanity and pride follows from the presumption of omnipotence. The American government at the moment does as it pleases, but instead of being met with objection, the ministers of the state find themselves swathed in applause. We betray our best hopes and principles in what was called a war in the Persian Gulf, and the country celebrates the defeat as if it were a victory. The savings and loan associations, and now maybe also the commercial banks, burden the public treasury with ruinous debt, but hardly anybody thinks to ask how it came to pass that so much was taken from so many by so few. The Supreme Court not only imposes financial conditions on the right to free speech but also restricts the right to habeas corpus (*McClesky* v. *Zant*) and rules (*Arizona* v. *Fulminate*) that the use of a coerced confession does not render a trial unfair. The government makes no secret of its contempt for the people whom it routinely plunders, but the people offer as little objection as the kitchen help in a Mafia hotel.

Sooner or later, of course, the foolishness and greed of the ruling class become so overbearing that the people lose respect for the name and image of authority. When the people also lose respect for the idea that their rulers supposedly serve and represent, the march of folly becomes a rout. Just as I can imagine Justice Rehnquist gazing anxiously into a vat of Brie, so also I can imagine him hiding from a host of beetles or an angry mob.

August 1991

JUSTICE HORATIO ALGER

One can always be kind to people about whom one
cares nothing.
—OSCAR WILDE

The Republican party has a talent for turning politics into puppet theater, and by next spring I expect that we can look forward to seeing the figure of Supreme Court Justice Clarence Thomas dancing in the strings once occupied by Willie Horton. The modern American presidential election apparently requires the presence of a representative black man who can be made to carry the party message and sing the company song. In 1988 the Republicans presented a

Victorian melodrama, and they cast the black man as the villain of the tale. Rapists and murderous bandits were said to be roaming the streets, a good many of them presumably free on bail raised by Democratic politicians and gorging themselves on the feast of public welfare. Enter Willie Horton, a convict on leave, grim-faced and barely literate, guilty of vicious crimes, and a man in whom the electorate could recognize the embodiment of its easiest fear. The Republican stage managers supplied the words and the music, and for two months on the nation's television screens Willie danced the dance of death.

But that was three years ago, before the glorious war in Iraq under the direction of General Colin Powell proved to the American audience the strength of its mercenary army, and before the Los Angeles police department demonstrated its capacity to keep the peace on the marches of the Foothill Freeway. If the electorate no longer doubts the need to deal as bluntly as possible with the ungrateful poor (whether in western Asia or East St. Louis), then maybe it is time to talk about rewards instead of punishments. If the Republicans wish to show themselves alert to the idiom of multiculturalism, they need a new black man to tell a new and friendly story. Enter Judge Clarence Thomas, dressed in a button-down shirt and living in an expensive Virginia suburb, a graduate of Yale Law School, an admirer of corporate finance and an apostle for the authority of the state. Horatio Alger in blackface.

If the political fables seem too cynical or too simple-minded, consider the way in which President Bush introduced Judge Thomas to the television cameras at Kennebunkport on 1 July, only four days after Justice Thurgood Marshall unexpectedly resigned from the Court for reasons of infirmity and age. Instead of talking about Judge Thomas's understanding of the law, Mr Bush told the story of his successful career. He might as well have been writing a letter of recommendation to the admissions committee at Augusta National or the Council on Foreign Relations. Behold, said President Bush, an excellent black man who had achieved his success without resort to liberal politics or the federal dole. The president began by saying—categorically and without further explanation—that Judge Thomas "is the best person for this position." He then proceeded to list the judge's schools and his scholarships, his service as a legislative assistant to Senator John Danforth of Missouri, his eight-year term as a federal bureaucrat under the tutelage of Ronald Reagan and the American Enterprise Institute, his appointment, in 1990, to the United States Court of Appeals for the District of Columbia. After praising Judge

Thomas as a "delightful and warm, intelligent person who has great empathy and a wonderful sense of humor," Mr Bush concluded his endorsement with an inspired non sequitur. "Judge Thomas's life," he said, "is a model for all Americans, and he's earned the right to sit on this nation's highest court."

The two clauses have nothing to do with each other. By virtue of the same false syllogism, the president could easily have submitted the name of Ken Griffey Jr or Michael Jordan or Arsenio Hall. Logic, of course, was irrelevant. So were the questions pertaining to the judge's wisdom or experience. Had the judge been white or green or blue, he would have had as little chance of sitting on the Supreme Court or standing in front of the cameras at Kennebunkport as Kevin Costner or Nolan Ryan.

Judge Thomas responded on key and in kind. He presented himself as an exemplary proof of the coming to pass of the American Dream, and his remarks could have served as an acceptance of an Academy Award. Instead of talking about the nature of the office for which he had been nominated, about the weight of the law or his countrymen's hopes of justice, he thanked the wonderful cast that "helped me to this point and this moment in my life—especially my grandparents, my mother and the nuns, all of whom were adamant that I grow up to make something of myself. I also thank my wonderful wife and my wonderful son." The judge glistened with egoism (seldom a good sign in a magistrate), but he spoke with tears in his voice, and the effect enhanced the photo opportunity.

For the next half hour the reporters in attendance on the lawn of the summer White House tried to ask hard questions. Was the appointment as cynical as it seemed? Wasn't it true that Mr Bush was trafficking in racial quotas? Wouldn't it be fair to say that in any other venue of the federal government Judge Thomas's nomination would be classified as an "affirmative action hire"?

None of the questions troubled the surface of the president's serene hypocrisy. No, he said, the nomination had nothing to do with racial preference. He had chosen Judge Thomas strictly on the basis of merit, and he didn't see "even an appearance of an inconsistency" with his previously stated opposition to the use of quotas. His denials were as condescending as they were dishonest.

QUESTION: Was race a factor whatsoever, sir?
PRESIDENT BUSH: I don't see it at all. The fact that he's a minority, you've heard his testimony, the kind of life he's had, and I think that speaks eloquently for itself.

The president rested his case on the biography, "on the kind of life he's had," and he left it to the press or the Democratic party to muster the courage to attack the story of a poor black boy born in a Georgia slum, deserted by his father at the age of seven, who learned his letters from Catholic nuns and who, by dint of his spiritual faith and moral effort, triumphed over the evil of segregation and went on to win fame and fortune in the imperial city that was Ronald Reagan's Washington.

The story was so good ("suckled by wolves; rescued by nuns") that the president didn't need to bother with more than a brief glance at Judge Thomas's prior thought and writing. The newspaper accounts suggest that he considered only one other name for the Court (Judge Emilio M. Garza of Texas) and that he reached his decision during a lull in his Saturday golf game. On Monday Judge Thomas was brought to Maine in an air force plane. The president granted him a brief audience (about twenty minutes in the presidential bedroom) and then, after lunch on the veranda (with Mrs Bush and a few of the president's senior advisers), presented him, like a prize fish, to the national media.

The president looked to be well pleased with himself. By nominating a black man to Justice Thurgood Marshall's seat on the Supreme Court, he had made what must have seemed to him a very deft and very clever move in the opening phase of the 1992 presidential campaign. If Judge Thomas didn't espouse Justice Marshall's liberal views (if, in fact, he was a doctrinaire conservative best known for his liege man's service to the mean-spirited bias that Marshall detested), well, then, too bad, and so much the worse for the adherents of the hated L word. Let the civil rights people bitch and moan and whine; let the National Association for the Advancement of Colored People worry about finding its way out of the maze of conflicted feelings. Overly sensitive advocates of racial justice had asked Bush for a black man, and he had given them a black man, and if they didn't like what they got, they could tell their troubles to Oprah Winfrey or the moon. The president's self-satisfaction expressed his contempt for the world of black political theory.

Together with his exemplary life, Judge Thomas possessed the attribute of a near perfect (and therefore blameless) silence on most of the principal issues likely to come before the Supreme Court. At the age of forty-three, he was one of the two youngest judges named to the Supreme Court in the last century (the other was Justice William O. Douglas). Because Judge Thomas had served on the Appellate Court in Washington for no longer than fifteen months, he hadn't yet had the chance to hand down any notable decisions, and because his published writings were so few (occasional journal articles and newspaper op-ed page pieces), he could be described as a man of few known opinions.

What he was known for was his bureaucrat's hostility toward the messy emotions associated with human and civil rights. In 1982 President Reagan had appointed Judge Thomas chairman of the Equal Employment Opportunity Commission, and for the next seven years the judge faithfully opposed the reckless and irresponsible use of the affirmative action laws. Together with a number of other black conservatives loyal to the Reagan cause, Judge Thomas beat the drum for the grand old Republican doctrines of individual initiative and free enterprise. Much of his own education had been paid for with government money, and he owed his career to racial preference and political patronage. But, like President Bush, he apparently didn't see any inconsistency between his ideological opposition to racial quotas and his dependence on those same quotas for his admission to Yale Law School.

For eight years the Reagan administration conducted a systematic assault against almost any civil right or civil liberty that anybody could name. Of the corruption so evidently in office during the 1980s, Thurgood Marshall once said, "I wouldn't do the job of dog catcher for Ronald Reagan." His likely successor on the Supreme Court doesn't permit himself so impolitic a view of things; over almost the whole of his career he remained as quiet as any other well-behaved functionary determined "to make it on his own." Senator Orrin G. Hatch of Utah predicted an easy confirmation in the Senate. "This man [Thomas] understands the difficulties of life. He has had a tough life, but he's made it all the way. Anybody who takes him on in the area of civil rights is taking on the grandson of a sharecropper."

Again, as with President Bush's encomium, it was the story of the life, not the temper of the thought, that defined Judge Thomas's place in the Republican puppet theater. It didn't matter whether he was made of straw or wood. The conservative scene painters and costume designers delighted in the task of furnishing the ideological decor. Writing in the *Washington Post*, the columnist George Will discovered in Judge Thomas a character who "could have stepped from the pages of those novels 19th-century readers loved. Novels of astonishing upward mobility by strivers who succeed by pluck and luck." Writing in the *Wall Street Journal*, Peggy Noonan (once-upon-a-time speechwriter to both Presidents Reagan and Bush) abandoned herself to the language of twentieth-century soap opera:

"Clarence Thomas made it in America because he was loved. His mother loved him. And when she could no longer care for him she gave him to her parents to bring up and they loved him too. . . . He got love and love gave him pride and pride gave him confidence that he had a place at the table."

Ms Noonan's sentiment appears on the opposite face of the coin of President Bush's contempt. On both sides of the coin Judge Thomas remains an ornamental figure—an emblem, a token, a medium of exchange. The president apparently thinks that he can play at racial politics as if it were a game of horseshoes.

The mistake is likely to be disastrous. If President Bush cares so little for the country's future or purpose that he stands willing to sell a seat on the Supreme Court for a short-term partisan interest, then from whom does he deserve either trust or respect? He humiliates Judge Thomas as a man, insults blacks as a race, debases the currency of the law and substitutes the cult of personality for the force of coherent thought. He degrades the office of the presidency by making it trivial.

It's possible that Judge Thomas might prove to be a capable justice of the Supreme Court. I know little or nothing of his mind, and I cannot presume to guess at what he might think or learn or say: I do know that he will be obliged to come to his decisions in a society that will insist more stridently on the loveliness of its stupidity and its superstition. He inherits the whirlwind financed by his patrons in the Reagan and Bush administrations, and his and our survival will require him to slip free of his puppet's strings and make good his escape from the stereotyped box of President Bush's Punch-and-Judy show.

September 1991

HISTORY LESSON

To tell about a drunken muzhik's beating his wife is
incomparably harder than to compose a whole tract
about the "woman question."
—TURGENEV

The coup d'état attempted in Moscow on 19 August (a.k.a. "The Putsch of Fools") came and went almost as abruptly as the hurricane that arrived that same Monday on the New England coast. Within a matter of hours a sizable bulk of the received wisdom of the last fifty years looked like the wreckage washing ashore in Narragansett Bay. The electricity in Rhode Island failed at noon, a few hours after the conspirators in the Kremlin told a press conference that Mikhail Gorbachev was nowhere to be found because "he has got very tired and needs some time to get his health back." When the electricity was restored (late in the afternoon on Friday), broken statues of Lenin were lying around on the grass in Gorky Park at the same aimless angles as the masts fallen into the sea at Portsmouth and Jamestown.

The Soviet Empire had dissolved, and the belief in communism had been canceled until further notice. Just as emphatically, and maybe more importantly, the failed coup d'état deleted the Marxist definition of history. As much an article of faith in the capitalist West as in the socialist East for the last half century, the Marxist orthodoxy promoted the thesis that history was a science, not an art, and that the character of particular individuals counted for less than nothing when plotted on the graphs of statistical projection. But in Moscow during the week of 19 August none of the leading incidents fit the measure of the familiar categories. The vagaries of the human spirit eluded the dragnets of the social sciences, and the traits of human personality proved more decisive than the forces of socioeconomic abstraction. Narrative triumphed over ideology, and the specific instance played havoc with the general theory.

What econometric model could have gauged the resonance of Boris Yeltsin's voice once he stood up to speak from the turret of a tank? Who could have foreseen the resistance of so many ordinary citizens, who refused to be cowed by the usual threats, or the resolve of the city officials (among them the mayor of Leningrad) who refused to obey the orders presented at the point of a gun? What policy institute could have guessed that the conspiracy of the reactionary Right (on paper as impregnable as the Lubianka prison) would stand revealed as a collective Wizard of Oz, a committee of timid bureaucrats, as divorced from the truths of their own motives as they were ignorant of the passions that moved the broad mass of the Russian people?

Like characters imagined by Chekhov or Gogol, the would-be saviors of the old order fell victim to their emotions (primarily fear and thwarted rage), and they so quickly lost sight of the grand blueprint of historical determinism (the one mentioned not only in the Soviet textbooks but also at the fear-mongering seminars sponsored by the American Enterprise Institute) that they neglected to arrest Yeltsin, cut all telephone lines, seize all radio stations and execute the captain of the Kremlin guard. Instead of parading their flags in the streets, they barricaded themselves within the maze of their beloved bureaucracy—issuing statements and decrees (about the shortages of food and the depletion of morals), ordering an immense printing of blank arrest orders and 250,000 pairs of handcuffs from a factory in Pskov, seeking to dam the flow of the future with a wall of paper.

By Wednesday they were consulting schedules for airline travel to central Asia. A cabinet minister retired to a hospital with a severe nervous disorder. A foreign secretary explained that his actions had been misinterpreted, his words badly misunderstood. A general left for the Crimea in the hope of apologizing to Gorbachev for all the confusion and noise.

Even as early as Tuesday, the second day of the putsch, I regretted the absence of Chekhov. Reading the accounts in the newspapers—by candlelight in a house as old as the Napoleonic Wars—I understood that the events in progress invited the perspective of a novelist, a playwright or a historian on the order of Macaulay or Gibbon. The circumstances didn't lend themselves to long and earnest discussions of ideological intent. The agony of the Communist *ancien régime* was a story about the strengths and weaknesses of character, about the stain of terror seeping across the face of a deputy secretary beginning to suspect that maybe he had divided his loyalties into too many parts, about Yeltsin's impulsiveness that was also Yeltsin's eloquence and Yeltsin's courage. Like the last Romanov czars, the Emergency Committee relied on the ancient tradition of ignorance and passivity said to have held the Russian spirit in chains for at least a thousand years. The people who gathered in the streets in the rain made do with a show of words and paving stones, knowing full well that in the event of gunfire their cause would be lost in twenty minutes.

By avoiding the risk of action, the conspirators were left with their own treachery and dithering incompetence. Their grandiose announcements reminded me of Chekhov's cast of provincial despots, of the ballrooms that he had described in Moscow and St. Petersburg, ballrooms crowded with pompous generals and complacent landlords bursting like sausages with news of the obvious and the sense of their own self-importance.

I invariably found myself trusting works of literature (if not Chekhov's stories, then the novels of Dostoyevski or Bulgakov) as the most reliable explications of the press reports. Within the entire canon of the collected works of Henry Kissinger and Zbigniew Brzezinski, not so much as a single sentence would have offered even the faintest appreciation of the behavior of Vasily Starodubtsev and Aleksandr Tizyakov, respectively the chairman of the Farmers' Union and the director of the military industrial lobby. Both gentlemen apparently embraced the cause of reaction in the hope of acquiring (at long last and after God knows how much delay and how many insults) the dignity of an office inside the Yellow walls of the Kremlin. All their lives they had wanted the importance of such an office, and nothing, not even the defection of the Tamanskaya division or the interior minister's suicide, could dissuade them from their purpose. From beginning to end, throughout the whole of the three days of the putsch, they remained fixed on the overriding question of moving furniture into suites 15 and 17. Tanks arrived and departed, and Vice President Gennadi Yanayev drank himself into an alcoholic stupor, but Starodubtsev and Tizyakov pressed forward with the great project, chivying the workmen, choosing wood grains, arranging the inkwells and the pencils. When Starodubtsev was arrested, he was still clutching the key to the kingdom so eagerly found and so irretrievably lost.

On Friday 23 August, the narrative of the bungled coup d'état changed into the story of the making of a new Russia, a new constitution, a new world, but it was still a story of human character (as opposed to the inevitable working out of political or economic doctrine), and through the scrim of the newspapers I could still hear the voice of the specific instance interrupting the broadcast of the general theory. As follows:

> An old-line Communist, arguing for the dissolution of the Soviet Congress: "The most disgusting thing in the world is a frightened deputy."
>
> A critic, age twenty-five, contemplating the troops standing disconsolately under the portico of the Bolshoi Theater: "That's not the way to do a coup. You remember how it was in Chile: fast and energetic. Ours was a thick porridge, a Russian idiocy."
>
> A parliamentary exchange between two disaffected politicians:
> FIRST DEPUTY: "Much of this congressional meeting has been undemocratic, I agree, and we've been put on our knees."
> SECOND DEPUTY: "It's not correct to say Congress was put on its knees. . . . This Congress was never off its knees in the first place."

During the last days of August events in Moscow moved so quickly that they could be seen as a single storm tide obliterating a shoreline or closing over the domes and towers of a lost world. Gorbachev returned to Moscow on a Thursday, expressing his gratitude to the democrats but still proclaiming his faith in the Communist party. On Saturday the Communist party all but ceased to exist, and by the following Tuesday the Soviet Union had sunk, like Byzantium or Troy, into the sea of oblivion. Leningrad had become St. Petersburg, and people greeting one another in front of the Winter Palace no longer used the term "comrade." In the parks and public squares the fragments of former monuments acquired the status of driftwood.

So also did the thesis of the American national security state. The work of deconstruction was more obvious in Moscow, but in Washington I could imagine an admiral interrupted in the midst of his briefing (to the Congress or the Joint Chiefs of Staff) on behalf of another fleet of nuclear submarines meant to confine the Soviet navy within the margins of the Baltic Sea. I thought of him in full uniform, pointing confidently at a map, reciting the ritual phrases of the old geopolitical liturgy that for forty years had alarmed the Council on Foreign Relations, comforted the faithful on the conservative and neo-conservative right, blessed the defense industries with the gifts of a merciful God. In the moment that the putsch in Moscow failed, the admiral might as well have been pointing at a map of the Assyrian Empire. Suddenly he was speaking a language as dead as Linear B, and the once numinous words and acronyms (Kremlinology, NATO, containment, domino theory, arc of crisis, and so on) referred to a dream of reality as distant in time as the Mayan worship of the sun. The shock must have been awful to behold. Just when everything seemed so promising for the military theorists in the aftermath of the victory in the Persian Gulf, American foreign policy had lost its shape and definition, and among the members of the *ancien régime* in Washington the tone of voice was elegiac: Lt Gen. Samuel V. Wilson, retired, once chief of the Defense Intelligence Agency said, "All my pillars of intellectual support are pretty well gone, because the Soviet Union and Soviet forces as I knew them no longer exist."

On 30 August, the day after the Soviet parliament declared the Communist party subject to criminal investigation, I noticed a story in the paper under the dateline Pompeii. A team of archaeologists had unearthed the bodies of eight more Romans who, on 24 August A.D. 79, failed to escape the cloud of burning ash descending so suddenly from the volcano on Mount Vesuvius. Their faces were turned toward the sea, fewer than 200 yards from the town wall, and in the vain hope of avoiding suffocation they had wrapped tunics around their mouths.

I thought of the Marxist historians and social scientists, not only in Russia but also in the United States, who for so many years had tried so hard to change the art of history into a system of averaging the data. They portrayed the individual as a puny anonym, helpless and irrelevant, trapped like a rabbit or a statistic in the nets and snares of ideological abstraction. The determinist fallacy provided the intellectual band music for the Cold War. The theory of historical inevitability allied itself with the doctrine of Mutual Assured Destruction, and the will to power (as opposed to the freedom of thought or the play of the imagination) imprisoned the nations of the earth in an attitude of fear. It wasn't only the threat implicit in the weapons, although the weapons were many and terrible. It was the habit and pattern of thought bent to the service of the slogan. The brutal simplifications made it hard to imagine the world as anything other than a military campground.

But it turns out that the world is a far more beautiful place than had been represented in the story told by the prison guards. Far more beautiful, and by no means prerecorded. As was made plain in Moscow in the last weeks of August, it is the individual who shapes the historical narrative, not (as the conspirators learned to their sorrow) the ream of blank paper that tells a story of its own. If the future is never any further away than the next sentence, the next gesture, the next best guess, then it belongs to the people who possess their own history, rely on their own experiments and speak in their own voices. The great argument going forward in the storm of the world is the same in the United States as it is in what was once the Soviet Union. To the best of my knowledge it is the same argument that enlivened the scaffolds of Renaissance Italy and the annals of imperial Rome. In brief and in sum, it is the old and often violent argument between time past and time future, between the inertia of things-as-they-are and the energy inherent in the hope of things-as-they-might-become.

Although the study of history resolves nothing, it offers the ceaseless example of man defining and redefining the meaning of his existence. Empires rise and fall, so do families and so do theories of aesthetics, but on their way to death men make their own immortality. If it is true that time destroys all things, then it is also true that men seek to preserve what they have found beautiful as well as useful, and all of us inherit the immense treasure of skills, manners, customs, poems, equations and sailing vessels rescued from the flood.

History can best be defined as the triumph of memory over the spirit of corruption, and if we draw comfort from the imaginative taking up of the experience of the past, it is because the study of history argues for a sense of community in the gulf of time, for a feeling of kinship with a larger whole and a wider self—with those who have gone before us and those who will come after.

If we can learn to see our own faces in the mirror of history, perhaps we can forgive ourselves for our weakness as well as fortify ourselves with the proofs of our strength. I don't know what Yeltsin will do tomorrow or next week or next year, but for the time being it is enough that he stood up on a tank in the square outside the Russian parliament on the morning of 19 August to say a few inspired words on behalf of the party of things-as-they-might-become.

November 1991

JOURNEY TO THE EAST

Academic and aristocratic people live in such an
uncommon atmosphere that common sense can rarely
reach them.
—SAMUEL BUTLER

Reading the newspaper accounts of President Bush's winter journey to Japan, I was reminded that people inhabit different periods in time as well as different coordinates in space. If I find myself talking to George Steinbrenner or Pat Buchanan, I know that I am listening to the news and opinions of the late Pleistocene; Henry Kissinger speaks to me with the authority of somebody fully in command of the wisdom of 1848; the conversation in the cafeteria at Bell Laboratories takes place somewhere in the second half of the twenty-first century.

For Mr Bush the time is 1945, and if the pomps and ceremonies of his Oriental tour had conformed to his inward state of mind, he would have arrived in Tokyo Bay on board the U.S.S. *Missouri*, dressed in a white naval uniform and very pleased to present the Japanese people with the sight of his baseball cap and gold braid.

As conceived by the Washington designers of photo opportunities, the pageant was meant to show a vigorous American president coming to Japan to demand economic justice from the old and duplicitous *Keiretsu*. The spectacle seen in the theater of the news presented the American president as a failed suppliant instead of a conquering hero—an ailing and pathetic figure dismissed with the smile of pity and the gift of some sweet candies shaped as miniature sculptures of the president's two dogs.

The embarrassment followed from the disjunction in time. In the autumn of 1945 it would have been hard to imagine that one day the United States might find itself pressed for cash, or that the lines of credit would run from East to West. Tokyo was in ashes, and the emperor had been informed by General Douglas MacArthur that he was no longer a god. The common wisdom held that everybody's image of the future looked like an American postcard. How was it possible to think otherwise? Was it not true that democracy, capitalism and social progress were all part of the same wonderful idea? Who could fail to embrace the American systems of value and the American theories of fair trade?

President Bush formed his understanding of Japan as a Navy pilot in World War II and apparently nothing in his subsequent experience has obliged him to amend his first impression. This lack of development is fairly common among people born to the assumptions of wealth and rank. They can afford to believe what they choose to believe, and they seldom find it necessary to revise the texts of the preferred reality.

Similar forms of arrested perception show up among people who stay too long in political office or become too accustomed to the privileges of corporate oligarchy. With Mr Bush, as with several of his principal companions on the journey to the East—notably Robert Mosbacher, the former secretary of commerce and now the president's general campaign chairman, and Lee A. Iacocca, the chairman of the Chrysler Corporation— a congenital weakness of mind has been made worse by their ceaseless exposure to the toxins of flattery.

First as vice president and then, even more elaborately, as president, Mr Bush finds himself constantly attended by a retinue of admiring servants—valets, Secret Service agents, appointments secretaries, chauffeurs, speechwriters, florists, stewards, outriders and food tasters. It is the business of all these people to comfort and reassure the president. He is never alone, never free of the din of hired praise.

Neither Iacocca nor Mosbacher can command quite so baroque a display of self, but they do the best they can, preferably at somebody else's expense. Iacocca travels with a suite of assistants and a choir of publicists. His vanity urges him in front of as many television cameras as he can charge to the Chrysler Corporation's account, and he draws an annual compensation of $4.65 million as a reward for selling junk merchandise and running a business that posted a loss of $892 million in the first nine months of 1991. The chairman of a Japanese company with a similar record of performance would have been obliged to resign in disgrace.

The prominence of Mosbacher and Iacocca on the pilgrimage to Japan made it all but impossible for the United States to sustain an impression of serious economic purpose. Had the president been traveling to Palm Springs to play golf with Jack Nicklaus or to Texas for the quail shooting, then Iacocca and Mosbacher might have been put to some sort of ornamental use. Both gentlemen possess many of the properties of highly polished wood, and if they can be placed at clever angles to the sun I'm sure that they can be made to reflect several hundred points of light.

But not to Japan, not to talk to people who still recognize a connection between labor and reward. Nobuhiko Kawamoto, the president of Honda, earns $360,000 a year for running a company that earns a profit and produces well-made cars. The Japanese ministers of trade almost certainly read (in English) more of the reports published by the US Department of Commerce than Mr Mosbacher can either identify or name.

Mr Bush's willingness to bring Mr Iacocca and Mr Mosbacher to Japan testified to his abiding faith in the certainties of 1945. The president learned the little he knows of money and trade during the era of American triumphalism, at the brief and aberrant moment in time when it was possible to believe that America owed its great place in the world to its military and moral virtue rather than to the weight of its currency. In 1945 the apprentice statesmen in Washington (almost all of them rich men as ignorant of money as the young George Bush) assumed that the United States owned a patent on capitalism. It was thought that capitalism was a uniquely American invention, like Coca-Cola or Yankee Stadium, that somehow it was synonymous with democratic government and Christian love.

The declaration of the Cold War in 1947 encouraged the United States to place its economic practice at the service of its ideological theory. Washington's obsession with Communist plots and conspiracies took precedence over anything so squalid as the mere counting of coins. Foreign aid was undoubtedly a good thing for humanity, but it was a far, far better thing if the beggar nations receiving the money agreed to join the Americans in the holy crusade against the Marxist infidels in Moscow and Peking. The denial of history (that is, of all the old world orders ever recorded in the memory of mankind) was as romantic as it was stupid. It didn't occur to the Americans that other people might be different, that they might have different ways of doing business or keeping score.

In Japan the mistake was as costly as it was humorous. Because the Japanese played baseball and because they so dutifully made tin souvenirs of the Empire State Building, it was assumed that they shared the American attitudes toward business and trade. But Japan did not base its economic system on the whim of the consumer, nor did the Japanese believe in making the largest possible profit in the shortest possible time. Unlike the Americans, the Japanese didn't draw much of a distinction between the public and the private interest. They conceived of their economy as an instrument of the national security, and they understood that in the balance of world power the sale of enough paper hats matched the speed of a Trident submarine or the throw weight of an ICBM. Business was war, and if the Japanese routinely rigged prices, stole patents and dumped their goods on foreign markets, they did so in the interests of a country that lacked America's natural resources (and therefore its careless faith in abundance) and on behalf of a people forced to live by their wits. If 95 percent of all Japanese high school students had to take six years of English, then that was the price of survival.

The Americans missed the points of cultural difference, and during the 1950s and 1960s Washington's attitude toward Japan remained condescending. It was thought that the Japanese were capable of only the very small things—assembling cheap toys or poor imitations of American toasters—and the impression of a third-rate country making fourth-rate products remained comfortably in place. A succession of American governments granted the Japanese unimpeded access to the American market, and the State Department remained indifferent to the menial details of international trade. During the 1950s the United States exported its steel and shipbuilding industries to Japan, but the fine gentlemen in Washington were enthralled by the grand opera of the Cold War, and the State Department didn't do floors and windows. What was the importance of a few miserable merchant ships when measured against the glorious arias about the nuclear navy?

The emergence of Japan as a rival economic power in the 1980s presented the Americans with an unhappy surprise. Before we figured out who did what to whom, or why nobody in Tokyo expressed more than a polite interest in our speeches about free trade and a fair price, we had lost our markets in cars and cameras and television sets. It was the loss of the cars that did the most damage to America's self-esteem. Cars were what America was all about.

Maybe that was the president's purpose in bringing with him to Japan not only Iacocca but also Harold Poling, the chairman of Ford, and Robert C. Stempel, the chairman of General Motors. Maybe he thought they were totems capable of casting spells. If the American automobile business could be restored to what it was in 1945, then Humpty Dumpty would be back on the wall, and the trade deficit, like the rain in the nursery rhyme, would go away and come again another day.

The wish proved as futile as the president's hope of blaming the Japanese for the failures of the American economy. Neither he nor any of his principal companions fully understood the mechanics of American trade policy, much less those of Japan. Stempel was as incompetent and self-indulgent an executive as Iacocca: a few weeks prior to his departure for Tokyo, GM announced the elimination of more than seventy thousand jobs and the shutting down of twenty-one assembly lines. The company reported an annual loss of $2 billion, but the board of directors awarded Stempel a compensation of $1.1 million a year.

The wonders of the American enterprise asked for charity in the form of managed trade (affirmative action on behalf of American cars), but they had the gall to present themselves as proponents of "the free market," as if they knew nothing about the myriad tariffs that the United States places on the import of foreign goods.

Nor did they appear to know much about Japanese politics. The prime minister, Kiichi Miyazawa, clearly would have liked to do a favor for his new friend George Bush (as well as for all of those ragged Americans standing in breadlines), but his word didn't carry much weight with the Japanese Diet or the Japanese *Keiretsu*. Japan had troubles of its own. The Tokyo stock market had lost a third of its value over the preceding eighteen months and the Japanese banks were by no means as rich as their clients wished to believe.

The president and his companions declined to acknowledge any realities other than the ones they chose to acknowledge. Mr Bush thrust himself into a game of *kemari* in the courtyard of a palace in Kyoto (a ball game he'd never seen before and didn't understand), and after a few moments of aimless play he said to his attending courtiers, "We won." He told various microphones that "world leadership is at stake" and made himself memorable to the Japanese public by fainting at a state dinner and vomiting on Prime Minister Miyazawa's suit.

Mosbacher meanwhile showed off his cuff links (generating additional points of light), and the automobile executives told everybody that they deserved to sell a lot of cars in Japan even though they refused to go to the trouble of building the cars with right-hand drive. Let the Japanese learn to drive with the wheel on the left, like the Americans.

The president's journey to the East ended as burlesque. Attempting to portray himself as a politician who cared about American domestic issues, he lost much of his stature as a statesman presumed to know something about foreign issues. He made it clear that he never understood the old world order, much less the new. On his return to Andrews Air Force Base, the president made a virtue of his ignorance. Because he had steadfastly refused to learn even the smallest lesson of experience, he could say to the assembled cameras that the journey had been a triumph. It was still 1945, now and forever, and he had carried the flag of the American working man to the uttermost ends of the earth.

The automobile executives went to Detroit to deliver the same brave message. Stempel spoke darkly of the thunderstorm of protectionism looming in the Congress. Iacocca told a crowd of businessmen at the Detroit Economic Club to beware the "insidious Japanese economic and political power within the United States."

The display of arrested perception on the part of so many of the travelers to the Orient (Bush and Mosbacher, the automobile executives, the food tasters) argues for an even more disastrous state of the country's affairs than has been suggested by the Democratic presidential candidates. For some years it has been obvious that we don't know how to build very good cars, but we used to know how to stage photo opportunities and make handsome and well-engineered lies.

March 1992

MELANCHOLY KINGS

Of comfort no man speak!
Let's talk of graves, of worms, and epitaphs,
Make dust our paper, and with rainy eyes
Write sorrow on the bosom of the earth.
Let's choose executors, and talk of wills.
For God's sake let us sit upon the ground
And tell sad stories of the death of kings!
—RICHARD II

Ten years ago this spring I listened to a smiling deputy secretary at the Treasury Department explain the mechanics of the economic miracle bestowed on his fortunate countrymen by the election of President Ronald Reagan. I remember that his office windows overlooked the White House lawn and that his voice was highpitched and thin, like the voice of a young man likely to have won a prep-school Latin prize. If I cannot now remember anything the deputy secretary said, it's because even at the time (in full view of the flip charts and free to ask questions) I didn't understand how the numbers proved the general theory of self-reliance. The young man wore a bow tie and was devoted to his faith in the Laffer curve. He was certain that if people followed the few simple rules of economic behavior provided for them in the computer models, the recession through which the country was then passing would vanish like an early morning mist or fog. Even teamsters and short-order cooks would find themselves promoted to the ranks of the prosperous middle class.

The deputy secretary's complacence was symptomatic of the age. Ronald Reagan had come to Washington with the promise of his salesman's smile and his repeated assurances that he meant to be president of a country in which it always would be possible—now and forever, world without end, Amen—for everybody to get rich. For a few years it looked as if he had made good on the guarantee of prosperity. Real estate prices improved, and cities as distant from the nation's capital as Omaha, Nebraska, acquired a taste for luxury. With funds borrowed from the Japanese, the country staged a show of opulence that could have been set to music by Cole Porter or Cecil B. De Mille. All the instruments of the mass media (backed up on piano and drums by the journals of the best literary and political opinion) agreed that wonders would never cease and that Paradise was at hand.

If not quite everybody was as fortunate as everybody else, the errors of omission merely proved that the benign deities of the free enterprise system moved in mysterious ways. During the spring and summer of 1982 a good many of the nation's farmers went broke, as did many of the factory workers stranded in the nation's old and technologically incorrect Rust Belt. Among the legion of the unemployed, blue-collar workers out-numbered white-collar workers by a ratio of two to one, and the congenial and popular wisdom of the age maintained that only poor people suffered the accidents of economic recession. The casualties were written off as the price of progress and the cost of doing business.

The timeless prophets of the moment (among them George Will, Pat Buchanan and William F. Buckley) explained that adversity was a blessing in disguise. Self-reliance was what America was all about, and hard times strengthened the sinews of character. The lessons were deemed especially useful to people who were illiterate, anonymous or poor, the kind of people otherwise inclined to lie around drinking milk or gin at the government's expense. Hard times taught them the value of a dollar, encouraged them to seize the reins of entrepreneurship, transformed them into honest Republicans.

The national news media wholeheartedly endorsed the same comforting sentiment, and for the better part of a decade (for as long as the façade of the Reagan prosperity remained more or less safely in place) the market in great expectations rose as steadily as the market in French silk and Italian leather. The seers employed by the American Enterprise Institute stepped forward to say that financial success was proof of moral or ideological virtue, and that a fortune in shopping malls was synonymous with a state of spiritual grace. The fashion magazines illustrated the good news with four-color advertisements for gold watches and castles in Spain. The texts and photographs flattered the subscribers with testimonials to their collective magnificence, and the expansive and upwardly mobile American middle class learned to admire itself as the eighth wonder of an envious world. The admissions committee welcomed new money in any and all denominations, and every week the lists of new members multiplied at a rate that brought joy to the hearts of the world's wine merchants, the world's tennis coaches, the world's hairdressers. The media were unstinting in their expenditure of adjectives, and as the decade reached toward its zenith the great American middle class stared at its reflection in the mirrors of the news and saw that it was good—successful, clear-eyed, hard-working, accustomed to the standards of excellence, dressed by Ralph Lauren, deserving of all things bright and beautiful.

If the flattery had stopped at this point, the subsequent destruction of the images of middle-class self-esteem might not have seemed so barbarous. But the oracles and the fashion consultants didn't rest content with the delusions of grandeur with which they already had decorated so many empty rooms. They pushed the envelope of fulsome praise even closer to the sun and awarded their patron the last and glittering attribute of self-reliance.

The adjective was preposterous—as preposterous as proclaiming Henry Kissinger the equal of Napoleon because both gentlemen were short—but such was the vanity of the age that a courtier's lying compliment passed as plain statement of good old-fashioned American fact. The joke was worthy of Molière. No class of businessmen in the history of the known world had been so cosseted by the servants of government than the class of American businessmen that enjoyed the grace and favor of the Reagan administration.

For ten years I have listened to self-styled entrepreneurs (men of vision, men of genius, and so on) bang their fists on grillroom tables and complain of the thousand and one ways in which government regulations strangled their initiative and bound the arm of honest labor. I'm sure that much of what they said was true, but never once did I hear any of them acknowledge their abject dependence on the gifts of government subsidy—the mortgage deductions on residential real estate, myriad investment credits and tax exemptions, preferential interest rates, Social Security payments, subsidies to entire industries (defense, real estate, agriculture, highway construction), tariffs, the bankruptcy laws, the licenses granted to television stations, the banking laws, the concessions given to the savings and loan associations. Of all the federal money distributed as transfer payments to individual Americans during the decade of the 1980s only a relatively small percentage found its way into the hands of the poor. The bulk of the donative sustained the pretensions of the mostly affluent and well-to-do. Without the help of the government, the self-reliant American middle class was as helpless as a child without its nurse.

In October 1987 some of the more alert children in the nursery (the ones playing closer to the doors and windows) noticed an ill wind blowing through the trees beyond the tennis court. The stock market lost 500 points in one day, and Nanny was so alarmed that she stopped reading the bedtime story by Tom Clancy. It was a swell story (all about tanks, Russians and planes), and if Nanny stopped reading it, maybe something was wrong.

Four years later even Nanny's slowest children (the ones in the center of the room playing with the blocks) knew that the storm of recession had blown away most of the sailboats on the lake. President Bush did his best to calm everybody's nerves (by staging a Tom Clancy story in the Persian Gulf), but by October 1991 the emotion loose inside the nursery was close to panic.

Something was clearly amiss with the general theory of self-reliance. An appreciable number of the nation's largest corporations (among them IBM, AT&T and General Motors) began to eliminate from their payrolls tens of thousands of dues-paying members of the middle class—educated people, people who carried briefcases and commuted from the suburbs, nice people, people who subscribed to *Time* and watched public television, white people, people who wore bow ties and won Latin prizes—and in the ensuing alarm and confusion it was discovered that the stern economic remedies so invigorating to the poor failed in their results when administered to residents of Fairfield, Connecticut and Brentwood, California. Once-upon-a-time advertising executives and bank vice presidents refused to square their shoulders and gratefully sweep the streets. They turned instead to drink and politics (some of them going so far as to threaten reprisals at the polls), and so the augurs at the American Enterprise Institute reexamined the entrails and understood that in at least one important particular what was good for the poor was bad for the rich.

After first ascertaining that in the current recession the ratio between the blue-collar and the white-collar unemployed stands at one to one, the augurs produced a slight amendment of the general theory—among members of the lower classes, failure was a property of individuals; among members of the middle classes, failure was a property of the state. A poor man failed because he was lazy or stupid or criminal. A rich man failed because of a tax policy or the Clean Air Act. Nobody knew why this was so. It was a great mystery, like the mystery of existence, but nobody, at least nobody important, doubted the truth of so sublime a paradox.

The media immediately changed their f-stops and framed the middle class in the melodramatic role of a citizenry betrayed. Victims all— seduced and abandoned, tricked by circumstance, delivered into bondage by vicious confidence men selling cheap imitations of the American Dream. The public-opinion polls suddenly acquired the aspects of a funeral march, and the mathematical proofs of pessimism began to show up in the newspapers like a procession of chanting monks. The still-timeless prophets of the age (among them George Will, Pat Buchanan, William F. Buckley) put on the robes of hired mourners, cherishing the wounds of the American body politic as if they were the stigmata of the murdered Christ.

The expressions of self-pity serve as another form of flattery because they presume a state of prior perfection. No matter how severe the adjectives, the emphasis remains fixed on a subject of supreme interest and importance—the beauty of the self, once glorious and now lost. The acknowledgement of weakness becomes proof of spiritual refinement, something comparable to a house in Nantucket or a feather boa bought at an auction on behalf of public television. The exquisite sorrow distinguishes its possessor from the anonymous crowd of stolid and capable citizens who endure their lives with a minimum of self-dramatization. Who pays attention to people who don't make piteous cries? Who wants to pay $100,000 for the movie rights to their chronicles of marriage and divorce? Who bothers to take their photograph for *Vogue* or travels to New Hampshire to buy their votes?

This winter's presidential campaign appealed to the emotions of self-pity, and as I watched the Democratic candidates carry their laments and promises through the snows of New Hampshire in January, I thought of Shakespeare's grieving Richard II returned to England to find himself abandoned by his mercenary armies. He had been deprived of his kingdom by reason of his extravagance and indecision, but he continued to believe himself omnipotent. His humiliation astonished him because it never had occurred to him that the indignities of hunger, loneliness and death routinely visited upon lesser human beings could be visited upon the majesty of an anointed king.

By the third week of January I understood that the phrase "the forgotten middle class" was a term of art, a euphemism for the modestly affluent and well-to-do, the not-poor and the non-black. Like the Republicans before them, the Democrats had learned to divide the country into only two classes—the middle class (both remembered and forgotten) and the underclass, which was invisible. The candidates were interested only in the first of these classes, in the prospective voters among whom they could recognize the presence of both money and resentment.

As I watched the gentlemen on C-Span, either debating one another or making their financial presentations in clean, well-lighted rooms, I understood that I was looking at a troop of mutual-fund salesmen, drumming up business among a crowd of nervous investors. With the exception of Jerry Brown, they had come to sell the suckers a choice of what Wall Street calls "financial products"—tax and investment credits, depreciation allowances, insurance policies, rebates and exemptions—and they canvassed the state, offering to perform (exclusively for those among the middle class who could still afford the price of admission) one or more of the hoped-for economic miracles. Were too many people out of work? Elect Tsongas or Kerrey or Clinton or Harkin and within a matter of months (if not weeks or days or hours), lo and behold, out of the ground or over the hills from Vermont, jobs will arrive by the regiment or battalion. Did too many people lack health insurance? Were too many people unable to buy a house or send their children to decent schools? Were too many people worried about the departure of the American Dream? Elect Tsongas or Kerrey or Clinton or Harkin and within a matter of months (if not weeks or days or hours), lo and behold, out of the sky or from lands far away . . .

None of which, of course, was new to the Republicans. On 28 January President Bush made of his State of the Union address the political equivalent of an automobile dealer's pitch for a Labor Day sale. He offered a complete portfolio of financial goods and services, but he improved the Democratic deal with cash back from this year's withholding tax and with an accelerated rate of depreciation for companies that bought expensive equipment (mainframe computers, corporate aircraft, and the like) between 1 February 1992 and 1 January 1993. The budget director, Richard Darman, explained the small print to the Senate Finance Committee, and as I watched him flip deftly through the finance charts, I wondered why he didn't sing a variation on one of those television car commercials in which the pretty girl tells everybody to buy now and save.

What was so dispiriting about the political presentation in both New Hampshire and Washington was the contempt with which the salesmen regarded their customers. They had come to buy votes, and they were willing to tell the suckers whatever the suckers wanted to hear, but only if the suckers lived in one of the richer zip codes and accepted the terms and conditions of the offering. A vote was a commodity; so was a tax break and so was medical insurance; and it wasn't going to do anybody any good to lose sight of the politics of the bottom line. The election was about what was in it for me—me the candidate, me the voter, me the purveyor of band music and public-opinion polls.

By consenting to define the election as a matter of narrow interests and short-term profits, the electorate and their paid representatives escaped the more difficult and fundamental questions about the long-term purpose of the common American enterprise. Nobody uttered a word or a phrase that might have been mistaken for idealism. All present complacently assumed that America, like Richard II, already existed in a state of moral perfection, and that what was wrong with the country could be corrected by a few judicious rearrangements of the bond portfolio and the porch furniture. But if we continue to believe our own self-congratulatory press notices—America the great and the good, America the invincible or, as President Bush put it in the State of the Union address, America the kindest, freest, strongest nation on earth—we will come, as did the dreaming King Richard, to a melancholy end.

April 1992

APES AND BUTTERFLIES

But man, proud man,
Drest in a little brief authority,
Most ignorant of what he's most assured,
His glassy essence, like an angry ape,
Plays such fantastic tricks before high heaven
As make the angels weep.
—SHAKESPEARE, *MEASURE FOR MEASURE*

*T*he theories of the new world order arriving these days from Washington move me to a feeling akin to pity for the nervous clerks assigned to write the sequel to the Cold War. I read their statements and formulations in the policy journals, as well as on the editorial pages of the *Washington Post* and the *New York Times*, and I remember the awful afternoon in the spring of my freshman year at college when I took the final examination in geology. I hadn't read the book or seen the slides, and I had missed all but one of the field trips. The essay question appeared in a language I didn't recognize, much less understand, and in a state of barely suppressed panic I wrote the answer in ottava rima. I had been reading Byron's *Don Juan*, and I cast my lot on the vain hope that the artful form of the essay might excuse its lack of content.

The Washington diplomatic establishment confronts a similar dilemma. Nobody knows the language in which to ask or answer the questions presented by the absence of the Soviet empire. The old vocabulary of threat and counterthreat—all the acronyms, all the CIA estimates, all the computer printouts and satellite photographs, the whole archive of lovingly annotated paranoia—is as remote as the gibbering of apes.

I was vividly reminded of the irrelevance of the Cold War diction by two texts published in the *New York Times* during the first eight days of March—a speech given by Václav Havel, the president of Czechoslovakia, and a Defense Planning Guidance composed by a committee of strategists at the Pentagon. Both texts addressed the same set of circumstances, but the difference of perspective and dimension was the difference between time past and time future. Havel spoke of a world in which the familiar geopolitical tropes and symbols no longer held any meaning. The Pentagon document could have been written by Teddy Roosevelt or Kaiser Wilhelm. It was the nearly simultaneous publication of the two texts that cast their differences in so clear a light. The excerpt from Havel's speech (to an audience in Davos, Switzerland) appeared on 1 March under the title "The End of the Modern Era," and I remember being surprised to come across it on a Sunday editorial page that I ordinarily associate with the amiable maxims of retired deputy secretaries of state.

Reflecting on the end of communism in Russia and Eastern Europe, Havel found the larger ending for a series of propositions inaugurated by the Renaissance, "an end not just to the 19th and 20th centuries, but to the modern age as a whole." The modern age he defined as the historical synonym for the dream of reason: "The proud belief that man, as the pinnacle of everything that exists, was capable of objectively describing, explaining and controlling everything that exists, and of possessing the one and only truth about the world."

Communism inflated this proud belief into the balloon of totalitarian absurdity, and Havel saw in its collapse the futility of the modern faith in systems of control and the supremacy of the scientific method, in ideological doctrine and statistical averages, in balances of power and the beauty of purifying abstraction.

Speaking as a politician besieged by what he recognized as the failure of "the technocratic, utilitarian approach to Being," Havel observed that the mechanisms of modern thought—in no matter what combination or how subtly geared to a Cray supercomputer—cannot formulate a coherent response to the most ominous threats to anybody's new world order. He had trouble enough with the Czech politicians bent on restoring the old Marxist world order in Prague (as well as with the Slovak politicians bent on restoring the old Hapsburg world order in Bratislava), but he knew (as the Pentagon clerks do not) that the urgent questions certain to be asked of mankind in the next century will be the ones about survival, not security—not the geopolitical questions about a coup in Panama or a war in Iran but the geophysical questions about the depletions of the biosphere and the holes in the ozone, about the disparity of wealth between the nations of the northern and southern hemispheres, about famine in Asia and disease in Africa.

Yes, said Havel, we can hold conferences and go to meetings and construct defenses against all these contingencies—new control systems, new scientific mechanisms, new institutions, new acronyms—but without the transforming power of a new idea or a new turn of mind, our efforts will matter as little as the baying of a postmodernist hound. As might be expected of a man who was once a playwright and a prisoner of the state, Havel argued for a politics grounded in the texts of feeling and experience—not only the summary reports that a politician reads every morning with the opinion polls but also the prompting of his own conscience, "the courage to be himself," and the constant practice of "humility in the face of a mysterious order of Being."

The *Times* published the Pentagon document a week later, on Sunday 8 March, and the juxtaposition with Havel's speech reminded me of Kaiser Wilhelm and the distances in time. The German empire in the early years of the century took a great and solemn pride in its military bearing, and the emperor, who was both theatrical and humorless, made it a point to appear every morning dressed in the uniform of a different regiment or fleet. His collection of martial costume was the wonder of the age—breastplates, Spanish top boots, plastrons, caps, medals, tunics of every conceivable color and design, gold braid, helmets, swords. He liked to sit on his horse for hours on end on the parade ground at Potsdam, and it was said that sometimes he confused himself with a statue of Mars or Frederick the Great. The pose apparently calmed his nerves and allayed his feeling of hysteria.

I assume that the authors of the Defense Planning Guidance aspired to a similar state of noble paralysis. Given the loss of self-definition in the E ring of the Pentagon, I expect that the panic must be difficult to suppress. Just as every action engenders an equal and opposite reaction, the fear of change invites the denial of change, and the more frightened people become the more they console themselves with the delusions of grandeur.

Henceforth, so says the draft document, America will dictate the terms of the world's peace. We will perform the labors of benevolent despotism in the name of liberty and on behalf of those of our friends whom we deem worthy of our interest and favor. Now that the Soviet Union has been stripped of the epaulets of empire, America will arrange the rough pageant of the world in a manner that befits the dignity of the world's only superpower. Never will we allow any rival power (present, emergent or reemergent) to stand in the sun of our supremacy.

Prior to its publication in the *Times*, the document was classified as secret, a memorandum internal to the higher echelons of Washington's policy planning staffs at the White House and National Security Council as well as at the State and Defense Departments—an *aide mémoire* meant to reassure the fine gentlemen seated, in Havel's phrase, at "the pinnacle of everything that exists."

The text furnishes the strategic theory justifying military expenditures of $1.2 trillion over the next five years, and its numerous appendices present seven "illustrative" scenarios for the kinds of small or regional wars that the American legions might be required to fight in the last decade of the century that we designate as our own. News of the seven scenarios had appeared in the *Times* on 17 February, and the patent fancifulness of the scripts—Russia attacks Lithuania and Poland; North Korea attacks South Korea; a coup in the Philippines, and so on—gave rise to expressions of mockery and disbelief among politicians wary of the Pentagon's appetite for large sums of money.

If the specific instances were fanciful, the general theory was grotesque. The draft document attributed the end of communism to the glory of American military power, not, as Havel had observed, to the larger powers of the human spirit, conscience, life itself. The collapse of the Russian Empire thus had little or nothing to do with its interior weaknesses and contradictions, and the failure of communism little or nothing to do with the mismanagement of the Russian economy. Germany and Japan owe their existence and their fealty to their American overlords because without the protection of the American fleets and armies (in 1992 as in 1945) they would stumble into the pits of anarchy and despair.

After establishing these convenient truths in the first paragraph, the Defense Planning Guidance sets forth the terms and conditions under which America consents to govern the earth—no smaller nations to pursue any interests that the United States doesn't think "legitimate," all nations to refrain from "even aspiring to a larger regional or global role," no irredentism, no wars or challenges to "the established political and economic order" without American permission, no impudence.

The draft document continues for several paragraphs in the same arrogant and condescending manner, but it is when the authors come to their sixth and last diktat that they achieve the sublime tone of an imperial calm. If I can be allowed to presume on the reader's patience, I will quote the passage at length:

> While the U.S. cannot become the world's "policeman," by assuming responsibility for righting every wrong, we will retain the pre-eminent responsibility for addressing selectively those wrongs which threaten not only our interests, but those of our allies or friends, or which could seriously unsettle international relations. Various types of U.S. interests may be involved in such instances: access to vital raw materials, primarily Persian Gulf oil; proliferation of weapons of mass destruction and ballistic missiles, threats to U.S. citizens from terrorism or regional or local conflict, and threats to U.S. society from narcotics trafficking.

In brief and in sum, and notwithstanding the modest disclaimer, America will act not only as the world's sheriff but also as the world's judge.

I wish I believed that the document was entirely cynical, an arrangement of toy boats and ornamental abstractions meant to defend the military budget and extract another $1.2 trillion from the federal treasury. But the pious certainty of the prose suggests the faith of true believers, and when I encounter a phrase as fatuous as "the U.S. must show the leadership necessary to establish and protect a new order," I know I'm in the presence of Kaiser Wilhelm and his horse. Within the Washington conference rooms where the strategic theorists decorate their maps with lines of force and arcs of crisis, the Pax Americana remains as it was in 1947, as permanent and serene as the dome on the Capitol or the stars in the flag. It is this notion that time can be made to stand still that comprises the worst of the news in the Defense Planning Guidance.

Almost as soon as the document was published, various White House and State Department officials took pains to disassociate themselves from its most obvious stupidities (the neglect of the United Nations, the insensitivity to the feelings of our creditors, the prohibitive cost of hegemony), but they voiced their objections in the same idiom of technological hieroglyphs. None of them questioned what Havel had called the proud belief in their capacity to explain and control "everything that exists."

The Cold War imprisoned the nations of the earth in the attitudes of fear. It wasn't only the threat implicit in the weapons, although the weapons were many and terrible; it was also the pattern of thought bent to the service of abstraction. As Havel remarked to the audience in Davos, the grim rituals of threat and counterthreat binding together the United States and the Soviet Union over the last fifty years also could be understood as a kind of alliance between the last citadels of the modern era making common cause against the ravages of time and change. Like antique generals in powdered wigs, still clinging to the old faith in rational self-interest, Machiavelli, systems analysis and the eagles of the Austrian empire, the two self-proclaimed superpowers propped each other up against the storm blowing from the abyss of a world dissolved.

For some twenty years now the standard theoretical revelations have failed to correspond to the text of events. What sovereign state can make good on its promises? How does it defend its borders against disease and the drug trade, or hold harmless its air or its water against acid rain drifting east across Canada or the radioactive cloud blowing west from

Chernobyl? The events of the last generation repeatedly have demonstrated (in Vietnam, in Iran, in Poland, in Cuba, in Eastern Europe and in Russia) that the freedom to act has passed from the larger combinations of power to the smaller concentrations of intellect and will.

The revolution alarms the Pentagon clerks who, like Richard Nixon, still think that we can "lose China" or "lose Russia" as if they were pieces on an American chessboard. Their dream of perfect security prompts them to see only the fearful aspects of a world escaped from the jails of doctrine—assassins sent by Libya or invented by Oliver Stone, fanatic environmentalists capable of poisoning a reservoir and holding for ransom the life and treasure of the status quo.

But to Havel, and to anybody else who thinks in the direction of the twenty-first century instead of the nineteenth, the passing of the modern age offers the peoples of the earth a chance to rescue themselves from their paralysis and inhibition, and with their newfound freedom of mind to deploy the forces of the moral imagination against the infantile wish for omnipotence. Havel's emphasis on feeling and experience assumes that men speak with authority only in the first person singular. They acquire wisdom and strength only by acknowledging their habitual stupidity and weakness, and to the extent that they can rid themselves of the language of abstraction, they can make and remake not only their lives but also their own world orders.

After reading the excerpts of Havel's speech in the *Times*, I sent for the complete text, and I noticed that as spoken in Davos it had a different and more hopeful ending. The version in the *Times* ended on a heavy phrase about "systemic and institutional changes," but in Davos Havel had gone on to talk about "the butterfly effect"—the "belief that everything in the world is so mysteriously and comprehensibly interconnected" that a slight, seemingly insignificant flutter of a butterfly's wing in Mexico City can provoke a typhoon in the South China Sea. He thought that the same effect was undoubtedly at work in the realm of politics, and that it was a mistake to believe that only gigantic bureaucracies could move against the armies of fear and superstition: "We cannot assume that our microscopic, yet truly unique everyday actions are of no consequence simply because they apparently cannot resolve the immense problems of today."

Precisely so. Take as proof of the proposition the feats of a small band of individuals (Havel among them, together with Walesa and Yeltsin) in arms against the supposedly impregnable fortresses of the nation-state.

If so few can do so much in the arena of politics, think how much more might be done in the less easily occupied reaches of the imagination. Seizing the radio station is an old story, but the leap of the human mind is always new.

May 1992

TRADING PLACES

> Should a man be appointed to a new post, praise
> of him pours forth, overflowing into courtyards
> and chapels, reaching the stair, the hall, the gallery,
> the whole of the royal apartment; one's quite
> submerged, one's overwhelmed by it. There are no two
> opinions on the man; envy and jealousy speak with
> the same voice as adulation; all are swept away by the
> torrent, which forces them to say what they think
> or don't think, of a man, and often to praise one
> whom they do not know. A man of wit, merit,
> or valor becomes, in one instant, a genius of the first
> rank, a hero, a demi-god . . .
> —LA BRUYÈRE, *CHARACTERS*

*L*ike the notables assembled under Louis XIV's roof at Versailles, official Washington divides the known world into only two parts. First there is Washington, and then there is everyplace else. The planes arriving and departing National Airport cross the only frontier of any consequence—the one between the inside and the outside—and all the truly momentous topics of conversation center on only one question, which is always and unfailingly the same: Who's in and who's out? The court might seem to be talking about something else—about war or peace or racial hatred or the deficit—but the words serve a decorative or theatrical purpose, and they are meant to be admired for their polished surfaces, as if they were mirrors or gilded chairs. What's important is what happens in Washington. Yes, it might be interesting to know that the United States now must pay $292 billion a year in interest on the national debt, and, yes, the poor blacks in the slums of Los Angeles obviously have their reasons to riot, but their suffering is far away and in another country, and what matters is the way in which the story plays tomorrow morning at the White House or the Department of Defense. Who will come and who will go? Who will occupy the office overlooking the lawn? Who will ride in the secretary's limousine, and who will carry the president's messages? Court ritual obliges all present to wear the masks of grave concern and utter the standard phrases of alarm ("America at the Crossroads," "The Crisis of the Cities"), but behind the façade of stately euphemism, the accomplished courtier learns to hide the far more urgent question: "What, please God, is going to happen to *me*?"

The masks come loose when the possession of the White House passes from one political party to the other and the would-be servants of the new world order parade their ambition in plain sight. The spectacle is marvelous to behold, and in the days and weeks following the election of Bill Clinton the news from Washington might as well have been extracted from an eighteenth-century book of court etiquette. On the Wednesday after the election the important columnists in town began making their bows and curtsies by comparing the new president with the young Jack Kennedy, and the more gracious members of the troupe professed to see rising from the mists of the Arkansas River the fabled towers of Camelot. Mo Sussman's, a restaurant much frequented by the city's principal careerists, added Arkansas Stew to its menu, and at the better markets in Georgetown the salesclerks murmured their appreciation of fried green tomatoes and sweet potato pie. The Securities Industry Association obligingly replaced its executive director, a Republican, with a Democrat who had known Bill Clinton at Oxford. Similarly abrupt exits and entrances took place in the executive offices of Hill and Knowlton, a consortium of prominent influence peddlers, and at the American Bankers Association.

On Thursday afternoon, less than thirty-six hours after the polls closed in California, Jack Kent Cooke, the owner of the Washington Redskins, discovered that he was acquainted with a surprisingly large number of Democrats. An invitation to sit in his box at RFK Stadium counts as one of the most visible proofs of rank within the Washington nobility, and during the fat years of the Reagan triumph and the Bush succession the sixty-four seats were comfortably stuffed with personages as grand as Edwin Meese, George Will and Robert Mosbacher. But on that Thursday, in answer to a question from a correspondent for the *New York Times*, Mr Cooke remembered that time passes and fashions change: "I'm a Republican, but strangely I have a great many Democrat friends. Dodd. Brzezinski. Greenspan—he's of indeterminate lineage. Sam Donaldson—what's he? Gene McCarthy and George McGovern."

The reporter asked if Mr Cooke knew of any football friends among President Clinton's circle of dependents and admirers. "'You must understand,' Mr Cooke said. 'The box is not used to ingratiate myself with the administration. Please quote me precisely on that. I invite people who are good company, happy, cheerful, good-humored people who love football.'"

Over the first weekend of the new revelation the publications that provide the court with topics of conversation—the *Times* and the *Washington Post* as well as *Time* and *The New Republic*—began rearranging the furniture in the drawing rooms of power. Previously resplendent figures much praised for their infallible judgement—among them James Baker, the once-upon-a-time secretary of state—were seen in the light of the democratic dawn as shabby impostors, as far behind the times as President Bush's collection of old tennis balls and the baseball glove that he had brought with him from the playing fields at Yale. Together with the work of revision, the court gazettes published the first in a long series of ornamental opinion pieces—from former ambassadors and deputy secretaries of state, directors of policy institutes, eager Harvard professors and economists in exile—meant to prove their authors deserving of an appointment to Paris or the National Security Council. Other voices in other rooms proclaimed their love of the environment and their interest in the saxophone, and at Wonder Graphics Picture Framing on Vermont Avenue, the owner of the store beheld a vision of prosperity: "'Everyone's going to have to hang up new pictures in their offices,' [he] said. 'They're going to be putting up new Clinton-Gore glad-handing pictures. They're going to need framing, and we do a very nice job.'"

The talented courtier possesses what Plutarch called "the soul of an acrobat"—that is, a man who discovers very early in his career that if he can learn to lick one boot he can learn to lick the boots of a regiment—and through the month of November, as the dance of grace and favor became both more desperate and more refined, I noticed that people long associated with Republican causes, with supply-side economics and weekends shooting quail in the company of Senators Simpson and Gramm, proposed themselves as voices of bipartisan conscience. Robert Strauss, the Washington lobbyist whom President Bush had appointed ambassador to Russia, appeared on network television to say that he once had been chairman of the Democratic National Committee and that he had voted, out of conviction and with a whole heart, for Bill Clinton.

Even in New York the conversations often veered off into the niceties of Washington protocol. One morning over breakfast at the Regency

Hotel with a government lawyer whom I had last seen in the twilight of the Carter administration, I was surprised to find myself talking about the Roman emperor Marcus Aurelius. The lawyer ordinarily didn't concern herself with events to which she couldn't attach living witnesses as well as a handsome fee, and I remembered her once telling me that history was the refuge of men who were afraid of the world. It wasn't until we had come to the end of the emperor's reign—his stoicism, his persecution of Christians, his bestowal of the empire on Commodus—that she informed me of Clinton's fondness for the late emperor's *Meditations*. She had been invited to a dinner given by one of Clinton's advisers, and she wished to make a subtle reference—as if derived from long reflection rather than a quick briefing—to the emperor's noble melancholy.

Three days later, in conversation with a professor of biochemistry at Yale, I was asked to speak for twenty minutes about the significance of Chico Mendes and Cordell Hull. The professor had heard that photographs of those two individuals were to be seen on the walls of Al Gore's office in the Senate (together with photographs of Rachel Carson and Yevgeny Yevtushenko), and if he could connect the metaphysical dots between the four names, then maybe when he went to Washington in a week's time to apply for a post at the Environmental Protection Agency, he might know what else to say after he had made his ritual devotions to the Manchurian tiger and the Japanese crane.

As long ago as 1831, passing through Cincinnati and Nashville, Alexis de Tocqueville was surprised by the virulence of what he called "the courtier spirit" among the supposedly plain and democratic Americans. He had thought that the citizens of the new democracy would prove to be homespun and rough-hewn people, direct in their actions and forthright in their address. He hadn't expected to find them so well schooled in the arts of servility. True, they didn't dress as well or as expensively as the ladies and gentlemen in France; their conversation wasn't as refined and neither were their manners, but they possessed a native talent for ingratiating themselves with anybody and everybody who could do them a favor or grant them a privilege. The effect was often comic—dandies in broadcloth instead of silk brocade, loud in their brag and fantastic in their gestures, bowing and scraping to one another while standing up to their ankles in the muddy street of a wooden town on the edge of a savage wilderness.

After considering the paradox for some years, Tocqueville concluded that in a monarchy the courtier spirit was less pervasive and less damaging than it was in a democracy. Even the most arrogant of kings seldom had the gall to speak in the name of the public interest. Louis XIV couldn't impose a military conscription, and he always had considerable trouble with the levying of taxes. The king's interest was clearly his own. But a democracy claims to serve the interest of the sovereign people, and so the officials who write and administer the laws can claim to act on behalf of anything that they can classify as the common good. The presumption allows for a more expansive abrogation of power than the divine right of kings, and because the figure of the prince in a democracy appears in so many different forms and disguises—as politician, network executive, corporate chairman, town clerk, foundation hierarch and Washington columnist—the anxious sycophant is constantly bowing and smiling in eight or nine directions, forever turning, like a compass needle or a weather vane, into the glare of new money. A democracy transforms the relatively few favors in the monarch's gift— sinecure, benefice or patent royal—into the vast cornucopia of patronage distributed under the nominally egalitarian rubrics of tax exemption, defense contract, publication, milk subsidy, tenure, government office.

Numerous writers over the last four hundred years have attempted to describe or define the courtier spirit, and on reading the news from Washington last autumn, I thought not only of Tocqueville but also of Denis Diderot's satirical dialogue, *Rameau's Nephew*. The text takes the form of a conversation set in a café in Paris in 1761, and the author presents himself in the character of a moral philosopher (very dignified, very grave) engaged in an antic dispute with Jean-François Rameau, a musician and music teacher who prides himself on his talents as scoundrel, rogue, flatterer, hanger-on, opportunist, hypocrite. The two men talk during the hour before a performance of the opera near the Palais Royal, Rameau berating himself for having committed the stupidity of telling his patron the truth and so having lost his place at his patron's table. He is a wonderfully comic figure, given to sudden and fanciful gesture, often interrupting himself to mime the stance and character of somebody whom he wishes to mock. At one point he performs the beggar's pantomime, the dance that he defines as the perfect expression of the courtier spirit and describes as follows:

> Then, smiling as he [Rameau's nephew] did so, he began impersonating the admiring man, the supplicating man, the complaisant man, right foot forward, left foot behind, back bent, head up, looking fixedly into somebody else's eyes, lips parted, arms held out toward something, waiting for a

command, receiving it, off like an arrow, back again with it done, reporting it. He is attentive to everything, picks up what has been dropped, adjusts a pillow or puts a stool under someone's feet, holds a saucer, pushes forward a chair, opens a door, shuts a window, pulls curtains, keeps his eyes on the master and mistress, stands motionless, arms at his side and legs straight, listening, trying to read people's expressions.

At the court of Louis XIV in seventeenth-century France, people occupied themselves with the work of making small distinctions—those greeted at the door, those offered armchairs, those deemed worthy of being seen off in their coaches. In official Washington in late twentieth-century America, the court occupies itself with similar distinctions—those granted government cars, those awarded parking spaces at National Airport, those invited to sit in Jack Kent Cooke's box at RFK Stadium. Against the sum of such tremendous trifles, the questions of yesterday's riot or tomorrow's debt beat as heavily as the wings of moths.

January 1993

SHOW AND TELL

The formula "Two and two make five" is not without
its attractions.
—DOSTOEVSKY

*T*he Clinton administration apparently means to define itself as a television program instead of a government, and although I admire what I take to be the theme of the show—restoring belief in the American promise—I don't know how it can please both its sponsors and its intended audience. The difficulty follows from the need to protect the interests of oligarchy (the people who put up the campaign money) and at the same time sustain the illusion of popular sovereignty among an electorate hoping for proofs through the night that our flag is still there.

The events attending President Clinton's inaugural might as well have been chosen as demonstrations of an untenable political theorem. Obliged to reward his patrons and comfort his fans, the president provided the former with the gifts of office and the latter with ritual songs and dances. On Capitol Hill the Congress went about the business of confirming the president's nominees to the cabinet—most of them corporate lawyers, several of them patently unqualified or inept, all of them loyal servants of the status quo that as a candidate the president had so often decried as timid, self-serving and corrupt.

More or less simultaneously, the president appeared as the friend of the common man in the series of *tableaux vivants* staged against the backdrops of Washington's best-known monuments—Bill Clinton at Monticello, departing for the Capitol under the aegis of Thomas Jefferson and riding through the landscape of the Civil War in a bus bearing the license plate HOPE 1; Bill Clinton by candlelight, approaching the Lincoln Memorial on foot; Bill Clinton ringing a replica of the Liberty Bell; Bill Clinton listening, transfixed, to Diana Ross sing "We Are the World" and to ten saxophonists play Elvis Presley's "Heartbreak Hotel"; Bill Clinton in tears at the Capital Centre, accepting the badges and emblems of democratic sentiment at the hands of Barbra Streisand and Michael Jackson; Bill Clinton swearing the oath of office in the presence of Maya Angelou, who read an ode to the multicultural text ("the Asian, the Hispanic, the Jew/The African, the Native American, the Sioux . . . the Gay, the Straight, the Preacher/the privileged, the homeless, the Teacher") of the American soul.

The juxtaposition of the two series of events—the one on Capitol Hill confirming the rule of entrenched privilege, the other a spectacle made for the hired help—established the plot lines and introduced the principal characters of the Democratic sequel to the Ronald Reagan show. The extravagant sum of money spent on the inaugural pageant ($17 million provided by the nation's leading business corporations) expressed the degree to which the nation's possessing classes were worried about the resentment still at large in the public-opinion polls. President Clinton clearly delights in the character of amiable television host, as he was glad to demonstrate at a televised "town meeting" in suburban Detroit in early February, but the audience is not apt to be as easily amused as it was in 1980, and the new star of political television lacks Mr Reagan's talent for looking presidential. To see him give a speech, or watch his wife ascent the steps of the Capitol, was to be reminded not of Thomas Jefferson or an act of Congress, not even of a documentary series produced by PBS, but of *Donahue* and *Designing Women*.

An election-year script obliges the candidate to campaign on the promise of social and economic change, as no friend of the corporate lobbyists and the status quo. Following the accepted practice, candidate Clinton from time to time had presented himself as a tribune of the people pledged to cleanse Washington of "the rich and special interests" that for twelve years of Republican misrule had robbed the American people of their tax money and their constitutional birthright. At the same time and sometimes in the same speech, he described himself as "pro-business and pro-labor," "for economic growth and for protecting the environment," "for affirmative action but against quotas," "for legal abortions but also for making abortion as rare as possible." His opinions were those that his audiences wished to hear, and never once did I hear him venture the word *justice*, presumably on the grounds that it might be mistaken, like the word *liberty* (a word he also avoided), for a criticism of his corporate sponsors.

The speeches were letter-perfect, but when it came time to name his cabinet and define his government, Mr Clinton lost his hustler's touch for the political shell game. In place of the diverse and unorthodox team of American talent that he had so often promised, he substituted the familiar trick of labels and tokens ("the Hispanic . . . the African . . . the Gay, the Straight, the Preacher, the privileged . . . the Teacher"), and instead of appointing at least a few citizens remarkable for their courage and independence of mind (the kind of people who might lend verisimilitude to the impression of change), the president assembled a company of functionaries burdened with an average term of service in Washington of thirteen years. The principal figures in his cabinet—Warren Christopher, the secretary of state; Les Aspin, the secretary of defense; Lloyd Bentsen, the secretary of the treasury—were men grown bleak and pale in the dim basements of politics-as-usual. For twenty-one years as a congressman from Wisconsin, and as chairman of the House Armed Services Committee, Secretary Aspin diligently forwarded the freight of the defense industry. During his 1990 congressional campaign, each of the nation's ten largest military contractors returned the favor with appreciative contributions. As the senior senator from Texas and the chairman of the Senate Finance Committee, Secretary Bentsen consistently supported the banking and insurance lobbies, voting in favor of each of President Reagan's major tax bills. As a corporate lawyer in Los Angeles and deputy secretary of state in the Carter administration, Secretary Christopher earned a reputation for his discreet silence, a man known and relied upon for his unwillingness to offend the consensus of opinion seated at the expensive end of the conference table.

Similar traits of mind and character distinguished almost the whole company of the new cabinet. As a prominent Washington lobbyist, Ronald H. Brown, the secretary of commerce, counted among his clients "Baby

Doc" Duvalier, the former Haitian tyrant, as well as the government of
Japan. On being raised to federal office, he was so gauche as to demand
exemption from the customary rules of pecuniary decency, and it didn't
occur to him to discourage the organization of a gala dinner party in his
honor that was to have been staged (three days before President Clinton's
inaugural) by a quorum of grateful business corporations, among them
J. C. Penney, Anheuser-Busch, Sony Music Entertainment and Pepsico.
Robert E. Rubin, the former cochairman of Goldman, Sachs & Company
whom President Clinton named chairman of the National Economic
Council, was equally careless of appearances. On his way to Washington
from New York, he sent letters to as many as one thousand corporate
clients (foreign and domestic), assuring them that both he and his firm
"look forward to continuing to work with you in my new capacity."

With only a few modest or senior exceptions, the collective tone of
voice of the new cabinet was that of the acquisitive and self-satisfied
child of the 1980s. Unlike the privy councilors appointed by President
Bush, most of whom enjoyed the status conferred by inherited wealth,
President Clinton's surrogates derived their presumption of privilege from
their institutional provenience, not by right of birth but by right of the
academic degrees bestowed by Harvard, Oxford and Yale Law School. The
seals and stamps embossed on their résumés certified their standing as
newly minted members of the nation's ruling oligarchy. Like their
contemporaries in Hollywood and on Wall Street, they had proved themselves equal to the tasks of self-promotion and adept at the arts of getting
rich. Almost without exception they were people whose moral reasoning
conformed to the circular design fashionable among the adherents of both
Presidents Reagan and Bush—what is good is rich and successful; what is
rich and successful is good; I am rich and successful, therefore I am good,
and so is my car and my theory of the just society. If the servants of the
Reagan and Bush administrations wished to divide the country into an
equestrian and a plebeian class, they at least were content to give up the
ornaments of conscience in exchange for the house in Virginia. The friends
of Bill Clinton apparently want it all—everything in both column A and
column B, the Zen garden and the BMW as well as the three-masted
schooner and the friendship of rap musicians.

The too blatant contradiction in terms both embarrassed and frightened
the Washington news media, who had thought that Mr Clinton knew how
to stage the play of appearances as adroitly as President Reagan. Certainly
as a candidate he had understood that people who would wear the masks

of populism must be careful to avoid the shows of vanity. The news media didn't object to the hypocrisy, which is as necessary to Washington as tap water, but they were troubled by the style of the hypocrisy, which was either twenty years out of date or five years ahead of its time. It was this latter possibility that compounded their embarrassment with the trace elements of fear. What if the Clinton administration was about nothing else except the projection of images? A collage of symbols made only for television? The president during his first few days in office toyed with a number of substantive political issues (campaign finance reform and the rescue of the Haitian refugees) as if they were as light as balsa wood or as transparent as a studio photographer's gauze. The feeling of weight-lessness corresponded to what was apparently the president's utter lack of conviction. Even President Reagan entertained at least two genuine beliefs (the Nicaraguan Contras were good; high taxes were bad), and three or four of President Bush's opinions held their shape from one week to the next.

But Mr Clinton apparently believes in nothing except the presentation of self. His rhetoric suits the uses of television because it can be cut into any convenient length (twelve seconds, thirty seconds, five minutes, forty minutes) and because it employs the diction of group therapy. Like the evangelist or faith healer, he delivers the good news in a language empty of existential context or historical reference. Politics is never about who has the power to do what to whom but always, as Mr Clinton said on the night of his election on the steps of the governor's mansion in Little Rock, and again when explaining to Congress the need for economic sacrifice, about the clash of giant abstractions—about "a fight between hope and fear, a fight between division and unity, a fight between blame and taking responsibility . . . and may God bless America."

By seeming to say everything, the president manages to say nothing. He defines himself as a man desperately eager to please, and the voracious-ness of his appetite—for more friends, more speeches, more food and drink, more time onstage, more hands to shake, more hugs—suggests the emptiness of a soul that knows itself only by the names of what it seizes or consumes. At the television gala presented in his honor the night before the inauguration, he couldn't prevent himself from mouthing the lyrics while Barbra Streisand sang "Evergreen." The cameras drifted away from Streisand—as Mr Clinton knew they must—and found the tear-stained face of the new president, devouring the words as if they were made of sugar or chocolate. His infant's dream of all-embracing celebrity would have been well understood by President William Howard Taft, who once was astonished to discover himself traveling on a train with Mary Pickford and Francis X. Bushman, the silent-screen stars who were then the wonder of the age. When he saw how the actress was mobbed by eager crowds at the station, he summoned Bushman into his presence and confessed that he envied him the adoration of the public. "All the people love you," he said to the actor, "and I can't have even the love of half the people."

Moved by a comparable feeling of melancholy and boundless desire, President Clinton at the televised town meeting in Detroit began by saying that after only three weeks in the White House he had learned "how easy it is for the President to get out of touch." He roamed across the soundstage like a starved animal, feeding on the questions from the audience as if they were the stuff of life and breath. In truth the Clinton administration might prove to be best understood as a ceaseless campaign or a never-ending talk show. At a White House press conference in the not-too-distant future, I wouldn't be surprised to see the president interrupt the discussion—about jobs or Bosnia or the debt—and turn graciously to the camera to announce a commercial break. I can imagine him saying, "Don't go away, we'll be right back," but as his smile dissolves into an advertisement for Bud Light, I can also imagine myself wondering what the show is about and why democracy at the end deteriorated into a child's game of show and tell.

April 1993

COSMETIC SURGERY

The lines of humanity and urbanity never coincide.
—GEORG CHRISTOPH LICHTENBERG

On the last Saturday in May President Bill Clinton named David R. Gergen, a prominent Washington journalist and once-upon-a-time Republican media operative, as his principal adviser and chief publicist, and over the next several days the public argument about the wisdom of the appointment took a form that I don't remember ever having seen before. Instead of dividing along political lines, the opposing voices of reason and conscience divided along geographical lines. Almost without exception, the people who favored the appointment, applauding it as an indication of enlightened and non-partisan judgement, lived in

Washington. Again by nearly unanimous consent, the people who detested the appointment, decrying it as an act of betrayal or a proof of bad faith, lived anywhere and everywhere else in the country.

The division of opinion was cast in high relief on the editorial pages of the *New York Times* and the *Washington Post*, two newspapers that ordinarily find themselves in bland agreement on most questions of the national health and safety. The editors of the *Post* welcomed Gergen's appointment as "a good idea," and they took considerable pains to present his character as that of the wise counselor and patient friend. President Clinton clearly didn't know how to manage his image, and here at last was "a man who might be able to help head off some of the disasters just waiting to occur and help organize the White House for getting the right things done without a lot of posturing and lip." The *Times* thought the appointment "not healthy," "non-partisanship run amok," and its editors presented Gergen as an artful sophist who had served the Reagan administration (as director of communications at the White House) by promoting policies "that coarsened the quality of social compassion, spread suffering among the most undefended citizens . . . " Stories published elsewhere in the paper reminded readers that it was Gergen who interpreted the Reagan presidency as a stage set, who polished the lenses of the "warm and fuzzy" photo opportunity, who presented the administration's economic theory (low taxes; high deficits) as the work of benign genius, who briefed the cadre of White House press agents (a.k.a. "the spin patrols") on the ways and means of misleading the national news media with the day's whisper of disinformation and who, most abominably, defended Reagan's habit of telling anecdotes about poor people using food stamps to buy vodka (or welfare money to pay for vacations in Paris) by explaining that the public didn't care about the literal truth of a statement "so long as the symbolic truth is defensible."

As in the public sectors of opinion, the private views of Gergen's appointment had more to do with the observer's occupation and address than with his or her theories of the common good. Throughout the first week in June I listened to various friends and informants in Washington speak of Gergen with palpable gratitude and relief. President Clinton had become the butt of too many jokes—about the women he kept failing to appoint to the Justice Department; about the sublime Cristophe, his Beverly Hills barber; about the game of hide-and-seek with his third cousin, the FBI and the White House travel bureau—and somebody had to teach him the rules of Washington ceremony and etiquette before he

brought down on his august office the slops of scorn and ridicule. The
American people were urgently in need of bold initiatives and exemplary
government, and official Washington could ill afford to discredit the
Democratic party. The weakness of George Bush had ruined the reputation
of the Republican party, and if President Clinton wreaked havoc among
the Democrats, then who or what would be left to the country except a
procession of demagogues on the order of H. Ross Perot?

The correspondents calling in their objections from the provinces—
from Boston and Detroit and Los Angeles—didn't care about the niceties
of political maneuver. They cared about the connections between word
and deed, and they still assumed some sort of agreement, if only tenuous
or speculative, between what a politician said and what a politician did.
The Republicans in their midst condemned Gergen as a blasphemer, a
man whose record of comfortable success as Reagan's propagandist should
have insured his loyalty to the interests that made him rich as well as
famous. The disaffected Democrats thought that Gergen's appointment
was tantamount to President Clinton's disavowal of the principles upon
which he had campaigned for office. Not only had Clinton promised to
revise or delete the economic program that Gergen had so diligently
promoted, but the budget that he submitted to Congress in February took
as its premise (high taxes; low deficits) the precisely opposite theorem of
the public welfare. If the president could hire as his chief publicist a man
whose name and reputation were synonymous with a vigorous defense of
the status quo, then who could take him seriously as an apostle of social
change? If the romantic dream of the man from Hope, Arkansas could
expire so quickly in the stale air of Washington intrigue, then how was
it possible to believe that Clinton spoke on behalf of the future instead
of the past?

While I listened to the many voices of remonstrance, it occurred to me
that much of the rancor in the country's politics follows from a failure to
properly understand the language spoken in the capital. Washington
is a city of words, but words perceived as ends in themselves (like marble
fountains or Roman sculpture), not as the means of expression or thought.
The art of government is the maintaining of the façade of government.
The sovereign rule of appearances sets the terms of the conversation, and
the uses of language bear resemblance to the uses of interior decoration. The
resident grandees acquire their opinions for reasons of fashion or state, as
if they were jewels or fans, and nobody cares what the words mean as long
as they convey a gratifying impression of grave importance. Different

opinions come into vogue with different administrations, and the deft careerist learns to clothe his ambition in both a Republican and a Democratic style. What does it matter how anybody wants to dress up the season's newest economic theory as long as the tax revenue continues to arrive in amounts adequate to the monumental tasks of social engineering?

The obsession with images is as evident in New York and Los Angeles as it is in Washington, but the difference in emphasis is the difference between people interested in thought and expression and people interested in power. It is the business of New York or Los Angeles to manufacture images (whimsically transforming unknown southern governors into presidential candidates), but it is the business of Washington to trade in those images as the currency of political truism. Once having made the image, New York grows bored with it. In Washington the image becomes useful only after it has acquired the stability of the received wisdom, hammered into the brass of a campaign slogan or worked into the lacquer of a cliché, a word or a phrase suitable for an appearance on *Nightline*.

At Versailles during the reign of Louis XIV the courtiers were required to play cards and scratch on doors with the little fingers of their left hands. Their knowledge in these matters proved their intimate acquaintance with the unutterable mysteries of the universe. At Washington in the late twentieth century the resident courtiers accomplish a similar purpose by writing op-ed pieces for the *Washington Post* and by knowing what to say to David Brinkley about Hillary Rodham Clinton's theories of medicine or the sorrow of the Haitian refugees drifting out to sea in open boats.

What is wanted is not a policy but the perception of a policy—a word or an image sufficient to sustain the fiction of virtuous authority, of a government that knows what it is about, of people who are in command of events, or who at least have some sort of idea in their dignified and well-dressed heads.

The successful Washington politician, like the accomplished Washington journalist, never makes the mistake of confusing the appearance of a thing with the substance of a thing. Appearances are light and substances are heavy. An appearance can be shifted as easily as a potted palm, and on different days of the week, or in different committees of the Congress, it can be transformed into something that it is not. Substance resembles alimony and steamer trunks.

If neither the White House nor the Congress takes much interest in correcting the country's more difficult or intractable social disorders, it is because solutions belong to the realm of substance. They imply pain, and pain is unacceptable because pain translates into resentment, and resentment loses votes. In place of solutions the courtiers at Washington stage the shows of appearance, and before what they hope will remain a forgiving public they perform the ritual masques and dances of democracy under the headlines of "War in the Gulf," "New World Order," "The Deficit."

Both in his writings and by the trajectory of his career, Gergen perfectly embodies the polished figure of the Washington courtier—a man who seldom stays too late or says too much, who regards himself as "a facilitator" and who never confuses a stratagem with a conviction or an expedient policy with a passionate belief. In the first bloom of his ambition he wrote speeches for President Nixon, and during the unpleasantness of the Watergate investigation he proved himself adept at arranging the adjectives meant to preserve his chief from any harmful contact with the truth. Subsequent to his employment in the Reagan administration he became a columnist for *U.S. News & World Report* and a resident sage on the *MacNeil/Lehrer NewsHour*. Once established as a man who could be counted on in any and all circumstances for the irreproachable platitude, he found it possible not only to work both as a fellow for the American Enterprise Institute (owned and operated by conservatives and for the John F. Kennedy School of Government (owned and operated by liberals) but also to maintain, through the long dark night of the Bush administration, a close acquaintance with Bill Clinton, then the Democratic governor of Arkansas.

To the White House press corps gathered in the Rose Garden on the morning of 29 May, the appearance of Gergen was like that of a god from a machine. He stood before the grateful company as a veritable Polonius, a court chamberlain of the most exalted rank who had arrived not a moment too soon. After four months in Washington, the president still didn't know which promises to keep or what smile to wear. Another four months of the same confusion and the public would begin to ignore the White House, and if, God forbid, the public ignored the White House, then what would become of the White House press corps's sense of its own importance?

The large and amiable presence of Gergen ratified the abdication of Clinton. Nobody had to put the proposition in quite so many words, but everybody knew that, for the time being at least, the assembled company was safe from ridicule and secure in its rightful place at the still center of the turning world. Who better than Gergen to teach the wayward president how to sustain the necessary fiction of a virtuous and well-ordered commonwealth? Gergen was one of the media's own, a man who knew that it was the sacred duty of a free press to protect the rulers of the state from the howling of the mob and preserve them (for as long as was decently possible) as images of wisdom and power.

The general sense of deliverance was so obvious that it could be seen that evening on the television news broadcasts. Before introducing Gergen, President Clinton made a polite little speech in which he said that he had been "very concerned that the cumulative effect of some of the things which are very much in the news has given to the administration a tinge that is too partisan and not connected to the mainstream, pro-change, future-oriented politics and policies that I ran for President to implement."

He might as well have been talking to the Washington Monument. Nobody paid the slightest attention, and when the president gave over the rostrum to Gergen, stepping diffidently behind his new tutor to lead the applause, it was clear to all present on the lawn that although he would continue to occupy the White House (and be allowed to keep the household staff and the Marine color guard), henceforth he would be seen as both captive and ventriloquist for the system he had said he meant to change.

August 1993

WASHINGTON PHRASE BOOK

The oldest, wisest politician grows not more human
so, but is merely a gray wharf rat at last.
—HENRY DAVID THOREAU

*L*ast year's presidential campaign raised the hope of moving the national government in some sort of new direction, and if none of the candidates could fix the precise compass bearing, at least they were sure that it pointed away from politics as usual, away from the mindless extravagance of a feckless and spendthrift Congress. The motion was approved and seconded by the public-opinion polls (almost all of which indicated profound disgust with the status quo in Washington), but apparently it was meant to be seen and not heard. As I listened to this summer's debate about President Clinton's budget—its virtue and presumed benevolence, its theory of deficit reduction, its taking from the rich and giving to the poor—I wondered what had become of all the navigational charts and maps. The election had come and gone, and the new direction was the old direction. Here were the same feckless and spendthrift politicians, not yet six months in office, demanding even more money (approximately $241 billion in additional tax revenues) in return for the same dubious promises to restrain their expenditures over the next five years by the sum of $255 billion.

Their specious accounting was as familiar as their smiling sophism, and although I could admire their gall, I found it hard to imagine the audience that they had in mind. Were they talking only to themselves, or did they seriously believe that the American people were likely to grant them immunity from the laws of cause and effect? Maybe they thought that the language spoken in Washington was so heavily encrusted with euphemism that it defied translation into the vulgar dialects spoken elsewhere in the country. The latter supposition prompted me to make occasional notes on the speeches in progress during the months of June and July, and by 6 August, the day that Congress ratified the president's budget (by a margin of one vote in both the Senate and the House of Representatives), I had worked out the meanings of a few of the principal words and phrases. On the assumption that the government will continue to find itself hard-pressed for money, I offer the definitions as program notes for what is likely to become a continuous performance of the Washington vaudeville revue variously entitled "Directions Lost" or "Promises Deterred." As follows:

TAX AND SPEND: What all elected politicians do for a living. An occupation, like nursing or carpentry, not an ideological program.

BUDGET PROJECTIONS: Federal arts projects, in which the numbers express the authors' indifference to money as well as their contempt for the bourgeois taxpayers who supply them with funds. In October 1990, President Bush also promised a $500 billion deficit reduction over five years in return for a tax increase. Even as soon as 1991, he said, the deficit would dwindle to the modest sum of $63.1 billion. Six months later, after receiving the favor of a higher tax rate, the government reported the 1991 deficit at $318.1 billion, and by the end of 1991 the sum had been raised to $384.6 billion—an error of $321.5 billion over the span of a single year's accounting.

GRIDLOCK: A comfort presented as an affliction. When speaking for the record, even a first-year congressman can be counted upon to nominate the condition as the chief obstacle to the just reforms that otherwise would take place no later than next Wednesday afternoon. Speaking privately, all present welcome the condition as the best of the available excuses for the failure to act. Inaction is always preferable to action because actions of even the smallest and most hesitant kind (subtracting the subsidy from the suppliers of mohair or closing down an ancient submarine base) imply friction, and friction is un-American because friction translates into resentment, and resentment loses votes. The trick is to convey the impression of progress and change while preserving the freeze-frame of the status quo. The adepts learn to speak of "processes," "structures" and "empowerments"; to postpone decision by referring the questions at hand to another committee, another authorization, another hearing, another signature. When properly managed, gridlock carries everybody safely forward to the out years.

THE OUT YEARS: The imaginary moment in time, invariably after the next presidential election, when the government reduces its expenditures and pays its debts. The most reliable authorities fix the happy day at a distance of four or five years in the future, and then only if the Congress still remembers that it was once moved by a vision of monastic simplicity.

As distinct from the spending cuts that occur in the out years, the higher tax rates take place in the world of historical event, retroactive to 1 January 1993.

THE DEFICIT: The dogma or slogan that serves as Washington's replacement for the Cold War. Not one politician in fifty can explain the theory of deficit reduction, but then neither could one politician in fifty explain the mystery of supply-side economics or the mechanics of the hydrogen bomb. Why quarrel with a great truth in which the public wishes to believe and for which it stands willing to pay?

SACRIFICE: Various forms of financial discipline applicable to the American people as a whole, not to the political hierarchies in Washington. Although the exercises are best performed by "the wealthy," they also can be practiced by "the middle class." The members of Congress often wish that they, too, could make sacrifices, but the burden of keeping up the appearances of good government obliges them to forgo the domestic pleasures available to ordinary citizens.

The Congress in 1992 allocated $2.7 billion to the cost of its own privileges and comforts. The comparable sum in 1970 amounted to $353 million; in 1980, to $1.2 billion. No other form of public expenditure has expanded at so grandiose a rate. Over the course of the last twenty years, Congress has increased the spending on itself by 705 percent—more than twice the 280 percent rise in inflation or the 311 percent rise in the defense budget. Each member of Congress (435 US representatives and 100 senators) receives an annual salary of $133,600, but the pay is augmented by perquisites (pension plans, health insurance, and so on) worth an additional $23,500 a year. The pensions, far more generous than those offered in private industry, allow quite a few of the members to retire with as much as $100,000 a year, and they support a good many other members with as much as $2 million over the course of their retirement. Together with the routine luxuries of free parking, subsidized meals, gymnasiums, attending physicians, valets, florists and hairstylists, Congress provides its members with the services of several dozen video producers, who arrange their publicity, and at least four upholsterers, who tend their office furniture.

TAXABLE INCOME: A donative granted by the state to a fortunate but sometimes ungrateful citizenry. What is given also can be taken away, and if the state imposes a retroactive tax or subtracts a percentage from a social security pension, it is because the state always has better uses for the national revenue than do the people from whose labor it is derived.

GUT-WRENCHING DECISION: Newspaper term for a Democratic politician's choice between two categories of self-interest. Which course of action most harms his or her chances of reelection—a vote that risks the anger of the electorate or a vote that prompts reprisals from the White House?

SOUND FINANCE: Lesson taught by precept rather than by example. Any American citizen who modeled his or her financial dealings on those of the American government would be declared bankrupt or be convicted of fraud.

ECONOMIC THEORIES: Acquired for reasons of convenience or fashion, as if they were hats or scarves. Different theories come into vogue with different seasons or administration. (high taxes or low taxes, deficit spending or fiscal restraint, Great Society or New World Order), and any or all of them can justify the demand for more money, more grandeur, more marble. Nobody in Congress needs to know what the words mean. What is important is that the money continues to arrive in Washington, more or less on schedule and in amounts sufficient to fund the deliberations about the meaning of justice and the rights of the unborn.

THE AMERICAN PEOPLE: Admired and excessively praised as an abstraction but distrusted when encountered in person. Too many of them cling to the superstition that their money is their own.

CONGRESSIONAL DEBATE: Ritual performances meant to sustain the belief in democracy. Like the church, the government derives its income from the tithes imposed on the faithful, and in a democracy the faithful require the proofs of principled disagreement and plain argument. All present on Capitol Hill share the same urgent need for money, but in order to obtain it they must make a successful show of their differences of opinion, belaboring one another with the props and catchphrases of political truism. When necessary, they exchange parts and reverse their theories of the public good. Championing President Bush's $500 billion deficit reduction in the autumn of 1990, Senator Bob Dole of Kansas employed the same arguments that he condemned as ruinous folly when they were presented by President Clinton, almost word for word, in the summer of 1993.

The older and more antic politicians in Congress sometimes have trouble keeping a straight face when reciting their lines. On a television talk show in late July, Senator Daniel Patrick Moynihan, who was charged with overseeing the passage of President Clinton's budget into law, barely could restrain his laughter when questioned by his hosts about the wickedness of the deficit. I remembered seeing the same glint of humor in his expression when we had been scheduled to appear on the same radio program some years ago in New York. While we were passing the time in the green room, Moynihan observed that no politician could possibly know or understand everything that his audiences expect him to know or understand. He ran through the long list of subjects on which he was supposed to be fully and definitively informed—education, health care, foreign policy, highway construction, the multiplication of cancer cells—and then he laughed at the absurdity of the proposition. "The thing is impossible," he said, "but I'm not allowed to admit that it's impossible. If the people guessed how little their rulers know, they might become frightened."

Given the expectations of infallibility, Moynihan said, the rulers of the state must pretend to know what they are doing or saying, and so government becomes representative in the theatrical, not the constitutional, sense of the word. "It's like a fourth-grade Christmas play," he said. "The little boy comes out onstage wearing a crown of paper stars and saying that he's the north wind. I do the same thing when I stand in front of a microphone and answer questions about the intelligence services or what happened to the Cold War."

He laughed again, more merrily than before, and when he was called into the studio, he paused in the doorway to strike a theatrical pose. Looking over his shoulder, he said, "Enter the north wind."

October 1993

ANSWERING THE CALL

He may be a patriot for Austria, but is he a
patriot for me?
—EMPEROR FRANZ JOSEPH

Anybody who reads the papers or who follows the political discussions on C-Span or *Larry King Live* presumably has been informed by now that the country suffers from a disastrous "crisis of leadership"—not only in the political circus but also in every other arena of the national endeavor afflicted with the signs of uncertainty and misfortune. For the last four or five years the phrase has been making the rounds of the prominent editorial pages and the public-spirited conferences at which panels of experts measure America's geopolitical standing in the world, and if not by the end of the first morning's first plenary meeting then certainly during the course of the luncheon address and in time for the next day's edition of the *Washington Post*, somebody says that if only we could find the proper leadership then we would know what to do about the crime and divorce rates—also about the high cost of heart surgery, the drivel in the schools and the war in Bosnia. The sentiment serves as both divine revelation and closing prayer. The speaker points to his or her final bar chart and regrets the absence of leaders capable of arresting the statistics of moral and economic decline, the panelists murmur the equivalent of a blessing, and all present nod their heads and know that they have been made wise. Why, of course, say the assembled corporate executives and government officials, leadership. By God, it's the leadership that's missing. We can photograph the moons of Jupiter and sell the joys of capitalism to the Communist Chinese, but we can't balance the federal budget or make safe the streets of East St Louis, and do you know why? For the same reason that the country—or the university, or the network, or the airline—is being governed by self-serving and incompetent fools. Because the leadership has gone out of our lives.

The phrase always makes a favorable impression, and I've noticed that it often has a soothing effect not unlike the sound of waterfalls or the distant chanting of monks, but lately I've begun to suspect that President Bill Clinton is the only man in America who thinks that it means something. He talks incessantly about leadership—its inestimable value and illustrious place in the history of nations—and when he addresses a joint session of Congress or a press conference in Detroit, he is forever sounding the trumpet or answering the call, constantly urging his fellow citizens forward against the enemies of progress arrayed like so many dark horsemen on the far shore of the Potomac, under the glittering banners of ignorance, superstition, cynicism and greed. Certainly he means to play the part of a heroic president—a leader, by God, like John F. Kennedy or Teddy Roosevelt—but although he makes an eloquent and heartfelt speech, nobody ever follows him out the door, or over the top, or into no-man's-land, or anywhere at all.

The result is comic because Clinton never seems to notice the absence of recruits. By presenting himself as an advertisement for leadership, he remains as reliably inert as a photograph meant to sell basketball sneakers or men's cologne, threatening nobody's interest and always glad to say something else at the next day's press conference. Does the economy languish? Yes, say the polls, and Clinton promises vigorous measures. Will Congress accept those vigorous measures? No, say the polls, and Clinton declares the economy cured of its sickness. Do the American people want better health care? Yes, say the polls, and Clinton announces a plan. Will the American people pay for the remedy? No, say the polls, and Clinton offers to rewrite the prescription. Is the war in Bosnia a crime against humanity? Yes, say the polls, and Clinton puts the marines on ready alert. Can an American military expedition bring peace to the Balkans? No, say the generals at the Pentagon, and Clinton orders the marines to stand down.

I don't doubt that the president means well, but the humor of his administration testifies to his too literal-minded attendance at too many conferences sponsored by the Ford Foundation and the Kennedy School of Government. The thought again occurred to me in early March at a symposium assembled in the grand ballroom of a New York City hotel to consider the question of foreign trade. It was the kind of conference that Clinton undoubtedly would have enjoyed—lots of important people busily taking important notes; lots of worrying about what was to become of the great, good American people (variously compared to a herd of alarmed buffalo or a colony of despondent ants); lots of solemn warnings. Over a span of five hours I counted twenty-six references to leadership lost, but by the end of the afternoon I had come no closer to an understanding of what it was that the country so sadly lacked. None of the speakers raised the corollary question of elitism— if leadership is good, why is elitism bad?—and neither did anybody express surprise or alarm at President Clinton's floundering in the shoals of the Whitewater affair.

The oracles on loan from the Brookings Institution and the American Enterprise Institute chose instead to speak of imaginary beings. Some of them apparently hoped for the arrival of an amiable despot, a smiling, uniformed figure who inspired the unswerving loyalty of the bond market and the news media. Others seemed to be describing a benevolent American plutocrat who could afford to ignore the trifles of mere self-interest and who expressed, both in his life and his person, the ideal of government as philanthropy. A few of the more literary respondents offered martial or sporting analogies, and when searching for exemplary proofs of leadership they mentioned military commanders, high-school football coaches and veteran police captains accustomed to administering precincts known for both the savagery of their inhabitants and the rat-like cunning of their elected magistrates.

As the speakers succeeded one another at the podium, adjusting the microphone and arranging their notes, I found myself hard-pressed to take seriously their fretting about leadership, possibly because I associate the word with the making of a moral rather than an athletic or managerial effort—with traits of character, not with a talent for leveraging a stock portfolio or stealing third base. Leadership is a strength not easily come by, and it declares itself in the practice of telling the truth. I think of a leader as a person who demands something difficult from other people, who imposes on himself as well as his followers, the burdens of conscience and self-restraint. The impositions seriously interfere with everybody's habitual pleasures and hypocrisies, and who in America at the moment would welcome such an individual to the annual board meeting, much less to the stage of the national political theater? Let the leader who was lost and then found begin to talk about sacrifices slightly more difficult than giving up cigarettes or the third whiskey before dinner, and he puts an abrupt and indignant end to the pious wish for his happy return. When Christ showed up in Jerusalem saying the kinds of things that leaders have an awkward habit of saying, the Romans quickly discouraged what seemed to them an overly zealous display of leadership.

I can imagine a leader cast as a parish priest or a personal trainer, even as a professor of seventeenth-century English prose, but not as a salesman or a politician. I look at President Clinton and think of a Mexican piñata—a plump but remarkably durable figure swinging back and forth in the wind of the news, bearing up under the blows of blindfolded lobbyists and delighted television correspondents, spilling forth the gifts of government in the form of defense contracts, smiles, hugs, farm subsidies, campaign promises, Fourth of July oratory and little, sweet-scented twists of backstairs gossip.

Given the premises of egalitarian democracy, I don't know how anybody (the twenty-six speakers in the grand ballroom, Rush Limbaugh or the editorial board of *The Wall Street Journal*) could expect a more high-minded result. Leadership that depends on something other than a talent for brokering the markets in special interest implies an aristocratic principle of government, which in turn implies the authority of an elite, which is, by current definition, impermissible. In the American conversation, even the word "elitist" serves as an insult—not quite as contemptuous as racist or sexist, but certainly as a synonym for social pretension and intellectual fraud.

Although nearly all Americans honor what they can perceive as honest achievement and willingly grant the prerogatives of authority to those elites who found their claims on the exhibition of skill or knowledge so narrowly defined as to fit within the categories of a profession (a divorce lawyer, say, or a tight end, or a cosmetic surgeon), they refuse to grant the patents of authority in the realm of political wisdom or virtue. Who can prove that the fine phrases consist of anything other than pompous sham? Every citizen sets himself up as his own moral entrepreneur, and somewhere in the back of the auditorium somebody raises the familiar American objection, "Oh yeah? Says who?"

The questions haven't brooked a satisfactory answer since the War of 1812, and if any of our modern grandees think that the lack of leadership is something new under the sun, they might take the trouble to study

Gordon S. Wood's *The Radicalism of the American Revolution*. Situating his argument in the years 1770–1810, Wood describes the transformation of the American political principle from something resembling the old Roman ideal of a republic—which was what both John Adams and Thomas Jefferson had in mind—into a commercial democracy shaped by the energy of money, which was more nearly akin to what Andrew Jackson had in mind. The authors of the Constitution assumed that their new government would be conducted by wealthy and disinterested gentlemen who had neither occupation nor narrow mercantile interests to promote, "men who," in Madison's words, "possess most wisdom to discern and most virtue to pursue the common good of the society." The assumptions expired in the economic wilderness of the 1790s. Too many of the society's "purest and noblest characters" went bankrupt, thereby forfeiting the leisure and the means to act the public part of either a natural or classical aristocracy.

Together with the freedoms of the press, the excitements of the revolution fostered vehement antagonisms against the British nobility—against its "certain Airs of Wisdom and Superiority," against its "Scorn and Contempt and turning up of the Nose," and after the war was won, a good deal of this same feeling settled upon the American gentry who had thought to govern the country for "the Honour and Pleasure of doing good." Just as republicanism (which asked of its citizens a high degree of moral effort and civic virtue) subverted the pretensions of monarchy, so democracy (which asks little of its citizens except the expressions of will and appetite) subverted the pretensions of republicanism. By 1801, in a speech to the townspeople of Wallingford, Connecticut, Abraham Bishop, a New Haven lawyer and a Jeffersonian republican, was busily castigating the wealthy and well-educated citizens of the state as "the deceiving few . . . well fed, well dressed, chariot rolling, caucus keeping, levee reveling federalists." Of the government newly arrived in Washington, which already was squandering on itself the luxurious sum of $42,000 a day, Bishop expressed nothing but loathing and contempt, and he cautioned his audience against the vainglorious wars declared by the heroic gentry but paid for, in blood and money, by "plain men like yourselves." Of great naval victories, he said:

> . . . [know] that privates must bleed by the thousands for the glory of admirals, commodores, and port captains; that the only glory to which the sailor or marine can arrive, is to have his name printed on the papers and

against it, *"thigh badly fractured, since amputated, and likely to recover,"* and in a few months after, *"bravely fighting in the maintop, cut in two by a chain shot,"* and just under it, "we are happy to announce that though not quite success-ful this time, yet *the admiral and officers are in high spirits* and having put into Jamaica to refit, intend to look at them again."

Elsewhere in the body politic, but most especially among "tradesmen, mechanics, and the industrious classes," the proto-businessmen of the age exhorted their listeners, in the words of George Warner, a sailmaker in New York, to do their "utmost at election to prevent all men of talents, lawyers, rich men from being elected." Similar sentiments directed the conduct of the country's cultural affairs, and by 1803, the Reverend Samuel Miller, besieged by a new and rude profusion of pamphlets, hand-bills, posters, broadsides and newspapers, was appalled to discover that America's intellectual leadership had fallen (then as now) into "the hands of persons destitute at once of the urbanity of gentlemen, the information of scholars, and the principles of virtue."

If not by 1805, the year that Lewis and Clark departed for the head-waters of the Missouri River, then certainly by 1812, the United States had traded the revolutionary generation's dream of a classical republic governed, in Wood's phrase, by "notable geniuses and great-souled men" for a democracy owned and operated by common people with a common interest in making money and getting ahead. The terms of the deal —vulgarity, rootlessness and anti-intellectualism as the price for economic and political freedom—apparently still confuse our own latter-day mercantile gentry. In their grandiose moments they imagine that they want leaders in the eighteenth-century naval tradition, officers of high purpose and resolve eager to engage the enemies of mankind on five con-tinents and seven oceans. Newspaper columnists puff themselves up like frogs and write stirring editorials about sending troops to Bosnia, redraw-ing the map of southern Europe, making an example of the thugs in Belgrade and Zagreb so that ruffians elsewhere in the world won't take it into their heads to leap and dance and blow up trains. But the mood soon passes, and the experts assembled in the grand ballroom remember that sometimes ships sink and armies perish. They consult the polls and their own fears and bargain for the kind of leadership that makes a brave show in the world but doesn't cost much more than the annual dues charged by the Council on Foreign Relations. No matter how loud their protestations to the contrary, and no matter how busily they take notes, they prefer as little leadership as possible, and in President Clinton they find the answer to all their prayers.

May 1994

TRIAL BY KLIEG LIGHT

If hypocrisy were gold, the Capitol would
be Fort Knox.
—SENATOR JOHN MCCAIN, 11 MARCH 1994

*T*hroughout most of the winter and much of the spring, the news media so diligently took up the cudgels of the Whitewater inquisition that by the second week in March I began to wonder why the Washington press corps wasn't suggesting that President Bill Clinton submit to a trial by combat or an ordeal by fire. Nearly every edition of every newspaper leaked fresh stains on the president's name and reputation, but the narrative made sense only if it was meant to be understood as a test of faith, as if the president were being asked to hold white-hot iron in his hands or walk on burning coals. Mostly the news was made of rumors—about the slovenliness of the president's ethics and the seediness of the president's friends—and after five months of headlines, the burden of the complaint amounted to little more than a set of variations on a theme by Rush Limbaugh. As follows:

1. While serving as governor of Arkansas in the late 1970s, Mr Clinton and his wife lost money in a real-estate speculation on the Whitewater River. Variously posted at $68,000, $46,000, $13,000 and $500, the loss was variously interpreted as a sign of financial negligence or political graft.

2. The Clintons formed a business partnership with James and Susan McDougal, neither of them the sort of person likely to be invited to dinner by Pamela Harriman.

3. Trading in several commodity markets, on an investment of $1,000, Mrs Clinton realized a profit of nearly $100,000. The trades were arranged by Robert ("Red") Bone, a professional cardsharp.

4. Vincent Foster, a White House lawyer who apparently had been managing Mr and Mrs Clinton's personal investments, committed suicide in July of 1993. Not even the oldest and wisest political columnist in Washington knew why he had done so, but it was assumed that because

Mr Foster had been a friend and law partner of Mrs Clinton in Arkansas, he had died under circumstances other than those described to the police. *The Wall Street Journal* suspected foul play.

5. Ten government functionaries, among them George Stephanopoulos, the president's aide-de-camp, received subpoenas from a Washington grand jury taking testimony about the failure of the Arkansas savings and loan once owned by Mr McDougal. Avoiding photographers as they passed in and out of the courthouse, the witnesses presented the pleasing appearance of criminal suspects.

6. During the ten years that Mr Clinton served as governor of Arkansas, a quorum of well-placed people in Little Rock made a lot of money, not always in ways that could be safely explained to the IRS.

Although I don't doubt that three or four of the points in question might be made into a losing election or a television mini-series, they don't add to a sum of high crimes and misdemeanors likely to impeach a president, and they reveal nothing of the president's character that wasn't obvious two years ago during his election campaign. Surely it has been clear from the outset that Mr Clinton is not Thomas Jefferson. As a presidential candidate he was known to have evaded the military draft during the Vietnam War and to have enjoyed the company of women to whom he wasn't married; the Arkansas newspapers knew him as "Slick Willie," and in the November election he received 40 percent of his votes from people who believed him to be an inveterate liar. Within six months of his triumphant arrival in Washington, the president showed himself abjectly beholden to the monied interests (in New York and Los Angeles as well as in Flippin, Arkansas), as a man who doesn't make good on most of his promises and drifts on the tide of the opinion polls—in brief and in sum, an ambitious American politician, circa 1994, loyal to the cause of expedience and intent upon seizing the bauble of fame. But why should the discovery come as a surprise or provoke the news media to a furious casting of stones and a frantic turning over of rocks?

The answers speak to the cynicism of the permanent government in Washington (that is, the Congress, the entrenched bureaucracies, the news media), which regards even the faintest prospect of genuine political reform as both an affront to its dignity and a calamity of nature. By extinguishing the little light of idealism that remained to the Clinton presidency as recently as last Christmas, the permanent government protects its own agenda, its own prerogatives, its own definition of politics as a synonym for the market in fear and greed. Let Mr and Mrs Clinton be seen as hypocrites, as venal as junk-bond merchants and as duplicitous as Michael Deaver or Ed Meese, and then maybe the American public could put aside—once and for all—the childish notion of a government animated by moral principle.

Acting their parts as the servants of the status quo and accepting hints and documents from both Republican and Democratic informants, the various divisions of the news media presented different stagings of the Whitewater morality play. On the nominally liberal left, the voices of aroused conscience in the *New York Times* and the *Washington Post* approached the topic of Mr Clinton's character behind the masks of unctuous concern. Once again sin had been discovered in the world, and the inspectors of souls viewed it with alarm. Having been too prudish to countenance the reports of the president's sexual indiscretions, they pursued the rumors of his financial misconduct with the zeal of a village busybody seeking to regain his authority as guardian of the public trust. If it was poor taste to talk about the Arkansas State Police arranging assignations for Governor Clinton in Little Rock motel rooms, surely it was always good taste to talk about money, even if the amounts were so small as to be scarcely visible. Borrowing the stock phrases with which they had memorialized the last days of the Reagan administration ("fluid morality" and "seedy appearances"), the editorial writers relied upon the same vocabulary of pious admonition in which they express their opposition to tyranny and their belief in freedom. Charles Peters, the editor of *The Washington Monthly*, struck the precise note of the preferred sanctimony—"I do worry that the White House's insensitivity to ethical issues is threatening the moral authority of the presidency. And that can have grave consequences."

Although no less fatuous than the piety of the left, the fulminations on the unambiguously reactionary Right were both more pointed and more absurd. Trembling with indignation and blinking in the television lights, Senator Alphonse D'Amato (R., N.Y.) made the rounds of the Washington talk shows to accuse the Clinton administration of "lies!" "distortions!" "secret cabals!" His hosts politely refrained from addressing him as "Senator Shakedown" (the name by which he is fondly known to his colleagues on Capitol Hill); nor did anybody remind the audience that D'Amato's habit of extorting campaign contributions had prompted the Senate Ethics Committee to chastise him for his too eager and too frequent displays of avarice. It was left to David Wilhelm, the Democratic National Committee chairman, to explain, off-camera, the humor of the proceedings. "Being attacked on ethics by Al D'Amato," he said, "is like being called ugly by a frog."

The editorial page of *The Wall Street Journal* meanwhile abandoned itself to paroxysms of hysterical glee. Once again, the contradictions were grotesque—cries of "corruption!" "chicanery!" "fraud!" from a paper that had staunchly supported the Iran-Contra arms deals and defined the savings-and-loan swindles as the patriotic labor of capital formation.

Admiring the hypocrisy of the *Journal's* editorial page in late January, I made the mistake of attributing the tone of near hysteria to the paranoid enthusiasms of Robert L. Bartley, its editor. An ardent believer in the mystical properties of "Star Wars," Bartley deeply reveres Lieutenant Colonel Oliver North, a hero whom he sometimes confuses with Napoleon or Alexander the Great, and thinks that the entire history of capitalism is explained by the Laffer curve. Anybody who fails to acknowledge the intellectual and moral purity of the 1980s, Bartley associates with the Antichrist. At a dinner party some years ago in New York, I remember him mistaking me for Teddy Kennedy and, seizing me by the tie, attempting to choke me to death. His editorials often fall into similarly violent passions, and the discovery of lacunae in President Clinton's tax records moved him to righteous scorn: "The financial life of Bill and Hillary Clinton reads more like the milieu of a David Mamet play, in which glib five-and-dimers swim along the edges of the real economy, living on fancy talk, cutting corners and hoping that one of the big boys will offer them a piece of the $100 sure thing."

At first I thought the thundering on the Right merely foolish. For all intents and purposes President Clinton is a Republican, friendly to a corporate view of the world, an advocate of the North American Free Trade Agreement, unlikely to question the wisdom of Merrill Lynch. As his chief financial advisers he had appointed Robert Rubin and Roger Altman, both of whom owed their fortunes to their success on Wall Street, and as secretary of the treasury, he had appointed Lloyd Bentsen, formerly the chairman of the Senate Finance Committee and known for his loyalties to the oil companies and the banks. Maybe Mr Clinton didn't know all the "big boys" in New York, and possibly he had spent too much time with the "five-and-dimers" in Arkansas, but quite clearly he didn't intend to threaten the established order. Why then Mr Bartley's feverish crying out against "fanatic propagandists" and "left wing lobbyists"?

Because in the public mind, if not in Mr Bartley's, President Clinton, no matter how flawed his character or how weak his efforts to shift the balance of political power in Washington, still embodies and represents the hope that the government might be used to improve the lot of ordinary citizens, that in at least some of its functions it might do something for people who can't afford to hire a lobbyist at the going rate of $400 an hour. Despite the embarrassments of his first eighteen months in office, President Clinton had been incautious enough to actually send a few bills to Congress proposing reforms of the environmental and campaign-finance laws, and his wife, anathematized in a *Wall Street Journal* headline as "Hillary in the Pits," was attempting to rearrange the national health-care system, which, as Mr Bartley's readers well know, is tantamount to messing around with 14 percent of the gross domestic product. Arguing that the Whitewater news proved the Clinton administration's false claim to the throne of virtue, the *Journal* recommended a prompt and happy return to the glorious year of 1985, back to the Cold War and supply-side economics and Nancy Reagan dancing with Alfred Bloomingdale under the stars in the Hollywood Bowl.

Like the *Journal*'s editorial page, the permanent government in Washington welcomed the Whitewater investigations as a means of making time stand still. A procession of Democratic politicians (very earnest, very high-minded) appeared on the Sunday-morning talk shows to say that the foul breath of scandal had paralyzed the friends of good government. They blamed the Republicans for the "crippling effect" that had postponed or delayed the passage of new and noble laws. Were it not for the din of rumor and the obstacles placed in the path of progress by a sensation-mongering news media, they would move at once to get on with the business of "solving the real problems facing this country." The pose was disingenuous, but nobody bothered to explain the joke. Extending to their Democratic guests the same courtesies offered to Senator D'Amato, the television anchorpeople refrained from pointing out that the Democratic party holds a majority in both the Senate and the House of Representatives, that if it wished to address "the real problems facing this country," it didn't lack the means with which to do so.

But in Washington the trick is always to achieve a perfect state of in-action. Congress warily avoids solutions to "real problems" because solutions invariably mean that somebody has to lose something or give something up; solutions imply change, and change is unacceptable because change translates into resentment, and resentment loses votes. In place of energetic politics, the permanent government substitutes theatrical spectacle, and the media set the terms of the courtship imposed upon the man who would prove himself fit for the hand of the republic. Medieval chroniclers tell of princesses who send Christian knights in search of dragons, requiring them to recover bits and pieces of the true cross and to wander for many days and nights in heathen forests. Toward the end of the twentieth century, in a country that prides itself on its faith in reason, presidents come and go within the flaming arc of klieg lights, weighed in the daily balance of the public-opinion polls, their voting records and childhood memories sifted through the labyrinths of *Crossfire* or *The McLaughlin Group*, answering, in twenty words or less, questions that cannot be answered in a thousand words.

Like President Reagan, President Clinton possesses an impressive talent for the part. Just as Mr Reagan established the authority of his presidency by making a joke of his gunshot wound—"Honey, I forgot to duck"—so also Mr Clinton earned the respect of the electorate by making a sermon on *60 Minutes* of his liaison with Gennifer Flowers. Generally admired for his capacity to bear insult and humiliation, the president again proved his mettle on the evening of 24 March before a mob of reporters assembled in the East Room of the White House. At ease in the klieg lights, preserving within the fastness of himself the imperturbable quiet of a public statue, Mr Clinton for thirty-eight perilous minutes answered questions about the Whitewater real estate deal, never once betraying the least sign of fear or disgust. On the strength of his performance he recovered ten ratings points in the opinion polls, and the news media the next day were unanimous in their praise—"Adroit, Adept, Ingratiating" (the *Washington Post*); "Magnificent" (ABC News); "Dramatic, high-wire clash" (the *New York Times*).

The presidency undoubtedly constitutes a fearful test of a man's capacities, but his capacities for what? Even if the electorate understood or cared about something as tedious as the mechanics of government, how does it choose between the rivals for its fealty and esteem? The one attribute that can be known and seen comes to stand for all the other attributes that remain invisible, and so the test becomes one of finding out who can survive the stupidity and pitiless indifference of the television cameras.

Why be satisfied with the play of mere words? Why not equip the president of the United States with a broadsword or an old crossbow and send him into the field against four horsemen in black armor or an infuriated bear? Assuming that the event is properly promoted and attractively staged, I don't see why it wouldn't draw a sizable audience, and I expect that any number of corporate sponsors could be counted upon to supply commercial messages touting the frontier spirit that made America great. I can imagine Peter Jennings or Connie Chung providing sententious commentary about the president's prior showings against a lion, a Ninja and a wolf, and some days later—assuming, praise Jesus, that the president survived—I can see him talking to Oprah, or Larry, or Jay about his lifelong love of manly sports.

June 1994

A BULL FOR APOLLO

First they lifted back the heads of the
   victims,
slit their throats, skinned them and
   carved away
the meat from the thighbones and
    wrapped them in fat,
       . . . And all day long
they appeased the god with song, raising a ringing
   hymn
to the distant archer god who drives away the
   plague.

—HOMER

*I*n the card rooms of the nation's better golf and racquet clubs, the members never suffer the indignity of handling tarnished coins or dog-eared dollar bills. The paper currency is always new, and although tradesmen sometimes bring smudged dimes onto the premises, the kitchen staff scours and then polishes the coins before the waiters presume to offer them as change on silver trays. Similarly diligent cleansings of the world take place most everywhere else in American society—in the universities and the media trades as well as in the philanthropies and the financial professions—but the rituals of purification in Washington aspire to standards no less exacting than those in force in Palm Beach, and when I read in the papers last June that Congressman Daniel Rostenkowski (D., Ill.) had been indicted on seventeen counts of corruption (among them embezzlement, conspiracy, tampering with a witness, and mail fraud) I thought of an old copper penny on which it was no longer possible to see the head of Abraham Lincoln. The congressman apparently had become so soiled by the commerce of the streets that the time had come to put him in the steam kettle with the dingy quarters and last night's spoons.

Because Rostenkowski had been chairman of the House Ways and Means Committee for thirteen of his thirty-five years in Congress, and therefore a politician of grave and venerable rank, the friends of conscience in Washington made an excited show of their horror and disgust. Eric H. Holder Jr, the United States Attorney who presented the evidence to a federal grand jury, characterized the defendant's conduct as "offensive," "reprehensible," so "corrosive" in its effect on the public trust that if left unpunished it was likely to "undermine the very principles upon which this nation stands." Announcing the indictment to a crowded press conference at the Justice Department, Holder mounted almost at once into the higher registers of virtuous indignation. He let it be known that "this is not, as some have suggested, a petty matter" but rather a damnable proof of betrayal, an assault on "our democratic system of government," and a mortal insult to "the vast majority of the members of Congress [who] have been, and are, decent and honorable public officials who work incredibly hard and follow all the rules."

The attending news media followed the instructions on the prosecutor's cue cards, and over the next few days in the *New York Times*, the *Wall Street Journal* and the *Washington Post* various columnists and editorial writers variously characterized the chairman as a "lost soul," a master maker of deals, "a throwback to an earlier era," "one of the most powerful men in the country," the arrogant spawn of a democratic majority too long in office in the House. The *Post* sternly reminded its readers that the defendant's crimes were "anything but petty; they can't be put in the everybody-does-it category either," and the *Wall Street Journal*, worrying about "the pervasive appearance of muck," compared Rostenkowski to "a modern George III—the product of a system in which the spheres of public and private life have merged into a single Presence."

Although admirable as works of rhetorical prose, the newspaper speeches, like the prosecutor's statement of egalitarian principle, were somewhat grandiose for the wickedness at hand. The seventeen specific instances of corruption set forth in the indictment didn't come close to supporting the weight or pretension of the collective reprimand. Congressman Rostenkowski stood accused of defrauding the government of roughly $600,000—a sum that Holder advertised as testimony to the defendant's gross appetite for graft—but on a careful reading of the forty-nine pages of the grand jury's true bill, the sum proved to have been assembled over two decades (1971–1993) in a series of transactions that seldom exceeded $30,000 in any one year. From time to time the defendant allegedly had gerrymandered his payroll accounts, abused his privileges at the House Stationery Store and the House Post Office, overspent his government allowance for leasing automobiles. On at least fourteen different occasions he allegedly had directed the House Finance Office to issue checks to persons who performed "little" or "no official work," mostly minor followers (the wife of a Chicago precinct captain, a housekeeper, a chauffeur, an assistant doorkeeper, a son-in-law) who mowed the defendant's lawn, picked up the defendant's laundry, painted the defendant's house, photographed his daughters' weddings and engraved, on commemorative brass plaques, the words "Friendship" or "Our Pal."

To his account at the House Stationery Store, the congressman was believed to have charged, improperly, the cost of sixty wooden armchairs (hand-painted and inscribed with the defendant's name), two hundred and fifty pieces of fine china (given by the defendant as wedding presents), and twenty-six pieces of cheap luggage, costing, in aggregate, approximately $2,200. At the slightly higher elevations of graft, the congressman compelled one or another of his dependents ("Employee number one," the photographer, and "Employee number six," the former son-in-law) to refund to him a percentage of his or her government pay, and at the House Post Office he occasionally exchanged his allotment of postage stamps for cash. Again the amounts were negligible ($1,000 here and $2,000 there), and they suggested the character of a man likely to indulge in careless extravagance rather than commit well-organized robbery.

Nor did anything in the indictment correspond to the defendant's opportunities to stage genuinely impressive raids on the federal treasury. The House Ways and Means Committee writes the nation's tax laws and superintends the division of the federal spoils, and between a late breakfast and an early lunch on any given legislative day, the chairman was accustomed to directing several hundreds of millions of dollars to its deserving allies and friends. On the afternoon of his fall from legislative grace, the kind of people who talk to the newspapers spoke of him as "a heavyweight," somebody who really knew how to price a bribe or rig the tax code, "a ward politician of the old school" who preferred rare steaks and cold martinis to Perrier water and grilled fish. In a front page dispatch to the *New York Times*, a reporter seeking to place Rostenkowski in historical perspective described what he remembered as a civics lesson in the defendant's office in November 1985, a few hours before the House Ways and Means Committee voted on that year's tax-reform bill. The chairman was talking on the telephone to the lesser members of the committee, reminding them of the tax exemptions that he had bestowed on sports stadiums in Cleveland and northern New Jersey, on a convention center in Miami and a waste-management plant in New York City, on parking garages in Memphis and Charleston, on a savings-and-loan association in his own dearly beloved city of Chicago. Impressed by the heft and size of the chairman's clout, the reporter formed a vivid impression of a consummate fixer of parking tickets never at a loss for the chance to collect a stray $100,000 on his way to the men's room or while standing around in the Capitol rotunda under the portrait of Tecumseh.

On the plausible assumption that prosecutor Holder's agents ransacked the congressman's files and records as thoroughly as police detectives breaking up the furniture in an escaped convict's mobile home, what is remarkable about the defendant is his vanity, not his dishonesty or his greed. Always a poor man in the company of well-groomed bankers and sun-tanned owners of football teams (people who earned upwards of $3 million a year and could afford to spend $25,000 a week on the company plane or the cocktail shrimp), the faithful Rostenkowski during all those years of brokering literally billions of dollars in government subsidy (and at the same time trying to keep up appearances as a guest at the table of oligarchy) served his corporate overlords as dutifully as an English gamekeeper looking after the squire's grouse. And in return for his service, what did the chairman ask for himself? A collection of souvenirs, some petty cash and a few personal attentions provided by the tenants of an apartment building that he owned in the not especially exquisite Fifth District of Chicago, on a street that almost certainly would have offended the sensibilities of George III.

As compared with the norms of financial courtesy that obtain everywhere else in official Washington—Clark Clifford billing a client $25,000 for a single telephone call, lecture fees in amounts upwards of $15,000 paid to William Safire and George Will by various corporate sponsors, lobbyists cheerfully paying $20,000 for the privilege of sitting at dinner with Secretary of State Warren Christopher—the defendant's needs were modest, his habits frugal. The chairman took so little when he could have taken so much, and in the wreckage of the indictment he stands revealed as a model of congressional deportment. He found his pleasure in the small proofs of his power—doing favors for some people and not for others, handing out cigars and tax exemptions, obliging self-important businessmen to wait in the anteroom or the rain, listening to people laugh at his jokes.

Why then the prosecutor's alarm and the pious mumbling in the news media? Set aside or take for granted the possibility of a Republican intrigue, and the question speaks to the air of nervousness in official Washington rather than to the name and number of the defendant's crimes. For the last five or six years, and most pointedly in the 1992 presidential election, the American people have not been shy about giving voice to their loathing and mistrust of the political status quo. H. Ross Perot constructed his campaign platform on little else except the premise of resentment, and in the November election, without declaring himself a candidate and despite his obvious likeness to both a demagogue and an autocrat, he received one fifth of the popular vote. In Virginia this summer, Lieutenant Colonel Oliver North stands for election to the United States Senate on a platform of contempt for the institution of which he hopes to become a precious ornament. Fourteen states have passed laws imposing term limits on their congressional representatives, and the opinion polls show a steadily rising curve of hostility toward official Washington—its habitual arrogance, its indifference to the concerns of the average citizen, its fatuous luxury and languid squandering of the public purse. The mood of populist suspicion lately has turned so ugly that even case-hardened politicians have begun to think the rewards of office no longer worth the labor of their acquisition. So far this year no fewer than nine senators and forty-six members of the House of Representatives have announced their intention to withdraw from the autumn elections, and when asked to explain their departures they mostly mention their unwillingness to see themselves reflected in the mirror of the news as villains and fools.

The unflattering image is by no means new, and in times past the Washington equestrian classes have managed to prevent too virulent an outbreak of cynicism (a terrible disease likely to lead to the ruin of the state) by performing the acts of ritual purification and sacrifice. Upon finding themselves too sorely burdened by the too public consequences of their cowardice or incompetence, they hurriedly search through the closets on Capitol Hill and discover—wonder of wonders and much to everybody's amazement—a scoundrel in their midst. With a loud blowing of horns and banging of drums, they decorate the once honorable gentleman with the proofs and symbols of corruption. The newspapers pass judgement, one or another of the courts pronounces sentence, the stinking, venal mess is carried off to jail or California, and the marble hall of government, cleansed of its impurities, regains its customary state of perfect innocence, in which, *pace* prosecutor Holder, the decent members of Congress "work incredibly hard and follow all the rules."

If the ritual destruction of public men invariably turns on a trivial amount of money, it is because the occasion for outrage arises only when the sums in question can be seen in company with some small and paltry purpose. The television audience lacks the patience to appreciate the intricacies of a big-time government swindle (the savings-and-loan deals, say, or the means by which the Pentagon budget every year gives up $40 or $50 billion to fraud), but nobody has any trouble following the plot of a petty theft—the $10,000 bribe from the dairy farmers that the late John Connally, then secretary of the treasury, stuffed in his pocket without bothering to look at the numbers on the check, Sherman Adams's vicuna coat, Congressman Jim Wright's $55,000 book deal, John Sununu's passion for limousines, Rostenkowski's $28,000 stamp album.

Not only do the small sums of money tell a better story (allowing the friends of the defendant to say, as somebody said of Rostenkowski to the *Times*, "It's almost Aristotelian—the tragic flaw"); they also bear witness to the shabbiness of the defendant's soul. In the American cosmology money is a synonym for God, and a politician who steals from the collection plate can be condemned as both a criminal and a heretic. Of the thirty or forty members of Congress led to sacrificial slaughter over the last ten years, all but three or four have trespassed against the majesty of wealth, and it is the tawdriness of the sum that imparts value to the ritual. By proving himself to be a poor man who needs the money—$1,000 here, $2,000 there— the defendant commits both the unpardonable American crime and the unforgivable American sin. Frank Mankiewicz, formerly an assistant to President John Kennedy and now a prominent public-relations man in Washington, explained the catechism to one of the newspaper reporters who wondered why Rostenkowski hadn't amassed a fortune in the bond market and why it was that Democratic politicians were more easily corrupted than their Republican confederates. "The lower classes steal," Mankiewicz said. "The upper classes defraud. The Republicans don't need walking-around money."

Year in and year out for as long as I have been reading the tale of American politics, the ritual cleansings of the government in Washington have followed one upon the other in a rhythm as certain as the changing of the seasons. The headlines come and go, and so do the defendants on the courthouse steps, but the habits of corruption remain as firmly in place as the Lincoln Memorial or the star of Bethlehem. Year in and year out the lobbyists continue to prosper and grow fat; the price of real estate moves steadily upward in Fairfax County, Virginia and next year's tariff proves as lucrative as last year's defense contract. Although the charges against Rostenkowski evolved from the discovery of a check-kiting scheme in the House Post Office in 1992, the members of the House over the last two years have voted—not once but twice—to suppress all further investigation of the scheme; nor has the House made good on its repeated promises to reform the campaign-finance laws. Even more tellingly to the point, Representative Joseph McDade (R., Penn.), the ranking Republican on the House Ways and Means Committee, was indicted two years ago for bribery and racketeering, but as of the present writing the legal embarrassment hasn't prevented him from continuing to oversee the management of the nation's finances.

As always, what is wanted in Washington is the illusion of reform, not the thing itself. The appetite for remonstrance grows with the rumors upon which it feeds, and as the readers of the tabloid press come to confuse the nation's politics with daytime soap opera (President Clinton in a motel with a Miss Arkansas, his wife speculating in the commodities market, one White House aide found dead in Fort Marcy Park, and another one going off to play golf in air force helicopters) the primetime audience demands gaudier entertainments, more solemn scourgings, richer sacrifices. Anxious to appease an increasingly restive electorate, the rulers of the state offer increasingly theatrical shows of their innocence. President Clinton travels to the beaches of Normandy to pose for photographs against a backdrop of military glory, and in Washington the servants of the great god demos lead forward to the altar of justice the prize bullock otherwise known as Congressman Daniel Rostenkowski, chairman of the House Ways and Means Committee.

No network news director could have made a happier casting decision. First and foremost, the chairman looks like a caricature of the corrupt politician—squinting and heavyset, a dissolute softness of the jowls, the expression in the eyes as lifeless as the expression in the eyes of a coroner. Secondly, the chairman had made a loud show of his skill at making deals, bragging to the press about his acquaintance with smoke-filled rooms. Thirdly, and by no means unimportantly, the chairman could be presented as an archaic figure inexplicably escaped from a prehistoric past. The newspapers earnestly stressed the latter point. The *Washington Post* was quick to reassure its readers that Rostenkowski "learned the game of politics in a bygone era . . . far different from the Washington of the 1990s with its independent counsels and ethics codes," and the *Times* was careful to observe that the defendant was "caught in a time-warp," an old ward politician who, like an extinct species of wharf rat, had failed to adapt to the evolving norms of clean and efficient government.

Until the week prior to the chairman's indictment, the ritual form of the sacrifice looked to be securely in place, and it was assumed that the bullock would go placidly to its fate. The newspapers supplied the proper quantities of front-page incense, and the defendant's lawyer, Robert S. Bennett, had agreed to a plea bargain with the Justice Department that allowed the defendant to resign from Congress, admit to a single felony (not related to his traffic in stamps with the House Post Office), pay a $38,000 fine and serve six months in prison. Official Washington was delighted with the arrangements. The chairman's own counsel—so deft a servant of the status quo that he also was defending President Clinton against the charges of sexual imperialism brought by Paula Jones—had sharpened the sacred knife with which the chairman was expected to cut his own throat. The ladies and gentlemen in the press gallery looked forward to a brief but poignant spectacle, after which everybody could go to lunch at Maison Blanche and know that once again the Republic had been led out of temptation and delivered from evil.

The script appealed to everybody but the bullock. Two days before the Grand Jury handed up the indictment, the defendant refused the plea bargain and, instead of accepting what the gossip in Washington described as "the deal of the century," issued a statement avowing his innocence. He hired new counsel (a Chicago lawyer, not a Washington lawyer) and said that he would gladly stand trial for seventeen crimes that he didn't commit.

If a jury finds the chairman not guilty, the verdict might mean that he is ahead of the times instead of behind the times and that the art and practice of representative government no longer can rely on the rely on the willing suspensions of disbelief. On the day that Rostenkowski was indicted, I listened to a Chicago radio show take calls from the defendant's constituents, and although they readily conceded that the gentleman was a crook, they didn't think him any different from the rest of the crooks in Washington. He had done what he had been elected to do and had brought back to Chicago more than its fair share of the federal spoils. Why then belabor him with the mockery of the law?

Comparable degrees of cynicism apparently sustain a number of the summer's political campaigns. Oliver North, a convicted felon, seeks election as the junior senator from Virginia; Marion S. Barry Jr, formerly mayor of Washington, DC, and not long ago released from jail, stands for reelection to the office in which he was last seen smoking crack; Representative Ken Calvert (R., Calif.) asks the voters in Riverside County to return him to Congress despite his having been found in what the papers called "a compromising position" with a prostitute in a car in downtown Corona.

By refusing prosecutor Holder's plea bargain, Rostenkowski gave up the gavel of the House Ways and Means Committee but retained his seat in Congress. Two days after being indicted for conduct so offensive as to "undermine the very principles on which this nation stands," he returned to the table over which he had been accustomed to preside, and although he was no longer chairman, his fellow members welcomed him with two standing ovations. On reading of their courtesy in the next morning's paper, I couldn't help but admire them for applauding the arrival of their own doom. If the rituals of purification no longer instill in the faithful feelings of reverence and awe, then who or what will protect Washington's equestrian classes from the wrath of the distant archer god? Let the laundering of politicians become as banal a procedure as the laundering of money in Switzerland or Grand Cayman, and the nervous court chamberlains on K Street can look toward to meeting (under circumstances probably unpleasant) a good many people to whom they haven't been properly introduced in the Cosmos Club or the White House Rose Garden.

August 1994

THUNDER ON THE RIGHT

It is muddleheaded to say, I am in favor of this kind of
political regime rather than that: what one really
means is, I prefer this kind of police.
—E. M. CIORAN

*D*uring the first weeks of the autumn election campaigns I noticed that when I turned on the radio and heard three or four people talking about politics, I couldn't tell the difference between the show's host, the congressman who had dropped by to drum up votes, the caller in Worcester disgusted with welfare cheats and the caller in San Diego who wanted to bomb Baghdad. By late October I understood that the distinctions didn't matter. Everybody was as angry as everybody else, and all present belonged to one or another of the parties of virtue and conscience. As often as not the host turned out to be a friend of Pat Robertson's, the callers—Della in Worcester and Bob in San Diego—had both learned their politics from the paintings of Norman Rockwell and the candidate, although he had served in Congress for twelve years, miraculously, had avoided the sloughs of corruption that had engulfed so many of his fellow pilgrims on Capitol Hill.

Once having established their various states of innocence, the guests proceeded to the great task of calling down the wrath of Moses or Teddy Roosevelt on the heads of their innumerable enemies. The catalogue of their resentment provided the text for most of the season's five hundred election campaigns, and well before the end of September the angry voices on the radio had become indistinguishable from the television commercials in which the candidates for federal, state and municipal office—like school-boys delighting in the hate speech so long forbidden in the universities —scrawled dirty words on a succession of blackboards for which they paid, in the major media markets, as much as $70,000 a minute. Campaigning for the Senate in Tennessee, the Republican candidate (a heart surgeon named Bill Frist with little to recommend him other than the magnificence of his inherited fortune) demanded "term limits for career politicians and the death penalty for career criminals." Running for governor in Florida, Jeb Bush, the son of the former president, indirectly charged the Democratic incumbent with murder; and in New York State the Republican candidate for comptroller, Herbert London, portrayed his opponent as a black racist likely to favor sending Jews to death camps.

Every now and then I made note of a remark that embodied the spirit of the campaign, and among these I find two that strike me as memorable. First, from Cal Thomas, a syndicated newspaper columnist with whom I found myself in conversation on C-Span almost a year before the election. Summing up the already prevalent feeling of revulsion for the federal government and all its smiling lies, Thomas said, "We ought to just put a full-body condom over the entire city of Washington and flush it out to sea." Second, on the last weekend of the campaign, Congressman Newt Gingrich of Georgia (now Speaker of the House of Representatives) fitting the news of tragic murder in the South Carolina to the specifications of self-serving political slogan. Taking note of the arrest of Susan Smith, the woman who drowned her two small children in a lake, Gingrich attributed her crime to the swarm of evils let loose upon the land by left-wing English professors and a prolonged Democratic majority in Congress. The poor woman's confusion, he said, "vividly reminds every American how sick the society is getting and how much we have to have change . . . [and] the only way you get change is to vote Republican."

The bitter slanders reflected a perception current among the propertied classes, predominantly white and suburban, that they were being robbed of their birthrights by a feckless government allied with the armies of the urban poor. Together with the citizens calling in their complaints to Don Imus or Rush Limbaugh—Della from her successful boutique and Bob from his profitable boat marina—even political candidates who had grown old in public office presented themselves as victims of a world they never made (one that had arisen mysteriously out of the mists of the 1960s behind the lyrics of a Bob Dylan song), and they gladly confirmed everybody's fondest fears of class warfare between the haves and the have-nots. Few politicians put the point so bluntly, but they knew which side to choose and, whether Democrat or Republican, they took their uncompromising stands—bold as eagles, brave as lions—under the beach umbrellas of the big money.

On 8 November the sum of the electorate's well-nourished grievances found expression in the vote that since has become the revelation of the reactionary dream of paradise regained. For the first time in forty years the Republican party gained command of the House of Representatives; together with a majority in the Senate, the party's candidates won gubernatorial elections in California, Texas, Pennsylvania and New York as well as control of eighteen state legislatures previously held by the Democrats. On the Democratic side of the ballot incumbent officeholders fell like rotted pears from wind-stricken trees, but among the Republicans not one sitting governor, senator or congressman lost an election.

Understood as a popular referendum against what since 1964 has been variously known as the Great Society, the New Covenant and the "L" word, the vote announced the loss of belief in the proposition that government, any government, can call into being the virtues of a civil society or the energies of high civilization. The vote matched the temper of a season in which the late Richard Herrnstein and Charles Murray's book *The Bell Curve*, a patchwork of dubious statistics and bogus theory, became a best-selling sensation on the strength of its good news that destiny was genetic, cognition hereditary and most black people justly sentenced at birth to lives of poverty and crime.

The post-election sifting of the vote confirmed the preelection impression of panic among the possessing classes—for the first time since 1970 more votes were cast by Republicans than by Democrats; in at least half of the six hundred elections to national, state and local office, and whippers-in of the Christian Right herded the faithful to the camp of the victorious Republican candidate, and in California, Proposition 187 (the one denying money and government services to illegal aliens) carried by a margin of three to two.

As was to be expected, the grand masters of the Republican fraternal lodges read the entrails of the election as proof of a happy return to the aesthetics of Cecil B. De Mille and the politics of Calvin Coolidge. But although I could understand the rejoicing on the Right as a euphoria not unlike the rapture of the deep, I expect that among the general public the feeling will prove short-lived, like the excitements associated with the smashing of champagne glasses and the tearing down of goalposts. Maybe it is unreasonable to ask or expect anything else of an election in which only 39 percent of those eligible bothered to go to the polls and 75 percent of the voters didn't know the names of their own representatives in Congress. Closely trimmed to the winds of rumor drifting through the headphones of the radio talk show hosts, the campaign gathered its emotional force from a series of imbecile non sequiturs cheerfully ignored by Della and Bob as well as by the celebrity host and the distinguished senator. As follows:

1. Populism in Cream

Much of the present unhappiness in the society, as well as most of the damage done to the nation's economy over the last fifteen years, descends from the Reagan administration's policy of increasing the wealth of the rich and reducing the means of the poor. Given the ceaseless muttering during the campaign about the lack of money and the loss of jobs, the electorate, had it been interested in cause and effect, might have been expected to direct its anger against the marble façades of the American oligarchy—against the Federal Reserve that has been steadily raising the interest rate (five times in the nine months prior to the election) or the corporations that have been busily winnowing the rows of middle management or shipping their back offices to Malaysia. But instead of blaming the rich, the voters blamed the poor, venting their spleen on immigrants, criminals, racial minorities and beggars—on the constituencies that can't afford a trade association or a high-priced lobbyist. The tone of the political advertisements aped the snide humor of the David Letterman show, the insults and put-downs—fatso, zit, liberal, wetback, and so on—meant to display the moral refinement of the politician paying for the jokes. The candidates made sport of poor people buying shrimp with food stamps; they said nothing about Wall Street speculators buying office buildings with tax-free junk bonds.

Several of the nation's leading newspaper columnists were at pains to point out that the trouble with the political season—its mean-spiritedness and absence of debate—followed from the country's straitened economic circumstances. The God-fearing American people were said to be out of money and out of compassion, feeling themselves under attack by tax collectors stealing their money and dark-skinned immigrants stealing their jobs.

But little about the election campaigns suggested that they were anything other than expensive entertainments presented at the pleasure of the rich for the amusement of their admirers among the would-be rich, a series of diversions on the order of the amateur theatricals staged by the particular friends of Marie Antoinette at the Petite Trianon. The prominent candidates were for the most part individuals possessed of sizable fortunes (Mitt Romney, Ted Kennedy, Frank Lautenberg, Michael Huffington, Jeb and George Bush, Herb Kohl, Richard Fisher and Bill Frist), and the audience to which they addressed their remarks was made up largely of the news media (the claque employed by the oligarchy to applaud its comings in and goings out) and those voters belonging to the wealthier echelons of the middle class. Far from being too poor to support its enthusiasm for politics, the country apparently was prosperous enough to spend upward of $500 million on the staging of an event that ESPN might rate as an attraction comparable to the East Asian golf tour or a wood-chopping tournament.

2. The Prom King

I can't remember a campaign in which so many people expressed such violent feelings of disgust for a sitting president. The objections were seldom political. Instead of condemning Clinton's legislative proposals or theories of government, the critics complained of the flaws in his character and deportment. They wished that he wouldn't give so many speeches or eat so many cheeseburgers. They didn't like his wife, or the sound of his voice, or the look of his hair. They thought him weak or too much obsessed by bureaucracy. Republican candidates everywhere in the country sought to identify their opponents as Friends of Bill, as if by merely establishing the association they proved the Democrat guilty of a dingy passion for government acronyms or Gennifer Flowers.

The perceptions were contradicted by the facts. Clinton shaped his politics to the conservative temperament of the times, and no Democratic president in recent memory had so eagerly attempted to expose himself as a closet Republican. During the 1992 campaign Clinton avoided being too often seen in the company of feminists and black people, and as president he had lobbied into law the three Republican initiatives dear to the heart of President Bush—deficit reduction, the crime bill and the North American Free Trade Agreement. His economic policies were as sound as the furniture in the boardroom of Goldman Sachs, but he made the mistake of thinking that the country was still interested in Democratic social policy, and by attempting to reform the health-care system he smeared his image as a good Republican and became the personification of big government, the inveterate busybody rummaging through desks and insurance claims, levying taxes and stamping death certificates.

Once having blundered into the morass of large-scale social reform, the president never could regain his footing as the Prom King elected to preside over what in 1992 both the voters and Clinton's corporate sponsors thought would prove to be a Republican government dressed up in the costumes of a television mini-series loosely based on the life of Andrew Jackson. The Democratic party had been morally and intellectually bankrupt for twenty years, the remnants of its principles sold at auction at increasingly low prices during the Reagan and Bush administrations, and nobody expected Clinton to take seriously the slogans found on old Hubert Humphrey buttons. Most of the time he didn't, but once or twice he forgot who was paying for the orchestra, and despite his innate conservatism and fondness for golf, the political audience chose to see him as a lost flower child at a Grateful Dead concert.

3. Uncle Sugar

So many of the opinion polls showed the electorate so implacably opposed to the existence as well as the theory of big government that one would have thought at least a few voters willing to give up their own particular subsidy—the tax deduction for home loan mortgages, say, or Social Security payments, or student loans, or Medicare. Della and Bob remained silent on the subject, and so did the candidates touring states and towns dependent upon the military budget or posing for photo opportunities in picturesque wheat fields enriched with the fertilizer of federal money. The damnable entitlement always proved to be somebody else's entitlement— somebody certainly undeserving and probably ethnic.

About the uses of government the contradictions were so many and so blatant that even Representative Gingrich often got lost in the labyrinth of his own sophism. He objected to the reckless squandering of public money on the shiftless and ungrateful poor, but he favored extravagant transfer payments to the appreciative and industrious rich, and over the span of his fifteen years in Congress his own districts in Georgia received gifts of federal largesse almost as lavish as those sent to Arlington County, Virginia and Brevard County, Florida.

Nor was Gingrich willing to relinquish the government's power to build the new Arcadia or justify God's ways to man. The Democrats upon whom Gingrich dripped the acid of his contempt ("welfare liberals," "McGoverniks," "Stalinists," "enem[ies] of normal Americans") had made the mistake of trying to reconstruct the social and economic order. Presuming to change black people into white people and Spanish Harlem into Palm Springs, they had sought to rectify the mistakes of a careless Providence that somehow had neglected to provide equal shares of intelligence, beauty and Microsoft Preferred to every child born under the American sun.

In the world according to Newt, the proposition failed not only because it was foolish but also because it substituted the lesser for the greater task. What was really important was the reconstruction of the moral order, nothing less than the "rescue of American civilization" from the pits of cynicism and despair into which it had been cast by hardened feminists and marijuana-smoking guitar players. The government, said Gingrich, must bring forth the spiritual analogue of the New Deal, must repeal the decade of the 1960s, clarify the distinctions between right and wrong, take Sunday school attendance, recall the American people (if necessary by force) to the shelter of "traditional morals," and bend the coercive powers of government to the reformation of the American character instead of the reconstruction of the American economy.

4. Past Perfect

No day passed without one or another of the candidates saying that "it's time for a change." The phrase appeared in eight of every ten television commercials, the implication being that whoever bought the time was advancing boldly into a future certain to be filled with prizes like the ones handed out by Vanna White on *Wheel of Fortune*. But the phrase was as empty as every other phrase in the campaign. What was wanted was the appearance of change and not its substance: a parade of new faces, even if they were as vacant as glass (see George Pataki, the governor of New York) and a rush of new words, even if they were nonsense rhymes.

Had either the voters or the candidates seriously considered the prospect of substantive change, the conversation presumably would have addressed specific legislative measures—about education, foreign policy, the deficit, health care, the GATT treaty, campaign finance and the environment. But instead of modest and therefore plausible reforms, there was Gingrich's grandiose "Contract with America," and instead of debate there was gossip—about Oliver North's felonies or Chuck Robb's mistress, about "McGoverniks" wandering in and out of pornographic movies, about the moral decay in downtown Toledo and drug dealers scouting the perimeter of Greenwich, Connecticut.

By way of allaying every voter's worry that he or she may have to give something up, the candidates new to politics put forward their ignorance of Washington as proof that they were the last people on earth likely to know how to operate the machinery of government and thus, by definition, incapable of changing even so much as a light bulb in the House of Representatives. It was as if a heart surgeon were to say that although he knew nothing of scalpels or anesthetics, and objected to the arbitrary discrimination between an artery and a vein, he was the man to perform the operation because he had adhered all his life to "Hoosier hometown values" and once had saved an Airedale from being run over by a train. Elect me, dear voter, because I am an ignorant fool. Even better, dear voter, elect me because, like you, I despise the office in pursuit of which I already have spent $24 million in promotional fees.

Campaigning for the Senate in California, Michael Huffington set the standard of absurdity to which so many of the season's campaigns so expensively aspired. With respect to his presence in Washington as a one-term congressman during the Reagan administration, Huffington said that all anybody did there was pass around unintelligible pieces of paper, a charade in which he for one certainly meant to take no part. "I'm against Washington," he said, "always have been. Congress has been in session for two hundred years, and all they do is make laws."

Taken as a measure of the popular and deep-seated preference for the joys of antipolitics, the belligerent non sequiturs of the fall elections all but guarantee another two years of legislative futility in Congress, which probably is the result that the voters had in mind. Gingrich confirmed the prognosis when he came to Washington three days after the election and said that as the probable Speaker of the House he was in no mood to bargain with anybody who didn't agree with his notions of America's moral reawakening. Speaking to a crowd businessmen at the Willard Hotel, Gingrich offered his intransigence ("cooperation, yes; compromise, no") as a testament to his righteousness, and to a reporter from the *New York Times* he said, "The White House can either decide to accommodate reality, or they can decide to repudiate reality. That's their choice."

Absent the prospect of useful compromise, and assuming that the new Republican majorities won't take much interest in President Clinton's "national conversation" or Hillary Clinton's "politics of meaning," what then will the members of the 104th Congress find to say to one another? Let the majority divide into the factions of the authoritarian and libertarian Right, and with any luck it will fall to arguing about how best to close the Mexican border, or whether to send troublesome adolescents to boot camps or Indian reservations, or when to schedule public floggings and where to build the next prison, or which grade of boiling oil to pour on the heads of undocumented maids. Given the presumption that government can contribute nothing of importance to the building of a secular common-wealth, what else can it do except distribute punishments and devise spectacles likely to excite the interest of a bored audience at the next election? It won't be easy to upstage the sensations of 1994. Possibly the congressmen will content themselves with the frequent openings of orphanages (loud applause when Gingrich cuts the ribbon), or with the ceremonial demolitions of federal office buildings (more applause and a release of balloons), or with costume balls staged in the courtyards of state prisons (dance music, the laughter of pretty women, Oliver North and Pat Buchanan both dressed as Napoleon). But the market for mass entertain-ment favors the trend toward violence, and in response to the clamor of the opinion polls I can imagine a party of committee chairmen outfitted by Banana Republic or Polo Sport, gunning for an endangered species of jackrabbit or Guatemalan on the Texas plains.

January 1995

SOCIETY

CIGARETTE, CIGARETTE SMOKING Assaults with a deadly weapon. Wax indignant.

ELITISM Admirable only among athletes, surgeons and divorce lawyers.

SEX advertising gimmick. Best confined to the telephone.

TWELVE STEPS Must be taken one at a time.

FREE LUNCH No such thing. Liberals believe in its existence, which is why they lose so many elections.

Who and What is American

There may not be an American character, but there
is the emotion of being American. It has many
resemblances to the emotion of being Russian—that
feeling of nostalgia for some undetermined future
when man will have improved himself beyond
recognition and when all will be well.
—V. S. PRITCHETT

Were I to believe what I read in the papers, I would find it easy
to think that I no longer can identify myself simply as an
American. The noun apparently means nothing unless it is
dressed up with at least one modifying adjective. As a plain American I have
neither voice nor authentic proofs of existence. I acquire a presence only as
an old American, a female American, a white American, a rich American,
a black American, a gay American, a poor American, a native American, a
dead American. The subordination of the noun to the adjectives makes
a mockery of both the American premise and the democratic spirit, but
it serves the purposes of the politicians as well as the news media, and
throughout the rest of this election year I expect the political campaigns
to pitch their tents and slogans on the frontiers of race and class. For
every benign us, the candidates will find a malignant them; for every neigh-
boring we (no matter how eccentric or small in number), a distant and
devouring they. The strategies of division sell newspapers and summon
votes, and to the man who would be king (or president or governor) the

popular hatred of government matters less than the atmosphere of resentment in which the people fear and distrust one another.

Democratic politics trades in only two markets—the market in expectation and the market in blame. A collapse in the former engenders a boom in the latter. Something goes wrong in the news—a bank swindle of genuinely spectacular size, a series of killings in Milwaukee, another disastrous assessment of the nation's schools—and suddenly the air is loud with questions about the paradox of the American character or the Puritan subtexts of the American soul. The questions arise from every quarter of the political compass—from English professors and political consultants as well as from actors, corporate vice presidents and advertising salesmen—and the conversation is seldom polite. Too many of the people present no longer can pay the bills, and a stray remark about acid rain or a third-grade textbook can escalate within a matter of minutes into an exchange of insults. Somebody calls Jesse Helms a fascist, and somebody else says that he is sick and tired of paying ransom money to a lot of welfare criminals. People drink too much and stay too late, their voices choked with anecdote and rage, their lexicons of historical reference so passionately confused that both Jefferson and Lincoln find themselves doing thirty-second commercials for racial quotas, a capital gains tax and the Persian Gulf War.

The failures in the nation's economy have marked up the prices for obvious villains, and if I had a talent for merchandising I would go into the business of making dolls (black dolls, white dolls, red-necked dolls, feminist dolls, congressional dolls) that each of the candidates could distribute at fund-raising events with a supply of color-coordinated pins. Trying out their invective in the pre-season campaigns, the politicians as early as last October were attributing the cause of all our sorrows to any faction, interest or minority that could excite in its audiences the passions of a beloved prejudice. David Duke in Louisiana denounced the subsidized beggars (that is, black people) who had robbed the state of its birthright. At a partisan theatrical staged by the Democratic party in New Hampshire, Senator Tom Harkin reviled the conspiracy of Republican money. President Bush went to Houston, Texas to point a trembling and petulant finger at the United States Congress. If the country's domestic affairs had been left to him, the president said, everybody would be as prosperous and smug as Senator Phil Gramm, but the liberals in Congress (blind as mollusks and selfish as eels) had wrecked the voyage of boundless opportunity.

The politicians follow the trends, and apparently they have been told by their handlers to practice the arts of the demagogue. Certainly I cannot remember an election year in which the political discourse—among newspaper editorialists and the single-issue lobbies as well as the candidates—relied so unashamedly on pitting rich against poor, black against white, male against female, city against suburb, young against old. Every public event in New York City—whether academic appointment, traffic delay or homicide—lends itself to both a black and a white interpretation of the news. The arguments in the arenas of cultural opinion echo the same bitter refrain. The ceaseless quarrels about the canon of preferred texts (about Columbus the Bad and Columbus the Good, about the chosen company of the politically correct, about the ice people and the sun people) pick at the scab of the same questions. Who and what is an American? How and where do we find an identity that is something other than a fright mask? When using the collective national pronoun ("we the people," "we happy few,") whom do we invite into the club of the we?

Maybe the confusion is a corollary to the end of the Cold War. The image of the Soviet Union as monolithic evil held in place the image of the United States as monolithic virtue. Break the circuit of energy transferred between negative and positive poles, and the two empires dissolve into the waving of sectional or nationalist flags. Lacking the reassurance of a foreign demon, we search our own neighborhoods for fiends of convincing malevolence and size.

The search is a boon for the bearers of false witness and the builders of prisons. Because it's so easy to dwell on our differences, even a child of nine can write a Sunday newspaper sermon about the centrifugal forces that drive the society apart. The more difficult and urgent questions have to do with the centripetal forces that bind us together. What traits of character or temperament do we hold in common? Why is it that I can meet a black man in a street or a Hispanic woman on a train and imagine that he and I, or she and I, share an allied hope and a joint purpose? That last question is as American as it is rhetorical, and a Belgian would think it the work of a dreaming imbecile.

What we share is a unified field of emotion, but if we mistake the sources of our energy and courage (that is, if we think that our uniqueness as Americans rests with the adjectives instead of the noun) then we can be rounded up in categories and sold the slogan of the week for the fear of the month. Political campaigns deal in the commodity of votes, and from now until November I expect that all of them will divide the American promise into its lesser but more marketable properties. For reasons of their own convenience, the sponsors of political campaigns (Democratic, environmental, racial, Republican, sexual or military-industrial) promote more or less the same false constructions of the American purpose and identity. As follows:

That the American achieves visible and specific meaning only by reason of his or her association with the political guilds of race, gender, age, ancestry or social class.

The assumption is as elitist as the view that only a woman endowed with an income of $1 million a year can truly appreciate the beauty of money and the music of Cole Porter. Comparable theories of grace encourage the belief that only black people can know or teach black history, that no white man can play jazz piano, that blonds have a better time and that Jews can't play basketball.

America was founded on precisely the opposite premise. We were always about becoming, not being; about the prospects for the future, not about the inheritance of the past. The man who rests his case on his color, like the woman who defines herself as a bright cloud of sensibility beyond the understanding of merely mortal men, makes a claim to special privilege not unlike the divine right of kings. The pretensions might buttress the cathedrals of our self-esteem, but they run counter to the lessons of our history.

We are a nation of parvenus, all bound to the hopes of tomorrow, or next week, or next year. John Quincy Adams put it plainly in a letter to a German correspondent in the 1820s who had written on behalf of several prospective émigrés to ask about the requirements for their success in the New World. "They must cast off the European skin, never to resume it," Adams said. "They must look forward to their posterity rather than backward to their ancestors."

We were always a mixed and piebald company, even on the seventeenth-century colonial seaboard, and we accepted our racial or cultural differences as the odds that we were obliged to overcome or correct. When John Charles Frémont (a.k.a. the Pathfinder) first descended into California from the East in 1843, he remarked on the polyglot character of the expedition accompanying him south into the San Joaquin Valley:

Our cavalcade made a strange and grotesque appearance, and it was impossible to avoid reflecting upon our position and composition in this remote solitude . . . still forced on south by a desert on one hand and a mountain range on the other; guided by a civilized Indian, attended by two wild ones from the Sierra; a Chinook from the Columbia; and our own mixture of American, French, German—all armed; four or five languages heard at once; above a hundred horses and mules, half-wild; American, Spanish and Indian dresses and equipments intermingled—such was our composition.

The theme of metamorphosis recurs throughout the whole chronicle of American biography. Men and women start out in one place and end up in another, never quite knowing how they got there, perpetually expecting the unexpected, drifting across the ocean or the plains until they lodge against a marriage, a land deal, a public office or a jail. Speaking to the improvised character of the American experience, Daniel Boorstin, the historian and former Librarian of Congress, also summed up the case against the arithmetic of the political pollsters' zip codes: "No prudent man dared to be too certain of exactly who he was or what he was about; everyone had to be prepared to become someone else. To be ready for such perilous transmigrations was to become an American."

That the American people aspire to become more nearly alike.

The hope is that of the ad salesman and the prison warden, but it has become depressingly familiar among the managers of political campaigns. Apparently they think that no matter how different the native songs and dances in different parts of the country, all the tribes and factions want the same beads, the same trinkets, the same prizes. As I listen to operatives from Washington talk about their prospects in the Iowa or New Hampshire primary, I understand that they have in mind the figure of a perfect or ideal American whom everybody in the country would wish to resemble if only everybody could afford to dress like the dummies in the windows of Bloomingdale's or Saks Fifth Avenue. The public opinion polls frame questions in the alphabet of name recognitions and standard brands. The simplicity of the results supports the belief that the American citizen or the American family can be construed as a product, and that with only a little more time and a little more money for research and development all of us will conform to the preferred images seen in a commercial for Miller beer.

The apologists for the theory of the uniform American success sometimes present the example of Abraham Lincoln, and as I listen to their sentimental after-dinner speeches about the poor country grown to greatness, I often wonder what they would say if they had met the man instead of the statue. Throughout most of his life Lincoln displayed the character of a man destined for failure—a man who drank too much and told too many jokes (most of them in bad taste), who was habitually late for meetings and always borrowing money, who never seized a business opportunity and missed his own wedding.

The spirit of liberty is never far from anarchy, and the ur-American is apt to look a good deal more like one of the contestants on *Let's Make a Deal* (that is, somebody dressed like Madonna, or Wyatt Earp, or a giant iguana) than any of the yachtsmen standing around on the dock at Kennebunkport. If America is about nothing else, it is about the invention of the self. Because we have little use for history, and because we refuse the comforts of a society established on the blueprint of class privilege, we find ourselves set adrift at birth in an existential void, inheriting nothing except the obligation to construct a plausible self, to build a raft of identity on which (with a few grains of luck and a cheap bank loan) maybe we can float south to Memphis or the imaginary islands of the blessed. We set ourselves the tasks of making and remaking our destinies with whatever lumber we happen to find lying around on the banks of the Snake or Pecos River.

Who else is the American hero if not a wandering pilgrim who goes forth on a perpetual quest? Melville sent Ahab across the world's oceans in search of a fabulous beast and Thoreau followed the unicorn of his conscience into the silence of the Maine woods. Between them they marked out the trail of American literature as well as the lines of speculation in American real estate. To a greater or a lesser extent, we are all confidence men, actors playing the characters of our own invention and hoping that the audience—fortunately consisting of impostors as fanciful or synthetic as ourselves—will accept the performance at par value and suspend the judgements of ridicule.

The settled peoples of the earth seldom recognize the American as both a chronic revolutionary and a born pilgrim. The American is always on the way to someplace else (toward some undetermined future in which all will be well), and when he meets a stranger on the road he begins at once to recite the summary of the story so far—his youth and early sorrows, the sequence of his exits and entrances, his last divorce and his next marriage, the point of his financial departure and the estimated time of his spiritual arrival, the bad news noted and accounted for, the good news still to come. Invariably it is a pilgrim's tale, and the narrator, being American, assumes that he is addressing a fellow pilgrim. He means to exchange notes and compare maps. His newfound companion might be bound toward a completely different dream of Eden (a boat marina in Naples, Florida instead of a garden in Vermont; a career as a Broadway dancer as opposed to the vice presidency of the Wells Fargo bank), but the destination doesn't matter as much as the common hope of coming safely home to the land of the heart's desire. For the time being, and until something better turns up, we find ourselves embarked on the same voyage, gazing west into the same blue distance.

That the American people share a common code of moral behavior and subscribe to identical theories of the true, the good and the beautiful.

Senator Jesse Helms would like to think so, and so would the enforcers of ideological discipline on the vocabulary of the doctrinaire left. The country swarms with people making rules about what we can say or read or study or smoke, and they imagine that we should be grateful for the moral guidelines (market-tested and government-inspected) imposed (for our own good) by a centralized bureau of temporal health and spiritual safety. The would-be reformers of the national character confuse the American sense of equality with the rule of conformity that governs a police state. It isn't that we believe that every American is as perceptive or as accomplished as any other, but we insist on the preservation of a decent and mutual respect across the lines of age, race, gender and social class. No citizen is allowed to use another citizen as if he or she were a means to an end; no master can treat his servant as if he or she were only a servant; no government can deal with the governed as if they were nothing more than a mob of votes. The American loathing for the arrogant or self-important man follows from the belief that all present have bet their fortunes (some of them bigger than others and some of them counterfeit or stolen) on the same hypothesis.

The American premise is an existential one, and our moral code is political, its object being to allow for the widest horizons of sight and the broadest range of expression. We protect the other person's liberty in the interest of protecting our own, and our virtues conform to the terms and conditions of an arduous and speculative journey. If we look into even so coarse a mirror as the one held up to us by the situation comedies on primetime television, we see that we value the companionable virtues—helpfulness, forgiveness, kindliness and, above all, tolerance.

The passenger standing next to me at the rail might be balancing a parrot on his head, but that doesn't mean that he has invented a theory of the self any less implausible than the one I ordered from a department-store catalogue or assembled with the tag lines of a two-year college course on the great books of Western civilization. If the traveler at the port rail can balance a parrot on his head, then I can continue my discussion with Madame Bovary and Mr Pickwick, and the two gentlemen standing aft of the rum barrels can get on with the business of rigging the price of rifles or barbed wire. The American equation rests on the habit of holding our fellow citizens in thoughtful regard not because they are exceptional (or famous, or beautiful, or rich) but simply because they are our fellow citizens. If we abandon the sense of mutual respect, we abandon the premise as well as the machinery of the American enterprise.

That the triumph of America corresponds to its prowess as a nation-state.

The pretension serves the purposes of the people who talk about "the national security" and "the vital interest of the American people" when what they mean is the power and privilege of government. The oligarchy resident in Washington assumes that all Americans own the same property instead of taking part in the same idea, that we share a joint geopolitical program instead of a common temperament and habit of mind. Even so faithful a servant of the monied interests as Daniel Webster understood the distinction: "The public happiness is to be the aggregate of individuals. Our system begins with the individual man."

The Constitution was made for the uses of the individual (an implement on the order of a plow, an ax or a surveyor's plumb line), and the institutions of American government were meant to support the liberties of the people, not the ambitions of the state. Given any ambiguity about the order of priority or precedence, it was the law that had to give way to the citizen's freedom of thought and action, not the citizen's freedom of thought and action that had to give way to the law. The Bill of Rights stresses the distinction in the two final amendments, the ninth ("The enumeration in the Constitution, of certain rights, shall not be construed to deny or disparage others retained by the people") and the tenth ("The powers not delegated to the United States by the Constitution, nor prohibited by it to the States, are reserved to the States, respectively, or to the people").

What joins the Americans one to another is not a common nationality, language, race or ancestry (all of which testify to the burdens of the past) but rather their complicity in a shared work of the imagination. My love of country follows from my love of its freedoms, not from my pride in its fleets or its armies or its gross national product. Construed as a means and not an end, the Constitution stands as the premise for a narrative rather than a plan for an invasion or a monument. The narrative was always plural. Not one story but many stories.

That it is easy to be an American.

I can understand why the politicians like to pretend that America is mostly about going shopping, but I never know why anybody believes the ad copy. Grant the existential terms and conditions of the American enterprise (that we are all bound to invent ourselves), and the position is both solitary and probably lost. I know a good many people who would rather be British or Nigerian or Swiss.

Lately I've been reading the accounts of the nineteenth-century adventurers and pioneers who traveled west from Missouri under circumstances almost always adverse. Most of them didn't find whatever it was they expected to find behind the next range of mountains or around the next bend in the river. They were looking for a garden in a country that was mostly desert, and the record of their passage is largely one of sorrow and failure. Travelers making their way across the Great Plains in the 1850s reported great numbers of dead horses and abandoned wagons on the trail, the echo of the hopes that so recently preceded them lingering in an empty chair or in the scent of flowers on a new grave.

Reading the diaries and letters, especially those of the women in the caravans, I think of the would-be settlers lost in an immense wilderness, looking into the mirrors of their loneliness and measuring their capacity for self-knowledge against the vastness of the wide and indifferent sky.

Too often we forget the proofs of our courage. If we wish to live in the state of freedom that allows us to make and think and build, then we must accustom ourselves to the shadows on the walls and the wind in trees. The climate of anxiety is the cost of doing business. Just as a monarchy places far fewer burdens on its subjects than a democracy places on its citizens, so also bigotry is easier than tolerance. When something goes wrong with the currency or the schools, it's always comforting to know that the faults can be easily found in something as obvious as a color, or a number, or the sound of a strange language. The multiple adjectives qualifying the American noun enrich the vocabulary of blame, and if the election year continues as it has begun I expect that by next summer we will discover that it is not only middle-aged Protestant males who have been making a wreck of the culture but also (operating secretly and sometimes in disguise) adolescent, sallow, Buddhist females.

Among all the American political virtues, candor is probably the one most necessary to the success of our mutual enterprise. Unless we try to tell each other the truth about what we know and think and see (that is, the story so far as it appears to the travelers on the voyage out) we might as well amuse ourselves (for as long as somebody else allows us to do so) with fairy tales. The vitality of the American democracy always has rested on the capacity of its citizens to speak and think without cant. As long ago as 1838, addressing the topic of *The American Democrat*, James Fenimore Cooper argued that the word "American" was synonymous with the habit of telling the truth: "By candor we are not to understand trifling and uncalled for expositions of truth; but a sentiment that proves a conviction of the necessity of speaking truth, when speaking at all; a contempt for all designing evasions of our real opinions. In all the general concerns, the public has a right to be treated with candor. Without this manly and truly republican quality . . . the institutions are converted into a stupendous fraud."

If we indulge ourselves with evasions and the pleasure of telling lies, we speak to our fears and our weaknesses instead of to our courage and our strength. We can speak plainly about our differences only if we know and value what we hold in common. Like the weather and third-rate journalism, bigotry in all its declensions is likely to be with us for a long time (certainly as long as the next hundred years), but unless we can draw distinctions and make jokes about our racial or cultural baggage, the work of our shared imagination must vanish in the mist of lies. The lies might win elections (or sell newspapers and economic theories) but they bind us to the theaters of wish and dream. If I must like or admire a fellow citizen for his or her costume of modifying adjectives (because he or she is black or gay or rich), then I might as well believe that the lost continent of Atlantis will rise next summer from the sea and that the Japanese will continue to make the payments—now and forever, world without end—on all our mortgages and battleships.

Among all the nations of the earth, America is the one that has come most triumphantly to terms with the mixtures of blood and caste, and maybe it is another of history's ironic jokes that we should wish to repudiate our talent for assimilation at precisely the moment in time when so many other nations in the world (in Africa and Western Europe as well as the Soviet Union) look to the promise of the American example. The jumble of confused or mistaken identities that was the story of nineteenth-century America has become the story of a late-twentieth-century world defined by a vast migration of peoples across seven continents and as many oceans. Why, then, do we lose confidence in ourselves and grow fearful of our mongrel freedoms?

The politician who would lift us to a more courageous understanding of ourselves might begin by saying that we are all, each and every one of us, as much at fault as anybody else, that no matter whom we blame for our troubles (whether George Bush, or Saddam Hussein, or Sitting Bull) or how pleasant the invective (racist, sexist, imperialist pig), we still have to rebuild our cities and revise our laws. We can do the work together, or we can stand around making strong statements about each other's clothes.

January 1992

Notebooks

MULTIPLE CHOICE

In large states public education will always be
mediocre, for the same reason that in large kitchens
the cooking is usually bad.
—NIETZSCHE

*T*he bulletins from the nation's educational frontiers continue to read like the casualty reports from a lost war. At least twice a month, and sometimes as often as once a week, yet another eminent committee publishes yet another melancholy communiqué about the defeat of the American schools. The witnesses tell mournful stories and cite gloomy statistics—about the poll showing that one-quarter of the adults interviewed were ignorant of the news that the earth revolves around the sun, about the majority of high-school seniors (93 percent) unprepared for college science courses, about the 70 million functional illiterates unable to read the Constitution or a complicated menu, about the high-school girl who thought the Holocaust was a Jewish holiday.

All the authorities agree that conditions keep going from bad to worse, and they worry, in solemn and poorly made prose, about the school system's failure to deliver "high-quality product to the infrastructure," about the inability of the next generation to operate the nation's political and economic machinery. Without notable exception they say that unless the kids settle down to their lessons, the United States could lose it all— the ball game and the farm, the Nobel Prizes as well as the cruise missiles, the stock options, the Pizza Huts and the condos in North Miami Beach.

I have been listening to this familiar dirge for more years than I care to remember—certainly since the National Commission on Excellence in Education noticed, in 1983, the "rising tide of mediocrity" inundating the country's classrooms—and I have labored through the heavy documents about declining verbal aptitudes and moral standards, about ESL, ETS and SAT, about programs for the gifted, the poor, the foolish, the outnumbered and the inept. But, try as I might, I cannot discover in myself the proper attitude of pious alarm. I listen to the chorus of lamentation, and I think of Buddhist priests beating ornamental gongs, of feathered shamans waving moleskin rattles at the evil spirits whom they mean to chase back into the forest, of Stanford professors in the studio audience of the Oprah Winfrey show holding up great books (as if they were silver crosses) in the face of the great vampire, television.

My lightheartedness follows from my conviction that the American school system over the last twenty-five years—far from having failed—has proved itself a roaring success. The award of a passing or failing grade depends on how one answers the prior questions about the nature and purpose of an American education. What is it reasonable to expect of the schools? Why do people go to school for sixteen years? To learn what?

For my part, I assume that American students do not go to school to acquire wisdom, to understand the literatures of antiquity and the loom of history or to acquaint themselves with what the ancient Greeks admired as "the glittering play of wind-swift thought." They go to school to improve their lot, to study the arts of getting ahead in the world, to acquire the keys to the commercial kingdom stocked with the material blessings that constitute our society's highest and most heavenly rewards.

These objectives conform to the popular theory of democracy. As Americans, we make the heroic attempt to educate all our citizens, to provide as many people as possible with as many opportunities as possible, to do for our children what we couldn't do for ourselves. The sentiment is as generous as it is romantic. Appreciated in its moral and social character, the American school system deserves to be ranked as the eighth wonder of the world. As long ago as 1937, Albert Jay Nock, an otherwise skeptical critic of the American pretension to the higher learning, was moved to a feeling of awe. He described the country's schools as "an expression . . . an organization—of a truly noble, selfless and affectionate desire."

That desire entails—unhappily and by definition—a corollary lowering of standards. Because the schools serve a political idea (as opposed to an intellectual idea), they cannot afford to make invidious comparisons between the smart kids and the dumb kids, between the kids who read

Shakespeare's plays and those who read the adventures of Spiderman. Under the rules of democratic procedure, the schools must teach everything to everybody (morals, hygiene, Plato's dialogues, the forward pass, macramé, the curveball, Marxism, cheerleading, table manners and calculus); even more wonderful, they must insist on the official fiction not only that everybody deserves to be educated but also, *mirabile dictu*, that everybody can he taught the same syllabus.

Translated into the measures of knowledge or talent or intellect, the proposition is plainly false—comparable to imagining that everybody can learn to write as well as Jefferson or compose equations as brilliant as those of Einstein. But, translated into the measures of worldly success, the proposition is demonstrably true.

Certainly it is not necessary to be well educated to make a success of an American life. It might be necessary to attend college for four years in order to meet the right people and acquire the right credentials, but little of what is useful will be found in books. Children learn by example as well as by precept, and they have only to look at Times Square and Disneyland—or consider the triumphs of individuals as culturally bereft as President George Bush, Madonna, Bob Hope and Donald Trump—to know that as a nation we care as little about the arts and humanities as we care about the color of the rain in Tashkent. The society bestows its rewards on the talent for figuring a market, not on the proofs of learning or the subtlety of mind.

The tide of mediocrity flows into the classrooms from the ocean that is the society at large. I'm sure it's true that relatively few high-school students can speak a foreign language or point to Czechoslovakia on a map; it's also true that President Reagan was hard-pressed to remember the provenience of the Civil War and that few American ambassadors can speak the language of the country to which they bought passage with money paid to a political campaign. I'm sure it's true that a great many college students don't know how to diagram a sentence or write a decent paragraph; the same can be said of most American tax lawyers and television anchor-men. The society doesn't expect its movie stars or its statesmen or its business magnates to have read Dante or Pascal or George Eliot. Nor does anybody imagine that the secretary of state will know much more of history than the list of dates printed in a sixth-grade chronology. If it becomes necessary to display the finery of learning, the corporation can hire a speechwriter or send its chairman to the intellectual haberdashers at the Aspen Institute. Education is a commodity, like avocado soup or alligator shoes, and freedom of mind is a privilege available only to those who can afford it.

I remember being introduced to the presiding attitude at Yale University in the 1950s when A. Whitney Griswold, then president of the university, welcomed the members of the freshman class to Woolsey Hall and reminded us in his opening remarks of the many feats of learning performed on our behalf by the venerable sages whose busts could be seen standing on pedestals along the walls. Western civilization apparently had been acquired at some cost, and the class of 1956 had an obligation to maintain it in a state of decent repair.

As an intellectual proposition, Yale proved to be a matter of filling out forms. Over a term of four years the celebrities of the human spirit (Cicero, Montaigne, Goethe, et al.) put in guest appearances on the academic talk show, and the audience was expected to welcome them with rounds of appreciative applause. Like producers holding up cue cards, the faculty identified those truths deserving of the adjective "great." The students who received the best marks were those who could think of the most flattering explanations for the greatness of the great figures and the great truths.

Before the winter of freshman year the students understood that the politics of a Yale education would have little to do with the university's statements of ennobling purpose. A Yale education was a means of acquiring a cash value. Whatever the faculty said or didn't say, what was important was the diploma, the ticket of admission to Wall Street, the professions and the safe harbors of the big money. As an undergraduate I thought this discovery profound; it had a cynical glint to it, in keeping with the plays of Bertolt Brecht then in vogue with the apprentice intelligentsia that frequented the United Restaurant on Chapel Street.

By the time I returned to Yale, briefly in the autumn of 1978 to teach a seminar in journalism, I understood that what I had thought was cynicism was nothing more than common sense. Schools serve the social order and, quite properly, promote the habits of mind necessary to the preservation of that order. The education offered at Yale (as at Harvard, Princeton and the University of Michigan) bears comparison to the commercial procedure for stunting caterpillars just prior to the moment of their transformation into adult moths. Silkworms can be turned to a profit, but moths blow around in the wind and do nothing to add to the wealth of the corporation or the power of the state.

From what I can tell by reading the historical record, the practical American mind has always looked upon the affairs of the intellect with a good deal of suspicion, in much the same way that a banker looks upon a fast-talking oil-well operator trying to borrow money for a deal in

Calgary. John Adams associated the arts with despotism and superstition and hoped that they wouldn't be encouraged in the new republic. Benjamin Franklin took a similar line. "To America," he said, setting the grain of American thought for the next 200 years, "one schoolmaster is worth a dozen poets, and the invention of a machine or the improvement of an implement is more important than a masterpiece of Raphael."

If it knows what's good for its career, intellect in America always takes the trouble to justify itself, like the Calvinist faithful, by its good works. The power of the imagination is all well and good if held severely in check, if in its commercial aspect it leads to some visible sign of improvement (preferably scientific or technical), if in its political aspect it serves the uplifting spirit of reform (usually rendered as a bureaucratic acronym), and if in its artistic aspect it remains purely decorative (something that can be framed in gold leaf or played on a banjo). I can wish that this wasn't so, and I can also wish that the $300,000 spent on a thirty-second television commercial (for face cream, say, or designer jeans) might be spent on books and school libraries. But wishing won't make it so, and until the society chooses to rearrange its order of priorities, I suspect that much of the money voted for education can be counted as a dole distributed to the downwardly mobile members of the clerical class.

The children, meanwhile, will learn as they always have learned in the United States—against long odds and despite the heavy atmosphere of sanctimonious indifference. The experience makes their achievement that much more valiant.

January 1989

THE OLD SCHOOL

Tradition means giving votes to the most
obscure of all classes—our ancestors. It is the
democracy of the dead. Tradition refuses to submit
to the small and arrogant oligarchy of those who
merely happen to be walking around.
—CHESTERTON

*L*ast month I suggested that it was unfair to blame the nation's schools for the failures of American education. Schools serve the wishes and expectations of the society to which they belong, and if society cares more about the labels in its shoes than it does about the words in its head, then our schools will train legions of rich but illiterate bond salesmen. They will continue to do so no matter how much money anybody donates to the new library or how many speeches the chorus of worthy elders addresses to the newspapers and the worried alumni. The point seemed to me obvious, but a surprising number of readers took surprisingly vehement offense. They wrote to say that I was cynical or feckless or impious or un-American—and demanded that I submit a program of uplifting reform. Easy enough, they said, to carp and criticize, but what, as a public-spirited citizen, did I propose to do?

I've never been very adept in the arts of practical advice, and I'm not even sure that the reform of the nation's schools can be safely construed as a good thing. What would be the political consequences in a society that so comfortably settles for the lowest plausible denominators? The triumph of the American dream presupposes the eager and uncritical consumption of junk in all its commercial declensions. Income doesn't express individual merit or value added to the society; if it did, the ranks of the unpaid would be terrible to behold. Think of the domino effect shuffling through the whole line of second-rate American goods and services—clothes that don't fit and household appliances that don't work, company presidents receiving salaries of $500,000 a year for achieving the miracle of bankruptcy, doctors who charge princely fees for misdiagnoses and bungled operations, university professors promoted for publishing unintelligible prose and a Congress that routinely makes laws as notable for their shoddy workmanship as a Florida condominium or an evening of primetime television.

But let us suppose—at least for the moment and the sake of argument—that the American people chose to rearrange their system of value and order of priority. Assume that they brought their interest in thought in balance with their passion for money. Given such favorable circumstances, I expect the correction of the schools could be carried forward with a minimum of trouble and expense. If I were assigned the task of revision (which in a well-ordered universe I wouldn't be), I would begin by citing the authority of Thomas Jefferson and Albert Jay Nock, both of whom argued that the business of education entails a ruthless winnowing of the available chaff. When Jefferson revised the Virginia Statutes in 1797, he drew up a comprehensive plan for public education that Nock, writing in 1937, summarized, approvingly, as follows:

Each ward should have a primary school for the three R's, open to all. Each year the best pupil in each school should be sent to the grade school, of which there were to be twenty, conveniently situated in various parts of the state. They should be kept there one year or two years, according to results shown, and then all dismissed but one, who should be continued six years. "By this means," said the good old man, "twenty of the best geniuses will be raked from the rubbish annually"—a most unfortunate expression for a Democrat to use! At the end of six years, the best ten of the twenty were to be sent to college, and the rest turned adrift.

Jefferson articulated a principle that today would be reviled as "elitist." Were he alive and well and living at Monticello, I can imagine him being dragged in judgement to the tribunal on *Nightline*. In the order of American insults the epithets "elite," "elitist" and "elitism" stand well above the lesser and preliminary invectives expressed in the terms "fascist," "racist" and "sexist pig." To denounce a fellow citizen as an elitist is to give the cut direct, to declare the final excommunication from the community of the ideologically pure in spirit. But without a frank acknowledgment of the differences between people, I don't see how the schools can be rescued from their difficulties.

Although extremely satisfying to the soul, the doctrines of egalitarianism make a mockery of the facts. Who could imagine a football coach recruiting his team to conform with a theory of social policy, or a baseball manager troubling himself with the niceties of affirmative action? College deans and high-school principals don't enjoy the same freedom of choice, and their obligatory disavowal of what they know to be true condemns the schools to amiable mediocrity.

Adapted to a modern circumstance, I can imagine Jefferson's purpose translated into a hierarchy of superior state schools (few in number and necessarily small in size) that would train (beyond the eighth grade) only those students who passed rigorous examinations in two or three languages. None of these schools would provide dormitories, athletic fields or psychiatric counseling. The curricula would be directed toward two fairly modest tasks: the teaching of languages, history and mathematics; and the instilling of intellectual confidence.

If the schools fail at either of these objectives, then all the rest—whether source readings from the syllabus of Western civilization or lectures on contemporary affairs from *ci-devant* secretaries of state—amounts to little more than a series of exhibitions preserved, like bank notes or trust funds, in the vaults of an intellectual museum.

The study of languages and mathematics provides the student with tools to work at the trade of learning. If he studies Latin, he will read Horace or Cicero or Juvenal; if French, Montaigne or Voltaire or Flaubert. It doesn't matter whether the student comes to appreciate the much-advertised "greatness" of these authors, or whether he can place them accurately within the chronologies of literary criticism. He reads the classical texts because they induce the habit of thought. If the student hopes to put the keenest possible edge to his mind in the available time, then a single chapter of Gibbon serves his purpose more effectively than the collected works of Henry Kissinger. A thorough knowledge of a few writers instills in the student the confidence that he cannot derive from selected passages printed, usually in bad translation, in an anthology chosen by a committee of pedants. If by the age of seventeen the student acquires fluency in three or four languages, this further bolsters his pride of intellect. He learns to distinguish between the hard coin of his own accomplishment and the inflated currency of fashionable opinion.

So also with the study of mathematics. The world rests on an architecture of numbers, and yet most of the students graduated from the nation's leading universities think of mathematics as a magical sequence of runes known only to the druids at IBM, NASA and the IRS. The mere thought of an algebraic fraction moves them to a feeling of holy dread. A thorough knowledge of high-school geometry would make them less anxious in a world that makes such common use of computer printouts and Einstein's equations.

As for courses in economics, music appreciation, sociology and political science, most of them contribute little or nothing to an understanding of their nominal subjects. Their deletion from the curricula would compare with the deletion of adjectives from a sophomore's impression of the moon rising over Sorrento. A summer spent working in a brokerage house or a brothel presents a clearer understanding of economics than does a textual analysis of all the memoranda published by the Harvard Business School; a casual but habitual reading of the Paris newspapers offers more insight into the nature of French politics than a seminar conducted by a government functionary under the rubric "Mitterrand, d'Estaing and the Invisible Left."

Together with its system of superior schools, the state also could provide a parallel (but less exacting) course of education (grammar and secondary schools as well as colleges) in which all students—no matter what their intellectual or financial capacities—could learn the rudiments of writing, reading, history and arithmetic. The instruction would be as systematic as the teaching of automobile mechanics. Literacy should be presented not as a suite of arcane or exotic studies but as a set of common tools that people learn to use in the way they use forks or compasses or chisels. The students would learn by doing—by ceaseless reading (primarily works of literature as opposed to textbooks), by ceaseless writing (letters, explanations, advertisements, narratives, campaign speeches), by the working of ceaseless calculation (of restaurant and department-store bills as well as interest rates and trade balances) and by the ceaseless study of historical chronologies. Because the schools would teach so few subjects, they could provide their students with the time and space in which to practice (during school hours) the habit of reading and writing.

Jefferson assumed that roughly 90 percent of the population was ineducable, but he didn't mean to imply that the majority of his fellow citizens were not otherwise fine people—decent, intelligent and possibly favored by fortune. He simply meant that most people were not suited to the atmospheres of the higher learning. Nor did Jefferson wish to prevent anybody from gaining experience of life (or escaping their parents or acquiring a trade or discovering the wonders of Los Angeles). Certainly everybody has a right to go somewhere, but not necessarily to academia.

If the Ivy League colleges and universities could be understood as clubs, the state universities as athletic camps and the professional schools (law, medicine, journalism, and so on) as medieval guilds, then everybody might feel less embarrassed by the need to feign an interest in Plato. Colleges like Harvard, Princeton and Yale could continue as they do now, but relieved of the burden to offer anything other than a pleasant four years under some very old trees in the company of some very fine buildings. The colleges wouldn't award marks or confer degrees. The students who wished to do so could read whatever books captured their fancies. They might also attend lecture courses and write as many papers as their tutors asked them to write. Otherwise they would remain free to learn how to tie their ties, where to go in the summer, which law schools lead to the most profitable careers. Corporations such as IBM, Honda or Citibank might accept apprentices as early as the age of thirteen.

Too often it is thought that an education can be acquired in the way that one acquires a suntan or an Armani suit, as if it were an object instead of a turn of mind. An education begins with two or three teachers and six or seven texts (maybe books, maybe equations or fossils or trees) that introduce the student to the uniqueness of his or her own mind. After that it's a matter of educating oneself. The best American minds, or at least the most generous and imaginative of American minds (I think of Lincoln and Melville and Edison), tended to be self-taught. Expressing a sentiment that Jefferson probably would have seconded, St Augustine observed that it is possible to learn only what one already knows.

April 1989

INSPECTORS GENERAL

> Our culture peculiarly honours the act of
> blaming, which it takes as the sign of virtue
> and intellect.
> —LIONEL TRILLING

W ere I to believe what I read in the newspapers, I would find it easy enough to imagine that the country has been seized by a convulsion of Puritan zeal. At least twice a week the papers bring word of a new committee established to impose a proper regimen of ethics on the moral sluggards who operate the nation's government and manage the nation's commerce. The bulletins often appear in conjunction with the news of a more stringent regulation governing the use of alcohol or tobacco, with the report of another television program forced off the air because of its sexual immodesty, with official statements and paid advertisements castigating junk bonds, the cocaine trade and poor muscle tone.

The announcements almost always bear the stamps of sanctimony and intolerance. The latter-day Puritans make no secret of their wish to blame and to punish and to cast what they trust will be the first of many stones.

As best as I can remember it, the current excitement about cleansing the nation of its impurities took hold of the public imagination at about the time that former Senator Gary Hart blundered through a silk curtain into the sin of lust. The media found him guilty of adultery, and Hart, marked with the equivalent of an A in the center of his chest, vanished into the Colorado wilderness. Within a matter of months the television and newspaper moralists discovered themselves to be as adept as Jonathan Edwards in the art of inspecting souls. Before another year was out, Senator Joseph Biden confessed to the sin of plagiarism, Judge Douglas Ginsburg admitted to the smoking of a marijuana cigarette and Jimmy the Greek apologized for making a tasteless comparison between the physical attributes of black and white athletes. All left by the nearest exit or the next train. The keepers of the national conscience seized their microphones and, like the man with the cane on the old vaudeville circuits, dragged them out of the light of respectable opinion.

Since then, of course, the compulsion to wash the sheets of the American conscience has become, if anything, more urgent. The stern and reproving winds of admonishment blow from all points of the moral compass. President George Bush apparently means to be judged and appreciated for his behavior, not his politics. During his first hundred days in office he has construed the duties of the president as a matter of winning prizes for conduct and deportment. It is as if he thinks that he need do nothing else except keep himself neat and tidy and clean, meet his schedule of appointments, play horseshoes, worry about the Russians and the environment, display sympathy for widows and orphans, show the media that he is a good and honest fellow and generally present himself in a manner befitting the exemplary American.

Bush's interpretation of the presidency as a sacramental office corresponds to the ceaseless manufacture of committees on ethics; to the proliferation of rules about the testing of the nation's blood, urine and speech; to the scourgings of former Senator John Tower and Representative Jim Wright. It was the scourging of Tower that first prompted me to wonder whether the excess of reforming zeal might not be better understood as rituals of purification, like the burning of sacrificial meats or the sprinkling of water and incense.

Surely Tower didn't deserve to be made to say his prayers on *This Week With David Brinkley* or to swear that he would never again drink distilled spirits if confirmed in his appointment as secretary of defense. Tower no doubt had committed his quota of indiscretions during his long and profitable service in government and perhaps he had been a little eager or a trifle hasty in his acceptance of $750,000 in consulting fees from his friends in the defense industries, but then, as he observed on more than one occasion, he had done nothing inconsistent with the common practice of his peers. In reply to the charges of drinking too much and taking too much money from lobbyists, he said: "I accept that the Secretary of Defense must adhere to a higher standard than members of the United States Senate, but my question is how much lower an acceptable standard is there for members of the Senate?"

The question was never answered. The media preferred to subject Tower to an inquisition that wouldn't have been out of place in fifteenth-century

Spain or present-day Iran. Self-appointed moralists as unlikely as Senator
Ted Kennedy dressed themselves up in the rhetorical equivalent of
a bishop's miter and examined the former senator for what the Puritan
magistrates in seventeenth-century Massachusetts would have defined
as witchmarks. Under different circumstances, and in a different time
and place, the spectacle might have been applauded as farce. But not
in America in the first hundred days of the Bush administration, not in
a country that spends almost as much money on soap and cosmetics as
it spends on weapons, the object of both expenditures being the defense
of the American body politic against the contamination of foreign
substances.

Still, despite the auto-da-fé imposed on Tower, despite the presiding
unctuousness of George Bush, I don't think that I could have anticipated
the moral indignation of Donald Trump. Trump is not a man known
for his religious assets, and although he likes to present himself as one of
the richest and most blessed real estate developers ever to walk the face
of an admiring earth, it is not yet certain that he has acquired waterfront
property in Heaven. He boasts of his long and faithful service to Mammon
and takes pride in the sharpness of his cunning and the sweetness of his
gall. Much of his income he derives from gambling casinos in Atlantic
City. And yet, on the morning of 1 May, Trump bought space in the New
York papers to ally himself with the voices of righteousness.

The full-page advertisement in the *New York Times* is worth quoting at
some length in order to indicate the violence of Trump's Puritan rebuke.
He takes as his text the rape and brutal beating of a young woman, white
and well-to-do, who had been jogging across the transverse road at 102nd
Street in Central Park when she was attacked by a band of black and
Hispanic teenage boys. Trump's advertisement divides into two equal parts,
the upper half of the page printed with nine words in 1½-inch capital
letters—BRING BACK THE DEATH PENALTY. BRING BACK
OUR POLICE!—and the lower half of the page crowded with a longish
statement, in smaller type, signed by Trump and beginning as follows:

> What has happened to our City over the past ten years? What has happened
> to law and order, to the neighborhood cop we all trusted to safeguard
> our homes and families, the cop who had the power under the law to
> help us in times of danger, keep us safe from those who would prey
> on innocent lives to fulfill some distorted inner need. What has happened
> to the respect for authority, the fear of retribution by the courts, society

and the police for those who break the law, who wantonly trespass on the rights of others? What has happened is the complete breakdown of life as we knew it.

Decrying the "dangerously permissive atmosphere" that has corroded the moral architecture of the city, Trump goes on to say that the time for mercy and compassion has long passed. "I want to hate these murderers and I always will," he says. "Mayor Koch has stated that hate and rancor should be removed from our hearts. I do not think so."

Possibly because Trump's language is so violent, the statement begs a number of unpleasant questions. Is not the story of Trump's much-advertised success the story of "some distorted inner need"? Why do so many of Trump's works and deeds testify to the rage of an insatiable appetite—for power and wealth and his name printed on any public surface (buildings, newsprint, airplanes, billboards, television screens) that he can seize from lesser mortals? Is it not true that Trump has prospered precisely because of the circumstances—the lack of "respect for authority," the wanton trespassing "on the rights of others"—that during the last ten years in New York have encouraged not only the killings in the streets but also the killings in the real estate market? Is it not also fair to say that the "twisted hatred" that Trump discovers in the city's criminals bears an unhappy resemblance to the "hate and rancor" that he asks the city's peaceful citizens to welcome into their own hearts? Trump apparently has as little use for the rule of law as Oliver North or General Manuel Noriega. In the name of virtue and the interest of municipal security, he invites his fellow townspeople to reduce themselves to a howling mob.

The vengeful squalor of Trump's moral code, like the scourging of former Senator Tower and the piety of Bush's presidency, suggests that the militant hyperbole of our latter-day purintanism is little more than a barbarous chant meant to preserve the illusions of innocence rather than to alter the mechanics of the status quo.

As a political candidate in 1988, President Bush promised to clean the waters of Boston Harbor and bestow on Washington the gift of honest government, but he based his campaign on the familiar tactics of smear and cheat and lie. Once arrived in Washington he continued to preach about conflicts of interest, but he neglected to press the point against those of his friends and companions (among them not only Tower but James Baker, the secretary of state; C. Boyden Gray, the White House counsel; and Brent Scowcroft, the national security adviser) who were asked rude questions about their finances.

The rituals of purification have been characteristic of American society since the first Puritans arrived at Plymouth and thought they had regained the states of innocence lost to Satan by generations of corrupt and inattentive Europeans. During the first three hundred years of the American settlement it was the sermon that served as the principal form of literary address among a people that enjoyed the favor of Providence. The times were always going from bad to worse, the congregation always in need of purifying words and hymns. Because most Americans (among them Trump and Bush) assume that they can do no wrong, they choose to believe that wickedness is a pollutant of one kind or another—something deadly or contagious that arrives, inexplicably, from the sea, the atmosphere or the slums. Because the innocent republic (or the innocent real estate deal) invariably finds itself betrayed, it always can justify the use of criminal or uncivilized means to defend itself against the world's treachery.

The rhetorical devices of a democracy trade in two markets—the market in expectation and the market in blame. The collapse of prices in one market entails a rise of prices in the other. To the extent that people expect nothing in the way of courage or idealism from the Bush administration, the public debate degenerates into accusations and the calling of names. Money—and the rumor of money—is what's left to talk about when nobody can think of anything else to say. To the extent that the newspapers become increasingly crowded with reports of theft and fraud—in the Pentagon or Drexel Burnham—so they also bring, often in adjoining columns, increasingly barbarous cries for spiritual reform. The more overwhelming the evidence of moral failure, the more vehement the denial that any such failure has occurred.

Given the prevailing mood of spiritual inquisition, the media ought to be clever enough to arrange even more frightful and instructive forms of penance. It's no good allowing the malefactors to drop unobtrusively from sight. Let them sit in Puritan stocks on national television. Let them be flogged during the halftime ceremonies in the Rose Bowl or made to wander disconsolately down Wall Street wearing a leper's bells. Let a correspondent from each of the network morning shows (somebody as affable as Willard Scott) make a daily tour of prisoners in the stocks, straightening their ties and reading aloud the list of their transgressions.

I expect that within another two or three years a board of examiners (appointed by CBS and Time Inc.) will require applicants to the public debate to fill out the moral equivalent of a financial disclosure statement. I can see a printed form, eight pages long and as incoherent as the instructions of the Internal Revenue Service. Under headings that encompass the entire repertoire of human behavior—sexual conduct, criminal offenses, racial bias, xenophobia, personal hygiene, and so on—the applicant will be asked to answer 2,000 questions about the status of his or her soul. It goes without saying that the forms would need to be filled out in triplicate, with copies submitted (together with urine and blood tests) not only to the media but to the relevant government authorities, university libraries and the offices of the Vatican.

In the meantime, of course, Trump can be counted upon to pay as little tax as possible to the city he purports to cherish, the Pentagon can be expected to pay overcharges of at least $2.1 billion a year and President Bush will go on wearing funny hats and serving afternoon tea.

July 1989

LEAD INTO GOLD

Man is a make-believe animal—he is never so
truly himself as when he is acting a part.
—WILLIAM HAZLITT

The *Wall Street Journal* last January took it upon itself to issue the equivalent of a writ of excommunication against a junk-bond salesman named Jeffrey "Mad Dog" Beck. The denunciation appeared on page one at the head of the right-hand column, under a promise of scandal:

SELF-MADE MAN

TOP DEAL MAKER LEAVES
A TRAIL OF DECEPTION
IN WALL STREET RISE

As I read the dispatch—extended to the unusual length of 5,000 words—I was hard put to discover what it was that poor Beck had done to antagonize the guardians of the nation's financial conscience, and I wondered why the *Journal* thought it necessary to print so sanctimonious a rebuke of so harmless a confidence man. The headlines could as easily have been affixed to the life and times of most of the financiers in New York still solvent enough to pay the check at The Four Seasons; with only a few changes of noun (substituting for *Wall Street* the word *Washington* or *Hollywood*), the same advertisement could serve as a pitch for a best-selling biography of almost any American politician or movie actress.

Why then the anathema called down on the head of the hapless Beck? By the *Journal*'s own account, Beck had committed no crime for which he could have been prosecuted in a court of law. True, he wore bow ties and told awful jokes, but he hadn't looted the customers' accounts or swindled his partners or cheated the government. What he had done was tell stories, puffing up the balloon of his own importance and improvising the narrative of a counterfeit life. (The same charge could be brought against George Bush or Joan Collins or Donald and Ivana Trump.) As works of the imagination, Beck's fictions proved to be as safe and as bland as the daydreams promoted on primetime television. He pretended that he had been born rich, that he had served with gallantry as an infantry officer in Vietnam and that every now and then (if Christendom trembled precariously enough in the balance of nations) he was called upon to perform a discreet service for the CIA.

In the context of the far more fanciful and opulent charades staged on Wall Street during most of the last decade, Beck's stories passed as hard currency among his fellow traders in the junk-bond markets. The oil and steel industries were being bought and sold with worthless paper and it was possible to believe anything. Who was going to take the trouble to doubt the provenance of Jeff Beck? He had a talent for meeting people and as a salesman (first for Oppenheimer and then for Drexel Burnham Lambert) he promoted a number of leveraged buy-out deals that turned into very big money. People thought him a fun guy to have around, a comedian who could be counted on to relieve the boredom between meetings. He once opened a window and said he was throwing himself twenty-five floors to the street unless somebody paid him his god-damned fee; on another occasion, seeking to impress a prospective client with his sangfroid, he ate an entire box of Milk Bones while discussing the fine points of financial strategy. If at the last minute he had to cancel a date with a woman, he telephoned to say that he was terribly sorry but his mother had just died.

For ten years he entertained the company at New York dinner parties with well-told tales. On a moment's whim or notice, he apparently would say whatever came into his head or whatever he thought the traffic would bear—Beck, the heir to a vast expanse of orange trees in Florida; Beck, the last male heir to the fortune amassed by the family that brewed Beck's beer; Beck, the captain of his college tennis team; above all and most importantly, Beck, the company commander in Vietnam, calling in napalm strikes on his own headquarters' tent, awarded the nickname "Mad Dog" by his devoted troops because he was always pressing heroic attacks against heavily defended artillery positions, on one occasion returning with only six of his fifty-three men after laying waste to a North Vietnamese regiment. If he mixed up his plot development (or if one of the women present remembered him telling a different story two weeks before in Miami), Beck affected the knowing smile of a man still at large on behalf of the CIA, the sort of man who sometimes had to tell more than one story in order to protect the secrets of state.

Beck's fortunes took a downward turn after he had a falling-out with Henry Kravis, one of the genuinely anterior figures in the leveraged buy-out business, with whom Beck had been associated on the margin of the RJR Nabisco deal. His jokes suddenly lost their antic charm, and his former friends, at least those few among them who hadn't vanished into the ratholes of bankruptcy and debt, no longer offered him a piece of the action.

If Beck had been more successful, if in fact he could have been ranked as one of the "top deal makers" on Wall Street, I doubt that the *Journal* would have chosen to punish him for his effrontery. But somebody had to be blamed for the wreckage in the financial markets after a decade in which so many of Wall Street's eminent financiers—almost all of them praised by the *Journal* as saviors of the republic—had distinguished themselves by virtue of their thievery, their swinishness and their greed. Like condemned veal left lying too long in the sun, Wall Street was beginning to attract a bad press. The collapse at Drexel Burnham threatened to annihilate what was left of the public confidence in the stock exchanges, and two books at the head of the best-seller list (*Liar's Poker* and *Barbarians at the Gate*) presented such unflattering portraits of the fine gentlemen operating some of the nation's better investment banks that unsuspecting readers might be led to abandon their faith in the miracle of free enterprise. Enter Beck, cast in the new and unaccustomed role of sacrificial ox. Beck, the embodiment of the sins of avarice and pride. Beck, the cautionary tale.

The judgement seemed to me so fraudulently pious that, as I read the text of the newspaper sermon, I found myself composing the lines of an argument in Beck's defense. What would happen to the much vaunted spirit of American enterprise if everybody was obliged to play it straight?

Was it not true that America was the land of the false promise and the tall tale? Of the new beginning and the second chance? Of anonymous wayfarers seeking to gerrymander the dignity of a name?

The native American vernacular, what Daniel Boorstin once called "the rhetoric of democracy," is the language of advertising. A democratic society concerns itself not so much with what is true as with what people believe to be true—with the image or the perception rather than the fact. How else could we sustain the markets in face cream and television prophecy and used Chevrolet trucks? To whom would we sell junk bonds and the national debt, the domino theory and the Laffer curve, the Evil Empire and Marlboro Country and Miller Time?

Like our commercial discourse, our political discourse relies on a vocabulary meant to persuade and seduce rather than to teach and inform. How else could we have elected Ronald Reagan or propped up our interest in the Strategic Defense Initiative? We live in a realm of jingles and slogans and popular songs, and we march off to war under the banners of a catchphrase or a nonsense rhyme, to make the world safe for democracy, because we remember the Alamo or the *Maine*. Our history, properly speaking, is not history but mythology; like our advertising and our politics, our remembrance of the American past takes place in the world of the will to believe. We cull the books and chronicles like the members of a traveling circus picking through the costume trunk. Invariably we choose the brightest colors and the gaudiest adjectives—the myth, the preferred memory, the old sales promotion.

Against the perceptions so solidly in place, it is all but useless to assert anything so subversive as a fact. Over the years, I have conducted a number of impromptu experiments with the density and mass of the Great American Truths, and I have found them impervious to the erosions of evidence or time. If I accost somebody with the news that George Washington (a.k.a. the father of our country) was probably sterile and that he also could be fairly described as a dandified, slaveholding real estate speculator, my newfound acquaintance stares at me as if I were as mad as the last Hungarian Communist. Similar expressions of alarm cloud the faces of people to whom I make similarly unauthorized observations—for example, that thirty-three of the forty-one American presidents have been rich men; that on the old American frontier it was customary to shoot one's opponents at long range, with a rifle, in the back; that Davy Crockett deserted his wife, strangled very few bears and didn't die at the Alamo; that throughout the eighteenth and most of the nineteenth centuries, the students at Harvard were ranked according to their social standing and religious piety, not in order of their scholarship or intelligence; that Americans never have been proficient in the arts of war, that General George Custer's incompetence proves the rule, not the exception, of the native talent for military command.

But among all the myths and folktales with which we comfort one another around the fires of our encampment in what is still a wilderness, none is more reassuring than the one about the happy hunting ground otherwise known as America. America is as much a work of the imagination as Jeff Beck's fictional orange grove. I don't know what else could have been expected in a country so little interested in history or geography. How else can so motley a crowd of hucksters agree on something so stately as a national identity unless they construe it as an ad campaign?

Prior to 1917, relatively few people in the country would have described themselves primarily as Americans. If they hadn't just arrived from somewhere else (thus inclining them to say they were German or Irish or Hungarian), they would have said that they were from Virginia or Texas or Ohio. Political authority was invested in the states, and the country understood itself as a constitutional assembly of regional interests, customs, habits of dress and rhythms of speech. The old order passed when the United States embarked on the adventure of the First World War. Obliged to explain why we were in France, we first had to know whom we included in the we. What did we mean by the words *America* and *Americans*?

The alarums and excursions in Washington coincided with the setting up of the movie business in Hollywood. In a very few years, the synthetic nationalism manufactured in Washington for reasons of state was sustained by the synthetic image of America made by the mythographers in California. The world out of time was superimposed on the world in time, and by the end of the Second World War it was considered un-American to discriminate between the fiction and the fact.

If Beck missed the brass ring of an American success, it was by the narrowest of margins, because he made a mistake with the publicity, not with the moneylenders or the police. As an American, he had been born with the obligation to construct a plausible self. Like the rest of us, he didn't have much of a choice in the matter.

April 1990

SERMONS AND SODA WATER

Fresh air and innocence are good if you
don't take too much of them—but I always
remember that most of the achievements and
pleasures of life are in bad air.
—OLIVER WENDELL HOLMES JR

Maybe not this year or next, but certainly before the end of the century and possibly before George Bush pitches his last game of presidential horseshoes, I expect to be interrogated by the Fitness Police. The surgeon general hasn't yet been granted the patents of supreme authority, and the federal government (at least to the best of my knowledge as of the end of last week) hasn't yet recruited the legion of spies and informers necessary for the strict enforcement of a punitive health code. But in stray and increasingly frequent moments of foreboding (while reading the Puritan apologetics for the war against drugs, or on being told that yet another battalion of previously unknown carcinogens has invaded the vegetable markets), I can sense the rising of a cold and purifying wind.

The national concern with pollutants of all kinds—in the atmosphere, the sea, the slums, the movie theaters—trembles on the verge of acute hypochondria, and too many signs point unerringly in the direction of a desperate and intolerant wish to cleanse the world of its impurities. Within the last few years the agents of the state have taken it upon themselves to examine the citizenry for flaws in its blood, its urine and its speech. The media amplify the din of incessant alarm by their ceaseless dwelling on the fear of disease, crime, sin, foreigners, poverty and death. Urgent bulletins reporting the whereabouts of the six un-American contagions make up most of what passes for the news. Every morning the papers publish dispatches from every section of the front:

• A woman in Wisconsin arraigned on charges of adultery.

• A politician in Washington censured for neglecting to send his financial statements to a decent laundry.

• The Supreme Court ruling in favor of police checkpoints at which motorists must submit to a summary search for drunkenness.

• A television columnist suspended for failing to scrub his language clean of racial and sexual opinions.

• The cardinal in New York insisting on the excommunication of Catholic politicians who approve the practice of abortion.

• The owner of a record store in Miami arrested for selling music besmirched with lyrics allegedly obscene.

If I correlate the news reports with the advertisements for abstinence and self-denial (for diet cola, nonalcoholic beer and no-color mascara), I know that the time has come to study the arts of innocence and stay off the streets after dark. A few weeks ago in an avant-garde restaurant in New York I committed the sin of smoking a cigarette and in the angry glance of the woman seated virtuously at the next table behind the monkfish, the tofu and the ferns I recognized the zealous glint of Madame Guillotine.

When I try to give form and shape to my apprehension, I see myself standing in a white and sterile room, arraigned on charges of smoking in a public park or trafficking in contraband nouns. Both my interrogators, young, blond, short-haired and of indeterminate sex, wear surgical masks and gloves of fine, translucent rubber. They sit behind a table of polished wood, reading the list of my prior crimes and misdemeanors—nineteen or twenty pages of small typescript in a plain manila folder. I shift uneasily under the artificial light, and I notice that the thin and processed air has been bleached with the scent of lemons. On the sound system I can hear, faintly and far off, the songs of birds and whales.

Judgement is an administrative formality, and I know that it is useless to attempt an excuse or an extenuating circumstance. I have been found out once too often (photographed at a distance of 300 yards on a Sunday morning in an open field), and the law is clear about the mandatory punishments—either a three-year term of aerobics at a rehabilitation camp up state or exile to one of the dingier cities of the Third World. In the Third World it is still permissible to burn coal and sell roasted meats to children under the age of twelve.

My interrogators take turns reading the charges and asking the questions. They do so in the manner of Hollywood celebrities announcing the nominees for an Academy Award. Their voices shine with the self-approval of obedient children. They know that they carry on their handsome shoulders the burden of the nation's conscience and the cost of its insurance. Like the theologians who conducted the Salem witch trials, they believe themselves engaged in a ritual of purification. Their faith in the peculiarly American dream of perfect health (both temporal and spiritual) is the same faith that sets up the markets for patent medicines, plastic surgery, evangelical religion and reform politics.

The national expenditure on health services (at last count more than $500 billion a year) deserves to be understood as an extravagant act of religious sacrifice. On the altars of eternal life the ancient Greeks presented gifts of burned meat to Zeus and Poseidon. Contemporary Americans profess their equivalent faith with the vast offerings of antiseptic gauze and needless surgical procedures.

The nation spends as recklessly on soap and cosmetics as it does on weapons, the object of both rituals being the protection of the American body politic against the contamination of foreign substances. Every drugstore in the country stocks hundreds of sprays, perfumes, ointments, powders, disinfectants, creams, fresheners, lotions and scents—all of them intended to preserve a specific part of the anatomy in a state of sweet-smelling grace! American food comes wrapped in plastic, supposedly cured of its impurities and often decorated with artificial colorings meant to disguise the baseness of its origins. The restaurants serving the minimalist abstractions of nouvelle cuisine go to considerable trouble to explain that nothing on the table was killed in a factory or caught in a net.

Transferred into the political arena, the doctrines of social sanitation oblige all candidates for public office to feign the clean-limbed innocence of college sophomores. Even the meanest of politicians has no choice but to present himself as one who would remove the stains from capitalism's bloody clothes and wash the sheets of the American conscience. The system in place is always assumed to be corrupt (a foul back room reeking of graft and cigar smoke), and the electorate expects its once and future presidents to present themselves as honest and wholesome fellows (not too dissimilar to high school football coaches) who know little or nothing of murder, ambition, lust, selfishness, cowardice or greed. The more daring members of the troupe might go so far as to admit to reading about such awful things in the newspapers, but the incidents in question invariably have to do with somebody belonging to the other political party or visiting from another world. President Bush conforms so amiably to the preferred image that the national media cannot bear to think of him as the kind of man who ever would have known—much less been associated with—villains so distasteful as General Manuel Noriega or Admiral John Poindexter. The society chooses to believe that the world's evil doesn't reside within the minds of men (as a consequence of their flawed and tragic nature) but exists, like the night air, in the space between their deodorants. The belief is consistent with the language of advertising and it encourages the frenzied consumption of more laws, more tests, more euphemisms, more regulations.

If microbes spawn and multiply as malevolently as the fiends in hell, then the criminalization of unhealthy behaviors follows as inevitably as the acts of contrition imposed on the Puritan congregations in seventeenth-century Massachusetts. I don't think it impossible that sooner or later (sooner in California, later in Ohio or Illinois) the state will demand jail sentences not only for smoking cigarettes but also for consuming too many calories, squandering carbohydrates and indulging a taste for saturated fats. The dealers in miracles pander to the belief that death is a disease for which somebody sooner or later will discover an infallible cure, but after too many promises have been proved false the frightened customers seek redress in the courts, and the laws begin to insist on the guarantee of immortality.

Let the laws prove insufficiently infallible, and sooner or later the country must come to resemble a well-disciplined boarding school (very clean, very Christian), governed by a headmaster (very hearty, very fit) who can be counted on to expel (to Dakar or Guatemala City) any careless pupil seen in the company of a filthy habit. I suspect that it won't be long before the surgeon general's elite guard begins to force overweight suspects up against glass walls in order to pat them down, not for guns or cocaine but for fatty tissues, for slack thigh muscles and for warts.

The only question that remains is the one about the design of the uniforms. Khaki tunics and white trousers, or khaki trousers and white tunics? Sneakers or riding boots? An athletic-director's whistle or a length of knotted rope?

August 1990

THE VISIBLE HAND

Money, which represents the prose of life, and which
is hardly spoken of in parlors without an apology, is,
in its effects and laws, as beautiful as roses.
—RALPH WALDO EMERSON

The mechanics of the savings and loan swindle become somewhat easier to understand if the reader remembers to bear in mind the comparison to the financial workings of a Soviet collective farm or a Bulgarian steel mill. The operative economic principle was socialist, not capitalist; the money came and went for reasons that were political and ideological, not because it obeyed the rules of supply and demand.

The story of the swindle makes a mockery of the national prayer to the idols of free enterprise. Instead of Adam Smith's benign and mysterious "invisible hand," what appears behind the curtain of fraud is the all-too-visible and familiar hand of venal and incompetent bureaucracy. As follows:

The American government conferred an urgent subsidy on an industry that certainly would have gone bankrupt if it had been left to the decision of anything as treacherous as a free market. In return for the subsidy, the grateful recipients (in Texas and California, as in Belorussia or the Ukraine) professed their fervent loyalty to the socioeconomic cant that enjoyed the blessing of the party in power. Whenever called upon to do so (in after-dinner speeches, while making campaign contributions, in letters to the editor of the *Wall Street Journal*), they expressed their belief in the joys of "risk-taking" and the wonders of "entrepreneurship."

Because everybody tacitly acknowledged the political text of the subsidy, the government neglected to insist on a strict accounting, and the newly minted bankers obligingly clothed the nakedness of their stupidity and greed in the false reports of unalloyed success.

Understood as the rule rather than the exception, and measured by any standard other than its handsome cost (currently estimated at $500 billion over the next thirty or forty years), the swindle was in no way abnormal or un-American. By and large, and certainly in its primary and steadier movements, the national economy depends not only on systematic price-fixing and noncompetitive bidding but also on the guarantee of government intervention. The theory of the free market works at the margins of the economy—among cabdrivers and the owners of pizza parlors, for small businessmen who make the mistake of borrowing $20,000 instead of $20 million—but the central pillars of the American enterprise rest firmly on the foundation stones of state subsidy. The federal treasury at the moment supplies 45 percent of the nation's income. Nearly three in every ten Americans live in a household receiving direct payments from the government; four of the remaining seven probably work for an enterprise dependent on the federal dole. The government subsidizes the growing of the nation's crops ($15 billion a year to the farmers) as well as the building of the nation's houses and the maintenance of the nation's roads. The television networks receive from the FCC the license that grants them (free of charge and without any risk) the use of the broadcasting frequencies. The commercial banks borrow money from the federal government at an interest rate two or three points below the rate they charge their best customers.

The politicians dress up the deals in the language of law or policy, but they're in the business of brokering the tax revenue. What keeps them in office is not their talent for oratory but their skill at redistributing the national income in a way that rewards their constituents, clients, patrons and friends. They trade in every known commodity—school lunches, tax exemptions, water and mineral rights, aluminum siding, dairy subsidies, pension benefits, highway contracts, prison uniforms—and they work the levers of government like gamblers pulling at slot machines. Explicating the point some years ago for the benefit of a touring civics class, William Greider, then an assistant managing editor of the *Washington Post*, described the acts of "buying, selling, swapping and hustling" as the fundamental means of expression occupying what he called "the poetic center" of the national capital.

As with the subsidizing of the farms and the defense industry, so also with paying off the bad debt acquired by savings and loan associations. Except for the taxpayers (who, as always, didn't know what was being promised in their name), nobody took the slightest risk. Always and whenever possible, the participants in the swindle zealously adhered to the fundamental American principles of "no money down" and "something for nothing."

The same economic maxims guided the settling of the old American frontier and the amassing of the gaudier fortunes synonymous with the decade of the Reagan prosperity. Sometimes it was the leveraged buy-out deal; sometimes it was the Wall Street practice of "insider trading;" sometimes it was a revision of the tax law or a contract bestowed by the Department of Housing and Urban Development. At HUD, the resident shills didn't even bother to pretend that they were playing with anything other than a marked deck. If the real-estate developer knew the right people in the administration, then he received the contract. If not, not. Explaining the procedure to a congressional committee investigating the extent of the fraud, DuBois L. Gilliam, formerly a deputy assistant secretary at HUD and now one of the few government officials serving a term in prison, described his public offences as " . . . the best political machine I've ever seen. We dealt strictly in politics."

Given the dependence of the economy on the grace and favor of Washington, I never know why the apologists for the American merchant class preach so many sermons on the sacred text of the "free market." Maybe it's because they know that they must make up in religious fervor what they lack in evidence.

During the course of the summer, at the same time that I was reading daily bulletins from the frontiers of the savings and loan swindle, I also had occasion to read the Spring issue of *Policy Review*, a quarterly journal published by The Heritage Foundation that embodies the orthodox wisdom of the Republican party, the larger corporations and the Wall Street banks. Under the title "The Vision Thing: Conservativism for the Nineties," the editors presented brief essays by no fewer than thirty-nine well-known voices of the conservative conscience, among them Russell Kirk, Senator Jesse Helms, Fred Barnes, Phyllis Schlafly, Fred C. Iklé, Ken Tomlinson, former governor Pete du Pont, William E. Simon and Pat Robertson.

They recited the national economic creed in the sweet soprano voices of a choir of castrati, and on reading their improving lessons, I was struck by the collective tone of inane complacence. It was as if I had been invited to an ideological variant of the Mad Hatter's tea party staged at an expensive conference center in Aspen or Palm Springs. I could imagine the guests dressed for croquet or golf, seated in white wicker chairs, admiring the post-card views of the sea or the mountains, busily arranging and rearranging their briefing papers, exchanging idiot solemnities with the aplomb of a club steward handing around the potted shrimp. Many of them had furnished the claptrap economic theory that justified the raids on the federal treasury during the heyday of the Reagan administration, but none of them seemed to have noticed the corollary damage done to the society's hope for the future. Nobody said a word about the debt, about the HUD or savings and loan swindles, about the numerous public officials indicted for theft or fraud, about the racial divisions in what's left of the American democracy, about the mismanagement of the military budget, about the squalor of the nation's cities and the wreckage of the nation's schools.

Everybody talked instead about the triumph of new money, which proved what one of their number described as the "moral superiority of the free economy over statism." Occasionally, they differed among themselves on what they regarded as minor points of doctrine (most notably with regard to the still troubling and unsettled questions of education and the environment), but on the principal articles of capitalist faith ("the free market," "economic liberty," "the commonwealth of freedom," and so on) all present expressed their calm and beatific agreement.

I read the anthology of self-congratulation with the mounting suspicion that it might have been intended as a parody. So many of the remarks were so far removed from the realms of experience that I began to wonder if any of the ladies and gentlemen in the lawn chairs had ever met a defense contractor, watched network television, traveled to New York or Miami, seen a slum or read an insurance claim. Every now and then one of their company admitted to having read something nasty in the newspapers or having heard—at a less refined conference—a really awful rumor (about illiteracy or crime or deviant sexual practice), but if the rumors were true (which they probably were not), then undoubtedly it was the fault of the "imperial Congress" or the "spiritual decay" said to be rotting the moral tissue of the nation's popular songs.

Nor did many of the guests of the symposium seem to have the least idea of what it might mean to sell their labor in a competitive market. Of the thirty-nine seers in residence, only a very few could be expected to pay their own bills. The majority owed their livings to some sort of subsidy or dole, either as politicians drawing an allowance of public money or as ministers of tax-exempt foundations relying on the largess of their corporate patrons.

The absurd humor of the performance in *Policy Review* was elaborated by George Bush in late June when he staged a show of fiscal conscience in the great hall of the Justice Department building in Washington. Wishing to express his alarm about the savings and loan swindle, Mr Bush appeared against the backdrop of American flags, seconded by the marine band playing "God Bless America" and "Hail to the Chief." To an audience of United States attorneys Mr Bush said, "These cheats have cost us billions, and they will pay us back with their dollars, and they will pay us back with years of their lives."

But the cheats always cost us billions. That is one of the great objects of the great American dream, and the reader who continues to cherish doubts on the point has only to consult the life and works of Donald Trump or reflect on the aerodynamic pretensions of the Stealth bomber. If Mr Bush were to pursue his vengeance across the whole table of organization of American business enterprise, he would find that an embarrassing number of his golfing companions had declared bankruptcy or had gone suddenly to jail. Life the friends of the March Hare and the Mad Hatter placidly trading economic theories over cups of tax-deductible tea, Mr Bush chooses to know as little as possible about the workings of the American economy. He prefers the mystical vision of "the free market" to the secular, workaday chores of the payoff, the kickback, the political favor and the cost overrun. If the distinction interested him, he could apply for an explanation to his son, Neil, a director of a bankrupt savings and loan association in Denver who granted himself opulent lines of credit (as much as $900,000) at virtually no cost.

The boy is obviously a born entrepreneur, and if the father took the time to study the son's arithmetic, I am sure that as a politician quick to follow a popular trend he would discover that his fellow countrymen have a profound aversion for anything that remotely resembles a free market or an honest risk. What they know and like is the rigged price, the safe monopoly and the sure percentage.

September 1990

OPENING THE MAIL

America remains democratic, not in the literal
sense of being a democracy, but in the moral
sense of consisting of democrats.
—G. K. CHESTERTON

*L*ast November in *Harper's Magazine* I published an essay decrying the palsied condition of the American democracy, and within a matter of days I was overwhelmed with letters to the editor taking me to task not for my pessimism but for my naivety and my romanticism. Few essays published in the magazine during the last two or three years have prompted so many interjections and further remarks, and at the end of a week I had enough text to make a short but instructive book. I read the letters with delight. Not only were they strongly phrased and free of cant, they confirmed Chesterton's distinction between the moral and literal meanings of democracy. None of the correspondents believed that the United States could be fairly described (not now, not in 1910 or 1826) as a textbook democracy. They chided me for being so foolish as to suppose that at some idyllic moment in the historical past the Americans ever had matched the ideal theory of democracy with a practice that was mercifully corrupt. And yet, again without exception, all the correspondents construed themselves as democrats, reserving the right to say what they thought, objecting, as much on instinct as on principle, to any encroachment on their liberties. They regarded the professional politician as what Paul Johnson once called "the great human scourge of the 20th Century," and they informed me that the republic always stands at risk, that its enemies, who are many and well fed, always ally themselves with more or less the same mob of selfish fears—with the pride of the rich and the envy of the poor, with the insolence of office and the wish for kings. Never mind, they said;

the country has survived the violence of thieves and the teaching of fools, and it is only our ignorance of history that makes it so easy for us to vilify our own age.

A correspondent in Keokuk, Iowa—R. G. (Buck) Buchannan, news director of KOKX radio—sent a revised draft of the Constitution that the Congress might well consider passing into law; seventeen students of senior English at the Deerfield Academy in Massachusetts sent a series of ripostes composed on assignment; John Colby Ney, the editor of *Collapse Watch*, an obscure and presumably anarchist journal committed to the acceleration of America's inevitable decline, cited, as proof of his thesis, T. S. Eliot's remark to D. H. Lawrence: "One can hardly have the phoenix without the ashes, can one?"

If a majority of the correspondents thought it absurd to expect that genuinely democratic government could promote the interests of a nation-state, possibly this was because so many of them had served on city councils and district school boards, as trustees of hospitals, or salt marshes, or museums. Their letters bore witness to what they had seen and heard in Rockport, Maine and Perkins, Oklahoma; in El Toro, California and Warren, Ohio and Sparks, Nevada. They reminded me that democratic government proves itself effective only in the smaller theaters of operation.

The sketchiness of the mail from Washington, DC (two letters and a postcard), sustained my impression of that city as the last outpost of the nineteenth-century British Empire. The uses of democracy (as opposed to the slogans of democracy) require the presence of fellow citizens who know enough and care enough about a common concern to argue about a water right or a fourth-grade English text, and in Washington I find functionaries instead of citizens. Maybe I have been unfortunate in my acquaintance, but in Washington I'm accustomed to listening to the mumble of abstractions, to policy intellectuals and under deputy secretaries who never permit themselves the luxury of an impolitic opinion. Their ambition tailors their thought to the prevailing political truth and they cannot afford the practice of democracy because they might find themselves declared *persona non grata* by the public-opinion polls.

The correspondents in Keokuk and Warren and Sparks understood democracy as a habit of mind necessarily at odds with the grand designs of the nation-state. The state defines power as the power inherent in things, and the people define power as the power inherent in dreams. To say that America is both a liberal democracy and a nation-state is to say that the

American eagle is both a bird and a fish. As the reasons of state gradually supersede the wishes and the interests of the people, the government increasingly must rely on subterfuge and the suppression of any opinion that contradicts the wisdom in office. The government may not wish to make the adjustments, but it has no choice in the matter. The larger a nation's sway and ambit in the world, the more likely that it will be obliged to abandon its principles. Troubled officials sometimes refer to what they call "the unhappy paradox" implicit in the waging of secret or undeclared war under the jurisdiction of a free, open and democratic society. Their embarrassment doesn't prevent the substitution of palace intrigue for candid debate or the preference, at least in official circles, for the virtue of loyalty as opposed to the spirit of liberty.

Both James R. Showalter of Peoria, Arizona, and Gordon Hilgers of Dallas, Texas, well understood the transmigration of the soul of the old American republic into the body of the new and improved American state. Hilger's comparison of the modern business corporation with a despotic city-state corresponds to my own observation. The larger corporations (Citicorp, Mobil Corporation, and so on) employ at least as many people as lived in Renaissance Florence or medieval Venice, and among the happy few who attain degrees of rank within the hierarchy, I have noticed the attributes of the accomplished courtiers. They laugh on cue and never neglect to marvel at the chairman's sagacity. When summoned to attend the ceremonies of the annual board meeting or quail hunt, they reflect the mood of authority as accurately as the still surfaces of an ornamental pond. The air of subservience remains constant throughout the whole honeycomb of the American oligarchy, a smiling and bowing attitude of mind as much in evidence at a television network or a newsmagazine as at an automobile company or a bank.

I also find persuasive Showalter's distinction between democracy and capitalism, two words that most Americans (George Bush not least among them) tend to regard as synonyms. The media ceaselessly compound the confusion, equating politics with economics and referring the customers, for social justice, to the notions counter in what they regard as the great, good American department store. Ever since the advent of President Ronald Reagan, I've noticed that even *soi-disant* leftist intellectuals think of themselves as crisis managers. As recently as last September, while passing a slow afternoon on a train between Baltimore and New York, I attempted to explain to a young entrepreneur (the owner, as I remember, of four beachfront motels) that capitalism wasn't a political idea, that Nazi

Germany endorsed the capitalist virtues and that had Saddam Hussein submitted his acquisitions policy to the Harvard Business School or the First Boston Corporation, he undoubtedly would have been congratulated for his aggressiveness and his search for excellence. The young man had considerable difficulty with the separation of his faith into its component parts, and on the way through Philadelphia I remember asking him what he thought was meant by the all-American phrase "Go for it."

Although most of the letters to the editor expressed varying degrees of skepticism about the outward and official forms of democracy, the authors retained their faith in the inward and unofficial expression of the democratic spirit, and it was on behalf of their hope for the best that they sent their corrections and amendments. A number of them, however, found fault with my failure to recommend a course of action. Easy enough, they said, to make dismal remarks about a system so obviously inept, but what would you, in fact, *do?*

I never know how to answer that question. I consider myself an editor by accident and a writer by design, and I regard neither profession as being especially congenial to the will to power. I would rather say what I think than go to dinner with Ted Koppel or Alexander Haig, and, for the sake of an apt phrase, I've lost, more than once, the chance of a fellowship or foundation grant.

That much having been said, and in the unlikely circumstance that I found myself standing for an election, I would rely on the precept that in a democracy the first question is not "Who is the best ruler?" but rather "Which ruler can do the least harm?" It is the law that must take notice of freedom, not, as in a military dictatorship or a jail, freedom that must take notice of the law. Believing that it isn't the business of the state to impose on the citizenry a system of moral belief or spiritual practice, I would rescind or greatly modify (citing the authority of the Ninth Amendment: "The enumeration in the Constitution, of certain rights, shall not be construed to deny or disparage others retained by the people") most of the laws of prohibition—on gambling, nude bathing, the use of drugs and the carrying of guns, pornography, prostitution, free speech (in all forms), abortion, polygamy or polyandry, aberrant religious beliefs, the habits of conduct, dress and deportment.

Given the further premise that democracy, by definition, is both an experiment and an inefficient mess, and given also enough time and the advice of wiser counselors, I might attempt a program of political illumination lively enough to enlist the enthusiasm of Robert Leonard of Roseville, Minnesota. Leonard replied to my November essay by describing his rediscovery of Tom Paine's admonition to the effect that "we have it in our power to begin the world over again" and to make the political alphabet new.

In July of last year, on his way to Spokane, Washington, Leonard and his wife stopped for the night in Bismarck, North Dakota, and on the grounds of the capitol building he discovered in progress a performance of "The American Visions Chautauqua." A company of local history professors dressed in period costumes, as Alexander Hamilton, Elizabeth Cady Stanton, Henry Adams, et al., was presenting selected scenes from American history, reviving, for one another, as well as for the crowd on the lawn, the language of American democracy. "What a delight!" Leonard wrote. "What an interesting and engaging way to learn, to be an active participant in a public discussion and debate—in the free-flowing atmosphere in a summer evening under a tent."

In an analogous spirit of free-flowing summer, and with the intention of opening a conversation rather than enforcing a regimen of discipline, I would put as many questions as possible to national referenda. Why not institute different means of government in different spheres of interest? The variants of democracy in those smaller jurisdictions (village, county, town, city, state) in which debate remains both effective and possible, and a federal jurisdiction, much reduced in size and authority, somehow reconstructed as a public utility or an international trading corporation. Why not an income tax that must be explained on no more than four pages of a government form? Why not nominate prospective candidates for Congress by lot, the names to be drawn from a list of candidates familiar with the rudiments of American history and at least five or six of the primary American political texts? The nominees would be required to show sufficient degrees of interest, knowledge and competence. Properly speaking, they wouldn't be politicians, and so they could be excused from the need to raise campaign money or trim their votes to the trends of the next election. Why not a period of national service (chiefly in the civilian sectors of the society) for any and all individuals (both domestic and foreign) who wish to hold government office?

With respect to the conduct of the nation's wars, I would make it a rule that no bureaucrat or intellectual mercenary should write weapons policy or act in an advisory capacity to the White House, Defense Department or National Security Council without a month's prior service in a war, a police precinct, a public hospital or a city morgue. The authors of the higher strategy also must have had occasion, at least once in their lives, to inform the next of kin of a death in a family.

In the matter of the government's obligation to the arts, I would limit the subsidies to well-established institutions—the National Gallery, the Metropolitan Museum, the New York Philharmonic—but on the condition that the subsidies be extravagant enough to maintain the institution in a state of easy affluence. Excused from the ignominy of perpetually begging for coins, the institutions could fix their attention on art instead of money. The shift in sensibility would improve the quality of both the management and the exhibits. No institution accepting a subsidy could solicit funds, charge admission or set up markets in posters, toys and scented candles.

Given another few thousand words, possibly I could come up with further questions which, with any luck, might encourage more practical people to break the habits of the old and draw the blueprints of the new. Probably I am too much of a romantic, not nearly cynical enough to welcome Mr Ney's forthcoming collapse, but so also is democracy a romantic idea, a thing of the spirit and the mind and by no means easy to sustain. More often than not it fails, as it did in Europe between 1920 and 1940 in Italy, Turkey, Portugal, Spain, Bulgaria, Greece, Romania, Yugoslavia, Hungary, Albania, Poland, Estonia, Latvia, Lithuania, Austria, Germany.

"A republic," said Franklin, "if you can keep it"; and as has been often said and often proved, democracy is never orderly or aesthetic or quiet or efficient, but it is the form of government that best preserves the spirit of liberty.

February 1991

ACHIEVEMENT TEST

Diogenes struck the father when the son swore.
—ROBERT BURTON

No American schoolmaster ever outlined the lesson at hand quite as plainly as did Woodrow Wilson. At the turn of the new century, while he was still president of Princeton University, Wilson presented the Federation of High School Teachers with explicit instructions: "We want one class of persons to have a liberal education, and we want another class of persons, a very much larger class of necessity in every society, to forgo the privilege of a liberal education and fit themselves to perform specific difficult manual tasks."

I came across Wilson's remark during the same month that President Bush announced yet another grand design for American education (one of possibly fifty such grand designs that I have heard announced by as many politicians over the past thirty years), and I was struck by both the constant and the variable. The pedagogical objective remains firmly in place, but the privileged classes have lost the courage to say what they mean. They continue to require the services of competent domestic labor ("decent help"), but they no longer write their own speeches, and their language has gone rotten with bureaucratic euphemism.

At a White House press conference on 18 April, posed against the familiar backdrop of the American flag, Bush made a show of presenting new plans and initiatives that he described as "revolutionary." "For the sake of the future, of our children, and our nation," Bush said, "we must transform America's schools. The days of the status quo are over."

Maybe on an otherwise slow afternoon this summer at Kennebunkport, somebody will explain to Mr Bush the meaning of the phrase "status quo." It is the ground and condition of his success as a politician, and if somehow it were to be abruptly removed (together with the helicopter, the applause and the campaign contributions), I suspect he might find it hard to get work in any kind of new social order that placed a high value on disciplined thought or an advanced degree of literacy.

The president left the business of explaining the lesson plan to its author, Lamar Alexander, the newly appointed secretary of education and the man best known for his financial sleights of hand. As governor of Tennessee and, later, as president of the University of Tennessee, Alexander proved himself extraordinarily adept at the art of the miraculous windfall. In one series of stock transactions he earned $569,000 without investing so much as a cent; in another deal he and his wife paid $5,000 for stock that proved within four years to be worth $800,000. He worked similar wonders with Whittle Communications, Kentucky Fried Chicken, the *Knoxville Journal* and various Tennessee banks. As a man obviously blessed with the entrepreneurial spirit of the age, Alexander approached the task of improving the nation's schools as if it were a problem in corporate management.

If the nation's intellectual infrastructure had fallen into as alarming a state of disrepair as its material infrastructure (that is, if its collective mathematical and literary skills had been as poorly maintained as its bridges, ports, prisons and roads), then what was needed was the stimulus of private enterprise. Operate the schools as if they were a chain of successful motels; impose uniform rules of procedure; cut costs; meet the customer's demands for better service; teach the kitchen staff to speak English; insist that the desk clerks know how to work the imported technology.

Alexander's brief addressed the profit-and-loss statements of the national economy, not the intellectual hopes or ambitions of the nation's children. What was wanted was a new generation of myrmidons fit "to perform specific difficult tasks." As long as the economy could make do with semiliterate or unskilled labor, then what difference did it make whether "another class of persons" learned to solve quadratic equations or read the novels of Henry James? Obviously, it made no difference at all, and so matters might have safely continued well into the twenty-third century if the economy hadn't suddenly found itself at a loss for workers familiar with the signs and digits of the new information order. For the past ten years committees of alarmed businessmen have been complaining about workers who cannot read or write or add or think or subtract. The corporate chairmen then go on to worry about the loss of America's place in the world, about our declining rates of productivity, about our failure to compete on equal terms with the Germans and the Japanese.

Attempting to allay these concerns, Alexander proposed a number of specific remedies: grants of public money for students qualified to attend private or parochial schools; standardized achievement tests (in English, math, science, history and geography); vocational requirements aligned with the requirements of the labor markets; construction of 535 new schools, presumably innovative, funded and designed by benevolent corporations. The federal government, of course, committed relatively little money to its new and revolutionary plan—no more than $690 million, a sum well short of what the Pentagon spent for the fireworks display in Iraq. President Bush and Secretary Alexander, offered their proposals more in the spirit of suggestions to the state and municipal authorities that pay most of the costs of American public education. But even if the administration had been willing to back its advice with cash, I'm afraid that the result would be as malformed as one of the secretary's business deals or one of the president's longer sentences. Change the schools into the intellectual equivalent of factories or sweatshops and you turn freedom of mind into an enemy of the state. The unauthorized answer slows down production and threatens to lower the average test score.

The difficulty, as Woodrow Wilson well and clearly understood, is political. It is the status quo that must be protected and transformed, not the children or the schools. But how do you teach people to solve the new equations unless you also teach them how to think? And if you teach too many people how to think, then how can you be sure that they won't ask the wrong kind of questions? Why would any politician wish to confront an informed citizenry that could read the federal budget, decipher the news from Washington and break down the election-year images into their subsets of component lies? Why would the purveyors of American goods and services choose to afflict themselves with a public intelligent enough to see through the scrim of the paid advertisements? The success of the American dream, like the success of MasterCard and the Republican party, presupposes the eager and uncritical consumption of junk in all its commercial declensions. Teach a man to think for himself and maybe he won't buy the after-shave lotion or believe that the glorious victory in Kuwait proves the need for a newer and more expensive collection of tanks. So troublesome a man might even bother to vote.

Recognizing the possibility of unrest implicit in too thorough a course of study, the schoolmasters of Woodrow Wilson's generation took it upon themselves to rig the curricula in a way that discouraged the habits of skepticism or dissent. They redefined democracy as "primarily a mode of associated living" (as opposed to a dedication to the belief in liberty), and they argued that American schools should cut the cloth of their teaching to what John Dewey called "the circumstances, needs, and opportunities of industrial civilization." They had in mind the training of a contented labor force, prospective members of the national economic team, "socially efficient" workers who understood that what was great about America was the greatness of its gross national product and not the greatness of its character and spirit.

The new program displaced the older republican hope of a citizenry schooled to the task of self-government. Jefferson had urged the teaching of political history so that Americans might learn "how to judge for themselves what will secure or endanger their freedom." The managers of the newly emerging nation-state, like Messrs Alexander and Bush, didn't have much use for citizens, especially citizens likely to see the would-be despot behind the mask of the popular general or the avuncular judge. Jefferson had asked, in effect, how could free men protect their liberties if they never learned that it was the business of most politicians to remove those liberties. The Wilson administration subtracted a good many liberties from the public domain during the First World War, and Wilson's propaganda ministry invented the syllabus of the great books of Western civilization (what we now know as "the canon") as a means of political indoctrination. The course was meant to quiet what a dean at Columbia University called "the destructive element in our society," to produce students who "shall be safe for democracy" and to make of the American troops in France what *History Teachers Magazine* called "thinking bayonets."

For the past seventy or eighty years the country's educational authorities have done their best to suppress the habit of critical thought. The objective (in 1991, as in 1905 or 1920) conforms to the requirements of a market geared to blind and insatiable consumption. Because the schools serve an economic system (as opposed to an intellectual ideal), they promote, quite properly, the habits of mind necessary to the preservation of that system. A successful American education bears comparison to the commercial procedure for changing caterpillars into silk instead of moths. Silkworms can be turned to a profit, but moths blow around in the wind and do nothing to add to the wealth of the corporation or the power of the state.

The American people have spent billions of dollars on education over the past forty years, and by now I would have thought that we might have acquired the wit or the courage to say that the condition of the schools accurately reflects our intent. We are a people blessed with a genius for large organizational tasks, and if we were serious in our pious blathering about the schools—if we honestly believed that mind took precedence over money—then our educational system surely would stand as the eighth wonder of the world. But we don't like, and we don't trust, the forces of intellect—not unless they can be tied securely to a commercial profit or a scientific benefit.

If many of our public schools resemble penal institutions, and if, despite the achievements of a relatively few gifted or fortunate individuals, the population at large sinks further into the sloughs of illiterate superstition, then I cannot help but think that the result is neither an accident nor a mistake. We make it as difficult as possible for our children to learn anything other than their proper place in the economic order because we fear the power of untrammeled thought. Most of what passes for education in the United States deadens the desire for learning because it fails to awaken the student to the unique value of his or her own mind. If the public schools employ the devices of overcrowded classrooms, recitations by rote, questions shaped to the simple answer of right or wrong, it is because the society regards the realm of thought as a subversive conspiracy likely to cause nothing but trouble. An inept and insolent bureaucracy armed with badly written textbooks instills in the class the attitudes of passivity, compliance and boredom. The students major in the arts of failure and the science of diminished expectations.

Outside the schoolroom we wage the same relentless campaign against free or unauthorized expression, and I think it is probably fair to estimate that the nation annually lays waste to roughly 50 percent of its intellectual capacity. George Orwell once observed that almost everything that goes by the name of pleasure represents a more or less successful attempt to destroy consciousness. The United States now spends upwards of $350 billion a year on liquor, pornography and drugs, and the Cold War against the American intellect thus constitutes a more profitable business than the old arrangement with the Russians. Subsidized by the state and supported by the peep-show operators of the mass media, the erotic entertainments tether the public mind to the posts of sexual fantasy. Liberty, said Jefferson, has ambitious enemies, and what they cannot gain with restrictive laws and the closing of as many libraries as possible, they accomplish with bread and circuses.

The idea of freedom stands in as much need of revision as the geography of the supposedly lost frontier. Within the circles of advanced opinion, it is taken for granted that the new technologies (if only we can train enough people to operate them) will save us all, that man has vanquished nature, that his machines have made nonsense of the seasons and subjugated the tribes of Paleolithic instinct. The illuminati who make these confident announcements then proceed to talk in a lighter and more conversational tone of voice about the corporate cul-de-sac in which they find themselves penned like so many sheep, about the faithlessness of their husbands or wives, the forgery of their tax returns, the silence of their children. Most people have the same hopes and aspirations—work in which they can find meaning and ways in which they can express their capacity to love. But if we haven't been taught to make the acquaintance of our own minds, how, in this most advanced of nations and most enlightened of times, can we manage to achieve those deceptively modest ends? And if our textbooks teach us that America is nothing more than the sum of its profits, then how do we expect to reinvent our politics, or our history, or our schools?

Some years ago, I published a few melancholy notes about the reduced circumstances of our political discourse, and, from a woman in Maryland, I received a stern reminder to the effect that the fault, dear Brutus, was not in our stars. "We do not," she said, "ask nearly enough of our-selves—not of parents, not of children, not of women, not of men, not of our institutions, not of our talents, not of our national or our personal character, not of our Constitution's promise, which we betray." In that one sentence, she said most of what needs to be said about the emptiness of the nation's politics and the shabbiness of the nation's schools.

If we could stop thinking of ourselves primarily as consumers, perhaps we could understand the lost frontier as being always and everywhere present—as near at hand as the wish to murder, cheat, steal, lie and generally conduct oneself in a manner unbecoming in an ape. Suppose that we could learn to recognize it in the death of a child in the next street, in any afternoon's proceedings in any criminal court, in the faces of people stupefied by their fear of poverty or the dark. Think how many of its large and various capacities the United States could put to use if only it knew why it was doing so.

July 1991

SENSE AND SENSIBILITY

The ocean is closed.
—SIGN POSTED AT 5:00 P.M. by the management of a
Miami Beach hotel

*O*n a Tuesday afternoon in late July, in a taxi stalled for an hour in traffic on the Brooklyn Bridge, I listened to a New York literary agent praise his daughter's gift for refined political sentiment. Twenty years ago a proud father might have praised a daughter's talent for music or gymnastics, but the times have changed, and it is the exquisite-ness of the moral aesthetic that prompts the cue for applause. The girl was fifteen, a student at one of the city's better private schools, already word perfect in her catechism of correct opinions. Her father was a successful dealer in high-priced pulp, and his daughter kept up with the latest cultural trends as they made their way around the beaches and lawns of East Hampton.

At the beginning of the spring term her biology class had taken up the study of primitive organisms, and the girls were asked to look through microscopes at a gang of bacteria toiling in a drop of water. The agent's daughter refused. No, she said, she would not look. She would not invade the privacy of the bacteria. They might be weak and small and without important friends in Congress, but they were entitled to their rights, and she, for one, would grant them a measure of respect. After what apparently was a moment of stunned silence in the classroom, the teacher congratulated the girl for her principled dissent. Of course she didn't have to look at the bacteria. She had taught the class a lesson that couldn't be learned from a microscope.

The story seemed to me proof of the inanity of much of what goes by the name of higher education, but the agent was so pleased with it, so suffused with the light of virtue, that I smiled politely and said something genial and optimistic about his daughter's chances of going to Harvard. By that time the taxi had crossed the bridge, and I was glad to escape into the less rarefied atmosphere of Second Avenue before the agent began to explain his theory of global harmony. I once had listened to him give a speech on the subject to a conference of publishers, and I knew that he was capable of long recitations in what he believed to be the language of the Oglala Sioux.

Two days later I was still thinking about the innocent and disenfranchised bacteria when I came across a news item on an inside page of the *New York Times* that matched the literary agent's story with its appropriate corollary. The narrative was very brief, no more than a few paragraphs, and sketchy in its details, but the moral lesson was as solemn as an auto-da-fé. Well after sunset on the evening of 16 July, an eight-year-old boy in Tampa, Florida looked through the window of a building near his home and saw a man and a woman (both unmarried and both in their middle thirties) making love in a hot tub. The hot tub was in the bathroom of a condominium that the man had rented three weeks earlier, and the blinds on the window had been drawn closed. The boy reported the event to his father, who called the sheriff's office. While awaiting the arrival of the men in uniform, a small crowd gathered outside the bathroom window, and another neighbor took it upon himself to record the scene in the hot tub on videotape. He was, he said, assembling evidence.

"They knew we were out there," he said. "They were exhibitionists. I shot right through the blinds."

Both the man and the woman were arrested on charges of committing a lewd and lascivious act. They spent the rest of the night in jail, and the next morning they each had to post $15,000 bail before being let loose in the streets.

The vigilant schoolboy in Florida reminded me of the sensitive schoolgirl in New York, and I wondered why it was that both prodigies seemed to partake of the same spirit. At first glance they seemed so unlike each other, and it was easy enough to contrast the differences of age, sex, education and regional prejudice. Their acts of piety expressed contradictory notions of the public good, and I could imagine each of their fathers thinking that the other father had stumbled into the snares of the Antichrist. The boy quite clearly had been born under the star of the political Right. Given world enough and time, he stood a good chance of growing up to vote Republican, enforce the drug laws and distribute Bibles or the collected works of Allan Bloom. The girl had been raised under the sign of the political Left, and once she completes the formality of the curriculum at Harvard, I expect that she will write funding guidelines for the federal government or scripts for Kevin Costner.

The ideological differences matter less than the common temperament or habit of mind. Both the boy and the girl apparently were the kind of people who sift the grains of human feeling and experience through the cloth of milk-white abstraction, and I didn't doubt but that they never would have much use for historical circumstance or the exception that proves the rule.

I wish I didn't think that such people now speak for the American majority, or that the will toward conformity crowds so close to the surface of so many nominally political disputes. The spirit of the age favors the moralist and the busybody, and the instinct to censor and suppress shows itself not only in the protests for and against abortion or multiculturalism but also in the prohibitions against tobacco and pet birds. It seems that everybody is forever looking out for everybody else's spiritual or physical salvation. Doomsday is at hand, and the community of the blessed (whether defined as the New York Yacht Club or the English department at Duke) can be all too easily corrupted by the wrong diet, the wrong combination of chemicals, the wrong word. The preferred modes of address number only three—the sermon, the euphemism and the threat —and whether I look to the political Left or the political Right I'm constantly being told to think the right thoughts and confess the right sins.

Passing through Portsmouth, Rhode Island, I see a sign on a public bus that says DO DRUGS AND KISS YOUR FEDERAL BENEFITS GOOD-BYE. I leaf through *The Dictionary of Cautionary Words and Phrases*, compiled by a tribunal of purified journalists (the 1989 Multicultural Management Program Fellows), and I learn that I must be very, very careful when using the words "man," "woman," "watermelon," "barracuda," "community," "banana" and "impotent." Given a careless inflection or an ambiguous context, the words can be construed as deadly insults.

The prompters of the public alarm sound their dismal horns from so many points on the political compass that I suspect that what they wish to say isn't political. The would-be saviors in our midst worry about the moral incoherence of a society distracted by its fears—fear of apples, fear of Mexicans, fear of bankruptcy, fear of the rain—and they seek to construct the citadel of the New Jerusalem with whatever materials come most easily or obviously to hand. Every few days the newspapers bear further witness to the jury-rigged orthodoxies meant to redeem the American moral enterprise and reclaim the American soul.

• The village of Chester, New York, passes a law to the effect that all the signs on all the stores of a new shopping mall must be painted blue. A merchant neglects to read the fine print on the lease and plans to put up the red sign under which he has been doing business for thirteen years. No good. Unacceptable. Either he paints the sign blue or he goes elsewhere. The village clerk, Elizabeth Kreher, overrules his objections with an air of sublime self-righteousness. "He shouldn't be complaining; he should be thankful to have such a nice place to move his store into. Plus it's a beautiful color—I just love blue."

• The chairman of General Public Utilities Corporation, a married man named Hoch, admits to a love affair with a woman employed by the company as vice president of communications. The news of their liaison arrived by anonymous letter. Hoch resigns, but the woman keeps her office and title. Various spokespersons explain that a public utility depends for its rate increases on the grace and favor of the federal government and therefore must align its manners with the prevailing political trends. The feminist lobby in Washington is as loud as it is judgemental. Goodbye Hoch.

• A waiter and a waitress working in a restaurant south of Seattle refuse to serve a pregnant woman a rum daiquiri in order to lead her out of the paths of temptation. When the woman persists in her folly, the waiter and waitress (both in their early twenties and very devout in their beliefs about health and hygiene) lecture her on the evils of alcohol and read her the surgeon general's warning about drinking and birth defects.

• A woman in California kisses her boyfriend goodnight on the steps of her own house, and a committee of disapproving neighbors reprimands her for lowering the tone and character of the block. For precisely the same reason, a committee of neighbors in Illinois censures a man for parking a vulgar pickup truck in his own driveway.

• Joseph Epstein, the editor of *The American Scholar* and a writer well-known both for his wit and neoclassical political views, publishes an essay in a literary journal in which he refers to "the snarling humorlessness" of various feminist critics and professors. He makes the mistake of repeating the joke about the couple in Manhattan who cannot decide whether to get a revolver or a pit bull in order to protect themselves against burglars. They compromise by hiring a feminist. The joke incites so much rage within some of the nation's more advanced universities that Epstein feels constrained to write a letter of explanation to the *New York Times* conceding that "one attempts humor at one's peril."

Like Queen Victoria and the National Endowment for the Arts, the Puritan spirit is not easily amused. Over the last seven or eight years I've noticed that my own experiments with irony or satire in mixed or unknown company require some introductory remark (comparable to a warning from the surgeon general) announcing the arrival of a joke that might prove harmful to somebody's self-esteem.

A society in which everybody distrusts everybody else classifies humor as a dangerous substance and entertains itself with cautionary tales. The news media magnify the fear of death by constantly reciting the alphabet of doom (abortion, AIDS, alcohol, asbestos, cancer, cigarettes, cocaine, and so on), and the public-service advertising extols the virtues of chastity and abstinence. The more urgent the causes of alarm, the more plausible the justifications for stricter controls. Stricter controls necessarily entail the devaluation of any and all systems of thought (most of them humanist) that make invidious distinctions between man and beast, man and moth, man and blood specimen, and I've noticed that the puritanical enthusiasms of the last several years complement and sustain the attitude of mind that assigns to human beings a steadily lower and more disreputable place in the hierarchy of multicellular life forms.

The rules and exhortations run to so many cross-purposes (more freedom and more rights, but also more laws and more police; no to fornication, yes to free contraceptives in the schools; yes to the possession of automatic weapons, no to the possession of cocaine) that it's hard to know what sort of perfect society our saviors have in mind. Presumably it will be clean and orderly and safe, but who will be deemed worthy of inhabiting the spheres of blameless abstraction? Maybe only the bacteria. Human beings make too much of a mess with their emotions and their wars. They poison the rivers and litter the fields with Styrofoam cups, and very few of them can be trusted with kitchen matches or the works of Aristotle.

I see so many citizens armed with the bright shields of intolerance that I wonder how they would agree on anything other than a need to do something repressive and authoritarian. I have no way of guessing how they will cleanse the world of its impurities, but if I were in the business of advising newly minted college graduates, I would encourage them to think along the lines of a career in law enforcement. Not simply the familiar and sometimes unpleasant forms of law enforcement—not merely the club, the handcuffs and the noose—but law enforcement broadly and grandly conceived, law enforcement as a philosophy and way of life, as the presiding spirit that defines not only the duty of the prison guard and police spy but also the work of the food inspector, the newspaper columnist, the federal regulator and the museum director. The job opportunities seem to me as numberless as the microbes still at large (and presumably up to no good) in the depths of the cold and unruly sea.

October 1991

MORE LIGHT

[A free people has] an indisputable, unalienable, indefeasible, divine right to that most dreaded and envied kind of knowledge, I mean of the characters and conduct of their rulers.
—JOHN ADAMS

*O*n the Tuesday after the Senate Judiciary Committee completed its hearings on the question of Judge Clarence Thomas (his character and sexual deportment), I found myself at lunch with several television and newspaper correspondents who were busy worrying about what they called "the unseemliness" of the proceedings on Capitol Hill. The tone of their conversation was genteel. The gentleman seated nearest to the ferns referred to "the spectacle of degradation." A woman dressed in silk said that she was "disgusted" by the "sordid" lines of questioning. All agreed that the hearings were "a national disgrace," that "something must be done" to correct a system of government so patently vile that it discouraged the participation of the good and true Americans (presumably present in large numbers somewhere west of the Alleghenies) who refused to descend into the sewers of politics.

Their sentiments echoed those of President Bush, Justice Thomas and the front page of the *New York Times*, and as I listened to their expressions of refined alarm, it occurred to me that we have become so estranged from both the spirit and practice of democracy in the United States that we no longer know what the thing looks like. Apparently we expect the business of government to be something orderly, decorous and safe— a stately pageant in which benign statesmen wearing white gloves pass noble documents to one another on silver trays.

The expectation is as foolish as it is absurd. For my own part I thought the hearings cast a clear and welcome light on the character and conduct of some of the disreputable politicians who govern the state. For a few hours over the Columbus Day weekend, against both the odds and the will of Congress, the American people were awakened to the shape and sound of their elected government. Politics consists in a ceaseless and bitter argument about who has the power to do what to whom, at what price, for how long and with what chance of redress, and here were people waging that argument in plain sight, telling one another the self-interested lies that they ordinarily manage to hide behind closed doors or disguise in the language of high-minded abstraction. The argument was often dishonest and sometimes comic, but it was an argument about the uses of power and the nature of justice, and its consequences undoubtedly will become apparent in an increasingly repressive definition of the nation's laws. If the hearings were sordid or disgusting, it was because the argument was lost to the champions of oligarchy, not because of the sexual aspects of the testimony or because of the vicious slanders brought by the Republican senators against the character of Professor Anita Hill. The American people understood precisely what they were looking at and why, and their appreciation of the rarity of the October hearings showed up in the Nielsen ratings. On the Friday evening Judge Thomas delivered his philippic against Anita Hill and the premises of democratic government, the two networks that broadcast the proceedings (ABC and NBC) received a 40 share of the audience. A championship baseball game appearing simultaneously on CBS received only a 19 share.

If the American people learned that liberty has ambitious enemies (among them Justice Clarence Thomas), they also learned that a democracy allies itself with social change and with the extensions—no matter how slight or how bitterly opposed—of human freedom and human possibility. Change is never easy and seldom fun; more often than not it takes place under circumstances that the apologists for the status quo invariably find "degrading."

The historical change at issue in Washington over the Columbus Day weekend was the one governing the shift in the alliance between men and women. For at least a century, but more insistently during the last twenty years, women have pressed their objections against the routine abuses of power (social, political, economic) with which the society holds in check their freedom of thought and action. Subtract academic feminist jargon from the argument and it is the same argument advanced by the aggrieved colonial gentlemen who signed the Declaration of Independence.

Like the British Parliament in the late eighteenth century, the United States Senate in the late twentieth century regards the prospect of social change (any social change) as both an insult and a nasty surprise. When presented with Professor Anita Hill's report of the sexual advances offered to her by Judge Clarence Thomas, the Judiciary Committee dismissed the statement as an irrelevant annoyance.

Nobody wished to reconvene the committee's researches into a matter that already had been satisfactorily arranged. The committee understood that Judge Thomas's nomination had little or nothing to do with his intelligence or his integrity or his knowledge of the law, but they also knew that they didn't want to change their votes and that any continuation of the hearings could bring them nothing but grief. They didn't have a choice. In the service of a Senate that lacks the courage of any conviction not endorsed by a public opinion poll, the Judiciary Committee went unwillingly to the television cameras, obliged to pay the price of the president's cynicism as well as their own.

They made a show of their venality and cowardice that was marvelous to behold. By turns angry, confused, embarrassed and malevolent, the members of the committee passed the weekend violating their own rules of procedure and protesting their innocence. It wasn't their fault that the hearings were still in session; it wasn't their fault that things had gotten so far out of hand; it wasn't their fault that Professor Hill's unsworn statement had found its way into the newspapers. The chairman of the committee, Joseph Biden (D., Del.), felt so sorry for himself that at one point he said to a witness, "I, too, have suffered."

With respect to the testimony of Anita Hill, none of the members of the committee (Democrat or Republican) understood what it was that she was talking about or why anything she said was important to anybody other than themselves. They ignored the historical and existential questions in the room (the ones about the evolution of the society's sexual mores), and they subjugated any questions of principle, conviction or conscience to the rules of Washington realpolitik. Uneasy with the testimony for reasons of their own, the Democratic senators made no attempt to shape her observations into a coherent narrative. The Republicans carried out the White House brief to do whatever was necessary to discredit the woman's statement. They did so with a meanspirited singleness of purpose that was as effective as it was dishonorable. Senator Orrin Hatch (R., Utah) distinguished himself by virtue of his smirking hypocrisy; Senator Alan Simpson (R., Wyo.), by his ignorance; and Senator Arlen Specter (R., Pa.), by his talents as a sophist and a bully.

The political question before the committee was the one about Judge Thomas's fitness to serve as an associate justice of the Supreme Court, and the answer to the question was apparent almost as soon as the judge began to speak. Testifying on Friday and again on Saturday, the judge revealed himself to be a man who despised the hopes as well as the mechanics of democratic government. His manner was that of an outraged British duke during the reign of George III, and his response to even the smallest whisper of seditious libel about the moral beauty of his soul could have been expressed in the phrase "How dare they?" Choosing to ignore the point that Professor Hill's statement referred to his abuse of public office (to sexual advances offered by the chairman of the Equal Employment Opportunity Commission to a woman dependent upon him for her livelihood and career), the judge refused to accept any senator's question about the text of his private life. He was as arrogant as he was vain and so contemptuous of what the commoners might have to say that he didn't condescend to listen to Professor Hill's testimony to the committee on Friday afternoon.

The judge's delusions of grandeur conformed to the specifications of his career as a loyal courtier pledged to the service of Republican money. For nearly twenty years he had kissed the rings of his patrons (Senator John Danforth, Ronald Reagan, Edwin Meese, George Bush, et al.), and he had become accomplished in the dance of grace and favor by which a man rises in the world not by reason of his merits but because of his connections.

The forced tone of his indignation followed from his long residence in the make-believe kingdoms of neoconservative rhetoric. Because he had never seen a lynching he could advertise himself as a victim of "high-tech lynching . . . destroyed . . . by a committee of the U.S. Senate rather than hung from a tree." Because he knew that if his accession to the Supreme Court failed he could return to lifelong tenure on the Federal Appeals Court and be comforted forever with the martyr's portion at the American Enterprise Institute, he could say that he had "died a thousand deaths" and would have "preferred an assassin's bullet to this kind of living hell." Pretending to know nothing of the art of political chicanery ("this sleaze, this dirt, this gossip") that had provided him with all his honors and all his offices, he could say to the Senate Judiciary Committee, "You are ruining the country."

On Friday morning he had the gall to present himself as a victim, a man who had been forced to endure the unspeakable agony of sitting comfortably in a chair for two weeks and being asked a series of facile questions to which he gave equally facile answers. He went on to say that "no job is worth what I've been through." Like much of the rest of his testimony, the statement was false. He wanted the job so badly that on Friday evening he returned to the witness table armed with the paint pots of racial hatred. Prior to the judge's evening testimony, nobody had smeared the proceedings with reference to anybody's color. Anita Hill was black and so was Judge Thomas, and the argument was about the abuse of power—about the humiliation that the master can inflict on the servant.

On Friday afternoon the executive producers directing Judge Thomas from the White House apparently told him that his confirmation was not yet certain, and they advised him to get busy with his paints and brushes. The judge did as he was told, and by nightfall he was talking to the television cameras about "bigoted, racial stereotypes . . . racial attitudes about black men and their views of sex" and so on.

His technique was that of a demagogue, and by the time he had given his third performance at the witness table it was abundantly clear that Judge Thomas was unfit to sit on the bench of a traffic court in Marina del Rey. He made the case against himself not on the evidence of what he said or didn't say to Anita Hill but on the proofs of his contempt for the entire apparatus of the American idea—for Congress, for the press, for freedom of expression, for the uses of democratic government, for any rules other than his own.

The Judiciary Committee did its best not to notice. The Republicans interpreted Judge Thomas's remarks as a patriotic variation on a theme by Lt Col Oliver North, and the Democrats were so intimidated that their chairman, Senator Biden, felt bound to apologize. "Please," he said, "I don't like this any better than you do, Judge."

The senator's embarrassment was as unctuous as his weasel's smile. Anita Hill was talking about sex, and Judge Thomas was talking about race, and where was it safe for a politician to hide? How was he going to get back to Delaware with all his votes intact?

He resolved the dilemma by substituting a legal question for the political question. If all the loose and possibly dangerous talk could be confined within the frame of a single inquiry (did Judge Thomas commit an act of sexual harassment against the person of Anita Hill ten years ago behind a closed door in a soundproof room?), and if the inquiry had the further advantage of being hopeless (for who except the judge and the professor could possibly know what happened ten years ago behind a closed door in a soundproof room?), then none of the Democrats on the committee would have to think for themselves, and all would be well.

The evasive maneuver allowed the Democrats on the committee to wait patiently for a miracle of divine revelation. Maybe somebody would come forward with proof that Anita Hill had spent five years in a mental institution in West Hollywood. Or maybe a messenger would arrive from Mt Olympus with documents showing that Clarence Thomas once toured the Italian Riviera with a pornographic dance troupe. Failing news of genuinely astonishing magnitude, the Democrats remained content with observations on the order of Howell Heflin's (D., Ala.) discovery that "one of them [Anita Hill or Clarence Thomas] is not telling the truth."

Once it was clear that the Democrats didn't wish to engage the political question, the Republicans had no trouble establishing the metaphor of a criminal trial. Here was a good man accused of a crime ten years after the fact by a woman who might be crazy (or lovelorn, or hostage to a feminist conspiracy, or the agent of a foreign power), and because this is America (land of the free and home of the brave), a man is innocent until proven guilty, and by God, we owe it to this fine jurist (this prince of righteousness who has endured the sufferings of Job) to grant him the benefit of the doubt. The metaphor carried without objection, and Judge Thomas's confirmation was assured well before the hearings ended and Chairman Biden waved his last, talk-show host's farewell.

The hearings provided the American people with John Adams's "most dreaded and envied kind of knowledge," but the news media didn't want any part of it, and they immediately took up the cause of suppression and denial. Senator John Danforth (R., Mo.), who sponsored Judge

Thomas's candidacy for the Supreme Court and who appeared throughout the weekend in the role of faithful shepherd, seldom managed to talk to reporters without giving the impression that he was on the verge of tears. On Sunday he stood in the rotunda of the Russell Senate Office Building and blamed the American democracy for Judge Thomas's ordeal. "This is a rotten system," he said, "rotten to the core." A similar tone of weeping moralism appeared almost simultaneously in the upper chambers of the press. As early as Saturday on the front page of the *New York Times*, R. W. Apple bemoaned the "lurid, gut-wrenching" scenes on Capitol Hill, and on Sunday, still appalled by "horrifying events" and "excruciating detail," he was suggesting that maybe the Congress should conduct its confirmations in secret, or at least come to some sort of prior arrangement with the White House about the kind of nominees who could be relied upon to refrain from embarrassing the children and the servants.

By noon Tuesday the figurative wringing of hands had become the wisdom in office. When I joined the company of the elect at lunch among the ferns on West Forty-sixth Street I noticed that I was the only journalist present who hadn't already appeared on a talk show to ask (*molto serioso* and while gloomily shaking the head) what was to become of a country in which louts, madwomen and irresponsible gossipmongers could foul the temple of government with the filth of self-interested lies. Somebody quoted Justice Thomas (or maybe it was George Bush, or David Broder, or John Danforth, or R. W. Apple) to the effect that the scenes on Capitol Hill were "intolerable . . . not the America we know."

But it was, of course, precisely the America we know. The America represented on the Senate Judiciary Committee is the America of the savings-and-loan swindle and the fraudulent defense contract, the America defaced by its crowded prisons and its wretched schools, the America that lies to itself about the wonderful prosperity certain to derive from an economic policy that places an intolerable burden on the weak, the old, the poor, the ignorant, the young and the sick. If we wish to give ourselves a decent chance to make an America that isn't as frightened or corrupt as the Senate Judiciary Committee, we will have to do the work in the honest light of day.

As Jefferson and Lincoln well knew (possibly because they were subjected to slanders far more vicious than those addressed to Clarence Thomas), the advancement of civilization is never a pretty sight. But we can't know what we're about, or whether we're telling ourselves too many lies, unless we can see and hear one another talk.

Great power constitutes its own argument, and it never has much trouble drumming up friends, applause, sympathetic exigesis and a band. But a democracy stands in need of as many questions as its citizens can ask of their own stupidity and fear. As many questions and as much light.

December 1991

CITY LIGHTS

Each person, withdrawn into himself, behaves
as though he is a stranger to the destiny of all the
others. His children and his good friends constitute
for him the whole of the human species. As for his
transactions with his fellow citizens, he may mix
among them, but he sees them not; he touches
them, but does not feel them; he exists only in
himself and for himself alone. And if on these
terms there remains in his mind a sense of family,
there no longer remains a sense of society.
—ALEXIS DE TOCQUEVILLE

*D*uring the first two weeks of May, I listened to a great many politicians worry about the scenes of urban apocalypse in South-Central Los Angeles, but the more often they mentioned "the crisis of the cities" or "the need for meaningful reform," the less convincing I found their expressions of concern. Most American politicians neither like nor trust the temperament of large cities, and their habitual animosity showed through the veneer of the speeches. They said what they were supposed to say—"healing the wounds of racial injustice," "a tragedy for us all," "human suffering," "rebuilding America's destiny"—and although many of them even went to the point of promising money— "enterprise zones," "relief funds," "bank loans"—it was clear that they would rather have been talking about something else. President George Bush appeared briefly in Los Angeles on 7 and 8 May, a week after rioting and fire had laid waste to roughly fifty square miles of the landscape, and his palpable uneasiness defined the tenor of the response from the leading manufacturers of the country's conscience and opinion. What he said wasn't much different from what everybody else said (compare the anguish in *Time* and *Newsweek*, Governor Bill Clinton's campaign statements, the anguish on *Nightline* and *Meet the Press*, Governor Pete Wilson's press conferences, the anguish of Dan Rather), but Mr Bush has a talent for embodying a falsity of feeling that lends itself to almost any solemn occasion, and his performance in Los Angeles admirably represented the attitudes of a social and political class that regards the city as its enemy. He arrived among the ruins of Vermont and Western Avenues at dawn on Thursday, riding in a heavily armed limousine under the protective escort of the Secret Service, the LAPD and the National Guard. His advisers allowed him to remain in the neighborhood for no longer than three hours in the early morning, before too many people were abroad in the streets, and his entourage had gone before most of the local residents knew that it had come. Walking through streets still sour with the smell of smoke, the president was obviously disturbed by what he saw of the wreckage, and his unscheduled remarks veered off in the direction of unfamiliar emotion. Speaking to a small congregation in a Baptist church, he said, "We are embarrassed by interracial violence and prejudice. We are ashamed. We should take nothing but sorrow out of all of that and do our level best to see that it's eliminated from the American dream."

Clearly the president was chastened by the sorrow and resentment of the people to whom he spoke, but his words were somehow tentative and contingent, as if they could be withdrawn on a month's notice. C-Span's television cameras followed him on his pilgrim's progress through the ashes of an urban slum, and as I watched him keep to his schedule of condolence I understood that it was a small drawing-room story about George Bush (his education, conduct and deportment), not a large and tragic story about a society that could inflict upon itself the despairing ruin of South-Central Los Angeles.

By Friday morning the president had recovered his optimisms and his sense of political proportion. He announced a gift of $19 million (for clinics and schools and the harrying of drug dealers) and he went to a hospital to visit a fireman severely wounded by gunfire on the first night of the rioting. Partially paralyzed and unable to speak, the fireman lay on his bed watching Mr Bush sign autographs and hand out tie pins. The president was cheerful but nervous, and in a moment of awkward silence he said to the fireman's wife, "This is fantastic. We're glad to be here. Absolutely."

To the wife of another fireman injured in the riots, the president, still trying to make polite conversation and meaning to show that he, too, was acquainted with grief, spoke of the heavy seas that had come last October to Kennebunkport: "I'm sorry Barbara's not here. She's out repairing what's left of our house. Damn storm knocked down four or five walls. She says it's coming along."

The American ruling and explaining classes tend to live in the suburbs, or in cities as indistinguishable from suburbs as West Los Angeles and the government preserves of Washington, DC, and their fear and suspicion of the urban landscape (as well as the urban turn of mind) would have been well understood by the gentlemen who founded the republic in Philadelphia in 1787. The idea of a great city has never occupied a comfortable place in the American imagination. Much of the country's political and literary history suggests that the city stands as a metaphor for depravity—the port of entry for things foreign and obnoxious, likely to pollute the pure streams of American innocence. Virtue proverbially resides in villages and small towns, and for at least two hundred years the rhetoric of urban reform has borrowed its images from the Bible and the visionary poets. Under the open sky (or a reasonable facsimile thereof) the faithful gather by the firelight to denounce the metropolitan sewers of crime and vice, and every now and then a knight errant—Jimmy Carter, Ralph Nader, Gary Hart, Ross Perot, et al.—rides off toward the dark horizon under the banners of redemption.

A similar bias informs the romantic spirit of American literature and provides the plots for popular melodrama. With remarkably few exceptions, the writers of genius decry the foul and pestilent air of the city and instead of staying in town to paint the portraits of society they wander off into the wilderness in search of spiritual salvation. Thoreau beside his pond, Melville in the vastness of the southern ocean, Hemingway off the coast of Cuba—all of them glad of their escape from the stench of commerce in Boston and New York.

The conventional hero of the western or detective story (sometimes known as John Wayne or Humphrey Bogart, at other times taking the alias of Gary Cooper, Clint Eastwood or Harrison Ford) rides into the dusty, wooden town and discovers evil in even the most rudimentary attempts at civilization. The hero appears as if he were a god come to punish the sin of pride and scourge the wicked with a terrible vengeance. After the requisite number of killings, the hero departs, leaving to mortal men and women (that is, wretched citizens) the tedious business of burial, marriage and settlement.

The movies and television series delight in showing the city as a killing ground. Predators of every known species (pimps, real estate speculators, drug addicts, prostitutes, dissolute prosecuting attorneys and venal police captains) roam the streets as if they were beasts drifting across the Serengeti plain. The successful protagonists learn to rely on their animal instincts. If they make the mistake of remaining human (trusting to the civilized virtues of tolerance and compassion), they die a fool's death in the first reel.

Given the preferred image of the city as godforsaken heath, it's not surprising that so many American cities come to look the way that the audience wants and expects them to look. The proofs of worldly ruin give credence to the theorems of transcendental grace. If American cities have the feeling of makeshift camps, littered with debris and inhabited, temporarily, by people on the way to someplace else, it is because we conceive of them as sulfurous pits in which to earn the fortune to pay for the country rose garden and the house with the view of the sea. The pilgrims come to perform heroic feats of acquisition and then to depart with the spoils to the comforts of Florida or the safety of Simi Valley.

To the extent that we measure the distance between the city and the suburbs as the distance between virtue and vice, we confuse metaphysics with geography and so imagine that blessedness is a property of the right address. During the Cuban Missile Crisis of 1962, in the early afternoon of the day on which the thermonuclear judgement was believed to be well on its way north from Havana, the city editor of the *New York Herald Tribune* sent me into Times Square to ask random citizens for opinions on their impending doom. Most of the respondents expressed a degree of anxiety appropriate to the circumstances, but I remember a woman from Lake Forest, Illinois who told me that I had addressed my question to the wrong person, and who smiled as agreeably as President Bush handing out tie pins in the Los Angeles hospital room. "I wish I could help you," she said, "but I don't live here, you see. I'm just visiting from out of town."

The spirit of the age is feudal, and the fear of the cities allies itself not only with the fear of crime and disease and black people but also with the fear of freedom. The energy of the city derives from its hope for the future, and the infinite forms of its possibility. The city offers its citizens a blank canvas on which to draw whatever portraits of themselves they have the wit and courage to imagine. Nobody asks them to constantly explain their purpose and they remain free to join the minorities of their own choosing. Among people whom they regard as their equals, who share the same passions for seventeenth-century religious painting or Edwardian licentiousness, they can come and go in whatever direction their spirit beckons. The freedom of the city is the freedom of expression and the freedom of the mind.

So precious are these freedoms that the citizens judge the city's squalor as a fair price for its promise. What suburban opinion deplores as unmitigated abomination—bad air, poverty, noise, crowds, crime, traffic, heavy taxes, exorbitant rents, cynical government—the citizen accepts as the cost of liberty. It is in the nature of great cities to be dangerous, just as it is the nature of the future to be dangerous. The complexity of life in the city engenders in the inhabitants an equivalent complexity of thought and a tone of mind that can make a joke of paradox and contradiction.

The ideal of the city as an expression of man's humanity to man never has enjoyed much of a constituency in the United States. The stones of Paris and London and Rome speak to the citizenry's high regard for the proofs of civilization. If it is possible to walk calmly through the streets of those cities late at night, it is not only because the government gladly spends money on public foundations but also because the other people in the streets take pride in their civility. Americans take pride in the building of roads and weapons systems as well as in their gifts for violence. We know how to mount expeditions—to the Persian Gulf or the California frontier or the moon—but we lack a talent for making cities.

The broad retreat to the suburbs over the last twenty or thirty years correlates to the fear of the future and the wish to make time stand still. The politics of the Nixon, Reagan and Bush administrations made manifest a San Diego realtor's dream of Heaven and defined the great, good American place as an exclusive country club. As the larger business corporations come to employ as many people as lived in Renaissance Florence, they acquire the character of fiefs and dukedoms, and by shifting their headquarters into landscapes luxurious with English lawns and avenues of trees, they signify the splendor of their superiority—both moral and financial—to the urban mob.

Whenever I read in the papers that yet another corporation has quit New York City for a country estate in Virginia or Connecticut, I think of the United States receding that much farther into the past. The company of the elect becomes too quickly and too easily estranged from the democratic argument. Already protected from chance and uncertainty by the walls of bureaucratic protocol, the ladies and gentlemen of executive rank become ever more fearful of strangers—of Al Sharpton and Puerto Rican Day parades as well as of rats, pestilence and crime—and their distrust of the city soon resembles the contempt so often and so smugly expressed by Vice President Quayle.

The fear is contagious, and as larger numbers of people come to perceive the city as a barren waste, the more profitable their disillusion becomes to dealers in guns and to the political factions that would destroy not only New York and Chicago but also the idea of the city. During the decade of the 1980s the federal government reduced by 60 percent the sum of money assigned to the nation's cities. Official Washington embraces the ethos of an expensive suburb, and the deductions embodied as a cultural prejudice as well as a political doctrine. The same bias shows up in the seminars conducted by professors of urban science who blandly announce—invariably with many smiling references to the wonders of modern telecommunications—that the United States no longer has need for large cities. From the point of view of civil servants and Baptist ministers, the revelation might be construed as good news, but not from the point of view of anybody still interested in freedom.

The hatred of cities is the fear of freedom. Freedom implies change, which implies friction, which implies unhappiness, which disturbs the nervous complacency of the admissions committee at the country club. Because the city promises so many changes and transformations (a good many of them probably dangerous or unhealthy), the act of decision presents itself as a burden instead of an opportunity. Confronted with the dilemma of making moral and existential choices, the friends of Vice President Quayle and Chief Justice Rehnquist seek to escape their confusion by declaring freedom the enemy of the state. They prefer the orderliness of the feudal countryside, where few strangers ever come to trouble the villagers with news of Trebizond and Cathay.

In the whole of the editorial autopsy conducted by the news media in the days following the Los Angeles riots, I never heard anybody say anything about the popular hatred of the freedoms of a great city. I know that the topic is not one that the political and intellectual authorities like to discuss, but without at least mentioning it in passing, the familiar indices of poverty and crime make little sense. Until we learn to value the idea of the city, we can expect to see the streets paved with anger instead of gold.

The more well-intentioned the reforms announced by the politicians and the more theatrical the anguish of *Newsweek* or Barbara Walters, the more clearly I could hear the voice of suburban triumph. The guests assembled on a lawn in Arlington or Kennebunkport nod and frown and piously confuse New York or Los Angeles with the Inferno imagined by Dante or Mel Gibson. A drift of smoke on the horizon confirms them in their best-loved suspicions and excuses their loathing for the multiplicity of both the human imagination and the human face.

July 1992

CAPTAIN MONEY

Thus much of this will make
Black white, foul fair, wrong right,
Base noble, old young, coward valiant.
. . . Why, this
Will lug your priests and servants from
   your sides
Pluck sick men's pillows from below their
   heads.
This yellow slave
Will knit and break religions, bless the
   accursed,
Make the hoar leprosy adored, place thieves
And give them title, knee and approbation
With senators on the bench. This is it
That makes the wappened widow wed
   again;
She whom the spital-house and ulcerous
   sores
Would cast the gorge at, this embalms
   and spices
To the April day again . . .
      —WILLIAM SHAKESPEARE
      TIMON OF ATHENS

*I*f H. Ross Perot were a poor man, or even a merely rich real estate developer blessed with a net worth of $100 million, his presidential ambitions would be seen and understood as comedy—a play by Molière or a movie with Chevy Chase. The newly minted plutocrat entertains delusions of grandeur, and the flatterers in his employ play court to his vanity: "Yes, my Captain, your wisdom is the wonder of the age." "You're right, my Prince, the cowboy hat is more democratic than the crown."

But H. Ross Perot commands assets in excess of $2.5 billion, and the miracle of his fortune preserves him from ridicule. So devout is the American worship of money that even the skeptics fall silent. They forget what they know about themselves and what they have observed in others; their reason fails them, as does their sense of the absurd, and before the majesty of Perot's balance sheet they prostrate themselves like slaves staring into Pharaoh's golden face.

The exit polls collected during the California primary elections in early June showed Perot enjoying extraordinary popular support when measured against both President George Bush and Governor Bill Clinton, and all the instruments of the media took up the theme of a mysterious descent by a god in a machine. How could such things be? Who could explain Perot's astonishing entrance onto the stage of the presidential campaign? Both in print and on television, every columnist and political analyst of any weight or consequence ran through the entire repertoire of solemn speculation—general disgust with the status quo, Bush's weakness, Clinton's irrelevance, end of the Cold War, wages of recession, collapse of a two-party system, hatred of Washington, triumph of television, era of new politics, democracy lost, democracy regained, and so on. But nobody remarked upon the exalted place of money in the American imagination, and the unanimous silence on the metaphysics of Perot's money—its divine radiance—answered all the questions about Perot's political triumph.

The commentators understood the joke implicit in the phrase "populist billionaire," but they discussed Perot's wealth only in its secular aspects—as the means with which to hire expensive political strategists and buy unlimited quantities of television time. What they neglected to mention was the spiritual meaning that Americans impart to the texts of money. Enthralled by the Dionysian beauty of cash, we blur the distinction between money as a commodity and money as visible proof of both grace and omnipotence. The blurring of the distinction persuades us to assign to money the powers that properly belong to the human spirit.

Ask any American what money means, and nine times in ten he or she will say that it is synonymous with freedom, that it opens the doors to feeling and experience, that citizens with enough money can play at being gods, do anything they wish—drive fast cars, charter four-masted sailing vessels, join a peasant rebellion, produce movies, endow museums, campaign for political office, hire an Indian sage, toy with the conglomeration of companies and drink the wine of orgy. No matter what their income, a depressing number of Americans believe that if only they had twice as much money, they would inherit the state of happiness promised them by the Declaration of Independence. At random intervals over a period of thirty years I have asked people of various means to name the combination of numbers that would unlock the vault to Paradise, putting the question to investment bankers and to poets supposedly content with metaphors, and the doubling principle holds as firm as the price of emeralds. The man who receives $15,000 a year is sure that he can relieve his anxiety if he had $30,000; the man with $1 million a year knows that all would be well if he had $2 million.

All respondents say that if only they could accumulate fortunes of sufficient sum and velocity, then they would ascend into the empyrean reflected in the best advertisements; if only they could quit the jobs they loathed, quit pandering to the company chairman (or the union boss, or the managing editor, or the director of sales); if only they didn't have to keep up appearances, to say what they didn't mean, to lie to themselves and their children; if only they didn't feel so small in the presence of money; then surely they would be free—free of their habitual melancholy, free to act and have, free to rise, like a space vehicle fired straight up from Cape Canaveral, into the thin and intoxicating atmospheres of gratified desire.

In a society that makes a god of wealth, the rich man can pretend to the airs and graces of a king. He can tell everybody else where and when to come or go, and he need never bend the courtier's knee to the pleasure of fools. By embodying the dream of unlimited wealth, Perot embodies the dream of perfect independence. The vision is immensely satisfying to people who cannot afford the luxury of doing as they please or saying what they think. The arts of obedience become both more galling and more refined as an always larger majority of the population finds itself dependent on the whim of a corporate or institutional overlord. In the first decade of the twentieth century roughly 40 percent of the American people were self-employed. For the most part they lived on small family farms and paid taxes that in the aggregate amounted to less than 5 percent of their annual income. By 1992 only 4 percent of the American people were self-employed. Mostly they lived in the cities and suburbs, paying taxes that in the aggregate amounted to 50 percent of their annual income.

The journalists who make their way to Perot's office in north Dallas all remark on the man's preternatural calm, and with a feeling akin to awe they gaze upon the smooth, uncluttered surface of his desk as if it were the still center of the turning world. Among a restless or disappointed people ceaselessly striving to become something else, the spectacle of a man content merely to be has a soothing effect. The man endowed with royal wealth presumably can afford the luxury of inner repose, and his exemption from existential doubt and common necessity might allow him to notice, possibly even to comfort and assist, people less fortunate than himself.

Properly understood, Perot inhabits the enchanted garden of celebrity and miracle portrayed in the supermarket tabloids—the realm of Elizabeth Taylor's marriages and the resurrection of Elvis Presley. Vast wealth is itself celebrity—a presence so luminous that the persons through whom it makes itself manifest serve merely as vessels for its glory. Perot entered the national political arena through the television analogues of the supermarket press—the Larry King show, *Donahue*, and so on—and he appeared as the figure of wealth incarnate, the revelation of the Godhead capriciously expressed in the person of an east Texas confidence man with an album of golden platitudes.

Had Perot not been worth $2.5 billion, he would have been seen as another salesman of economic self-help touring the circuit of the television talk shows in order to hustle his theories of financial redemption ($21.95 in hardcover; $9.95 in paperback; $27.50 for the videocassette), and his political views would have been understood for what they were—the commonplace axioms of a pretentious businessman prompted to play the part of statesman and sage. The role is a familiar one, and over a span of thirty years I've seen it performed by automobile manufacturers and presidents of oil companies as well as by authors of best-selling recipes and diets. It is the role of the newly arrived millionaire on the speaker's dais at the annual convention, of the season's wealthiest entrepreneur at the Friday morning executive seminar initiating the faithful into the mysteries of his management techniques and his vision of the next generation, the next century, the next millennium.

The audience invariably listens with an attentiveness precisely calibrated to the net worth of the man on the podium. Banality in the mouth of a failed businessman or an unpublished novelist sounds banal; in the mouth of David Rockefeller or Tom Clancy the same words acquire the weight of oracle. Similar protocols regulate the size and duration of the applause meted out at fund-raising dinners. Whether pledged to African orphans or victims of muscular dystrophy, $200,000 always gets a bigger hand than $50,000. On the announcement of sums in excess of $500,000, the audience customarily rises to its feet, the warmth of its ovation appropriate to the welcoming of a newly elected head of state or the return of a triumphant general.

If even a secular religion can be defined as those sets of attitudes that people take for granted, then it is by our unquestioning allegiance to the rule of money that as Americans we make good the proofs of our faith. The bottom line is the judgement of God. We find it impossible to conceive of a world in which money doesn't have the last word, and we construe the rich man as being both good and wise. The syllogism is idiocy, and would be understood as idiocy in any society other than our own, but it makes the market in celebrity.

Happily for Perot's presidential ambition, his fortune presents itself in the costume of the old American West. Had the money been eastern or inherited, or if Perot were the sort of man who was fond of limousines and Armani suits, his political views would seem as silly as the paid advertisements that Donald Trump used to place in the *New York Times* announcing his answers to the questions of the trade deficit or metropolitan crime. But Perot looks and sounds like a small-town druggist, jug-eared and homely, a common man who went west with the wagon trains and the banjo music and happened to come across a gold mine. Both in his voice and his person—as well as in his collection of the works of Frederic Remington and Norman Rockwell—Perot expresses the preferred image of the nineteenth-century western frontier.

If the American dream is about nothing else, it is about the victory of hope over experience, and on the way west—no matter how many children died, or how bad the weather, or how many animals were lost—the pioneers encouraged one another with the telling of the great story about their conquest of Paradise. They subscribed to the doctrine that hard work and true grit overcome all obstacles, that people who believe that nothing is impossible can sometimes succeed in accomplishing the impossible. Against the odds and in the teeth of the wind, they proved themselves a courageous and inventive people adept at the arts of improvisation. No matter what their provenance or point of origin, they held in common a talent for inventing myths and real estate promotions. They chose for their captains men who could organize and persuade, who knew how to get folks to do things together, who could rekindle the flickering candles of their belief with descriptions of an imaginary Eden on the far side of the sunset. What was wanted was a salesman and a booster, a good fellow with an easy smile and a fool optimism. The doctrine of the second chance carried with it the good news that the battle was never lost, and the promise of a new start in a new line of country glimmered on the horizon like the hope of tomorrow's rain.

The aura of myth and dream preserves Perot not only from ridicule but also from the standard assaults of a suspicious media. Every day for two weeks after Perot's putative victory in the California primary, the *New York Times* published an account of one or another of the ways in which Perot's record as duplicitous charlatan makes a mockery of his pose as savior of the republic. The paper was at considerable pains to describe Perot's fortune as the product of government subsidy, Perot as friend to venal politicians (most notably Richard Nixon and Jim Wright), Perot as conspiracy theorist believing the stories about the nonexistent American prisoners of war in Vietnam, Perot as real estate speculator hustling the Alliance Airport deal north of Fort Worth, Perot as autocrat eager to build prisons and dispatch the police to search, without cause or warrant, entire neighborhoods presumed to be harboring drugs.

None of the discoveries and revelations diminished the noncandidate's standing in the polls. Perot's image continued to float as blithely as a campaign balloon over the heads of mortal politicians doomed to answer the questions. Allegations deemed awkward or inconvenient Perot either flatly denied or dismissed as the impiety of the godless eastern media. He disarmed his critics with his homespun humor, referring to the directors of General Motors, with whom he once had unpleasant dealings, as "pet rocks" and saying of that company's standard of incompetence, "I never could understand why it takes six years to build a car when it only took four years to win World War II." Pressed to explain the discrepancy between his theory of law and order and the spirit of the Constitution, he said, "We can amend that dang Constitution if we have to," and on the question of the environmental summit meeting in Rio de Janeiro, he said, with similar insouciance, "I don't know a thing about it."

But no matter what Perot said or didn't say, his lack of hesitation between the thought and the word recruited new believers (among them Hollywood movie celebrities and Washington political mercenaries) to his peasants' crusade. Here at last was a man whose every statement wasn't prepared by a speechwriter or geared to an opinion poll, and Perot's apparent independence of mind—seemingly unfettered by any political debt or calculation—canceled the objections that might have been raised against the tone and substance of his remarks. The illusion of perfect freedom served the same purpose as the illusion of unlimited wealth commonly projected by the most artful salesman of fraudulent financial schemes. The swindler poses as a man of immense fortune, and the mark, no matter how well off, imagines that the man richer than himself stands that much nearer the Godhead. Early in the 1980s, at about the same time that Michael Milken was rigging the market in junk bonds, a California investment manager named J. David Dominelli, a.k.a. "Captain Money," borrowed a few thousand dollars to set up a Ponzi scheme in the basement of a Mexican restaurant in La Jolla. Within five years the scheme attracted $200 million, and Captain Money, like the sorcerer's apprentice, didn't know how to shut down the flow of cash. He bought everything he could think of—three jet aircraft, dozens of $100,000 sports cars, racehorses worth $650,000, ski condos in Colorado and beach property in Del Mar—but still the customers kept coming. The richer the captain seemed, the more desperately the suckers wanted to deal themselves into the catastrophe.

The history of the United States is synonymous with the dream of riches, but throughout most of our two hundred years as a republic we have managed to temper the furious energies of that dream with some sort of moral or spiritual restraint. Well before the American colonists declared their independence from Britain, they declared themselves of two minds about the purposes of their new Jerusalem. One faction thought that money was merely a commodity (as drab as wood or straw or cloth) and that the American experiment was about the discovery of a moral commonwealth. Another faction, equally idealistic, but not so pious, thought that money was a sacrament and that America was about the miracle of self-enrichment. The argument between these two temperaments runs like a theme for trumpet and drums through all the music of our history, literature and politics.

Although money always has occupied an exalted place in the American imagination, never in the history of the republic had that place been raised so high as in the years of the Reagan ascendancy. President Reagan's gaudy inauguration in 1981 cost $8 million and established the standards of conspicuous consumption characteristic of both his terms in office. By 1985 the new style had congealed into a tasteless opulence expressed in fur coats for Cabbage Patch Kids and advertising copy that read, "Feel gloriously rich," "Satisfy your passion for gold," "Rich is better." The dreams of avarice glittered in the shop windows of every American city large enough to support a market in German engineering and Italian silk, and the lists of best-selling books, both trade and mass market, attested to the public delight in the beauty and power of money: who has it, how to groom and cherish it, what to wear in its presence, where it likes to go in the summer.

The wonder of H. Ross Perot rises from the light-mindedness of an age eager to believe that it was possible to buy the future. Like Perot, Reagan projected an aura of imperturbable calm, and he taught the country that it wasn't necessary for a president to know anything about law, or foreign policy, or free speech, or trees, or black people, or whales. Government was a salesman's smile and a gift for phrase. Reagan's speechwriters understood that the more complicated the circumstances, the more desperate the wish for prophetic certainty and grand simplification.

Perot offers the same comforts, but with the difference that he translates the hope of freedom into the passive voice—freedom from instead of freedom to. The political analysts like to say that Perot has not defined his politics, that he has not articulated his position on the issues, that he stands before the electorate as a mystery and an enigma. Their profession of ignorance is disingenuous. Character is policy, and like other billionaires who have devoted their lives to the amassment of wealth, Perot doesn't have much use for any ideas that cannot be yoked to a government contract. Speaking to his talk-show hosts, he avoids mention of the word "liberty," and his rules of economic salvation could have easily been posted on the wall of a Bulgarian textile factory in 1953 by a committee of Communist commissars.

With surprisingly few exceptions, all of Perot's associates—former, current, commercial and political—testify to the authoritarian temper of his mind. One is either with him or against him; he lacks the patience for compromise; anybody who disagrees with him is either a fool or a knave. As president of EDS, the computer services company on which he founded his fortune, he imposed on the hired help codes of dress and deportment. When a Texas newspaper printed a story that Perot thought unflattering, he berated the publisher with the threat of blackmail.

The incidents add to the sum of a priggish and vindictive autocrat, a man who delights in his sobriquet of "the billionaire scoutmaster" and who clearly would prefer to conduct the affairs of government as if he were the warden of a prison or the abbot of a monastery. Though the media prefer not to recognize the portrait of so clownish a potentate (a figure on the order of Johnny Carson's Karnak the Magnificent), Perot's enthusiastic supporters readily welcome what they see and hear as the promise of benevolent despotism. His admirers wear T-shirts emblazoned with the motto ROSS FOR BOSS, and they recognize in Perot the efficient manager of a utopian real estate development in Arizona or southern California—the kind of walled town or private community likely to be named Sunset Estates or Rancho Paradiso. The dream of freedom embodied in Perot's fortune turns out to be the dream of escape from the storm of the world.

Like Marie Antoinette, Perot plays at the rituals of innocence. In the park at Versailles the French queen built a replica of a country farm and amused herself in the role of a simple milkmaid. Perot prefers the pose of the humble, plain-speaking democrat. His "electronic town hall" is a replica of democratic government, as artificial as Marie Antoinette's farm or a theme-park attraction called "Democracy-land." Stirred by feelings of nostalgia, and voting their fear instead of their courage, the residents of Rancho Paradiso presumably would be happy to visit the diorama, ride in the colonial horse carriages, listen to actors in eighteenth-century costume recite the speeches of Franklin and Jefferson. If only Captain Money will keep them safe from the passage of time (as well as from foreigners, bad news, existentialism, crime and contradiction), why not paint all the houses blue and trim all the rosebushes to the regulation height of two feet six inches? The pittance of a few civil rights or liberties is a small price to pay for a vigilant sheriff and a decent gardener.

In a society that was less afraid of the future, Perot's presidential ambitions would play as satire or farce. The strength of his showing in the public-opinion polls speaks to the retreat from democracy, not to its passionate reawakening or return. On the assumption that even despots have their benevolent afternoons, a democracy doesn't ask the question "Who is the best ruler?" It asks, instead, "Which ruler can do the least harm?" The mechanism of checks and balances places as many obstacles as possible in the way of the fears and passions of the moment, and by so doing it preserves the principle of freedom against the promise of miracles and the wish for kings.

August 1992

MUSIC MAN

Kings are for nations in their swaddling clothes.
—VICTOR HUGO

Anybody glancing at the television talk shows over the last four or five months would have been hard-pressed to escape the grinning presence of H. Ross Perot, the would-be captain of the American soul who promotes himself—to Larry King and Jay Leno and Charlie Rose and the folks at NBC news—as a political masterpiece. The performance is like that of the crow in Aesop's fable who thinks it can sing as sweetly as the nightingale, but it draws a crowd, and the crowd grows larger and more attentive as President Bill Clinton's approval ratings drift lower in the public-opinion polls. When not otherwise promised to a television host, Perot travels to Washington to teach the Congress the lessons of good government that he learned from his long and careful study of the works of Norman Rockwell. Again the spectacle is grotesque, but what is more grotesque is the deference of the politicians who applaud his screeching as if it were the wisdom of Jefferson or the music of Mozart.

Between late February and early May Perot testified before three congressional committees, and he invariably arrived with a claque of true believers who occupied the back rows of the hearing rooms and provided the silent veneration and spontaneous applause. Also invariably, Perot addressed the members of the committees as if they were schoolchildren arraigned on disciplinary charges before a headmaster determined to make them say their prayers and drink their milk. He established the pose in early March, for the benefit of a committee considering the possibility of congressional reform. Instead of addressing the questions at hand, Perot delivered his standard lecture about a corrupt government squandering the nation's treasure on idle luxuries and useless toys. Portraying the servants of that government (among them all the politicians present in the hearing room) as a crowd of spendthrift fools, he recited his familiar list of complaints about the deficit, foreign lobbyists, extravagant expense accounts, private gymnasiums, idiot welfare programs, cut-rate haircuts and preferred parking spaces at Washington's National Airport. He ended the lecture with a warning and a threat. If the members of Congress continued to misbehave and failed to heed his sound advice, then on election day the great, good American people would drive them from the temple. Perot knew that this was so because the great, good American people had appointed him their champion and surrogate, and they were not in a mood to tolerate any trifling with their affections. Grinning for the cameras, comforted by the murmuring of the true believers in the back row, delighting in the wonder of his own virtue, Perot said, "I urge you, on behalf of millions of ordinary people who are out there earning a living: Stand on principle. Don't compromise. You will have their support. I can guarantee you. I can deliver if I have to."

What was shocking about the remark was the servile acquiescence with which it was received. Nobody laughed in the man's face. Perot had dressed up the nakedness of his own ambition in the Halloween costume of the public-opinion polls, and he might as well have threatened to summon an army of hooded elves, or Caesar's legions, or the terrible wrath of Ramtha, the ancient warrior from the lost continent of Atlantis who speaks to

Shirley MacLaine, but nobody asked him why he wasn't wearing his Batman mask or his wizard's pointed hat. The politicians lacked the courage to laugh because, like President Clinton and the oracles of the Washington news media, they accepted the existence of what they called "the Perot vote" as if it were as real as Mexico and as lucky as a winning lottery ticket. If Perot could attract 19 million votes in last year's presidential election without bothering to declare himself a candidate, and if, four months later, his approval ratings stood at 51 percent (as opposed to 24 percent in September 1992), then clearly his voice was the voice of God. The polls were the polls, and what was the use of objection or dissent to people frightened of both the future and the electorate?

Senator William S. Cohen (R., Me.) expressed the presiding sentiment of the committee when he welcomed Perot, and Perot's contempt, with a flatterer's eager smile: "I walked in here from a meeting with the President, and there were as many people waiting to get in to see you as there had been waiting to see him. And I said 'Who won the election?'"

The question took the measure of the fear and trembling on Capitol Hill. During Perot's guest appearances before various committees, most of the politicians offered him easy cues in the manner of Larry or Charlie or Jay. The two politicians brave enough to ask rude questions— Representative Donald M. Payne (D., N.J.) and Senator Harry M. Reid (D., Nev.)—noticed that Perot drew his strength from the general loss of faith in the institutions of democratic government. The question, Payne said, is not "Whom does he help?" but rather "Whom does he hurt?" Reid said, "I've come to realize that people are afraid of Ross Perot."

But afraid of what? Perot is a charlatan, and the Perot vote represents no interest and no constituency. Like the Bermuda Triangle or the Land of Mordor, it is a fiction, an anthology of grievance or a reservoir of unspecific anger and resentment. Last November it mostly consisted of the disillusion with the purpose as well as the practice of politics, and as President Clinton continues to disavow his campaign promises (bowing or curtsying to almost any corporate lobbyist dressed in a loud voice and an expensive suit), it manifests itself as an inchoate feeling of nostalgia for a world of kings and queens and fairy tales.

During the last six months, I've listened to as many as forty people declare their belief in H. Ross Perot, but aside from their aversion to Bill Clinton and perhaps higher taxes, I can't imagine their agreeing with one another on any specific political theory, program, policy, issue, philosophy, plan or initiative. Unlike the people who comprised the vote for Governor

George Wallace in 1972, or the supporters of Theodore Roosevelt in 1912, they stand for nothing except their own unhappiness. Democracy is about consenting to lose an election, about the balancing of particular interests and the making of always imperfect compromises between specific constituencies, but Perot's admirers think democracy is a movie by Frank Capra.

Among their disparate company I've counted automobile salesmen, environmentalists, English professors, social engineers, monopolists, remittance men and friends of Ralph Nader. What they hold in common is an agenda of miscellaneous complaint. Everyone knows what he or she detests (most especially media spokespersons wearing dark suits and red ties), but hardly anyone knows how a caucus works or who paves the roads. On a Friday afternoon in April, over the course of two hours on a train, I met a young woman who said that she voted for Perot because President Clinton had betrayed Kirtland's warbler as well as the spotted owl, and an older man, retired and living in Naples, Florida, who said that he had reduced his interests to three—the Bible, the Social Register and his gun. At a wedding reception in New York City in early May, I ran across an angry gentleman in a tweed suit who jammed a forefinger into my chest while making repeated and emphatic points about Perot's strength, Perot's decisiveness, Perot's resolve, Perot's grit. Yes, he said, he had considered all the weak-kneed objections, but he was sick of politics, sick of feeling sorry for people who, when you really thought about it, got what they deserved. He didn't think it necessary to specify the tasks to which Perot's grit might be applied, but I was left with the impression that he wouldn't think it amiss if Perot began the work of reclamation by placing the members of Congress under house arrest or stringing them up by their thumbs. What was wanted was some strong authoritarian medicine to purge the country of its moral relativism (or its limousines, or its liberal media, or its grasping real-estate developers), and Perot clearly was the man to write the prescription.

I suspect that Perot's admirers value him at his true worth. His temperament is apparently that of a vindictive prig, a man who would prefer to conduct the affairs of government as if he were the abbot of a monastery or the warden of a prison. With surprisingly few exceptions, all of his associates—former, current, commercial and political—testify to his autocratic cast of mind. One is either for him or against him, and anybody who is against him is either a fool or a knave. Certainly he doesn't respond well to even the mildest criticism, and he engages in nominally democratic debate only when he has been assured the privilege of the last word. His pose as the country's candid friend—the honest man speaking truth to power—is so patently false that I'm surprised it doesn't turn rancid in the heat of the television lights. Perot is more accurately described, in G. K. Chesterton's phrase, as the "uncandid candid friend," the smiling and unctuous man who says, "I'm sorry to say we are ruined," but is not sorry at all. He doesn't love what he chastises. The love of country follows from the love of its freedoms, not from the pride in its armies or its gross domestic product. Perot loves his own picture of America, and like the latter-day Puritans who take it upon themselves to examine the citizenry for flaws in its blood, its urine and its speech, he makes no secret of his sanctimony and intolerance, of his wish to blame, punish and cast what he trusts will be the first of many stones.

The rising of Perot's image over the horizon of the news suggests that the traditional American political narrative has lost much of its force and most of its coherence. None of the contradictions in Perot's character—the avowed autocrat championing the cause of populist revolt, the humble and plain-spoken servant of the people asking, in effect, to be elected king—dissuades his admirers from the belief that he embodies the country's only hope of regeneration.

Perot picked up the scent of Clinton's weakness as early as February, when Clinton submitted his budget message to Perot's approval before presenting it to Congress. In March Lloyd Bentsen, the secretary of the treasury, made a pilgrimage to Dallas to ask Perot's blessing for the president's crusade against the deficit. Perot ignored the flattery and sharpened the edge of his sarcasm. Within a month of the inauguration he had returned to the talk shows, and to one of the television reporters in attendance he said, "My role is as a grain of sand to the oyster." He canvassed the country as the bringer of bad news, speaking to rapt audiences in California, Texas, Colorado, Florida, Maine, testifying before Congress, presenting two half-hour advertisements for himself on NBC (at a price of $500,000 each), and in answer to questions about the business of state, he relied on his gift for the caustic phrase:

On the North American Free Trade Agreement—"A worn-out inner tube."

Of the Clinton administration's attempt to stimulate the economy— "Like a faith healer who knows nothing about medicine trying to cure cancer with aspirin."

Of the United States Congress—"It's time to pick up a shovel and clean out the barn."

Of the White House advisers assigned to formulate an energy policy—"Poets, philosophers and bee-keepers."

Of the secrecy protecting Hillary Clinton's deliberations about health care—"This is not a nuclear bomb program."

The witticisms achieved their intended effect, and as the winter passed into spring, President Clinton worried as much about the Perot vote—its demography, average age, racial composition, throw weight and mystical significance—as he worried about his budget proposals and the war in Bosnia. In early April, speaking to the American Society of Newspaper Editors at Annapolis, in a tone of voice that was nearly that of a hurt and puzzled child, he was saying that 85 percent of his economic program was "what Ross Perot recommended in the campaign." Clinton didn't know how to placate or appease Perot, and his nervousness was unbecoming in a president. He looked too much like a toadying courtier and the impression hastened his descent in the public esteem.

By early May Clinton and Perot were exchanging insults in the newspapers (referring to each other as liars and rumormongers), and it had become embarrassingly clear that the gentlemen resembled rival talk-show hosts competing for the same audience. To the extent that authority is invested in persons instead of ideas or institutions, the politician stands on no platform other than the scaffolding of self-dramatization. The rule of love supplants the rule of law, and instead of addressing fellow citizens, the commoner who would be kind seeks to recruit fans.

If the media had wished to do so, they could have discredited Perot and the Perot vote as easily as they did the Branch Davidians or Oliver Stone. But the news media, like Perot, adopted the pose of the uncandid candid friend, and they preferred the melodrama of the wealthy scoutmaster at odds with the wayward son of the South. Perot as clown didn't sell papers, but Perot as Sir Lancelot sold in the markets of superstition to the same sort of people who read Rush Limbaugh and *Women Who Run with the Wolves*. The loss of distinction between who is real and what is fictitious sustains the market for movies on the order of Francis Ford Coppola's *The Godfather* (*Parts I–III*) and books in the manner of E. L. Doctorow's *Ragtime*, for the art of lip sync and the New Age dreams of a shaman's return from Atlantis. Perot commissions Ken Follett to write a heroic version of his life under the title *On Wings of Eagles*, and Gloria Steinem, always a bellwether of the going trend, aligns the passion for witchcraft with feminist political doctrine: "The healers and wise women of pagan times knew what they were doing when they made covens of thirteen witches—small enough so everyone could talk, large enough for diversity and an uneven number so decisions were not deadlocked."

The transformation of politics into soap opera makes nonsense of the sham distinctions between Democrat and Republican, liberal and conservative. Our political discourse becomes synonymous with advertising—a mob of images notable for the strict separation of cause and effect—and the inferior forms of credulity, on a par with astrology and fortune-telling, comprise the tailor's remnants of what was once a public debate. The less that people understand of what politicians do, the more urgent their desire to appoint politicians to the ranks of the immortals.

The founders of the American republic entertained few illusions about the perfection of human nature, but as an advance over the pagan belief in a pantheon of gods and heroes, they proposed the contervailing ideal of a civil government conducted by mere mortals. The proposition was as courageous as it was optimistic, but it doesn't meet the expectations of an age that worships celebrity and defines itself as the sum of its fears.

As the world comes to be seen as a more dangerous and complicated place than was dreamed of in the philosophy of Walt Disney, people become impatient with rulers in whom they all too easily can recognize weaknesses embarrassingly similar to their own. The news broadcasts swell with proofs of catastrophe—murder in the suburbs and riots in the cities, civil war in Bosnia and bankruptcy in Washington—and an anxious public yearns for the shows of omnipotence, not only on the part of its presidents but also from its scientists, its ball players, its divorce lawyers and its first-term congressmen. Because omnipotence doesn't exist in the state of nature, it must be manufactured, and the supply increases with the demand. The best-seller lists promise the miracles of rescue and deliverance (in the form of diets, exercise machines and manuals of spiritual recovery), and on the stage of the national political theater the cast of democratic magistrates gives way to a procession of miraculous mandarins offering prayers and sacrifices to the sun or the moon or the deficit. Some of them sing and dance, and some of them, like H. Ross Perot, draw diagrams and astonish Jay Leno with the great news that they also play drums.

July 1993

YELLOW BRICK ROAD

Not to know what happened before one was
born is always to be a child.
—CICERO

*I*n any new publishing season most of the books that touch on
the questions of the national well-being do little more than preach
the conventional sermons of doom—violent crime advancing
into the suburbs, no city street safe from riot or disease, the government
bankrupt, and the air thick with poisonous smoke. Few of the authors
allow the chance of humor or escape, but once they have furnished their
long and obligatory lists of statistics (about the sum of the federal debt or
the number of homicides in Brooklyn or Miami) they rest content with
what have become the ornamental cries of alarm, as harmless as Halloween
stories and as safe as short-term, tax-exempt bonds.

Against the familiar and best-selling trend, I had the good luck in
early September to come across a book that avoided the usual piety and
inspired me with the hope that all is not yet lost. The book, *Land of Desire*,
by William Leach, is a history of consumer capitalism in the United States
between 1880 and 1930, its conscious invention and immediate success,
the nature of its iconography, its early alliance with the banks and business
corporations, the zeal of its first promoters and its eventual subjugation of
the American mind. The book is a pleasure to read, not only because Leach
writes well but because he presents the culture of consumer capitalism as a
historical and time-bound phenomenon—a sequence of events like other
sequences of events, (the Cold War, say, or the ascendancy of the Caliphate
of Córdoba), and therefore possessed of a beginning, a middle and an end.

What is so heartening about Leach's book is its argument, entirely
persuasive, that consumptionism is made of a set of attitudes as artificial
and deliberately contrived as the movements of a mechanical bird. Prior to
1880 it did not exist in the forms that we now know it, and its corollary
behaviors and habits of mind cannot be mistaken for the laws of human
nature. The point is often and easily lost in the din of advertising that
composes the entire text of our modern American civilization, and for as
long as I can remember, but most especially over the last twenty years, I've
listened to nothing but contrary messages from the leading oracles of the
age. They might quarrel about matters of minor distinction between Karl
Marx and Henry Ford, but they all devoutly acknowledge the primacy of

consumptionism and inflate its operative values (pleasure, security, comfort, money the measure of all things) into general principles of existence—as immutable as the fixed stars, the multiplication tables or the sea. Nobody questions the assumption that money rules the world, and the voices on the political Left join with those on the political Right to sing the antiphonal hymn to Mammon. It is a matter not only of how people behave and to whom they show deference but also of what the society looks like and how it administers both its spiritual and temporal rewards. The language of commerce is the *lingua franca* that knits together all the voices of American pluralism, the one national vocabulary in which people express their worth and their meaning.

But it was not always so, and Leach locates the origin of the aesthetic of desire in a specific time and place. Leach begins his narrative with the appearance of the modern department store—Marshall Field's in Chicago, Siegel-Cooper's in New York, John Wanamaker's in Philadelphia—and he follows the rapidly improving art of merchandising through the evolution of the poster, the mailorder catalogue, the billboard, the advertising slogan and the display window. The spectacle is wonderful to behold, in no small part because so many of the strategies of enticement spring full-blown from the head of a capitalist Zeus, and because so little of the rhetoric has changed over the course of the last one hundred years. All the principal characters in Leach's tale speak and think in a language that would be immediately intelligible to any modern audience looking at magazine advertisements and television commercials. Here is L. Frank Baum, now chiefly known as the author of *The Wonderful Wizard of Oz* but who, in 1898, all but invented the art of window display, exhorting his fellow window trimmers to let the lamps and tin pots "come alive" as if they were figures on the stage, to "bring the goods out in a blaze of glory," and make them look like jewels. "Suggest possibilities of color and sumptuous display that would delight the heart of an oriental."

Here is Elbert Hubbard, who wrote what he called "publicity preachments" and edited a magazine entitled, appropriately, *The Philistine*, addressing a meeting of advertising men in 1911: "Everybody should advertise while they are alive. The man who does not advertise is a dead one, whether he knows it or not." Or Katherine Fisher, another of the earliest copywriters, saying in 1899 that the trick is to direct the popular mind into the mirrored galleries of limitless desires because "without imagination, no wants . . . without wants, no demand to have them supplied." Or, lastly and most tellingly, Simon Patten, the country's most influential economist at the turn of the century and the guiding spirit of the Wharton School of Economics, indignantly refuting the idea that "consumption of luxuries and the indulgence in them" is somehow inglorious, preaching the doctrine of "wish pulses and wish structures" that urge mankind forward into the great and liberating task of ceaseless spending.

Well before the advent of the First World War, the United States gives birth to what Leach calls "the brokering class," intermediaries of various kinds and descriptions (corporate lawyers and dealers in easy credit as well as art instructors, popular novelists and university professors) who fabricate, burnish and promote the retail merchant's dream of Heaven that we now accept as the authoritative and universal vision of the good life. Leach extends his observations across the whole canvas of American society, finding the lines of historical perspective not only in the beginnings of the toy and public-relations industries but also in John Wanamaker's staging of the Garden of Allah fashion show in New York in 1912, the Gimbel Brothers busily decorating their stores with paintings by Picasso and Cézanne, the founding of the Harvard Business School in 1908 on the premise that consumption was far more important than production.

Between 1880 and 1930 the land of desire replaces the older religious and political ideals that sustained the American people in the century before the Civil War—ideals that embodied the values of thrift, productive labor, the ownership of land, republican government, Christian poverty and plain speech—and within the span of two generations America becomes synonymous with the culture of acquisition and consumption, with the cult of the new and the belief that money is the alpha and omega of all human existence. It is a dismal story, and it was understood as such as early as 1902 by William James, who remarked on the appearance of the consumer society in *The Varieties of Religious Experience*: "We have lost the power even of imagining what the ancient idealization of poverty could have meant: the liberation from material attachments, the unbribed soul."

I read Leach's book in conjunction with September's news from New York and Washington about the country's present economic miseries, and it was impossible to ignore the syllogism connecting Baum's *obiter dicta* about decorating display windows (Use the best art to "arouse in the observer the cupidity and longing to possess the goods") to a spendthrift society gone rotten with a surfeit of sales promotions. The sum of the national debt and the grotesque maldistribution of the nation's wealth reflect the monetization of political thought and the commercialization of the moral imagination. It isn't the political system that has failed the United States over the last fifty years but rather the ideas that buttress and undergird that political system. Or, as one of President Clinton's advisers might someday have the wit to say, "No, its *not* the economy, stupid," it's the imbecile belief that government is another word for a department store and that money in sufficient quantities can redress the balance of the world's grief, water the deserts of the earth and bring forth in the bright sunshine of finance capitalism a race of happy and satisfied customers.

Over the last half century we have invested a stupendous fortune in our belief that we can buy the future, but what has been the result? If money were the answer to all our prayers, by now, surely, we might have expected to see some proof of its glory. But Dorothy's yellow brick road leads nowhere except into bankruptcy, or possibly onto the stage of a musical comedy by Rodgers and Hammerstein, and in the aftermath of Ronald Reagan's performance as the Wizard of Oz the once infinite promise of the consumer culture begins to look faded and old. If even the largest corporations (among them IBM, Procter & Gamble, General Motors and AT&T) cast off hundreds of thousands of workers as if they were used paper cups, what becomes of the horde of eager customers still solvent enough to buy up the inventories of the nation's goods? Consumptionism assumes the ceaseless gratification of the ceaselessly expanding desire diffused throughout the population, but what happens to the Emerald City of Oz when the population no longer can afford to buy all the toys and balloons?

Despite the persistent casualty reports along the whole line of the economic front, I have yet to meet anybody who seriously believes that the Clinton administration can make good on its promises of economic deliverance, and last summer I noticed that a good many of the people writing letters to *Harper's Magazine* understood that the time had come to talk about something other than yesterday's sales promotion or tomorrow's dance band. As opposed to the professional journalists who write for the large media syndicates, and who therefore must compose the advertisements for reality (in the manner of Messrs Wanamaker, Gimbel and Baum), the magazine's readers don't labor under the same constraint, and a letter from John L. Chapman in Camarillo, California, expressed the general tone and sense of the correspondence: "Why do we not see the gross incongruity of a world that A) cannot stop hunger but B) depends so heavily on a system demanding constant consumption—not only of food but automobiles, beer, houses, VCR's, and whole universes of gadgetry and questionable services."

Answering his own question and foretelling the extinction of America's business civilization, Chapman went on to argue, I think correctly, that the events of the last fifty years have shown our belief in money to be a superstition as pathetic and outworn as an ancient Egyptian's trust in Osiris. If the condition of the biosphere is even half as precarious as the environmentalists suggest, then the twenty-first century must, of necessity, abandon the theory of value so lovingly displayed in the windows of Bloomingdale's. The capitalist ethic lacks the intellectual and moral capital necessary for the preservation of the world's oceans and atmospheres. If there is a profit to be made by poisoning a river or burning a forest, and if profit is a manifestation of the divine, then how does the believing capitalist condemn either practice without committing blasphemy? The question allows for one of two answers—the poor fool either sacrifices his life on a pyre of Excelsior, or he looks for a new religion.

The loss of faith in Simon Patten's "chemistry of wishes" shows up throughout the whole of the society, not only in the letters to *Harper's Magazine* but also in every afternoon's television confession to Oprah or Sally or Phil, among the legion of recruits to one or another of the recovery movements and in Hillary Rodham Clinton's search for "a politics of meaning." Not surprisingly, human beings don't care to define themselves as servo-mechanisms tagged with the prices they bring in somebody else's auction. As an idea or a habit of mind, the consumptionist mystery no longer inspires hope in the future, but as yet we haven't found the words in which to express our presentiment of a new order of value. Among all the urgent tasks of the next ten years, probably the most urgent is the revision of our notions of profit and loss. At the moment we are all Marxists, still enthralled by the doctrines of economic determinism and the Dionysian beauty of the cash nexus, and two hundred years from now the historians will write about our solemn rituals of getting and spending as if we were children worshipping stones. By way of seeing our predicament in a historical perspective, we would do well to reread the writers Leach mentions at the end of his book, among them William and Henry James, Elizabeth Flynn, Thorstein Veblen and Henry George. Although contemporaries of Baum and Patten and Hubbard, they spoke on behalf of the older American traditions, and their voices were the voices of dissent. They recognized the land of desire as another fraudulent real estate speculation (not unlike so many of the swindling land deals that accompanied the closing of the American frontier), and against the enticements of the Emerald City they argued for a more spacious vision of what it meant to be human. Knowing that the good was not in "the goods," that goodness inheres in men, not things, they understood that the goal of life cannot be a continuous improvement of material conditions because as the conditions become better, the people become worse.

Looking through the plate-glass windows of a new department store on lower Fifth Avenue in 1904, Henry James knew that he beheld the tyranny of commercial empire. He saw the windows as "invidious presences" meant to bring in money, "and was not money the only thing a self-respecting structure could be thought of as bringing in?" Edna Ferber was similarly appalled when she looked into one of the new business windows in Chicago in the winter of 1911. "It is a work of art that window," she said, "a breeder of anarchism, a destroyer of contentment, a second feast of Tantalus." Henry George began his treatise on political economy by observing that the bulk of life is spirit, not matter. Place on one side of the scale the collective energies of the human mind—the immense and restless mass of perception, feeling, imagination and idea—and no matter what one places on the other side of the scale—the nuclear arsenal, the island of Manhattan, $4 trillion in dimes—the balance tips toward the weight of spirit.

November 1993

MORTE DE NIXON

A frivolous society can acquire dramatic significance
only through what its frivolity destroys.
—EDITH WHARTON

When Richard Nixon resigned the office of the presidency twenty years ago this summer, I thought it possible that in his own peculiar and crooked way he might have done his countrymen an honest service. It wasn't the one that he had in mind, and honesty was never a trait for which he had much liking or use, but by so conspicuously attempting to suborn the Constitution and betray every known principle of representative government, he had allowed the American people to see what could become of their democracy in the hands of a thoroughly corrupt politician bent upon seizing the prize of absolute power. The civics lesson was conducted in plain sight over a period of eighteen months on network television and memorably illustrated by the singular ugliness of Nixon's character. The more obvious aspects of that character (its hypocrisy and self-pitying rage) had been made, as he so often said, "perfectly clear" during his prior years in public office, but the congressional hearings preliminary to his certain impeachment showed that he was also vindictive, foulmouthed and determined to replace the rule of law with corporate despotism. Nixon's distrust of any and all forms of free speech was consistent with his ambition to shape the government of the United States in his own resentful image, and when he left for the beach at San Clemente, as grudgingly as a dog giving up its bone, I remember watching his helicopter rise for the last time from the White House lawn and thinking that his fellow citizens wouldn't soon forget the constitutional moral of the tale.

The assumption was mistaken. When Nixon died on 22 April in New York City, at the age of eighty-one, the national news media pronounced him a great American and told the story of his life as sentimental melodrama. The assembled dignitaries on the weekend television shows solemnly mourned the passing of a benevolent sage, a figure of "historic proportions" and "towering size," who had weathered the storms of obloquy and defeat and so proved the theorem of an American success. The Sunday newspaper sermons reiterated the theme of redemption, and William Safire, the *New York Times* columnist who had once served as Nixon's speechwriter, provided the middle A to which the rest of the media orchestra tuned their instruments: "Richard Nixon . . . proved there is no political wrongdoing so scandalous that it cannot be expiated by years of useful service; no humiliation so painful that it cannot be overcome by decades of selfless sagacity . . . "

The sentence deliberately shifts the weight of judgement from the public to the private man, from the realm of law (in which magistrates uphold sworn oaths) to the realm of conscience (in which citizens answer only to their good intentions and their aerobics instructors), from the political forum to *Oprah*. The choir of sound opinion hummed the requiem in an arrangement by Lawrence Welk: "An Indomitable Man, An Incurable Loneliness"—the *New York Times*; "He would have been a great, great man had somebody loved him"—Hugh Sidey; "Figure of gentle pathos . . . impossible not to feel, simply, sorry for him"—*The New Yorker*; "So much kin to the rest of us that I never felt the faintest impulse to apologize for liking him"—Murray Kempton; "Inspired and inflamed the American imagination for half a century . . . a giant, right up there with Citizen Kane and Moby Dick"—the *New York Times*.

Stray voices of dissent appeared in *The Nation* and *The New Republic*, but for the most part nobody addressing a large audience said more than a few polite words about the Vietnam War or the deceased's manifest contempt for the American people. The prominent eulogists spoke of Nixon's "triumph over adversity," not of the numberless dead in Indochina; of Nixon as "the comeback kid," not of the damage he had inflicted on the nation's political culture; of Nixon's youth and early sorrows, his loneliness, his "vulnerable awkwardness" and "longing for respect." All present agreed that what Nixon had done he had done for the most American of reasons —because, as he himself once said to somebody who asked him why he told so many lies, "I had to win. That's the thing you don't understand. The important thing is to win." Unable to contradict so patriotic a truism (offered by one of the news magazines as a further proof of the former president's subtle grasp of world affairs), the eulogists absolved Nixon of his sins and pardoned his crimes because he had worked so hard to commit them, thus demonstrating, in another of Safire's sophisms, "a gutsy engagement with life."

The flattering sentiment accompanied Nixon's body west to California, and on the Tuesday that it was brought to Yorba Linda the dispatch in the *New York Times* began with a flourish of Shakespearean trumpets and drums: "In a scene worthy of 'King Lear,' the usually sunny California sky unleashed thunder, lightning, rain and hail today as Richard M. Nixon's body returned to his birthplace in a plain wooden coffin covered by a flag." At the burial service on Wednesday afternoon the illusion of grandeur was somewhat more difficult to sustain, possibly because so many of the well-manicured mourners at the grave resembled the guests at a Mafia funeral, but a military band played "Victory at Sea," the tune that comforted Nixon during his last paranoid months in the White House in the summer of 1974, and the speeches expressed the proper sense of pious grief. Henry Kissinger, on the verge of tears, praised Nixon for his "visionary dream" of a new world order intended "to give new hope to mankind"; Senator Robert Dole, also in tears, proclaimed the second half of the twentieth century "The Age of Nixon" and said that "in the end what matters is that you have always lived life to the hilt"; President Clinton, who, at a banquet the previous Saturday in Washington, had said of Nixon that "he taught me what it means to be an American," observed that the dearly departed would have enjoyed the proceedings and approved the subsequent press releases.

The service ended with the playing of "The Battle Hymn of the Republic" and "America the Beautiful," and as a bugler played taps and a flight of air force planes passed overhead in the missing-man formation, I wondered what had become of our historical memory and why so many people were so eager to award Richard Nixon the headline of an apotheosis. Even in the best of times Nixon's performance in the national political theater tottered precariously close to the comic and grotesque. Look at him askew or in an odd light, and it was always frighteningly easy to mistake him for an old vaudevillian who had stumbled into a production of *Macbeth*, an inspired clown traipsing around the stage declaiming stately gibberish.

I could understand President Clinton wishing to divert the media's attention from his own misdemeanors by so charitably overlooking Nixon's felonies; I could understand Kissinger justifying a failed foreign policy that was, in point of fact, his own; I could understand Dole wanting to present himself, in time for the next Republican National Convention, as a man of the people; and I could understand a reluctance on the part of the ladies and gentlemen of the fourth estate to admit that they spend their time dressing up thugs and mountebanks in costumes signifying high and noble deaths. But even when taken all together, the several specific motives and agendas don't account for the grace bestowed on so wooden and paltry a politician as Richard Nixon, and I suspect that his translation into a statue follows from our common wish to declare, now and forever, world without end, our collective innocence. If Nixon is innocent, we are all innocent; if Nixon can murder nearly 1 million people in Indochina (among them 21,000 American kids) to no purpose other than his own self-aggrandizement, then who among us cannot cheat our children, or falsify our tax returns, or swindle the customers, bribe the judge and abandon the girl. Forgive Nixon and we forgive ourselves. Why else go to the trouble of transforming the lying congressman and the disgraced president into the elder statesman and wise diplomat remarkable for his telling of geopolitical truths?

Certainly it was a metamorphosis accomplished against long and heavy odds. Nixon's incompetence as a president shows up on almost every page of the published record, and a close reading of the small print suggests that his gifts as a statesman can best be compared to John Grisham's genius as a novelist or Madonna's talent for dancing. It's true that as president, Nixon pursued the opening to China, which, given the circumstances, was a feat of diplomacy comparable to conceding the existence of the Pacific Ocean, and it's also true that most of the time he knew which telephones to tap, but with respect to the more difficult questions confronting his administration (most especially the ones in Indochina), Nixon was consistently and pitiably wrong. He believed in the chimera of the domino theory, and he thought that the United States could win the Vietnam War if only the air force dropped another twelve tons of explosives on another four peasants. He was wrong about the effects of the secret bombing and the subsequent invasion of Cambodia—the North Vietnamese sanctuaries that he meant to destroy didn't exist. At the end he was even wrong about the character of the American people. Thinking that they would applaud his cleverness and what he was pleased to imagine as his striking resemblance to both Teddy Roosevelt and Charles de Gaulle, he never understood why so many college students hated the sound of his voice.

Nor did Nixon's record on domestic affairs provide the iconographers with many proofs of "historic proportions" and "towering size." As ignorant as Kissinger about the economic consequences of his foreign policies and indifferent to the concerns of the American electorate, Nixon (again for reasons having solely to do with his own reelection) set in motion a corrosive inflation as well as a divisive racial politics from which the country has yet to recover.

The publicists also encountered various technical difficulties washing the laundry of Nixon's gangsterism. Whenever possible he substituted palace intrigues for candid debate, and the standard biographies suggest that he felt freely at ease only in the company of his own toadying courtiers or in the presence of military despots like Ferdinand Marcos and the Shah of Iran, and I think it probable that he envied the Soviets their freedom of criminal maneuver.

He was constantly scribbling furious directives in the margins of the daily press summaries, instructing his henchmen to rid him of enemies both real and imagined. His verbs were always violent—"Get someone to hit him," "Fire him," "Freeze him," "Cut him," "Knock him down," "Dump him." His hatred of free speech was apparent in his every gesture and expression, and when confronted with an obstacle to his will, he invariably exhibited the autocrat's instinct to coerce, break in, lie and suppress. On one of the tape recordings impounded by the Watergate investigation, Nixon speaks to Chuck Colson about the great task of chastising the legion of his enemies in a voice hard to reconcile with the image of the benevolent sage: "One day we will get them . . . Get them on the floor and step on them, crush them, show no mercy. And we'll stick our heels in, step on them hard and twist . . . right, Chuck, right?"

Although by the summer of 1987 the standard iconographies routinely mentioned Nixon's "brilliant" intellect and "enigmatic" character, neither adjective is easy to align with the noun. As Nixon's national security adviser, Kissinger used to make fun of Nixon's "meatball mind." He often telephoned his more sardonic confederates to read aloud from the president's memoranda, laughing at the pomposity of the language that glossed over the threadbare emptiness of the thought. Nixon's several books extend and annotate the joke. The writing is poor, the arguments trite, the author's voice as sententious as that of a latter-day Polonius. Fond of belaboring the obvious and very pleased with himself in his wizard's hat, Nixon is forever telling his readers that the Russians cannot be trusted, that a surprising number of people exist in a state of poverty and that war isn't a game of Parcheesi.

Nor does the record show Nixon among the more complex, let alone enigmatic, figures appearing on the American political stage over the last thirty-odd years. Although he was unstable, he was also tiresomely predictable. His principal biographers unanimously attest to the rigidity of his character and its uncanny lack of development; even his mother said of him, "I never knew a person to change so little." Loyal only to his invincible selfishness, Nixon in any and all circumstances could be counted upon to adhere to three inflexible rules of procedure: (1) To tell the expedient and self-serving lie, (2) To ask only one important question of the other people at the table ("What's in it for Richard Nixon?"), (3) To unctuously proclaim his own innocence.

Bryce Harlow, another of Nixon's counselors, once compared him to "a cork . . . push him down and he pops right back up." Precisely like a cork or a mechanical toy, Nixon is forever saying, "I am not a crook," or "When the President does it, that means it is not illegal," and because it always turns out that he is a crook (or a liar, or a shill, or a cheat) the story is never very interesting. Neither are the adventures of a cork.

Corks, however, possess the virtue of predictably rising and falling like the caricatures made for afternoon soap opera, forever scaling the battlements of melodrama and falling back into the moat of bathos, and it was in his capacity as an actor temporarily on loan from *As the World Turns* that Nixon served the purposes of the mass media. Reassuringly incapable of further development, he never failed to come up with the *cliché juste* (about his wife's "respectable Republican cloth coat" or "the little cocker spaniel dog, Checkers"), and he was always there, as he once famously said, "to kick around" like a cheap toy or a stuffed bear.

Like most everything else made by and for the mass media, Nixon was a collaboration, a product of the corporate imagination in the manner of a Broadway musical, a Hollywood action film or the CBS evening news. He was cast as the suspect wanted for the murder of everyone's brightest hopes and best instincts, and the caricature was so broadly drawn that it could absorb or blot out very high quotients of guilt, fear and self-loathing. Diverted by the melodrama of Richard M. Nixon, the lonely urchin from Whittier, California, who found fame and fortune in the nation's capital (found it and lost it and then found it again), we could forget what it was that he did—forget what was at risk in the Watergate conspiracies and Indochina, forget how many people died. The bias of the mass media favors the personal over the impersonal, the actor over the act, and the caricature of Nixon allowed us to preserve the innocence of the American dream by transforming a bleak and terrible tragedy into primetime situation comedy.

As is the habit of actors, Nixon brooded over the worth and beauty of his image in the press, often peering through the newspapers for two and three hours at a time, and when I listened to Washington reporters talk about his obsessive marking up of their copy I thought of the mechanical toy reading the label on its box, trying to figure out what it was that the manufacturers had in mind. I'm not sure that he ever fully understood the instructions, which possibly explains why he so often mistook his own character or felt compelled, especially in his later years, to speak of himself in the third person. Prior to his first meeting with Russian Premier Leonid Brezhnev in the spring of 1972, Nixon directed Kissinger, who proceeded him to Moscow, to announce him as a man who was "direct, honest, strong." He was, in fact, devious, dishonest and weak, but Kissinger at the time was still wearing the White House livery and let the remark pass without amendment. On the eve of another of his departures to Moscow, Nixon compared himself both with Dwight Eisenhower on the morning of D-day and with William the Conqueror on the afternoon prior to the Norman invasion of England in the eleventh century.

Among the reported sightings of Nixon impersonating a public statue, the most recent appeared in *The New Yorker* on 9 May, in Michael Korda's breathlessly admiring account of an August 1989 dinner party at Nixon's house in Saddle River, New Jersey. Nixon always liked to conduct impromptu seminars on the topics of geography and world history, and while the brandy was being handed around, he took it into his head to enlighten and improve two Chinese diplomats recently arrived from Beijing. Meaning for his words to be carried grandly back to China (as if they were emeralds on a velvet cushion), Nixon, speaking very slowly, very solemnly, said, "When Nixon was President and Leader of the Free World, he found that *firmness paid*. You tell them that." Somewhat later in the evening, while showing his guests around the house, he opened the door to his study and announced, "This is where Nixon works." "This is the desk at which Nixon wrote all his books."

The next question, "Who wrote Nixon?" Korda was too polite to ask, but if I had to answer it, I would guess that we all wrote Nixon. Even citizens as nominally liberal as Tom Wicker and Murray Kempton found in the caricature the hope of redemption. Wicker's biography of Nixon, *One of Us*, derives its melancholy and elegiac tone from the author's sense of his own failures, and Kempton, writing his maudlin farewell on the occasion of Nixon's death, said, "His sheer vulnerability so fills the memory as to expel all musings about his place in history." No wonder the media were so loud with lamentation. So many of us have so much for which we wish to be forgiven that I wouldn't be surprised if in the not-too-distant future President Clinton suggests naming a national holiday in Nixon's honor.

July 1994

DEVOUT OBSERVANCES

The world is not a prison house, but a kind of spiritual
kindergarten where millions of bewildered infants are
trying to spell God with the wrong blocks.
—EDWIN ARLINGTON ROBINSON

*T*en years ago the foreign journalists passing through New York City wanted to talk about America's weapons, the subtlety of their engineering and the certainty of their moral purpose, their extravagant cost and likely destinations. Now the correspondents ask about America's hospital bills—about the medical-industrial complex instead of the military-industrial complex—and during the second week in August I met with more or less the same set of questions from a British magazine editor, a French social critic and a Japanese television producer. They had been following the progress of the health-care reforms promoted by President and Mrs Clinton as well as by five committees in Congress, but although they had a fairly clear sense of the political and financial arguments at hand, they were baffled by the surrealism of the conversation.

Under what Alice in Wonderland rule of illogic did the Americans spend so much money on the care and protection of their health (nearly $1 trillion in 1993) and yet, simultaneously and with no apparent sense of contradiction, so recklessly indulge their passions for alcohol, chocolate, tobacco and criminal violence? If they meant what they said about the failures of their health-care system, then why didn't they amend the behaviors that sent so many of them to the emergency wards? The United States possessed the world's finest collection of CAT scanners and artificial hearts, but every day fourteen American children were killed by gunfire, and the ratio between the country's shelters for battered women and its shelters for stray animals stood at three to one in favour of the animals. Had the Americans no notion of cause and effect? Did they imagine that their Constitution, or their American dream, or their genius for tinkering with machines, held them harmless against the laws of nature? Why was nobody saying that death admits of no known cures, or that there isn't enough money in the world, let alone in the treasury of the United States, to guarantee every man, woman and child in America the inalienable right to long life, perfect eyesight and freedom from suffering?

Long ago in the days of the evil Soviet empire and the once-urgent questions about the prospect of World War III, I learned that the grand designs of American policy invariably resist a too-literal-minded reading of the text. I never could explain to the gentleman from *Le Monde* the sublime romanticism in the Strategic Defense Initiative (a.k.a. Star Wars) because I couldn't get across the point that the technology on which it presumably was based not only didn't exist but was impossible to construct, that if the system were to serve the magical purpose that President Reagan assigned to it, the air force would need to lift into orbit a space platform roughly the size and weight of the state of New Jersey. President Clinton's prescription for universal health care belongs to the same order of imaginary numbers as President Reagan's remedy against universal nuclear annihilation, and if the foreign journalists were having trouble with the metaphysics it was because few of them grasp the doctrine of American exceptionalism, and they fail to appreciate the degree to which we construe physical well-being as the most perfect of earthly goods. We now spend more money on health than we spend on any other service or commodity in the inventory of human happiness—more than we spend on cosmetics, or cocaine, or weapons deemed invincible—and for the promise of immortality, even a false promise made by an itinerant quack or an unlicensed saint, we will gladly pay the price of bankruptcy.

What we have made of the health-care debate over the last two years offers a specific proof of the general proposition. For nearly the whole of President Clinton's term in office the political and administrative classes have kept up a constant hum of words about the need to revise the country's diplomatic relations with death, but after God knows how many hours of talk and how many pages of print, what has anybody said? A great deal about the protocols of the treaty and little or nothing about its substance. Rather than address the hard questions—the ones about why the rich enjoy a comfort of doctors unknown to the poor or how to organize the inevitable rationing of medical care in a way that won't be perceived as both cruel and unjust—we discuss, without interruption and at interminable length, the progress of this or that bill through the reception rooms on Capitol Hill, President Clinton's standing in the opinion polls, the guile of the insurance companies, the bureaucratic tissue of this or that HMO, the proliferation of high-priced lobbyists, the cost of television commercials meant to frighten Democratic congressmen or pensioners over the age of fifty, the conspiracies of druggists. We might as well have been arguing about the number of angels that can dance on the head of a pin.

The most expensive debates in any age resolve themselves into the question "Why do I have to die?" Even as recently as 1945, the question still could be addressed in the United States by poets and clergymen. The events of the last half-century remanded the question to the politicians, who know the whereabouts of the nuclear weapons, and to the scientists, who perhaps will discover the wells of eternal youth. The aura of divine radiance shifted its locus from cathedrals to research laboratories, from theaters and concert halls to atomic accelerators and hospital operating rooms. The pilgrims of the thirteenth century delighted in the wonder of stained glass and saw the reflection of divinity in the rose window at Chartres Cathedral. The patients of the late twentieth century look for the face of God in the smooth surfaces of a computerized axial tomography scanner.

The American hospital-going public now asks of its medical advisers what medieval Christendom asked of its priests and saints—the remission of sins (of the flesh if not the spirit) and the hope of everlasting life—and we approach the topic of our individual health. Alone on the physician's examining table, or assembled as a constituency in the consulting rooms of the public policy debate (as the audience listening to Ira Magaziner or Senator Orrin Hatch juggle contradictory sets of meaningless statistics on CNN), we await the coming of miracles. In the meantime we prefer to know as little as possible about the precise terms of our own mortality, about the ebb and flow of our bodily fluids or the "health product procurement procedures" that supposedly will take effect in the year 2002—in the promised land known to the politicians as "the out years," when all the deserts bloom and there is always enough money to pave the streets with gold.

The acronyms and the technical jargon inoculate us against the virus of doubt, and we remain grateful for the benedictions pronounced in the language of chemical compounds, reassured by Hillary Rodham Clinton's synod of nearly 500 registered experts that met in secret to write some 1,300 pages of an unintelligible prescription. The tenets of faith overrule the objections of experience, and as practiced by its physicians and encountered by its patients, American medicine is best understood as a quasireligious ritual that satisfies both the native trust in technology and the native worship of money. Wonders come to pass at sufficiently regular intervals to justify the heavy tithes imposed on the faithful by the insurance companies (the modern equivalent of the old ecclesiastical bureaucracies) and to sustain the popular belief in divine rescue.

Over the last fifty years the volume of superstition in the country has expanded at almost the same rate as the achievement of our science, and I suspect that both variants on the theme of immortality followed upon the American victories in World War II. Prior to 1945 few Americans imagined themselves masters of the universe and therefore entitled to immunity against the evils afflicting the lesser nations of the earth, and the medical professions performed very few miracles. For most illnesses the treatments were largely therapeutic, and doctors relied on common sense, a few rudimentary surgical procedures, the natural resilience of the human body and the steadily preserved hope that by next week or tomorrow morning the patient somehow would show signs of improvement. The presiding spirit within most American hospitals still retained something of the old stoic idea that the strength to confront suffering was to be found in the people, not in the machines.

As a boy of eleven in 1946, I used to accompany an older cousin on his Sunday morning rounds through the wards of a public hospital in San Francisco, and although the walls were badly in need of paint and nobody had enough of anything—not enough light, not enough anesthetic, not enough time—I came to think of a hospital as a place where otherwise ordinary people, both doctors and patients, performed acts of extraordinary courage. My cousin was then in the second year of his residency, and occasionally he arranged for me to sit with the students in the surgical amphitheater, where I acquired a rudimentary knowledge of human anatomy and learned that although sooner or later even the most artful physician had to bow to the superior force of "the senior practitioner"—the pale and humorless figure whose judgement was final and whose presence announced the sack of the capital city—the doctors fought tenacious diversionary actions, postponing and delaying the inevitable defeat and making sure that death claimed its victory under the rules of civilized warfare in order that the patients need not humiliate themselves. I don't remember any specialists. Probably I was too young to know what a specialist was.

I do remember that my cousin admired the writings of Seneca, the Roman essayist and politician forced by the Emperor Nero to commit suicide in A.D. 65. Seneca wrote his *Letters from a Stoic* for the specific purpose of teaching himself to meet his own death in a manner that he wouldn't find humiliating. My cousin was particularly fond of a line that I soon had verbatim—"Rehearse death. To say this is to tell a person to rehearse his freedom. A person who has learned how to die has unlearned how to be a slave."

The old stoic spirit was no match for the medical technologies brought forth by the inventive genius of the Second World War. Armed with a newly acquired pharmacopoeia of genuinely miraculous drugs, a new generation of doctors found itself capable of genuinely astonishing cures. As the supply of miracles increased, so did the demand. Infirmities one considered natural to the human condition (old age, anxiety, weak chins, infertility, adolescence) were promoted to the status of illnesses deserving of a specialized vocabulary and government money. The expanding definitions of what constitutes disease supported parallel expansions within the health-care industries, which now employ upwards of 10 million people and account for 14 percent of the national economy. As medical spending surpassed defense spending, the crusade against death acquired many of the characteristics of the crusade against godless communism. In the five years since the end of the Cold War, the number of new recruits to the health establishment has increased 43 percent, and most of them have learned very quickly to speak the hieratic languages proper to the custodians of the unutterable mysteries. During the heyday of the Cold War, not one citizen in 10,000 could measure the throw weight of an ICBM or describe the circumference of annihilation likely to surround a nuclear explosion. In the midst of the current proliferation of medical strategies, not one patient in

10,000 can read an X-ray or make sense of a hospital bill, explain the chemistry of aspirin or locate the position of his or her own spleen.

By and large we count our ignorance a blessing, and all present can recite fabulous stories (heard from Oprah or the *National Enquirer*, if not from a friend) about a man with the glass lung and the woman safely returned from the grave. The media cater to our superstitions by their incessant dwelling on the fear of disease, and the headlines bring word not only of cholera in Africa and AIDS in Hollywood but also of flesh-eating bacteria in Connecticut and the mysterious advance of liver spots among sunbathers in Sarasota Springs. Our credulity invites the contempt of our appointed saviors, and during the brief span of my own lifetime the practice of medicine in the public hospitals increasingly has become a dreaded ritual that assigns to the patient the role of paying victim—an ordeal by committee that requires rather than alleviates the postures of humiliation.

Because so much of modern medicine is a matter of faith, a good many of the procedures that its critics condemn as "waste" or "mismanagement"—the ceaseless filling out of forms, the ceremonial taking of blood, the solemn murmuring of acronyms—also can be understood as what Thorstein Veblen in *The Theory of the Leisure Class* defined as "devout observances." The goods and services in question conform to what Veblen called the canon of honorific waste, proving their inestimable worth as sacrificial offerings and acts of piety by virtue of their futility and superfluous expense. The more opulent the technology or the more costly the physician's fee, the more benign the presumed result. The supposed "fat" in the system is its bone and marrow.

We hold fast to our beliefs despite a considerable bulk of evidence to the contrary. In 1991, the cost of health care in Greece and Spain amounted respectively to $404 and $848 per capita, and yet both countries reported longer life expectancies than did the United States, which, in that same year, measured the cost of its health care at $2,868 per capita.

Late last autumn, in response to an article by Willard Gaylin published in *Harper's Magazine* under the title "Faulty Diagnosis: Why Clinton's Health-Care Plan Won't Cure What Ails Us," I received a letter from Jack Heggie, a subscriber in Boulder, Colorado, who extended the line of argument with a number of mordant observations drawn from his close reading of various medical journals—that when doctors go on strike, as happened in Los Angeles in 1976, the death rate declines; that in many hospitals as many as 40 percent of all medical diagnoses (as subsequently verified on autopsies) are wrong; that as long ago as 1974 American hospitals performed 2.4 million unnecessary surgical operations at a cost of $4 billion and 10,000 lives.

The parallels with the weapons industry require little elaboration. The hospital surcharges for an aspirin or an artificial limb bear comparison to the markups paid by the Pentagon for a cruise missile or a wrench. Like the military-industrial complex, the medical-industrial complex invites the practice of large-scale fraud (conservatively estimated at $100 billion a year in false billings), and neither enterprise concerns itself with the niggling questions of supply and demand. Disease serves as an appropriately expensive substitute for Bolshevism, and the prompters of the public alarm direct their patriotic anger at the fellow-travelers in our midst who neglect their aerobic exercises, continue to smoke cigarettes and fail to eat their arugula.

Even if President Clinton manages to rearrange the country's health-care system, I doubt that his reforms will have much effect on the American attitudes toward sickness and health. Judging by this summer's newspaper accounts, all the familiar superstitions remain comfortably in place. The medical ecclesiastics came and went, speaking of HMOs and DRGs and HIPCs, of "global budgets" and "managed competition," but none of the interested parties (certainly not the government or the insurance and pharmaceutical companies) raised awkwardly existential questions about the limits of medicine or the unwillingness of the American public to make its peace with death. Still reluctant to call his campaign promise by its right name (a chimera projected onto the screen of the out years), the president redefined the term "universal health coverage" to mean 95 percent of the citizenry (a figure that excluded 13 million people) and set his countrymen the lesson of how to be a slave—how to bow and stoop and bend the knee not only to the special interests and the day's opinion polls but also to the belief that death is a mistake and disease an accident distinctly un-American.

At the end as at the beginning, the debate relapsed into an expectant silence papered over by the chatter of a lobbyist's "process points." After two years of waiting for a miracle—from MetLife, from the American Medical Association, from almost anybody with a stethoscope or a formula for spinning straw into penicillin—the still unanswered questions about who pays for what had been remanded from the secret convocation of Hillary Clinton's oracles to the equally discreet proceedings of a conference committee on Capitol Hill instructed to reconcile the unreconcilable differences between a sham hypothesis proposed by the House and a sham hypothesis proposed by the Senate. Although every politician in Washington could fairly guess that any law passed by Congress under the rubric of health-care reform was likely to provide the American people with less care for more money, all present professed devout faith in the sublime paradox summed up by Senator Bob Kerrey (D., Nebr.) in the phrase "All we have to do is to spend more in order to spend less."

The choir of voices singing the praise of the medical-industrial complex borrowed the liturgies of the old military-industrial complex and replaced the doctrine of mutual assured destruction with the doctrine of mutual assured salvation. The notion presupposes a strenuous leap of faith, but then so did the theories about surviving a nuclear onslaught, and so does the story of Satan's fall from heaven.

October 1994

ART AND ANTIQUES

So long as we read about revolutions in books, they all
look very nice—like those landscapes which, as artistic
engravings on white vellum, look so pure and friendly:
dung heaps engraved on copper do not smell, and the
eye can easily wade through an engraved morass.
—HEINRICH HEINE

*B*efore attending a State Department dinner on the evening of 6 October, I had thought that the notions of an exemplary American empire (seat of virtue, light unto the nations, hope of mankind, and so on) had dropped below the horizon with the lost city of Mycenae. By the time the waiters replaced the grilled rockfish with the roast pheasant, I understood that instead of being abandoned or mislaid, the geopolitical romance had been transposed into the realm of pure form, and during the interval between the champagne and the cassis sorbet I knew that if sometimes I had misjudged American diplomacy over the last thirty years, it was because I had failed to appreciate its character as an art exhibition.

The recognition took me by surprise. Earlier in the evening I had arrived at the building on C Street inclined to feel charitable toward anybody obliged to make foreign policy in a world where the old portfolio of theory so seldom speaks to the new sets of facts. Together with the reports from Haiti, the newspapers that morning mentioned the mutilated bodies of twenty Bosnian Serbs on Mount Igman southwest of Sarajevo, a civil war in Liberia, a political assassination in Mexico and a rumor or Iraqi troops massing on the border of Kuwait. Given so many emergent and simultaneous occasions, in what sort of perspective was it possible to fix the coordinates of a national interest? The traditional practice of diplomacy assumed the existence of frontiers meant to hold in check the movement of peoples and the passage of time, but the velocity of modern communications joined with the weight of mass immigration yields a new equation of human energy. It is an equation that presents the rulers of large and supposedly sovereign states with a hard problem in political mechanics. If nothing is foreign and nobody is an alien, then with what set of blueprints does the state construct such a thing as a foreign policy?

The questions accompanied me as far as the elevator hall on the eighth floor, the first of the sixteen reception rooms, each of them splendidly furnished in the architectural styles of the late eighteenth century, that occupy the whole of the building's uppermost floor and contain the State Department's permanent exhibition of early American virtue. Admiring the Roman architraves framing the elevator doors and being careful not to walk too heavily on the King of Prussia marble (the largest expanse of such marble known to mortal man), I proceeded through a gallery and another entrance hall (both passages distinguished by the presence of rare and priceless furniture), and so into the John Quincy Adams State Drawing Room, where a string quartet was playing the music of Haydn. Under the arched fanlight in the south wall, George F. Kennan, the evening's guest of honor, stood in a receiving line with Strobe Talbott, the deputy secretary of state, and as I waited my turn to shake hands with the two men, I had a good deal of time in which to reflect upon the provenience of both the paintings and the other guests.

The two sets of forms didn't agree with each other, either in character or in historical period. The objects in the room are representative of the early American republic—Gilbert Stuart's portrait of John Jay, paintings by Benjamin West and Charles Willson Peale, Thomas Jefferson's writing desk, a silver bowl made by Paul Revere. The people in the room were servants of the American nation-state—individuals on the order of Robert

S. McNamara and Richard Helms and Katharine Graham—who had inherited the presumptions of quasiimperial grandeur that the United States had found among the other spoils of victory in the Second World War. Almost without exception they belonged to the American oligarchy, the kind of people who own banks and racehorses and newspapers, anti-democratic in spirit and apt to define liberty as the power of money rather than the freedom of mind. Roughly one hundred in number, the guests graciously accepted glasses of wine and mineral water handed around on silver trays and exchanged the small tokens of the day's gossip—about the sad figure of Warren Christopher, the secretary of state (humiliated by former President Jimmy Carter in the Haitian negotiations), about President Clinton (vanishing like the Cheshire cat), about Bosnia (a tragic story), about gunboats (very expensive to maintain).

Over the shoulders of a woman in a black taffeta dress, I noticed McNamara standing under Charles Leslie's portrait of John Quincy Adams, and I remembered that during the Vietnam War he had thought that by teaching the natives the arithmetic of kill ratios and body counts the United States could transform them into loyal subjects of the American Express card. Adams, in his Fourth of July speech in 1821, had made a quite different point—the republican as opposed to the imperial argument—saying that America didn't go abroad "in search of monsters to destroy," that if we were to enlist under banners other than our own, "were they even the banners of foreign independence, we would involve ourself beyond the power of extrications, in all the wars of interest and intrigue, of individual avarice, envy and ambition."

The difference between the two statements of the American purpose was the difference between people who think they can buy the future and those who have the courage to imagine it. The founders of the Republic expected America to rise as a power in the world not because of its fleets or its armies but because of its experiments, and they defined liberty not as the freedom to conquer but as the freedom to make and think and build. Their heirs and assigns tend to think of liberty as a dangerous and probably criminal substance, something best placed under surveillance or preserved behind glass.

Thinking that Adams's remark might well have been addressed to Jean-Bertrand Aristide or the Emir of Kuwait, I further remembered that I most recently had come across it in a speech that Kennan delivered in March to the Council on Foreign Relations, and on reaching the head of the receiving line it occurred to me that of all the people in the room he probably was the closest in temperament to the Doric entablatures and the Chippendale chairs. The most eminent as well as the most senior of the country's statesmen, Kennan had entered the foreign service in 1927, in the last years of the Coolidge administration, and throughout the whole of his career he had argued against the grand simplifications so beloved by the managers of the national security state. At the age of ninety he stood with the strength and bearing of a much younger man, still persuaded that the United States needed sound principles rather than global strategies, that it was better advised to learn the contingent lessons of history than to proclaim the slogans of a world-encircling dogma. During the Second World War he was posted to the American embassy in Moscow, and in 1947, under the pseudonym "Mr. X," he published an article in *Foreign Affairs* setting forth the theory of containing the Soviet presence in Europe ("by the adroit and vigilant application of counterforce at a series of constantly shifting geographic points") from which eight American presidents subsequently derived the premise of the Cold War. Kennan intended the policy of containment as an expedient and temporary measure, a diplomatic task preliminary to useful discussion. Never had he expected it to become the justification for a permanent state of military readiness. Appalled and embarrassed by so gross a misreading of his text, Kennan resigned from the State Department in 1953, and except for a brief term as ambassador to Yugoslavia in 1961–63, he has devoted the last forty years to the teaching of diplomatic history at the Institute for Advanced Study in Princeton.

For at least thirty of those years, the State Department has been constructing its masterpiece of stage design, and despite the distractions of three undeclared wars, and in the midst of God knows how many lesser alarms, interruptions, rebellions and armed interventions, the great labor apparently has never ceased, not since that awful day in January 1961 when Mary Caroline Herter, the wife of the secretary of state during the Eisenhower administration, burst into tears at the prospect of receiving the queen of Greece in rooms that reminded her of an airport lounge. The unhappy woman had a point. The State Department building never has been admired as a work of architecture, and even the *New York Times*, a paper ordinarily willing to forgive the government's failures of policy or taste, once pronounced it "utterly banal, institutional, and graceless . . . at best a credible period piece from the late 1950's." The original reception rooms expressed the commercial aesthetic of the early Holiday Inns—wall-to-wall carpeting on concrete floors, the exterior walls of glass and steel—and Mrs Herter, who had been brought up as a Standard Oil heiress, was unaccustomed to turquoise drapes. To an attending aide-de-camp she said, "I've never been so mortified in my life as an American woman."

The secretary's wife was concerned with the questions of etiquette, but as the work of decoration progressed, room by room and carved ceiling by carved ceiling, it acquired a didactic purpose. What had begun as a show of manners became an uplifting text expressed in the language of architectural ornament, a gallery of sermons intended to improve and edify the sometimes brutal or loutish heads of state arriving in Washington from the less fortunate places of the earth.

The work swelled and expanded over the same period of time in which the State Department was steadily being diminished as an instrument of moral, intellectual or political force. A succession of American presidents got into the habit of making their own foreign policy in the basement of the White House, preferably in secret and often without reference either to the Constitution or a reliable map; the larger banks and transnational corporations, like the fiefs and principalities of medieval Europe, arranged their alliances and détentes through the embassies of their own overseas subsidiaries, and only after the treaties had been signed did they look to the clerks at the State Department to draft the press releases. But even as the office of the secretary of state was being reduced in both power and rank, the workmen on the eighth floor—carpenters, stonemasons, plasterers, furniture restorers, painters—were busily concealing the futility of time present with the glorious façade of time past.

On the way to dinner through the Thomas Jefferson State Reception Room, most of the guests paused to admire the carving of a gilded eagle, the magnificence of the Turkish rug, the plaster bust of John Paul Jones. Standing with the others in the dress circle of American privilege and leading opinion, I wondered whether we were part of the exhibit—like Governor De Witt Clinton's china plates or Copley's portrait of Mrs John Montresor (in red riding habit and velvet hat)—or whether we were meant to take from the display the same kind of instruction directed at personages as various as Manuel Noriega, the king of Saudi Arabia and the late Ferdinand Marcos. Had Noriega returned to Panama with the thought of submitting his political enemies to less strenuous regimens of torture? Would Richard Holbrooke or Strobe Talbott disavow their knowledge of caviar or send their children to public schools? Did everybody present know that the entire art collection was worth $75 million? That the pedimented glass doors had been copied from designs made for Jefferson's house at

Monticello? These latter advisories were probably a good deal more urgent than anything being done or said in Baghdad or Port-au-Prince, but what was the lesson to be learned, and how did it affect the prices of *gravitas* at Sotheby's?

The string quartet followed the guests into the Benjamin Franklin State Dining Room, and as the dinner ran its course the music proceeded from the eighteenth to the nineteenth century, arriving with the coffee at the terminus of Brahms. The windows in the south wall overlooked the Lincoln Memorial and the Potomac River, and in the distances of the autumn night I knew that the radio frequencies and television broadcast bands were loud with incoherent signals—not only the coded transmissions arriving on the State Department's lower tiers from Kigali and Zagreb but also Rush Limbaugh preaching the gospel of an imbecile realpolitik and Oliver North campaigning for election at Virginia on a platform of grinning and bald-faced lies. The voices were as many and as disparate as their points of origin and degrees of amplification, but heard together in chorus they were questioning the democratic premises of the American idea as well as the doctrines of American exceptionalism and the symbols of American supremacy, and who among all the important people in that important room knew what to say by way of an answer? In place of words, they had a collection of antiques. The parliament of images handsomely illustrated the book of American virtue, but in all that brilliant assembly of marble console tables, Chinese export porcelain, Queen Anne chairs and block-and-shell carved writing desks, which of them could speak?

Warren Christopher, the secretary of state, attempted the feat after the coffee had been served, but the speech had been written by somebody else, and it sounded like an advertisement meant to sell American democracy as it if were a brand-name detergent justly famous for its credibility and resolve. Christopher began by saying that both Nelson Mandela and Boris Yeltsin had passed safely through Washington during the previous six days, and because they had come and gone without incident and because as yet no American soldier had been killed in Haiti, "pessimism has had a bad week." He was glad to report that in the final decade of the century denominated as America's own, the national ship of state had weathered the really difficult storms—the ones that George Kennan's generation had confronted in Korea and Eastern Europe—and had come at last into smooth water and easy sailing. New markets for democracy were opening up in Asia and Latin America, and the success of the Haitian expedition had shown what could be done with some first-rate sentiment, enough helicopter gunships and 20,000 combat troops.

The guests rewarded Christopher with a gust of imperial applause, and Kennan, speaking in the dry and piping voice of an emeritus professor, followed with a brief parable about a buzzing fly that imagined itself a great king. Borrowed from an old Chinese text, the story served as a subtle correction of the evening's grander moments, but most of the guests were seated so softly on the cushions of self-congratulation that they missed the point about the vanity of princes and applauded Kennan as admiringly as they had viewed the colonial silver and the remnants of the American Revolution. Weighed in the scale of value held up by the style section of the *Washington Post* (the standard measure of judgement accepted by most of the people in the room), Kennan was a priceless antique, as rare in his own way as any of the other objects in the State Department's collection.

December 1994

TRAVELER'S TALE

All things are artificial, for nature is the art of God.
—SIR THOMAS BROWNE

*T*hree days before Christmas last year, on an afternoon train from New Haven to New York, I found myself sitting opposite a woebegone young man in his late twenties who seemed so alarmed by the direction of his own thoughts that I was reluctant to unsettle him further with a careless remark about Newt Gingrich or the weather. I took him to be a student in one of the Yale graduate schools, but by his appearance I couldn't guess at the topic of either his dissertation or his unhappiness. He was wearing blue jeans, a worn but once well-tailored overcoat and the remnant of a gray cashmere sweater. His round and naturally pleasant face was gaunt and drawn, and although the melancholy expression in his eyes suggested the possibility of an unpublished poet, he could just as easily have been studying law or architecture.

We were among the few passengers in an unheated car, and during the first twenty minutes of the journey he stared absently out the window at the rain, his hands thrust dejectedly into the pockets of his coat. When at last he chose to speak, he didn't turn his head. The obliqueness of the statement surprised me less than its hollow tone.

"You know, of course," he said, "what they can do to mice."

I didn't know—either which they or what mice—but I understood that my companion had been asking himself a series of questions for which he had found no good answers and that his observation followed from a dismal line of reasoning that he no longer could suppress.

"It's Christmas," I said. "The end of the year. The *fin de siècle*. Everybody's depressed."

He ignored the remark as an irrelevance, and as he shifted the angle of his gaze, I could see that he was calculating the precise degree of my probable ignorance.

"Have you ever heard the term 'germ-line cell therapy'?" he asked. "Do you know how many thousands of human embryos are lying around in cold storage?"

I said that I had heard rumors about the human embryos but had assumed that most of them were harmless. The young man regarded me with a superior smile, as if from a cold and condescending height. Identifying himself as a doctoral candidate at the Yale Divinity School, he asked me whether I had noticed either of the two reports published on the front page of the *New York Times* within the space of the last six weeks, one of them about experiments with the sperm cells of mice at the University of Pennsylvania, the other about a mouse inflated with a gene causing it to become grotesquely obese. I remembered the photograph of the fat mouse, which had a bow around its neck and looked to be about the size of a pet rabbit.

"If they can eliminate the gene for obesity," he said, "it's only a matter of time before they can eliminate the gene for sloth."

Before the train reached Bridgeport he had informed me that the news in the biomedical sciences was by no means good. He had been diligently collecting journal articles about transgenic fish and children born to their grandmothers, also newspaper dispatches about the molecular rearrangement of cows and dinosaurs soon to be hatched from old rocks. The new biological world order, he said, was much nearer in time than anybody supposed. Becoming suddenly animated and beginning to wave his hands, he lurched into a projection of the life forms likely to inhabit the next millennium.

"Synthetic salmon as big as killer whales, my friend. Huge and omnivorous creatures devouring all the minor fish in the Gulf of Alaska. Mutant tomatoes as round as basketballs. Insects in the shape of parakeets. Chickens crossed with rats or Quentin Tarantino."

Apparently what troubled him was the prospect of a world from which all traces of human imperfection had been removed, like mud on a boot or stains on a rug. Who then would have need of his services? Of what use was the Old or New Testament among people bred to the design specifications of Steven Spielberg or the Walt Disney Company?

"Perhaps you can explain to me," he said, "the point of preaching sermons to people who look like Yoda and know nothing of sin and remorse."

"Journalists like to write about miracles," I said. "They exaggerate things."

The young man dismissed the objection with an abrupt and impatient gesture, and between Bridgeport and Darien he summed up the result of his research in so rapid a rush of words that I had trouble keeping track of the distinctions between "xeno-grafts" and "the genome project," between the "polymerase chain reaction" and Cenozoic insects preserved in beads of amber. Other passengers came and went, but the divinity student took no notice of them, and he never once was at a loss for another terrible sign or portent looming just below the biomedical horizon. In the station at Stamford he mentioned the two hundred genetically engineered organisms released into the environment over the last ten years (all of them suspect and some of them missing), and passing through Cos Cob he mocked the pretensions of literary theorists.

"At Yale," he said, "people think deconstruction is something that happens in the English department." And then, with scornful laughter, "Guys in beards writing commentaries about Proust. They think of themselves as revolutionaries."

But it is the cellular biologists, he said, who revise the texts of human meaning, adding or deleting gene sequences like semicolons. By the time the train entered Westchester County, the divinity student had worked himself into so agitated a state of mind, part despairing prophecy and part antic improvisation, that he had attracted the respectful attention of three teenage girls wearing red woolen caps that made them look like Christmas elves. The apocalyptic tenor of his remarks followed from his assumption that within a matter of not too many years the wonders of corporate science would bring forth a market in genetic home improvements (intelligence, skin color, athletic ability, and so on) as profitable as the market in cosmetics.

"If I can give my dog blue eyes and a dancer's feet," he said, "why can't I do the same for my daughter?"

As long ago as February 1993, he said, the United States government approved the patenting of new life forms, and by so doing granted genetic engineers the right to own specific traits and characteristics. The Patent Office's ruling pertained to animals, but in view of the 1980 Supreme Court decision that the patent laws refer to "anything under the sun made by man," the divinity student foresaw the arrival of the biomedically engineered Eden in three stages, all of them brief.

First, the deployment of the genetic codes to fend off hereditary diseases. Identify the gene for obesity or breast cancer, remove it from the embryo and thus preserve the child from at least one of the scourges of the flesh.

Next and not long afterward, the molecular biologies made to serve the pleasures of the rich. Philip II of Spain collected dwarfs, and what was to prevent the latter-day lords of creation—Michael Jackson, say, or Matsushita, or Bill Gates—from collecting centaurs or two-headed golfers or miniature reproductions of Henry Kissinger? The divinity student could imagine private zoos in Colorado; limited editions issued by the Franklin Mint; bizarre auctions under the chandeliers at Sotheby's.

Last, once the techniques had become both reliable and cheap, the better drug- and department stores selling celebrity-sponsored sperm cells as if they were shades of lipstick. The masculine and feminine ideals of beauty no longer would need to be left to chance, and instead of taking up the questions of faith and conscience, people would graze like sheep among the displays of attractively designed tubes, priced at $49.95 and filled with genetic reprints of Elizabeth Taylor's eyes or Frank Sinatra's voice.

"Who will want to listen to the word of God," he said, "when they can change themselves into whales or movie stars?" The three girls looked at him in amazement, obviously thrilled with the news of their deliverance.

At the station in New Rochelle the train stopped for nearly ten minutes, and the young man fell abruptly silent. His long exigesis apparently had exhausted him without relieving him of his depression. He stared bleakly at the passengers crowding through the doors, most of them noisily excited with the hope of a festive evening in the city, and I wondered what I could say to him that might bring him some small measure of holiday cheer.

He was undoubtedly overstating the speed of scientific advancements (as well as confusing the practice of genetics with the theory of eugenics), but if I was sure that the new biomedical dispensation would arrive at a much later date than he supposed, I was also sure that on his principal existential point his fears were well founded. The pitiless logic of the capital markets eventually would overrule the moral objections from the sentimentalists in the choir loft. The Pope and Pat Buchanan might rail against the blasphemy of commercial mutation, but the bioengineering industries already have invested as much as $30 billion toward the manufacture of improved human beings, and too much money stands to be made from the sale of a heart-shaped mouth or a longer life.

If I couldn't comfort the divinity student with psalms, at least I could console him with assurances about the vanity and greed of his fellow man. I remembered that the Yale Divinity School had been founded in a very strict and Puritan tradition, and the faculty possibly had neglected to introduce the young man to the writings of the more sardonic authors. I suspected that he had read too much of Thomas Aquinas and not enough of Voltaire; too much Martin Buber and John Bunyan, not enough Mark Twain and Ambrose Bierce.

"Have faith in Mammon," I said, "and trust to the quibbling of lawyers. Rely on the cowardice of politicians."

The train slowed down for its passage through the desolation of the South Bronx, and I explained that whereas the devil offered Faust knowledge and power in return for his soul, the modern corporations would offer traits and characteristics for a percentage of the gross and that, with any luck, the lawsuits would last a thousand years.

The trace of an approving smile flickered briefly at the corners of the divinity student's mouth, but then he thought of the numberless charlatans unable to resist the temptation of promising biological utopia, probably not much different in its landscape of good behaviors than the one envisioned by the Republican signers of the Contract with America—Sunday school rows of obedient citizens, all of them blameless and most of them blond, none of them committing crimes, nobody telling lies.

"I can hear the speeches," he said. "No more racial hatred. No more citizens physically or intellectually challenged. An end to war and aggression, and literacy furnished at birth. Welcome to the New Jerusalem."

I assured him that even the Christian Coalition would come to its senses and everyone would remember that the end of war is also the end of finance capitalism, that by relieving the human race of its stupidity and grief, the apostles of everlasting happiness also would be evicting themselves from the office in Washington and the pulpit in Palm Springs.

The young man frowned, still worried about the lack of souls to save, and I again assured him that although nobody could afford to put the proposition quite so plainly, a consensus of the country's best and most respectable opinion would discover that an excess of virtue debases the currency of free will and subverts the meaning of the Constitution. The train was on the railroad bridge crossing the East River into Queens, and out the windows to the west we could see the triumphant Manhattan skyline glittering in the dusk.

"Of what else is the city made," I said, "except the sins of mankind?"

Without avarice, I said, what would become of Wall Street? Deprive a broker of his inalienable right to insider trading, and the market would empty of both buyers and sellers. Without lust, what would happen to the news and entertainment media? The few remaining journalists would be reduced to making lists of yesterday's temperature readings. Without wrath, who would go to see Steven Seagal movies or the Super Bowl? Without pride, what hairdresser would survive an afternoon's appointments? What tailor could sell another suit? Delete the stain of envy from the national genome, and the entire apparatus of the American economy—the glory of its markets and the grandeur of its laws, the whole magnificent edifice of steel and glass and neon light—would crumble as surely into dust as the colossal wreck of Troy.

"It would never do, you see," I said. "Human perfection is the ruin of the state."

In Pennsylvania Station a Salvation Army band was playing "Joy to the World." The young man walked with me toward Seventh Avenue, both of us pushing against the current of the holiday crowd festooned with shopping bags from Tiffany's and Bloomingdale's and The Gap. But in all that vast throng of wayward souls, hurrying home to Christmas and the suburbs, bearing overpriced gifts and long lists of New Year's promises they already knew they couldn't keep, I noticed very few who didn't look to be angry or tired or late. Reminded of the vanity of human wishes and the heavy burden of human sorrow wrapped up in so many red and green ribbons, I clapped the student on the back and told him to take heart, rejoice in the spirit of the season and know that he saw before him a lifetime guarantee of steady work.

"Fear not," I said. "Even if by some mischance Bristol-Myers Squibb isolates the gene for peace on earth and goodwill toward men, the poor couldn't afford it and the rich would want something more amusing."

The young man almost smiled—not as yet a broad smile, not a smile that anybody would associate with Santa Claus or think to put on a Hallmark Card, but nonetheless a brighter expression than the one with which he had boarded the train in New Haven. In the distance I could hear the Salvation Army trumpet taking up the tune of "Good King Wenceslaus," and as the divinity student walked off into the traffic and the rain changing to snow, I thought I noticed a stronger set to his shoulders, as if somehow it had occurred to him that toy mice and the futures market both bear witness to the art of God.

February 1995

CULTURE

ROME (ANCIENT) Corrupt. The important people spent most of their time going to sexual orgies. Refer to it when talking about the degradation of network television.

MIDDLE AGES Poetic time. Nobody was interested in money, and most of the women knew how to talk to rabbits and birds.

WESTERN CIVILIZATION Defunct. Destroyed by television and the English departments at Duke and Stanford universities.

EIGHTEENTH CENTURY All the women were beautifully dressed, but by the age of forty they went bald and lost their teeth. The century was good at music and politics, but it had no sense of hygiene.

Adieu, Big Bird

*O*ver the last twenty-odd years I've probably read several hundred civic-minded documents, mostly foundation studies or government briefing papers, intended to reform one of the society's institutions or repair one of the society's misfortunes, but I don't think I've ever read such a forlorn text as the report published last summer by the Twentieth Century Fund Task Force on Public Television. The title of the report took the form of the question "Quality Time?" which could be understood as either plaintive or sardonic, and well before I turned to the "Summary of Task Force Recommendations" I wondered why all present didn't simply hand in the pencils and adjourn to the nearest hotel bar to drink a bottle of California chardonnay in memory of a hope that had long since been lost.

But it is not in the nature of task forces, especially ones outfitted with high moral purpose, to abandon their missions without a decent show of optimism and resolve, and the twenty-three prominent citizens assembled by the Twentieth Century Fund to worry about the future of public broadcasting carried out their instructions to the last syllable of sound advice.[1] In the summer of 1992 the fund had invited them to review the record of public television since it was established by Congress in 1967—the sources

---

[1] The complete list of the names and titles of the attending magi cannot be easily compressed into a footnote, but as an indication of the quality of the company, the following names may be considered representative: Vartan Gregorian, Task Force Chair, President, Brown University; Peggy Charren, Founder, Action for Children's Television; Henry R. Kravis, Founding Partner, Kohlberg Kravis Roberts & Co., and Chairman of the Board of WNET/Channel Thirteen; Lesley Stahl, CBS News Correspondent, Co-editor, *60 Minutes*.

of its funding, the extent of its audience, the character of its programming, its former triumphs and present sorrows—and with these topics in mind the task force devoted the better part of a year to the proposition that public television should "enrich" and "strengthen" American society by advancing "our basic values." The preamble to the report amplified the sentiment in language suitable to an annual banquet or a Hallmark card: "Inherent in that mission [of public television] is its role as an alternative to commercial television, which is driven by concern for the marketplace, and therefore fails to capture many of the values we hold dear, such as excellence, creativity, tolerance, generosity, responsibility, community, diversity, concern for others and intellectual achievement."

The task force endorsed each of these fine values, regretted their temporary absence and took note of the several obstacles that cruel fate had placed in the way of their joyful expression. But not wanting to offend any prospective underwriters, or possibly arouse the suspicions of Senator Jesse Helms, the twenty-three voices of conscience were very, very careful in their choice of words. Whenever possible, they preferred euphemism. They didn't dwell on public television's abject dependence on its corporate sponsors or its eagerness to hustle toys to children through the friendly offices of Barney and Big Bird. They spoke instead about "competition for viewer's attention," about relying, perhaps too strongly, on "business underwriting," about "the lack of adequate funds" that prompts, unhappily, so many stations "to resort to broadcasting 'mass appeal' programming in order to attract viewer contributors during on-air fundraising drives."

When the task force came at last to its recommendations, it found public television in need of bracing reform in all sectors of its operations, but despite the repeated urging of "fundamental structural change" and the frequent use of the words "must" and "should," the admonitory paragraphs lacked conviction. It was the languid emptiness of the prose that made the noble thoughts seem so forlorn. One paragraph in particular I could imagine being read in the key of C minor, accompanied by mournful flute music and the slow tapping of a toy drum: "Editorial balance and objectivity are requirements, but the system should be flexible enough to require them over a period of time, rather than within every individual program. Otherwise there is no way in which public television can be anything except bland, unexciting, undemanding, and unintelligent—all of the things it was designed not to be."

Like the fine phrases and the fine values that decorated the rest of the task force's report, the brave words about editorial balance were as familiar as the Cookie Monster, and I wondered how it was possible that their rank hypocrisy still could provoke me to mockery and anger. Why go to the trouble? By now, surely, everybody must know that the conditions of public television's existence—most especially the conditions that govern the making of the primetime programs distributed by the Public Broadcasting Service (PBS)—require its strict conformity to the norms of expression deemed proper by the corporations that sustain its pretensions to intellectual freedom. People have been making the point for twenty years. Even the Carnegie Commission, which conceived the purpose embodied in the Public Broadcasting Act of 1967, understood, as long ago as 1979, that its good intention had gone astray. In that latter year the commission published a second report, to the effect that public broadcasting didn't come close to meeting the original specifications, that it had failed to serve as "a forum for controversy and debate" or as "a voice for groups in the community that may otherwise be unheard."

Why, then, the late-arriving complaint? Not only had I seen the programs and read the reviews but I also had met quite a few of the dramatis personae. As the producer of *Bookmark*, a half-hour talk show for PBS, during the seasons 1989–91, I'd encountered a complacent bureaucracy so frightened of new ideas that it no longer knew how to do anything except go to meetings. Some of my querulousness I can set down to the private accounts of a spirit ill-suited to the environment.[2]

On the plane of a public argument my objection proceeds from a sense that public television does the country a disservice by refusing to open its institutional mind to the social, technological and political changes abroad in the world. We have before us an entirely new set of circumstances—new means of telecommunications, new blocks and definitions of national interest, new vocabularies in the arts and the sciences—but the Public Broadcasting Service inhabits a world according to Alistair Cooke. The broadcast year is still 1973, and nobody has heard of Ted Turner or imagined the possibility of five hundred cable channels selling gold

---

[2] A round-table discussion with the authors of newly published books, *Bookmark* was never well regarded by the management of PBS. The show was in many ways flawed, but the criticisms had to do with its subject matter: when I first offered the program to WETA in Washington (together with $1 million in prospective funding), the station's chief programming officer, Ward Chamberlin, declined the offer on the ground that the important people in the country didn't have time to think about books. WNET in New York agreed to broadcast the program on condition that I hired its own expensive producers, augment it with film clips and pay the station a surcharge of $250,000 for its friendship and public-relations counsel.

jewelry and performances of Japanese No plays. Without the presence of PBS in 1973, Big Bird and Bill Moyers might never have become household names, but nobody at PBS appears to have noticed that both the times and the rules have changed. Instead of trying to bend the new technologies to new forms of programming, or asking themselves what the broadcast and cable networks neglect to carry, or how to address an American citizenry sorely in need of relevant information, the happy few in the public-TV studios in New York or Washington or Sioux City think they do the American public a great favor if every now and then they show a painting by Van Gogh or play a tune by Beethoven.

The Twentieth Century Fund report appeared in July, the same month that PBS presented the schedule of its 1993–94 season to a gathering of television critics in Los Angeles. Reading the newspaper accounts of the press conference during the same week that I was reading "Quality Time?" I was moved to a feeling akin to pity for the twenty-three worthies who had labored so long and so earnestly to come up with language that smudged the likeness between PBS and the commercial vaudeville circuits.

Among the principal new series: *The Secret of Life*, *The Nature of Sex*, *The Great Depression*, *Death: The Trip of a Lifetime*. Among the series originally produced but then abandoned by the networks: *I'll Fly Away*. Among the special programs grouped under the heading "In the Spotlight": *Sade: Love Deluxe*, *Joe Cocker: Night Calls*, *Billy Joel: River of Dreams*.

The PBS publicity introduced the new programs with an overture of inspiriting verbs ("inform," "inspire," "illuminate"), but each of them could as easily have been bought by any one of several cable channels—by Discovery, or A&E, or CNN—and quite clearly they were intended for an audience much weakened by its prolonged captivity in the theater of celebrity. It wasn't that the programs were dull, or fatuous, or poorly conceived, but rather that they had little or nothing to do with the public interest as it was defined by the Carnegie Commission in the optimistic winter of 1967 and confirmed by the Twentieth Century Fund in the melancholy summer of 1993. They made no attempt to provide the American people with a visible means of support for "the values we hold dear," and instead of offering an alternative to the Roman circus of commercial television, they presented a show of slightly less expensive lions.

Appearing at the podium in Los Angeles as patron of the new PBS season, Jennifer Lawson, executive vice president of national programming, took the occasion to announce a forthcoming development deal with Brandon Tartikoff, the Hollywood studio executive formerly at NBC and Paramount Pictures. Fortunately for PBS, she said, Tartikoff had agreed to produce what she called "a watercooler comedy" for the 1994–95 season, a comedy that was to be set in New Orleans, in a bar warmly reminiscent of NBC's immortal *Cheers*: Entitled *Under New Management*, the comedy would invite a racially balanced cast to showcase the political and cultural wisdom of the day.

The newspaper story neglected to quote Ms Lawson on the subject of social relevance, but in my mind's eye I could see her pitching the concept and working the room, and I remembered how she once had explained to me—patiently, as if to a child—the funding priorities of public television. I had come to Washington to ask for $200,000 to defray some of the cost of producing *Bookmark*, which was then appearing in its third season on 140 PBS stations. The Bell Atlantic Corporation had paid the full cost of the first three seasons, but the company had shifted the venue of its good works to the promotion of golf tournaments and if I were to produce a fourth season of the program, I needed at least a little money from Washington to prove to other underwriters that the system awarded it some measure of esteem. Of the $250 million that the federal government allots every year to public television, Ms Lawson reserves roughly $55 million as a production budget for programming that she thinks deserving of a national audience, and her decisions seldom brook argument or appeal.

We met for lunch at the Four Seasons Hotel, but before we ordered the mineral water and the arugula with walnuts, I knew that my cause was lost. Ms Lawson quite clearly was a woman of the theater, and what had she to do with editors who wanted to talk, God help us, about the play of ideas? I might as well have been offering Socratic dialogues to Barry Diller or Larry Tisch. The proposition was patently absurd, but, knowing that we both knew it was absurd, I could enjoy Ms Lawson's company and admire her candor. As expected, she didn't have much use for what she called "cheap little half hour service shows." She was interested in expensive productions geared to the primetime hours of 7:00–10:00 P.M., glossy stuff with music and helicopter shots and famous names. "Bring me big projects," she said. "Bring me Streisand or the Civil War. I'd rather give you $2 million than a paltry $200,000."

During the three years of my acquaintance with PBS, I noticed that most of the important bureaucrats, notwithstanding their mandate to commission "alternative" programming, liked to mistake themselves for

Hollywood agents. Their budgets seldom allowed them the use of limousines and cellular phones, but, whenever these comforts could be arranged, they received them with the smiles of faint acknowledgement that they had learned from their study of Fred Astaire. Maybe public television wasn't as big or as rich as ABC or Fox, but what it lacked in the way of substance, it supplied with the airs of entitlement.

The effect was always comic because the presiding sensibility belonged to the Age of Aquarius, and everybody was expected to show a poet's disdain for commerce and trade. We were all engaged in the great work of bringing truth and light to a grateful populace, and a cant phrase about the venality of the commercial networks was understood as a mark of refinement and taste. The humor in the conversations followed from the contradiction between the pose of principled bohemianism and the stultifying preoccupation with funding—its source and durability, its innate loveliness and resemblance to the waters of the Nile—that reduced all present to a state of near paralysis. Given the system's medieval financial structure, the effect is probably unavoidable.

Properly understood, public television is not a network. It is an anthology of 351 stations, each of them jealous of its own rights and privileges, each of them suspicious of Washington and envious of one another, loyal to their own interests, their own board of trustees, their own definitions of the public good. If the system were to be represented on a geopolitical map, it would resemble the Holy Roman Empire during the last years of its decaying hegemony—351 petty states and dukedoms, each with its own flag, court chamberlain and trumpet fanfare.

Dependent on Washington in varying states of subservience, the stations enjoy different privileges of wealth and rank, and they divide into four different degrees of vassal—the metropolitan stations that produce most of the programs seen on public television (WGBH in Boston, WNET in New York, WETA in Washington); the stations operated by universities, mostly in basements; the stations owned by a city or state, all of them beholden to local political agendas; the stations controlled by boards of education, which supply primary and secondary schools with televised classroom assignments.

Taken all together, the annual subsidy to public television amounts to $1.4 billion, but it derives from so many different sources under so many different conditions and restrictions that most of the people in the system seldom have time to think about anything other than the protocols of money. Less than a fifth of the total sum (roughly $300 million) is allocated to the making of national television programs. The bulk of the subsidy pays the operating costs of the 351 stations, each of which believes itself entitled to the glory that was Greece and the grandeur that was Rome.[3]

The inevitable quarreling between so many antagonistic interests and ambitions assures the system's lack of coherence, which almost certainly was what Congress and the Nixon administration had in mind in 1970 when they grudgingly agreed to provide funds for the Public Broadcasting Service. The opposition to the Vietnam War had given tongue to too many voices of dissent. What would the government want with an independent or television network likely to make more trouble than was already present in the streets? By dividing the money into the smallest possible denominations and the editorial authority into the smallest possible constituencies, and by setting the big stations against the little stations and the city stations against the country stations, the government made sure that the Carnegie Commission's alternative ways of looking at the world would be strangled at birth. The Reagan administration continued and refined the practice during the 1980s by further reducing PBS's accustomed pittance, and the corporations filled in the blank spaces with programs best understood as advertisements for a preferred reality and with what the servants of the system learned to call "enhanced underwriter acknowledgments."[4]

I don't know why so many people persist in the superstition that PBS reflects a Leftist political bias. It's true that every now and again the system broadcasts a documentary film shot from a feminist, black or homosexual point of view, but the occasions are so infrequent and the films so cheaply

---

[3] The federal government supplies a relatively small proportion of the subsidy, no more than $285 million, or 20 percent, of the total sum. Subscribers contribute $296 million (in dues and membership fees); state governments contribute $230 million and the corporations another $230 million; the remaining balances arrive from state colleges, foundations, local governments, private colleges, public colleges and auctions. Although the corporations contribute direct production costs in the amount of only $90 million per annum, their opinion of the larger projects adds to the weight of their importance. The metropolitan stations assign as much as 85 percent of their production budgets (as well as 85 percent of their time and thought) to those projects that bring with them the promise of matching grants.

[4] In return for their production money, PBS allows the corporations to affix image advertising to the completed film, much in the manner of seventeenth-century Dutch painters who placed their wealthy patrons in the foregrounds of classical or biblical scenes, pious figures kneeling at the gates of Jerusalem or holding the stirrups of the captain's horse.

produced that they can safely be understood as acts of private piety, not as statements of public purpose. By and large and as a general rule, political discussion is not encouraged in the drawing room with the leather-bound volumes of *Masterpiece Theatre*, the handsome sporting prints (mostly of waterfowl and wolves) and the collectible celebrities arranged at the table with Charlie Rose, but for the sake of civic-minded appearance the system permits occasional seminars on topics of current interest—provided, of course, that the participants come dressed in decent clothes, with their hair neatly combed and their arguments stamped with the seals and permissions of a reputable corporation. The regularly scheduled news and talk shows serve at the pleasure of their corporate sponsors, and as I read through the press material describing the 1993–94 season, I noticed that the names of the weightier pundits coincided with the heavier concentrations of wealth. As follows:

Washington Week in Review—Ford Motor Company

Wall Street Week with Louis Rukeyser—Prudential Securities Inc.; Travelers Corp.; Massachusetts Financial Services

Tony Brown's Journal—Pepsi-Cola

Technopolitics—Pfizer, Inc.; Anheuser-Busch Companies; Kraft General Foods

Adam Smith—Metropolitan Life Insurance Company

The MacNeil/Lehrer NewsHour—The Archer Daniels Midland Company; The New York Life Insurance Company; Pepsico

Firing Line—The John M. Olin Foundation; Annenberg Foundation

The McLaughlin Group—General Electric[5]

What surprised me during my encounters with PBS was the lack of objection to the terms of its medieval servitude, and at the system's program fair in Dallas in June of 1990 I remember thinking that I had wandered onto the set of a costume drama in which the assembled notables imagined themselves acting the parts of the Duke of Essex or the Duchess of Anjou. Each of the 351 broadcast fiefs within public television supports the sensibility of both a program and a station manager (either of whom is likely to

---

[5] By the estimation of Fairness and Accuracy in Reporting, the clear majority of the guests presented on public television news and talk shows (at least 70 percent) speak for the interests of the professions, the government or the corporations. Only 10 percent of the respondents appear as common citizens or as members of "the general public." On the Corporation for Public Broadcasting, the supervisory body that distributes the congressional subsidy to PBS, the board of directors reflects an unashamedly conservative political bias. The chairman is Sheila Burke Tate, who was Nancy Reagan's press secretary.

detest the other), and these individuals, together with their trains of followers, come to the fair to look over the next season's leading attractions.
They look at highlight reels, make the rounds of the hospitality suites and
complain about the arrogance and stupidity of their overlords in Boston and
New York. Although most of the stations must present the ten or twelve
programs that Washington deems obligatory (*Nova, The MacNeil/Lehrer
NewsHour, Great Performances,* and so on), they remain free to do as they
please with the rest of the programming day, and instead of presenting Bill
Moyers on Zeus or *Frontline* in Somalia, they can show old Ginger Rogers
movies or the complete archive of *Star Trek,* or, as WTTW in Chicago chose
to do last October, a home shopping service. Nor do the stations have
to present a program at a uniform time. Washington might broadcast a
program at 6:00 P.M. on Sunday, but Seattle can show the tape at 2:00 A.M.
on the following Tuesday. San Francisco might choose to hold the program
for six months, until Saturn enters the house of Virgo. Dominion over the
schedule and the time slots encourages attitudes of hauteur, and sometimes
the affectations can be very grand. In particular, I remember a program
manager from Sacramento who informed me that if she was going to talk
about books at all, she preferred to talk about Chaucer or Ezra Pound, and
that if she had to make aimless conversation with what the system calls
"a talking head," she preferred it to be a famous talking head.

The fair lasted nearly a week, and because the temperature never
dropped below 100 degrees, nobody ever left the hotel. Ms Lawson arrived
with a suite of retainers from Washington to explain the year's division of
the spoils, and the metropolitan stations sent wandering celebrities
(among them Bill Moyers and Jim Lehrer) to astonish the impresarios from
Boise and Wichita Falls and maybe cajole them into broadcasting their
news. Not until the third day of the fair did I discover the distinction
between program managers and station managers, and that by persuading
one of them that five of John Updike's paragraphs made a weight equal
to a hundred photographs of Princess Di, I was apt to make of the other
a sullen enemy.

Within the hierarchies of commercial television, the ebb and flow of
patronage runs in fairly straight lines, and even the most arrogant of studio
executives seldom has the gall to speak in the name of the public interest.
His interest is clearly his own. But PBS claims to serve the interests of the
sovereign people, and so the functionaries who distribute the national
largesse claim to act on behalf of anything they can classify as the common
good. Because the figure of the prince appears in so many different

disguises—as foundation executive or corporate sponsor, or friend of Louis Rukeyser—the expectant courtier is constantly bowing and smiling in eight or nine directions, forever turning, like a compass needle or a weathervane, into the glare of the new money.

If much of the programming seen on public television takes place in the kingdom of perpetual blandness, it's because nobody present can afford the risk of giving offense. Any controversial opinion, any rude or unwelcome noise, inevitably provokes objections, if not from Senator Helms, then from the Gay and Lesbian Task Force or the chairperson of the board of trustees. Mindful of the imminent complaints, and all too aware that prestige within the system accrues to the accounts of intellectual cowardice, the curators of the nation's conscience tailor their programming to the measure of a college commencement speech.

On the last night of the fair, in the only hotel bar that stayed open past midnight, I met a producer of public-affairs programs who was staring bleakly into his drink and calculating the cost-benefit ratios within PBS between sophistry and candor. Although he favored the second form of expression (describing himself as "a maker of winter opinions instead of summer hats"), he knew that he couldn't afford the luxury of honest criticism, "not if I want to continue to guide the country into a free, open and democratic debate." He laughed lightly at his own bitter joke and explained that everybody within the chateau of public television talked mostly about the forms of funding and the sources of funding because everybody knew that the ideas didn't matter. Ideas were as cheap and as perishable as moths, he said, but Pepsico lived forever, and so did the Ford Motor Company and The John M. Olin Foundation.

By the time I read the report of the Twentieth Century Fund's task force, I had seen enough of the system to recognize the tone of pious euphemism as its defining characteristic and voice. A dissenting opinion appended to the report as "Supplemental Comment from Eli N. Evans" was the exception that proved the rule. As the president of the Charles H. Revson Foundation, Evans had invested a great deal of thought and money in his belief in the possibilities of public television. He also had served on the staff of the Carnegie Commission that drew up the original brief in 1967, and as a member of the second Carnegie Commission in 1979. Having seen his hopes courteously but implacably mocked for the better part of thirty years, he had decided that the best thing to do was "to begin again," "to sweep away this history and create a new national entity that will lead the system to a new world."

Evans didn't think that the important questions were about money. The system was always short of money, and even if it hit the lottery in forty-three states at least once every six months for the next fifty years, it still would be short of money. More to the point, PBS had nothing to say that wasn't being said by somebody else. Maybe the system never had anything to say, but in the context of the changes that have reshaped the means of communications over the last ten years, and as one of many instruments in what has become an entirely new media orchestra, PBS no longer can be heard to be making a distinctive sound.

I suspect that Evans is probably right, but as I read the last dismal pages of the report I found myself wondering what PBS would look like if it attempted to do what it was intended to do—if it didn't dance for ratings points and curtsy to the whim of the corporations. PBS was meant to address the American people in their capacity as students and citizens (rather than in their capacity as buyers of life insurance), and if it had the wit to extend the practices of C-Span and National Public Radio, I could imagine its cameras in state legislatures and city halls, in university lecture rooms, in the nation's teaching hospitals, in research laboratories and town meetings, in the capitals of foreign countries and on the decks of wandering ships.

Of the vast energy and intelligence at large in the world, I have not the least doubt, and it seems to me no hard trick to place a camera in a room with people excited by their journeys toward the horizons of the human mind. Maybe some of them don't speak in sound bites, and maybe some of them go on too long about the aerodynamic absurdity of the hummingbird or about last week's hearing on property taxes, but the play of ideas assumes the active participation of the people who come to watch. PBS insults its audience by speaking to them as children who must be cease-lessly amused and entertained. At the bidding of the corporations that gaze upon the images of their own magnificence, PBS resigns its task of looking outward into the world and turns inward upon the reflections in a courtier's mirror.

December 1993

Notebooks

BELLES LETTRES

K. ——, the publisher, trying to be critical, talks
about books pretty much as a washerwoman would
about Niagara Falls or a poulterer about a phoenix
—EDGAR ALLAN POE

For some years now the big publishing syndicates have been playing a game not unlike Monopoly or musical chairs. At least once
a season two or three of the smaller publishers discover that they
have been sold (like antique silver or African ivory) to Rupert Murdoch,
the Bertelsmann Verlag, or Time Inc. Although I had been reading the
reports with the respectful attention owed to large sums of money making
a stately progress across the pages of the newspapers, I didn't appreciate the
consequences of these events until, last Tuesday in an Italian restaurant on
West Fifty-sixth Street, I saw poor Hastings scribbling diagrams on a
tablecloth. Earlier that morning he had asked me to meet him for a late
lunch, and by the tone of his voice, which was one of poorly suppressed
panic, I understood that we weren't going to talk about the youth and early
sorrows of either Goethe or Joyce.

Hastings looked even worse than I had expected. He is a large and ordinarily optimistic man, subject to passionate enthusiasms (for a promising
novelist, an obscure poet or a new book of Czechoslovakian stories), given
to wearing the same rumpled tweed suit for weeks on end, constantly
rummaging through his pockets for a stray pencil. For twenty years he has
been content to work as a senior editor for one of the city's most eminent
publishing houses, and for twenty years he has been telling anybody who

would listen to him that the long-awaited revival of American literature was about to astonish the world with its brilliance. At innumerable conferences, he could be counted upon to appear as a bringer of good news, almost always carrying a boxed manuscript in which, so he said, he had discovered the portents of genius.

But on Tuesday Hastings had the furtive look of a man no more than twenty-four hours ahead of the police. He seemed somehow smaller than usual, smaller and quieter and much too carefully dressed, as if he had thought to disguise himself in the cloak of corporate rectitude. Seated at a corner table, pouring gin into his coffee and smoking too many cigarettes, Hastings was attempting to draw the organizational chart of the conglomerate that had bought his imprint for a price said to exceed the gross national product of Peru.

"I don't know which one of the divisions owns me," he said. "I've been to nineteen meetings in the last two weeks, but I still don't know which of the voices in the room is the one that sings the melody."

He had been told to acquire manuscripts that stood at least a three-to-one chance of arriving on the best-seller lists (in *Publishers Weekly* as well as the *New York Times*), and the instruction had cast him into the void of existential doubt that he previously had associated with the writings of Albert Camus or T. Coraghessan Boyle. His new editor-in-chief was a woman who used to decorate department-store windows. Books priced at $24.95 she construed as luxury goods meant to be carried to the beach with the Bain de Soleil or placed gracefully on glass tables with the flowers and the enameled snuff-boxes. To the best of his knowledge she had never read any book that couldn't be mistaken for a catalogue or a travel brochure.

"But if I don't come up with something by Friday afternoon at three o'clock," he said, "I'll know what Beckett was trying to say in *Waiting for Godot*."

He had composed a preliminary list of titles, but he wanted the benefit of a second opinion before presenting it to his board of examiners. With an air of apology and embarrassment, explaining that he still had daughters in college and a mortgage on the house in Putnam County, he handed me a typescript so heavily marked up with changes and crossings out that it looked like the first draft of a lyric by Dylan Thomas. As follows:

1. *The Priapus File:* Case histories of the twenty-five most depraved men and women in the annals of psychoanalysis. Foreword by Dominick Dunne or the editors of *Vogue*.

2. *The Third World Diet:* Exotic recipes, with results proven by the

experience of people starving in Zaire, Mexico, Mozambique and the Sudan.

3. *Aladdin's Lamp:* The one and only true secret of investing in the stock market, by Ivan Boesky or Michael Milken. Complete with 400 pages of graphs and a list of competent criminal lawyers.

4. *Jane Fonda's Book of Pets, Jane Fonda's Book of Guerrilla Warfare, Jane Fonda's Book of Antique Cars.*

5. *My Funny Valentine:* The letters and diaries of Al Capone.

6. *Geopolitics Made Simple:* A portfolio of maps, together with a glossary of terms ("détente," "window of vulnerability," "hegemony," "arc of crisis," and so on). Introduction by former president Richard M. Nixon.

7. *The Last Berwick:* A long novel set against the vivid pageantry of the history of the world. The author, preferably an attractive woman (for the photograph on the dust jacket), begins the chronicle of the Berwick family at the Battle of Troy.

8. *More for Me:* An anthology of tips about how and where to buy anything and everything. Entries arranged alphabetically by commodity (ascots, bread, chinoiserie, debutantes, and so on). Commentary by Tom Wolfe.

9. *The 250-Minute Orgasm:* Ancient Hindu techniques discovered in the carvings on a wall in Khajuraho. Verified after years of painstaking experiments by a board of medical authorities connected with the Beverly Hills Institute for Creative Human Relations. Illustrated.

While I was reading the list, Hastings stared at me with an expression of acute anxiety. I knew what it had cost him to compose the list, and I wished that I could have spared him the pain of criticism. I didn't have the heart to tell him that he was about four years behind the trends, that nobody wanted to hear any more disquieting news about money or war or sex. The buyers of books at $24.95 a copy wished to applaud the excitements of jogging and contemplate the stillness of gardens.

"It's not a bad list, Hastings," I said. "Certainly you're on the right track. But the conceptions are still too literary, and you haven't got a sense of what is truly commercial. There's no Hollywood book; no life of Jesus; nothing about sports or Elvis or the zodiac; no sensational murder; no guide to a healthful and happy divorce; not enough celebrities."

We continued the conversation for another hour or so, but Hastings couldn't fix his attention on what was being said. He drank a fourth and fifth tumbler of gin and began to talk about taking up a career as a trainer of performing elephants. He had always been fond of the circus, he said, and with an animal act you knew where you stood with the crowd.

June 1989

WALTER KARP, 1934–1989

The world is given to those whom the world can trust.
—WALTER BAGEHOT

Walter Karp died on 19 July—at the age of fifty-five, without prior notice, quite possibly as the result of a hospital's error or neglect—and it was as if a steady and familiar light had been blown away in a sudden wind. Karp had been a contributing editor of *Harper's Magazine* for eleven years, and because I admired him both as a writer and as a man, his death seems to me a grievous loss. I know that I have lost a friend in whose presence I invariably found myself added unto, and I don't think it too much to say that the American public has lost a vigilant and courageous advocate of its civil liberties. Karp's was a voice of dissent—often angry, sometimes comic, always impassioned.

He was a stormy petrel of a man, small and excitable, delighting in the rush of his words and the energy of his ideas, loyal to his convictions, indifferent to his material circumstances, trembling with a furious intensity that was both moral and intellectual, remorseless in his pursuit of what he thought was the truth. I remember him as being somehow constantly in motion, barely able to contain himself, quick to doubt and to question, never satisfied with what he called "the official version of things."

His passion was politics, and his precepts were simple and few. He believed that in America it is the people who have rights, not the state, and that the working of a democratic republic requires a raucous assembly of citizens unafraid to speak their minds. He thought that if only enough people had the courage to say what they meant, then all would be well. His reading of American history (especially the writings of Jefferson and Madison and Adams) taught him that the boon of liberty never could be taken lightly or for granted and that the American Constitution assumed a ceaseless and bitter struggle between the interests of the few and the hopes of the many, between those who would limit and those who would extend the authority of the people.

Karp enlisted himself in the ranks of the many, and the articles and essays that he published in *Harper's Magazine* (seventeen of them between

September 1978 and July 1989) mostly had to do with what he called "the wanton abuse of power" on the part of government officials, both elected and appointed, who minted the currency of the public trust into the base coin of their own petty ambitions. His method was one of investigative reading, and he approached his study of politics as a historian less interested in the news of scandal (which he accepted as a constant) than in what John Adams once called "that most dreaded and envied kind of knowledge" about the character and conduct of the nation's rulers.

Karp thought that the meaning of political events revealed itself more plainly in the reading room of a public library than in a White House press conference or in private conversations with well-placed government officials, who, as Karp well knew, entertained their respondents with welcome and self-serving lies. Once embarked on a line of inquiry, he read everything pertinent to the composition of a reliable record—newspapers, documents, journals, congressional testimony—and with his facts in hand could measure the distance between what politicians said and what they did. He described his method as "simply a matter of paying attention to public deeds that have been largely ignored or made light of"; and the dismantling of the grandiose fictions behind which "the lying pantaloons" in Washington concealed the shabbiness of their acts moved him to wild and derisive outbursts of sardonic glee. He liked the old and straightforward words that were synonymous with American political writing in the late eighteenth century—"oligarchy," "tyranny," "elective despotism"— and he wrote his essays in a language bright with fierce eloquence.

Karp had little use for the customary reduction of political discourse into the vocabulary of decorous abstraction. He understood politics as a series of not very difficult answers to the not very difficult questions of who does what to whom, for how long and at what cost to the common good. Nothing so moved him to mockery and scorn as the assumption that the sequence of historical events could be assigned to the "unseen workings of indeterminate forces" or that the art of political chicane could be attributed to the paltry desire of money.

I remember arguing the point with him on more than one afternoon in a downtown café, and I can still see him glaring at me across the table and denouncing me as a fool too easily caught in the net of facile cant. "The hardest way to make a million dollars," he said, "is to become a United States senator. Any vicious, impudent, brazen, shrewd, gifted person can think of an infinite number of better ways to become rich than to become a crooked politician."

Not that Karp didn't think that most politicians weren't brazen or impudent or crooked, but he understood that they savored the sweet and palpable pleasures of exercising power, and I can still hear him laughing at the "absurd notion—very popular in the news media and the universities" that somehow political power was of no interest to the people who held and enjoyed that power.

Following Madison, Karp believed that popular government without adequate information, or the means to acquire it, was "prologue to a farce," and he was habitually wary of official attempts to stifle or suppress the informed debate on which a democratic republic relies for the knowledge of itself. During President Reagan's two terms in office, the government mounted a systematic assault on precisely those habits of free expression that Walter Karp deemed inestimably precious. In defense of what he construed as the fundamental American premise, Karp wrote first an essay, "Liberty Under Siege" [*Harper's Magazine*, November 1985], and then a book of the same title [Henry Holt, 1988] in which he announced, in grand and noble prose, his grand remonstrance. He began, as always, with a summary of the facts, setting forth the record of an administration that over a period of five short years (in the name of efficiency, thrift or national security) had asserted the government's "right to confidentiality"; authorized the CIA to question American citizens; withheld documents from Congress under the rubric "executive privilege"; subjected academic and scientific research to the government's "review and oversight"; attempted to eliminate postal subsidies for schools, libraries and the blind; obliged government functionaries with access to "sensitive information" to sign agreements saying that they never would write or speak about what they had heard or seen without prior permission; restricted the circulation of published books and journals; excluded the press from the invasion of Grenada; defined reporters (in the words of Secretary of State George Shultz) as being "always against us"; defined press leaks (in the words of Assistant Attorney General Richard Willard) as "consensual crimes"; set up an Official Secrets Act; attacked not only the accuracy but also the legitimacy of the press.

At the end of his essay Karp allowed himself a peroration, which I ask the reader's pardon to quote at length because it so well expresses the spirit of the man.

> Imagine a venerable republic, the hope of the world, where the habits of freedom are besieged, where self-government is assailed, where the vigilant

are blinded, the well-informed gagged, the press hounded, the courts weakened, the government exalted, the electorate degraded, the Constitution mocked, and laws reduced to a sham so that, in the fullness of time, corporate enterprise may regain the paltry commercial freedom to endanger the well-being of the populace. Imagine a base-hearted political establishment, "liberal" as well as "conservative," Democratic as well as Republican, watching with silent, protective approval this lunatic assault on popular government. Imagine a soft-spoken demagogue, faithful to nothing except his own faction, being given a free hand to turn Americans into the enemies of their own ancient liberties.

Karp's methods and convictions, to say nothing of his language, put him at odds with the rules of deportment and the canons of taste that regulate the tone of contemporary American journalism. He published eight books and countless magazine articles but never was generally acknowledged as an important writer; he never earned more than $30,000 in any one year, and he received few of the ornamental honors, subsidies and flattering reviews that the journalistic profession bestows upon the virtues of solemn orthodoxy. Karp's enemies, who were many and envious, dismissed him as "cranky," "old-fashioned," "too literary," "too historical."

The world didn't trust Walter Karp and rewarded him with nothing in its gift. I doubt that he expected otherwise. I think he would have been insulted if he had been offered a Pulitzer Prize. He would have thought that he had said something too easy, too obvious, too polite. Mainstream American journalism was a profession that he held in contempt, because he understood that the press, by and large, takes its prompts from the government, that it repeats what it is told by official sources (the Congress, the White House, the Defense Department), that it is in the business of defending the interests of the few against the hopes of the many. To Karp's mind the media were passive by nature and subservient by habit, accepting "leaks" and "handouts" as if they were gratuities offered to a butler or a gamekeeper.

Because Karp didn't court the grace-and-favor of those in office, he didn't depend for his opinions on the whispers and rumors current among the best people on the Sunday morning talk shows. He had the courage to think for himself, a writer cut in the American grain who could count among his antecedents spirits as restless and various as Ambrose Bierce, Albert Jay Nock, and H. L. Mencken. Despite his mocking pessimism he was never cynical, and he retained his faith in the energy and imagination of the American people. Confronted with another proof of mindless folly in the day's newspapers, he was fond of citing Jefferson's dictum that "we are never permitted to despair of the commonwealth."

Even so, I think Karp was surprised by the lack of public objection to the Reagan administration's assault on his beloved habits of freedom, an assault that continues unabated under the Bush administration. The government effectively stuffed the mouths of any and all public officials who had tasted of the forbidden fruit of sensitive information, and yet, except for a few squeaks of ceremonial alarm in the nominally liberal sectors of the Congress and the news media, the decree was received as amiably as the report of yesterday's stock prices.

Across the whole spectrum of the political debate the silence has become almost audible, and I sorely miss Walter Karp's passionate dissent, just as I miss his sardonic wit and his antic improvisations on the themes of oligarchy and elective despotism. He was a historian of the best kind— an excited amateur who didn't allow the weight of footnotes or the fear of a faculty committee to impede the line of his argument or the enthusiasm of his thought. I took courage from his example, and I thought of him as one of the magazine's principal voices not only of dissent but also of conscience—restless, uncomfortable, uncowed, prodding me to eschew cant, to remember the uses as well as the right of free speech, to do better.

October 1989

ENDGAMES

The *fin* is coming early this *siècle*.
—ANGELA CARTER

T he conjunction of the end of the century and the end of the millennium has not gone unnoticed by the journals of advanced opinion, and if the early portents mean anything, then it is safe to assume that over the next ten years the markets for dire prophecy and piteous lamentation will become almost as profitable as the markets for free-range chickens and sun-dried tomatoes. Strictly speaking, of course, the *fin de siècle* hasn't yet arrived, but nervous editors in New York and Washington already have been seized with the compulsion to be the first into print with the worst possible news. The summer issue of *The National Interest* announced "The End of History?" and scarcely two weeks later, so early in September that all the leaves were still on the trees, *The New*

Yorker announced "The End of Nature." It's hard to know how the news-magazines and the television networks can sustain so uncompromising a standard of finality, but I'm sure that somebody will think of something ("The End of the Molecule," "The End of Art," "The End of the Solar System," and so on), and maybe by the end of the season Ted Koppel will be walking around Washington dressed in a magician's robe and a wizard's pointed hat.

Ordinarily, I don't read the reports from the frontiers of the apocalypse (for the same reasons that I have never been attracted to science fiction or to the paintings of Salvador Dalí), but the two essays in question excited a flurry of gossip among the kinds of people paid to promote trends, and I was curious to see how and when the authors had chosen to end the story of man's immense journey from the Precambrian sea.

To my surprise, I found the essays alarming. Not for the reasons the authors intended, but because I hadn't expected to come across so loath-some a callowness of feeling tricked up in so shallow a veneer of thought. I was also struck by the fundamental similarity of the two tracts, which, at first glance and judging by their provenance and style of address, seemed to arrive from opposite points on the ideological compass.

"The End of History?" written by Francis Fukuyama, a deputy director of the State Department's policy planning staff, appeared in a quarterly journal owned and operated by neoconservative policy intellectuals allied with the interests of the Reagan and Bush administrations. As testi-monials to the essay's importance, the journal published accompanying comments from, among others, Irving Kristol, Senator Daniel Patrick Moynihan and Allan Bloom. Fukuyama presents his thesis in a bureaucratic prose that is fatuous, smug and clotted with abstraction, but in Washington, a city not known for its literary judgement, his essay was applauded as a work of genius. "The End of Nature" plays to the super-stitions of the environmental Left. The author, a young man of sensibility named Bill McKibben, strives for a sanctimonious effect that is earnest, doom-ridden, precious and tear-stained. In New York, a city not known for its farms or its morals, his essay was received as a work of rural piety.

Despite their political differences, Fukuyama and McKibben share a profound love of self, and it is their corrosive narcissism, combined with their revulsion for anything smeared with the mud of human experience and desire, that joins the essays in their common campaign against death and time. Two representative passages suggest the presiding tone of ennui and disdain:

The end of history will be a very sad time. The struggle for recognition, the willingness to risk one's life for a purely abstract goal, the worldwide ideological struggle that called forth daring, courage, imagination, and idealism, will be replaced by economic calculation, the endless solving of technical problems, environmental concerns, and the satisfaction of sophisticated consumer demands. In the post-historical period there will be neither art nor philosophy, just the perpetual caretaking of the museum of human history.

—Fukuyama

The end of nature probably also makes us reluctant to attach ourselves to its remnants, for the same reason that we usually don't choose new friends from among the terminally ill. I love the mountain outside my back door —the stream that runs along its flank, and the stream that slides down a quarter-mile mossy chute, and the place where the slope flattens into an open plain of birch and oak. But I know that in some way I resist getting to know it better—for fear, weak-kneed as it sounds, of getting hurt. I fear that if I knew as well as a forester what sick trees look like I would see them everywhere. I find now that I like the woods best in winter, when it is harder to tell what might be dying, but I try not to love even winter too much, because of the January perhaps not so distant when the snow will fall as warm rain. There is no future in loving nature.

—McKibben

Neither writer can imagine a world other than the one shaped in his own image. Fukuyama knows as little of history as McKibben knows of science, but both writers accept their ignorance as further proof of their good fortune, because it allows them to display the delicacy of their sentiment without worrying too much about the silliness of their pretensions.

Fukuyama defines history not as tragic narrative but as a set of theories and abstractions current (like ivory bibelots) in the parliaments and *grands salons* of western Europe since the end of the French Revolution. He notices that over the course of the last two hundred years the attitudes associated with what he calls liberalism have triumphed over all the other isms— socialism, communism, absolutism, despotism, fascism, and so on—and because everybody who matters in the world (the wealthier citizens of the large industrial nations that comprise the "universal homogeneous state") has embraced, thank God, the values of finance capitalism (that is, everybody who is anybody wants a refrigerator, a VCR and a constitution), the world has arrived at what Fukuyama discerns to be "the end point of mankind's ideological evolution and the universalization of Western liberal democracy as the final form of human government."

Because the principles of Western liberal democracy cannot be improved upon, they will govern, now and forever, the material world. Fukuyama admits to a few unresolved differences of opinion among the rabble outside the palace gates, but these he dismisses as minor because they only concern the backward natives of the Third World, people still "mired in history." He concedes that it still might be necessary to mount a few police actions against terrorism, and he expects some "ethnic and nationalist violence" from "Palestinians and Kurds, Sikhs and Tamils, Irish Catholics and Walloons," but in the clean, well-lighted conference rooms at the center of the universe (among the people who count and the money of consequence), there really isn't anything more to do or say. History is something that happens to poor people; it is a story of the slums.

McKibben's definition of nature is as fastidious as Fukuyama's definition of history. He doesn't refer to the whole of the creation but rather to a "certain set of human ideas about the world and our place in it." The certain set of ideas proves to be his own idea, which is cozy and sentimental and cute and safe. In McKibben's view, nature was once a "sweet and wild garden," the realm of innocence, J. R. R. Tolkein's Hobbiton, the mise-en-scène of *Winnie-the-Pooh*. Wicked, wicked men have spoiled this fairy-tale demesne, and even though McKibben understands that the planet might remain habitable, he knows that "IT WILL NOT BE THE SAME!" That is the sum of his lament. He recites the familiar catechism of forthcoming doom—boiling seas, endless drought, dying forests, acid rain, rising temperatures, poisoned birds—but all of these events merely provide background effects in the heartbreaking melodrama that might as easily have been entitled "Bill McKibben's Broken Toy." Bill is very, very upset. The wicked, wicked men have taken away his little blue blanket and his old teddy bear, and now when he walks out of his wonderful, wonderful house in the Adirondack Mountains and looks up at the stars and the rain and the moon, he knows that he is looking at damaged goods.

His voice is petulant, like that of the Hollywood Studio Executive Who Has Read Thoreau examining the grilled salmon at a new restaurant in Santa Monica and wanting to be very sure that the fish never swam—not once, not even for five minutes when it was young and foolish and didn't know any better—in a dirty stream.

McKibben doesn't take the trouble to conceal the nakedness of his disgust for human beings. To McKibben's mind everything artificial is bad because it has been corrupted by the hands of men. Man is vile, a hideous, many-headed beast ceaselessly replicating itself, spewing pollution into the innocent atmosphere and the blameless sea. From time to time the word *human* occurs in one of McKibben's sentences, and his first association is invariably with something foul—a stinking automobile, a noisy chain saw, an ugly condominium. He approves of landscapes in which he can find "nothing to remind me of human society—no trash, no stumps, no fences," and he thinks of human beings as inanimate objects, barely distinguishable from dustbins—for example, "over the last century, a human life has become a machine for burning petroleum." So contemptuous a view of mankind condemns McKibben's argument to futility. Given the scale of the environmental catastrophe that he so lovingly foresees, who else except man can find a way out of the morass? Certainly not a gasoline engine or a stone marten. Certainly not McKibben, who is too busy caressing his despair.

Fukuyama is more languid and less hysterical, but he writes with the bureaucrat's dandified distaste for "the mire of history" (the breeding ground for McKibben's human vermin), and, like McKibben, he reduces human experience to the mechanics of consumption and the mathematics of statistical analysis and projection.

Neither Fukuyama nor McKibben has any use for the reaching of the human mind or the courage of the human spirit. It never occurs to them to admire the works of Homo Faber or Homo Ludens. Cathedrals, gardens, drawings, poems, hymns, recipes, prescriptions, plays—all these manmade things Fukuyama and McKibben consign to the dungheap of history, artificial waste products rotting in the sun, as futile and irrelevant as the lives of the men who built the Roman aqueducts, recorded the teachings of Lao Tse, made maps, sailed over the edge of the world, invented logarithms, studied the circulation of the blood, survived Auschwitz and walked on the light of the moon.

"Numberless are the world's wonders," said Sophocles, "but none more wonderful than man." Ancient Athens styled itself the "nurse of men," and Pericles in his funeral oration boasted not of the objects collected in the city, although these were both many and beautiful, but of the character of the Athenian citizen—"self-reliant, loyal, public-spirited, resourceful, versatile, marked by refinement without extravagance and knowledge without effeminacy." The Renaissance made of man the measure of all things. "What a piece of work is man," said Shakespeare. "How noble in reason, how infinite in faculties . . . the paragon of animals."

Fukuyama and McKibben don't think so. They prefer the modernist ("post-historical") portrait of man as a weak and filthy creature, and they place their self-righteousness and their ignorance at the service of dealers in miracles and redemptions. Like the late Ayatollah Khomeini and the gamekeepers of the thousand-year Reich, they believe that the world must be cleansed of its impurities and the human herd thinned out with the techniques of sustained yield management. If their essays can be read as signs and portents, like the entrails of sheep once studied so closely by the old Roman augurs, then the omens must be said to be unfavorable.

November 1989

PLAY ON WORDS

The world of politics is always twenty years behind the
world of thought.
—JOHN JAY CHAPMAN

O n a rainy Thursday night in late February, at the Cathedral of St John the Divine in northern Manhattan, a choir of celebrities staged the political analogue of an Academy Awards ceremony in honor of the president of Czechoslovakia, Václav Havel, and on the way uptown in the subway I wondered if I could expect to see Ivana Trump and the Solid Gold dancers. The invitation listed the names of some of the illuminati scheduled to appear on the program (among them Warren Beatty, Henry Kissinger, Meryl Streep and Sting), and the sum of their collective Q ratings foretold an evening decorated in pious tinsel. In Czechoslovakia, actors and playwrights maybe have an aptitude for politics—the Civic Forum, Havel's first constituency in Prague, met in the basement of the Magic Lantern Theater—but in the United States the arrival of more than two or three celebrities at the scene of a political event ordinarily means that whatever meaning that cause or question once might have possessed already has been broken up into photo opportunities and sold for scrap to network television. Because I had admired Havel from a distance, for both his courage and his eloquence, I was reluctant to see what I knew of the text of his life translated into an advertisement for the moral beauty of somebody else's social conscience.

The venue of the cathedral compounded my sense of foreboding. The place is known for the trendiness of its sentiment, and during a long and reluctant acquaintance with its spiritual repertoire, I have become accustomed to doves of peace fluttering through the sacristy, aging guitarists playing Bob Dylan songs in the apse, minority dance troops performing to choral works dedicated to the memory of the lost counter-culture or the Twelve Nations of the Sioux. Every autumn, to commemorate the Feast of St Francis, the bishop bestows his blessing on pets and small animals, and one year, in the crowd of children holding their dogs or their rabbits or their birds, I remember seeing a pale and presumably sardonic child walking up the steps of the west portico with a pet lobster on a long, embroidered leash.

Thinking about the lobster and the doves of peace (some of which had been festooned with red and blue ribbons), I walked the few blocks from the subway to the cathedral in a state of mind by no means friendly to the evening's diversion. Between Broadway and Amsterdam Avenue, I refused to give money to three different beggars, annoyed with myself for being so foolish as to take part in a spectacle that I could imagine Tom Wolfe describing under the rubric "Radical Czech."

But when I turned north at the corner of 111th Street and saw the crowd standing in the rain outside the cathedral, a much bigger crowd than I had expected, it struck me that maybe I had been too quick and easy with the smart jokes. From what I could tell by looking at the patient and serious expressions on the faces of the several people nearest me at the end of the line, nobody had come for the publicity. I was relieved to notice the absence of limousines and photographers, and while I waited for the cathedral to open its doors, I had time to reflect on my own reasons for taking the uptown train.

On 1 January, a few days after Havel took up his duties as president of a country lately released, like himself, from captivity, he had given an extraordinary speech to the Czechoslovakian people. Reading the text in the paper, I had been moved by the force of his words in a way that I hadn't thought possible. The man apparently was trying to tell the truth, and because I had never heard an American president try to tell the truth, the effect was both violent and shocking, as if somebody's anarchist cousin had fired a pistol in the midst of a cocktail party meant to raise funds for the New York Public Library. Almost two months later, I could still remember the opening lines of the speech:

"For forty years," Havel had said, "you have heard on this day from the mouths of my predecessors, in a number of variations, the same thing: how our country is flourishing, how many more millions of tons of steel we have produced, how we are all happy, how we believe in our government.

I assume you have not named me to this office so that I, too, should lie to you."

The American public, of course, pays its politicians (and pays them handsomely) to tell as many lies as might be necessary to sustain the romance of the afternoon headlines, and yet here was a man—on his fourth day in office and not yet familiar with the silver tea service and the comforts of power—willing to risk the loss of his newfound privilege for something as plain and unprofitable as the truth. For an American politician, Havel's opening statement would have been—quite literally —impossible. American politicians long ago gave up the burden of speaking in their own voices or forming their own words. Their owners and speechwriters don't permit them to take idiot chances with any text that hasn't been approved by the investment committee.

Havel proceeded to make matters worse by informing his fellow citizens that they were all responsible for their own troubles. "It would be very unwise," he said, "to think of the sad heritage of the last forty years only as something foreign, something inherited from a distant relative."

Havel went on to say that the Czechoslovakian people—himself among them—had become "morally ill" because "we are used to saying one thing and thinking another," because "we have learned not to believe in anything, not to care about each other, to worry only about ourselves."

In the mouth of an American politician, Havel's words would have been condemned as blasphemy (because, as everybody well knows, nothing is ever America's fault), and as I stood outside the cathedral that evening in New York, I called to mind the scene in Washington on the previous day, when Havel had addressed a joint session of Congress. Again he had made the point that politics was about the willingness to say what one meant, about finding a language in which to express not only the theory but also the practice of liberty. He began by recognizing the absurdity that is often synonymous with improvisations on the theme of freedom:

"The last time they arrested me ... I didn't know whether it was for two days or for two years. Exactly one month later, when the rock musician Mikhail Koscak told me that I would be probably proposed as a presidential candidate, I thought it was one of his usual jokes."

As recently as 27 October of last year, Havel had been an outlaw, imprisoned by one of the most repressive communist regimes then still extant in Eastern Europe. By profession a playwright, he had invented too many characters who voiced too many opinions deemed offensive to the wisdom in office, and he had spent five and a half of the last thirteen years in prison. The period of enforced silence prompted him to reflect on the nature of political power, and so, standing before the members of the House and the Senate, he had said, "A person who cannot move and live a somewhat normal life because he is pinned under a boulder has more time to think about his hopes than someone who is not trapped this way."

Although he acknowledged the military and economic victories of the United States in the years after the Second World War, he didn't think that the triumph of capitalism was quite as triumphant as it had been made to seem in the pages of the *Wall Street Journal*. Nor did he think that the Western nations had come to the end of history:

"We still don't know how to put morality ahead of politics, science, and economy. We are still incapable of understanding that the only genuine backbone of all our actions, if they are to be moral, is responsibility —responsibility to something higher than my family, my country, my company, my success."

The assembled senators and congressmen, most of them illuminated with the smiles of self-congratulation, interrupted the speech with five standing ovations and repeated shouts of "Bravo." If their effrontery had been staged in a theater—in a play by Dürrenmatt, or Havel, or Beaumarchais, or Brecht—the scene would have played as bitter comedy. Not one American politician in twenty-five has read both the Constitution and the Bill of Rights; not one in fifty knows of any higher good than "my interest, my party, my success;" not one in a hundred finds any connection, whether logical or allegorical, between what he says and what he means.

The last of the day's light faded before the cathedral doors opened, and as the line lurched slowly forward I fell into conversation with the woman next to me, a librarian at Columbia University who was writing a monograph about Shakespeare's surprisingly thorough knowledge of music and the law. She didn't share my suspicion of the American governing classes or my too easily awakened anger at their insufferable hypocrisy, and on my way up the cathedral steps I noticed that my humor had been amended by her delight in words, and I found myself wondering what had become of the lobster that had so cautiously made the same ascent.

I found a seat in the nave, about half the distance between the west door and the pulpit, and as the immense and dimly lit neo-Gothic space gradually filled with people come to pay their respects to a brave man, I studied the mimeographed program and guessed at the weight and length of the camera boom placed in the crossing between the transept and the nave. Among other spectacles and diversions, the revised edition of the program promised remarks by Milos Forman and Eli Wiesel; readings from Havel's speeches by Paul Newman and Gregory Peck; songs by Dizzy Gillespie and Roberta Flack; and a good many orchestral performances of music by Dvořák and Mozart.

The camera boom, fifty or sixty feet long and balanced with a block of lead, was so large and so prominently situated that it dwarfed the human figures in the cathedral. It looked oddly prehistoric, as if it were some sort of monstrous and omniscient insect. The rights to the evening's entertainment had been awarded to Czechoslovak television as well as to the American Public Broadcasting System. Across the aisle, about four rows nearer the camera and the pulpit, I noticed one of New York's wealthier literary agents in conversation with an author noted for his patriotic fictions on the theme of America the Invincible and America the Good. They looked as sleek and soft as otters, both of them expensively manicured and glittering with gold jewelry. It occurred to me that neither would have had much trouble serving the Communist *ancien régime* in Prague. Not, if the times demanded a change of ideology and a rearrangement of the political furniture, would they find it difficult to serve any other state (fascist or monarchist or social democratic) that generously rewarded them for their hired loyalty and praise.

I was estimating the likely speed of their change of costume when Havel entered the cathedral through a side door, forty-five minutes late, invisible in a crowd of friends, dignitaries and Secret Service agents. He was so far away that I was aware only of blurred movement, as if I were watching a wind passing through distant grass. Although almost nobody else in the cathedral could see him any better than I, the entire congregation, maybe as many as 4,500 people, instinctively rose and applauded.

The program began with a fanfare played on a herald's trumpet and the ringing of the cathedral bells. Milos Forman spoke a few words of welcome to his longtime friend and fellow dramatist, Placido Domingo sang an Agnus Dei written by Bizet and Paul Newman read a brief passage from one of Havel's reflections about the difference between the uncomfortable truth and the expedient lie.

Newman read the lines with an emphasis and inflection better suited to a bad movie, and yet, much to my astonishment, I felt myself infiltrated by a feeling of irrepressible hope. If I had come to mock the proceedings as a work of synthetic glitz, I was mistaken. The words rang true, even in a voice as false as Newman's, and for the next hour I was filled with an elation as reckless as that of a truant child. Listening to the voices in the cathedral (Susan Sarandon reading Havel's letters from prison, Arthur Miller addressing Havel as the first avant-garde president), I thought that it might yet be possible to invent or discover a new politics expressed in a language capable of telling a straight story. The Brooklyn Philharmonic Orchestra played a passage from Mozart's *Don Giovanni* (which was first performed in Prague in 1787), and I thought, if the Czechs can slip the bonds of cynicism and cant, then might not the Americans make good their own escape? All that would be required would be a few people willing to say what they meant and to bear the responsibility for their own voices. The music shifted into a major key, and I could feel myself shrugging off my accustomed wariness as if it were an old and heavy coat. I glanced across the aisle at the well-stuffed literary agent, and in the enthusiasm of the moment, I understood that on a rainy Thursday night in upper Manhattan, the dogs of selfishness, ambition and greed had been brought briefly to heel. For the time being, at least, maybe because of a trick of the light or the abruptness of the modulation away from a minor key, I thought I saw the agent's expression of habitual avarice softening into the lineaments of conscience and thought.

The camera that had reminded me of an insect reappeared in a completely different kind of metaphor. The crane and boom moved so effortlessly —gliding forward and drawing away, rising and falling in a slow, dream-like motion—that I could imagine it as a living soul, weaving the thread of immortality on the loom of time. The image was more in line with what Havel had been trying to say. More than anything else, we have need of a believable story, because without a believable story we have no means of connecting the past to the present, the dead to the living, the citizen to the state, the now to the then.

So great was my excitement with the prospect of the feats of the political imagination that might yet be performed with a new company of actors under the direction of a new theater management that my era of good feeling, again to my astonishment, survived the entrance of even so famous a fool as Henry Kissinger. Until Kissinger appeared in the pulpit, the evening had passed without embarrassment—the music was good, the emotion genuine, the speakers brief and to the point. The instant Kissinger's name was announced, the ceremony lost a good deal of its optimism. The entire sum of Kissinger's life and work testifies to the success that can be chiseled from a degraded politics with the journeyman's tools of presumption, dishonesty and betrayal. A man seated directly behind me screamed, "Murderer!;" I could hear people shouting boos and catcalls elsewhere in the cathedral. Prior to Kissinger's sententious homily on the text of the Cold War, all the speakers had tried to describe the shape of an idea larger and higher than themselves, looking, at least figuratively, upward. Kissinger looked down, condescending to bestow on the congregation the favor of his advice. Instead of talking about Havel, he talked about himself. "When I was in Prague in 1968," he said, "I tried to warn my good friends the Czechs, but they wouldn't listen to me. . . . " He continued in the same manner for more than five or six minutes (nobody else having spoken for more than one or two minutes), and the effect was turgid and pompous.

Kissinger was followed by Gregory Peck and by Lukas Foss conducting the Largo from Dvořák's *New World* symphony, and for a moment it looked as if the evening might regain its balance. The chance was lost with the appearance of Barbara Walters and Saul Bellow. Like Kissinger, Walters and Bellow spoke, adoringly, of themselves. Walters said that she had been thrilled to be in Prague last Christmas, in time for the wonderful, thrilling experiences associated with the collapse of a Communist regime. Bellow was glad to know that when Havel was in prison he had remembered to read Bellow's novel *Herzog*. As a reward for Havel's intelligence and taste, Bellow had brought an autographed copy of the novel *Herzog*, which he hoped the obviously perceptive president of Czechoslovakia would accept as a token of his, Bellow's, esteem.

The evening collapsed inward on itself like a dead star, and it ended on a sustained note of mummery—with the presenting to Havel of a meaningless "spirit of freedom award," with the passing around of candles for everybody in the cathedral to light, and with the playing of Aaron Copland's disingenuous *Fanfare for the Common Man*.

Havel didn't give a speech. He explained that because he didn't spend the afternoon in prison he hadn't had time to compose his thoughts, and he confined himself to saying thank you in a voice obstructed by obvious emotion and a heavy accent.

Even so, I counted myself fortunate, and I left the cathedral in high spirits, willing to consider the possibility that even Henry Kissinger and Barbara Walters might one day learn to doubt their own magnificence. It was still raining, but more lightly, and I figured that if all of us were at fault for the shambles of the American enterprise, then I had as much of an obligation as everybody else to try to find the words, or the rush of words, that could be bound to the task of telling a believable story.

May 1990

A PARDONER'S TALE

A city for sale, and doomed when it
finds a buyer.
—JUGURTHA, COMMENTARY ON ROME, C. 104 B.C.

A s an editor with twenty years' service in the media trades, I
count myself reasonably well versed in both the cunning and
the sorrow of Grub Street. I'm used to the effrontery of book
publishers and the insolence of critics, and when I read the memoirs of an
old politician or a new talk-show host, I know that I might as well be
reading the report of last week's press conference with the late Elvis
Presley. Presented with two variants of more or less artful fraud (Hitler's
Diaries, say, and Henry Kissinger's *White House Years*), I can draw the fine
distinctions between the modified fact and the self-serving lie.

Book publishing was never a business for the pure in heart. As long
ago as 1839 in Paris, Balzac took the trouble to codify the nine standard
swindles with which the publishers of his acquaintance gulled both the
writer and the reader. Maupassant amended and revised the rules of
unctuous procedure in 1885, and George Orwell did the same in 1946.
Then, as now, most publishers would rather sponsor works of literary
merit, but few of them can afford to make a habit of the practice. The temper of the times demands freaks and wonders, and the publishers meet the
specifications of the market with the iconography of the rich and famous.
It doesn't matter if the celebrities can think, or write, or even talk. The
wisdom of Millie, the White House dog, commands a higher value in the
bookstores than the aphorisms of Seneca. It is always possible to hire ghost-
writers, invent scenes of an imaginary childhood, provide wise sayings and
dire prophecies, and construct heartwarming anecdotes about the subject's
intimate acquaintance with a sexual fetish, a notorious crime or a large sum
of money. What matters is the manufacture of an object wrapped in a
photograph familiar to thousands of people passing by B. Dalton's window
in downtown St Louis.

Numerous publishers have explained these subtleties to me over a
period of years, and until last November I considered myself current with
the vanguard of literary cynicism. I was, as usual, wrong.

On the day after last November's election, the morning mail brought a
book from Simon and Schuster bearing the title *An American Life*, by
Ronald Reagan, and when I read the blurb on the dust jacket, I knew that

giants still walked the earth. With consummate, barefaced gall, the publishers presented the book as both an "autobiography" and "a significant work of history." Either statement standing by itself would be offensive enough; joined together they achieved a degree of shamelessness that I had thought beyond the reach of the propagandist's art. To imagine that Mr Reagan would take the trouble to write anything at all (a simple, declarative sentence, much less a manuscript running to 726 pages) is to imagine that he reads Voltaire in French and devotes his afternoons to the study of the Kirtland's warbler and the Burgess Shale.

Curious to see how the publishers justified the sales pitch, I turned to the acknowledgements page and noticed that Reagan (or whoever was writing the page in his name) conceded that he "had a great deal of help, for which I am most appreciative." The otherwise anonymous author went on to express his gratitude to himself in a phrase as ingenuous as a campaign promise: "Robert Lindsey, a talented writer, was with me every step of the way."

The book doesn't bear reading. By way of taking the measure of the text I read the whole of Part Five (pages 469–543), entitled "Iran-Contra." The sequence of events subsumed under those two words is one to which I have given considerable thought and study, and so I have some basis for comparison with Reagan's rendering of the same chronology. The account presented in a plausible imitation of Reagan's voice assigns the blame for any inconvenience or embarrassment to Israel, the United States Congress, the American media and the accidents of fate. The author excuses himself by saying that he relied on his friends and counselors, and besides, he was busy with other, more important matters elsewhere in the world. The Reagan of the book, like the Reagan of the White House script and the trumped-up press release, maintains the fiction of his perfect innocence, repeatedly insisting that he never traded weapons for hostages and never dreamed of dishonoring the law, the Constitution or his oath of office. The tone of voice is cloying and sweet, like "God Bless America" arranged by Lawrence Welk and played, at a slow tempo, on an accordion. If the reader thinks that judgement too harsh, I refer him to the final paragraphs of discussion of the Iran-Contra deal. The passage is consistent with the remainder of the text:

> On the day that John Poindexter came to the Oval Office to resign, I didn't ask him the questions I now wish I had. If we hadn't acted so quickly, maybe he and North would have told me some of the things that are still a mystery to me after all this time.

If I could do it over again, I would bring both of them into the Oval Office and say, "Okay, John and Ollie, level with me. Tell me what really happened and what it is that you have been hiding from me. Tell me everything."

If I had done that, at least I wouldn't be sitting here, writing this book, still ignorant of some of the things that went on during the Iran-Contra affair.

The demonstrable falsity of *An American Life* leaves unanswered the questions of motive and result, and I can imagine the lenient reader asking why Reagan's book is any worse than Nixon's book, or Kissinger's book, or Millie's book. Reagan, after all, is an amiable fellow who thought he was doing everybody a good turn, and if people take comfort in his homilies and his smile, then where's the harm in that?

Surely Reagan cannot be blamed for an act of all-American commerce. What else is an old song-and-dance man to do? If a Japanese automobile company wants to rent his presence for a speech in Beverly Hills or a series of lectures in Tokyo, why not charge the going rate of $25,000 a night or $2 million a week? If he bestows the blessing of his name on a bad book in return for a reputed $6 million as an advance against royalties, how reprove him for accepting a fee much smaller than the sums routinely paid to entertainers as prominent as Dustin Hoffman or Joe Montana?

And how blame Simon and Schuster, which is owned by Paramount, which in turn possibly hopes to employ Reagan as an actor (costarring with Bob Hope and George Burns in the sequel to *The Golden Girls*) or as an agent for another book deal? A publisher is only as rich as his last sale, and in some future negotiation the former president might agree to serve as a lobbyist putting in a telephone call to Margaret Thatcher (for her own memoirs) or to Senator Jesse Helms for a favorable reading of the antitrust laws.

Certainly the big media found no fault with Reagan's gerrymandered life. The *New York Times*, ABC television and *Time* magazine received the publication of the book in the adoring posture of the Magi come to Bethlehem to praise the arrival of good news. Christopher Lehmann-Haupt, the principal critic for the daily *Times*, gratefully accepted the fiction that Reagan somehow had written the text. Choosing his adjectives with the obsequious tact of a salesclerk behind the perfume counter at Bloomingdale's, Lehmann-Haupt discovered in the book a "distinct and personal voice" as well as a "sense of authenticity." Barbara Walters on ABC's *20/20* barely managed to restrain her impulse to kneel. The book, "like the man himself," she pronounced "humorous and gentle."

But the most egregious flattery appeared, not surprisingly, in *Time*, which published expensive excerpts from the book in its 5 November and 12 November issues under the headline AMERICAN DREAMER. The prefatory remarks, written by *Time*'s deputy chief of correspondents, introduced Reagan as "this avuncular American . . . a sweet soul with firm if simple beliefs." The deputy chief of correspondents conceded that "Dutch Reagan's own recollections" might be taken to task on a few niggling points of omission. It was true that the narrative was "celluloid thin," and it was also true that Reagan didn't quite answer all the questions asked by the vicious critics in the meanspirited quarters of the media. But the critics never understood that good old Dutch was a wonderful man forced to bear heartbroken witness to the awful things done (by other people, all of them nasty) to his hope of "morning in America." The critics didn't know, as the deputy chief of corespondents knew, that Reagan "was and remains a stubborn dreamer, a radical reformer out to rid the world of nuclear war and Big Government . . . a man totally without guile operating in a world of cunning rascals."

Trying manfully to edit the tears out of his copy, the deputy chief of correspondents ended his preface with an evocation of that far-off, blessed day in Washington when Reagan stepped forward to deliver his first inaugural address at precisely the same moment that a shaft of sunlight descended through the gray clouds to certify the miracle of his advent.

In a society fortified with some sense of its own dignity and worth, the publication of *An American Life* would be understood as an act of contempt. Contempt for a public that the media deem to be so debased that it will bear any insult and suffer, without objection any jeering mockery. Contempt for the uses of language and the meaning of words. Contempt for the immense labor with which people struggle to tell the story of what they have seen and thought and known. Contempt for the continuum of human feeling and experience in which people preserve what they have found beautiful as well as useful on their voyage through the gulf of time.

If we accept the Reagan autobiography as anything other than an insult and a mockery, we commit a kind of suicide. History embodies the triumph of memory over the spirit of corruption, and if we deny the truth of our existence, we lose the right to our own names.

The machinery of the big media is as indifferent to the force of intellect as it is to the first person singular. Although the individuals operating the equipment might wish it were otherwise, the media as a collective entity cannot help but speak in the voice of a ventriloquist's dummy, a voice as false as the one in which the artificial Ronald Reagan tells the parable of an artificial life. The media mean to please, never to teach or bear witness. The networks and the big publishing syndicates address themselves not to an answering mind but to an empty and silent crowd. They mount spectacles and sell cures for unhappiness and misfortune. Collectively, they perform the function of the monkish pardoners of medieval Europe who carried on a profitable traffic in Christian relics. To the fourteenth-century markets in superstition the pardoner sold fragments of the true cross and feathers said to have fallen from the wing of the archangel Gabriel. To the twentieth-century trade in desperate wish and childish dream the media sell pages said to have dropped from the hand of a Dutch uncle.

On the Monday following Reagan's cameo appearance with Barbara Walters, one of the darker mysteries of modern communication was revealed to me in a SoHo restaurant by a man who had tuned the tenor of his mind to the lute music of an earlier century. I noticed him as soon as I walked into the place because he looked too expensive for the setting, too sleek and self-assured, too much like a work of art temporarily on loan from the Upper East Side. The restaurant caters to a downtown crowd, mostly writers and would-be writers habitually slow with the rent. The gentleman at the next table looked to be in his middle forties, and he was dressed as if for a photograph advertising Ralph Lauren's theory of the leisure class. The woman with whom he was eating dinner could have posed for the same advertisement—blond, maybe ten years younger than the man, wearing a silk blouse and a strand of reassuringly heavy pearls. They both examined the menu with a diligence befitting their status as model students of the good life. I lost track of them during the soup course, and so it was with some alarm that by the time the salad arrived I noticed that the man had worked himself into a fit of inarticulate rage. More alarmingly, the welter of his confused ill-feeling appeared to be directed at myself.

I had been talking at some length about Reagan and Reagan's rotten book, and the gentleman apparently had taken offense. He didn't wish to be associated with the vilification of a great and true American, but he was too polite to denounce me as a traitor and a spy. Lacking the nerve for speech, he reached into his briefcase for a copy of that morning's *Wall Street Journal*, and then, very carefully, he opened the pages between our two tables as if the double spread of paper were a hospital screen placed next to the bed of a patient afflicted with a contagious disease.

Or maybe he meant the paper to stand between us as a kind of magical shield, like the one that the Red Cross Knight carried to Jerusalem on Holy Crusade. The *Wall Street Journal* faithfully had preserved President Reagan from harm or censure during his two terms in office, and it occurred to me that the corporate gentleman might have endowed the paper with the power of Moses' rod. In his briefcase lying open on the floor I noticed a number of objects believed to express and contain the wonders of modern technology (an electronic calculator, a portable phone, a sheaf of computer spread sheets, a Mont Blanc pen), and I thought of Charles V, the French king who adorned his royal chapel with his collection of relics and who, by the time he was thirty, in the year 1368, had acquired, among other objects, the top of John the Baptist's head, Christ's swaddling clothes, the crown of thorns and a flask of the Virgin's milk.

I could imagine the corporate gentleman acquiring the text of *An American Life* in the same spirit of humility that so inspired and uplifted the pious king. But I didn't think that his lady friend would be as easily satisfied. At a price of $25 the copy, she presumably would expect a further sign of Reagan's beatitude, and I could imagine her asking the salesclerk to repeat the publisher's guarantee to the effect that Reagan's photograph on the back cover would, given world enough and time, weep genuine tears.

January 1991

TRAINED SEALS AND SITTING DUCKS

Journalism consists in buying white paper at
two cents a pound.
—CHARLES A. DANA

*B*etween the two campaigns waged by the American military command last winter in the Arabian desert—one against the Iraqi army and the other against the American media—it's hard to know which resulted in the more brilliant victory. Both campaigns made use of similar tactics (superior logistics, deception, control of the systems of communication), and both were directed at enemies so pitiably weak that their defeat was a foregone conclusion.

The bombardment of Baghdad began on 17 January, and within a matter of hours the newspaper and television correspondents abandoned any claim or pretension to the power of independent thought. It was as if they had instantly enlisted in the ranks of an elite regiment, sworn to protect and defend whatever they were told to protect and defend by the generals who presented them with their morning film clips and their three or four paragraphs of yesterday's news.

By the end of the first week I no longer could bear to watch the televised briefings from Washington and Riyadh. The journalists admitted to the presence of authority were so obviously afraid of giving offense that they reminded me of prisoners of war. The parallel image appeared on cue five weeks later when what was left of the Iraqi army stumbled across the desert waving the white rags of surrender.

The Iraqi troops at least had suffered the admonitions of gunfire. The American media surrendered to a barrage of propaganda before the first F-16 fired its first round at an Iraqi military target. The Pentagon's invitation to the war carried with it a number of conditions—no reporters allowed on the battlefield except under strict supervision, and then only in small task forces designated as "press pools;" all dispatches submitted to the military censors for prior review; no unauthorized conversations with the allied troops; any violation of the rules punishable by expulsion from the theater in the sand.

The media accepted the conditions with scarcely a murmur of protest or complaint. Who could afford to decline even so ungracious an invitation? The promise of blood brings with it the gift of headlines, audiences, single-copy sales, Nielsen ratings, Pulitzer prizes and a swelling of the media's self-esteem. A television network on assignment to a war imagines itself outfitted with the trappings of immortality. The pictures, for once, mean something, and everybody has something important to say.

On the fourth day of the bombing Dan Rather confirmed the Pentagon's contemptuous opinion of a media cheaply bought for a rating point and a flag. He appeared on a CBS News broadcast with Connie Chung, and after reading the day's bulletin, he said, "Connie, I'm told that this program is being seen [by the troops] in Saudi Arabia. . . . And I know you would join me in giving our young men and women out there a salute." Rather then turned to the camera and raised his right hand to his forehead in a slightly awkward but unmistakably earnest military salute.

The salute established the tone of the media's grateful attendance at what everybody was pleased to call a war. Had anybody been concerned with the accurate use of words, the destruction of Iraq and the slaughter of an unknown number of Iraqis—maybe 50,000, maybe 150,000—might have been more precisely described as a police raid, as the violent suppression of a mob, as an exemplary lesson in the uses of major-league terrorism. Although the Iraqi army had been much advertised as a synonym for evil (as cruel as it was "battle-hardened," possessed of demonic weapons and a fanatic's wish for death), it proved, within a matter of hours, to consist of half-starved recruits, as scared as they were poorly armed, only too glad to give up their weapons for a cup of rainwater.

But the American media, like the American military commanders, weren't interested in the accuracy of words. They were interested in the accuracy of bombs, and by whatever name one wanted to call the Pentagon's trade show in the Persian Gulf, it undoubtedly was made for television. The parade of images combined the thrill of explosions with the wonder of technology. Who had ever seen—live and in color—such splendid displays of artillery fire? Who could fail to marvel at the sight of doomed buildings framed in the glass eye of an incoming missile? Who had ever seen the light of the Last Judgement coursing through a biblical sky?

Most of the American correspondents in Saudi Arabia experienced the war at more or less the same remove as the television audience in Omaha or Culver City. They saw little or nothing of the battlefield, which was classified top secret and declared off-limits to the American public on whose behalf the war presumably was being waged. The military command provided the media with government-issue images roughly equivalent to the publicity stills handed around to gossip columnists on location with a Hollywood film company. Every now and then the government press agents arranged brief interviews with members of the cast—a pilot who could be relied upon to say hello to all the wonderful folks who made the plane and the ordnance, a nurse who missed her six-month-old son in Georgia, an infantry sergeant (preferably black) who had discovered that nothing was more precious than freedom. But even this kind of good news was subject to official suspicion. A reporter who said of some pilots that the excitement upon returning from a mission had made them "giddy" found the word changed to "proud."

The Pentagon produced and directed the war as a television mini-series based loosely on Richard Wagner's *Götterdämmerung*, with a script that borrowed elements of *Monday Night Football*, *The A Team*, and *Revenge of the*

Nerds. The synchronization with primetime entertainment was particularly striking on Super Bowl Sunday. ABC News intercut its coverage of the game in progress in Tampa with news of the bombing in progress in the Middle East, and the transitions seemed entirely in keeping with the spirit of both events. The newscasters were indistinguishable from the sportscasters, all of them drawing diagrams in chalk and talking in similar voices about the flight of a forward pass or the flare of a Patriot missile. The football players knelt to pray for a field goal, and the Disneyland halftime singers performed the rites of purification meant to sanctify the killing in the desert.

The televised images defined the war as a game, and the military command in Riyadh was careful to approve only those bits and pieces of film that sustained the illusion of a playing field (safe, bloodless and abstract) on which American soldier-athletes performed feats of matchless daring and skill.

Like the sportscasters in the glass booth on the fifty-yard line, the newscasters standing in front of the palm tree or the minaret understood themselves to be guests of the management. Just as it never would occur to Frank Gifford to question the procedures of the National Football League, so also it never occurred to Tom Brokaw to question the ground rules of the war. When an NBC correspondent in Israel made the mistake of talking to New York about an Iraqi missile falling on Tel Aviv without first submitting his news to the local censors, the Israeli government punished his impudence by shutting down the network's uplink to the satellite. The embargo remained in force until Brokaw, at the opening of *NBC Nightly News*, apologized to Israel for the network's tactlessness.

Between representatives of competing news organizations the protocol was seldom so polite. The arguments were about access—who got to see whom, when, why and for how long—and the correspondents were apt to be as jealous of their small privileges as the hangers-on attached to the entourage of Vanilla Ice. When Robert Fisk, a reporter for the British paper the *Independent*, arrived at the scene of the fighting for the town of Khafji, he was confronted by an NBC television reporter—a licensed member of the day's press pool—who resented the intrusion. "You asshole," the television correspondent said. "You'll prevent us from working. You're not allowed here. Get out. Go back to Dhahran." The outraged nuncio from NBC summoned an American Marine public affairs officer, who said to Fisk, "You're not allowed to talk to U.S. Marines, and they're not allowed to talk to you."

Even under the best of circumstances, however, print was no match for television. The pictures shaped the way the story was told in the papers, the newsmagazines and the smaller journals of dissenting opinion. Although a fair number of writers (politicians as well as scholars and plain citizens) took issue with the Bush administration's conduct of the war, their objections couldn't stand up to the heavy-caliber imagery delivered from Saudi Arabia in sorties as effective as the ones flown by the tactical fighter squadrons. *Time* and *Newsweek* followed the pictures with an assault of sententious rhetoric—"The greatest feat of arms since World War II . . . Like Hannibal at Cannae or Napoleon on a very good day."

At the end as in the beginning, the bulk of the writing about the events in the Persian Gulf was distinguished by its historical carelessness and its grotesque hyperbole. The record strongly suggests that the Bush administration resolved to go to war as early as last August, almost as soon as Saddam Hussein made the mistake of invading Kuwait. If the war could be quickly and easily won, then the administration might gain a number of extremely desirable ends, among them the control of the international oil price, a revivification of the American military budget, a diversion of public attention from the sorrows of the domestic economy, a further degradation of what passes for the nation's political opposition, a cure for the mood of pessimism that supposedly had been undermining Washington's claims to world empire.

But none of these happy events could be brought to pass unless a credulous and jingoistic press could convince the American people that Hussein was a villain as monstrous as Adolf Hitler, that his army was all but invincible, that the fate of nations (not to mention the destiny of mankind) trembled in the balance of decision. It wouldn't do any good to send the grand armada to the Persian Gulf if the American people thought that the heavy guns were being wheeled into line to blow away a small-time thug.

The trick was to make the sitting duck look like the 6,000-pound gorilla. Much later in the proceedings Lieutenant General Thomas Kelly could afford to say, amidst applause and self-satisfied laughter at the daily press briefing at the Pentagon, that, yes, sending B-52's to carpet bomb a single Iraqi Scud site was, come to think of it, "a delightful way to kill a fly." But in the beginning the generals were a good deal more careful about the work of disinformation. By October, Washington was besieged with ominous reports—about Hussein's chemical and biological weapons, about the price of oil rising to $50 or $100 a barrel, about the nuclear fire likely to consume the orchards of Israel, about the many thousands of body bags being sent to Saudi Arabia to collect the American dead. All the reports derived from government sources, and all of them proved to be grossly exaggerated.

The advantage of hindsight suggests that President Bush and his advisers chose Saddam Hussein as a target of opportunity precisely because they knew that his threats were mostly bluster and his army more bluntly described as a gang of thieves. The media never subjected the administration's statements to cross-examination, in large part because the administration so deftly promoted the fiction of a "liberal press" bent on the spiteful negation of America's most cherished truths. The major American media are about as liberal as Ronald Reagan or the late John Wayne, but in the popular mind they enjoy a reputation (undeserved but persistent) for radicalism, sedition and dissent. The administration well understood that the media couldn't afford to offend the profoundly conservative sympathies of their primetime audience, and so it knew that it could rely on the media's complicity in almost any deception dressed up in patriotic costume. But for the purposes of the autumn sales campaign it was necessary to cast the media as an antagonist as un-American as Saddam Hussein. If even the well-known "liberal press" could be brought into camp, then clearly the administration's cause was just.

The media loved the story lines (especially the ones about their own dread magnificence), and by Christmas every network and every magazine of respectable size had designed for itself some kind of red, white and blue emblem proclaiming its ceaseless vigilance and its readiness for war. When the steel rain at last began to fall during the second week of January, most of the national voices raised in opposition to the war had been, as the Pentagon spokesmen liked to say, "attrited." Through the five weeks of the aerial bombardment and the four days of the ground assault the version of the public discourse presented in the media turned increasingly callow. *Time* and *Newsweek* published posters of the weapons deployed in the Persian Gulf, and the newspapers gave over the majority of their editorial-page space to columnists gloating about the joy of kicking ass and kicking butt. Andy Rooney on *60 Minutes* struck what had become the media's preferred note of smug self-congratulation. "This war in the Gulf," he said, "has been, by all odds, the best war in modern history. Not only for America but for the whole world, including Iraq probably. It was short and the objectives of victory were honorable. In spite of all the placards, the blood was not for oil. It was for freedom. We did the right thing."

The return of the nation's mercenary army was staged as a homecoming weekend for a college football team, and the troops arriving in Georgia and California found themselves proclaimed, in the words of *Life* magazine, "Heroes All." Many of them had spent several uncomfortable months camping in the desert, but few of them had taken part in any fighting. The number of American casualties (125 dead in action, 23 of them killed by "friendly fire") once again posed the question of whether America had gone to a war or to a war game played with live ammunition. But it was a question that few people cared to ask or answer.

Maybe the question is irrelevant. In the postmodern world maybe war will come to be understood as a performing art, made for television and promoted as spectacle. Maybe, as the producers of the charades on MTV would have it, Madonna is Marilyn Monroe, true love is a perfume bottle and George Bush is Winston Churchill.

Certainly the administration succeeded in accomplishing what seemed to be its primary objectives. The cost of oil went down and the prices on the New York Stock Exchange (among them the prices paid for Time Warner, the Washington Post Company, CNN, and the *New York Times*) went up. The country welcomed the easy victories in Kuwait and Iraq with band music, ticker-tape parades and speeches to the effect that once again it was good to be American.

Still, I find it hard to believe that the American people feel quite as triumphant as they have been made to appear in the newsmagazines. The cheering rings a little hollow, as if too many people in the crowd were shouting down the intimations of their own mortality. The elation seemed more like a feeling of relief—relief that so few Americans were killed and that almost everybody, this time at least, got home safely.

Maybe the war in the desert was a brilliant success when measured by the cynical criteria of realpolitik, but realpolitik is by definition a deadly and autocratic means of gaining a not very noble end. The means might be necessary, but they are seldom admirable and almost never a cause for joyous thanksgiving. If we celebrate a policy rooted in violence, intrigue, coercion and fear, then how do we hold to our higher hopes and aspirations? We debase our own best principles if we believe the gaudy lies and congratulate ourselves for killing an unknown number of people whom we care neither to know nor to count. How do we tell the difference between our victories and our defeats unless we insist that our media make the effort of asking questions other than the ones that flatter the vanity of the commanding general? Like the seal balancing the red, white and blue ball on the end of its faithful nose, a servile press is a circus act, as loudly and laughingly cheered by a military dictatorship as by a democratic republic.

May 1991

AGITPROP

> We have rudiments of reverence for the human
> body, but we consider as nothing the rape
> of the human mind.
> —ERIC HOFFER

Among the several shams being promoted this summer by the Republican presidential campaign, the most fanciful as well as the most dishonest is the one about "the cultural elite"—the presumably sinister conspiracy of liberal opinion in New York and Los Angeles said to be corrupting the texts of American virtue. Both President Bush and Vice President Quayle describe the conspiracy in words unctuously chosen to convey the impression of a vast company of anonymous malcontents whom it would be too dangerous to confront or to name. In answer to a question from Barbara Walters in late June on ABC, President Bush frowned at the camera and said, "I can't define what cultural elite means, but I know it when I see it."

He could as easily have been talking about modern art. Tacitly invoking the authority of a former director of the Central Intelligence Agency, the president indicated powers not lightly trifled with, and he left it to Barbara, and to the 18 million viewers presumably at home in the good and true America—the America blessed by its churches, its Little League baseball teams, its lawns and family picnics—to draw their own ominous conclusions about the threat to their moral safety.

Vice President Quayle has been slightly more forthcoming with his winks and smiles and brightly polished innuendos. If he has provided only a few names—those of Mario Cuomo and Murphy Brown—at least he knows the whereabouts of the conspirators, and he isn't afraid to say—as countless all-American demagogues have said before him—that they can be found in Hollywood film studios, in faculty lounges, in the offices of the news media. Pressed for more specific identifications on the *MacNeil/Lehrer NewsHour*, Quayle wagged his finger like a reproving nursery-school teacher and said, "They know who they are."

296

Quayle first raised the hue and cry against the cultural elite in May, and by the Fourth of July, in time for the small-town Independence Day parades, he and President Bush had let fall enough hints and whispers to allow for the composition of a police artist's sketch of the suspects wanted for the murder of the American dream. As the delegates to the Republican convention assembled in Houston in August, the all-points bulletin supplied the following description:

> A man or woman in "jaded" middle age, likely to be driving a foreign car and speaking in sarcasms. Urban temperament. Dark or sallow complexion, possibly Jewish. Consorts with known homosexuals and approves the practice of abortion. "Sophisticated" taste in seafood and sexual fetishes. Jeers at babies in carriages and avoids performances of *Oklahoma*. Often seen mocking the American flag. Numerous prior arrests for cutting the American moral fiber into strips of Surrealist verse or pornographic film. Armed with liberal catchphrases and feminist slogans. Likely to be angry and believed to be dangerous.

The Republican caricature of an American cultural elite is as grotesque as the old Communist caricature of an American ruling class. The White House propagandists mean to condemn as wicked and immoral most of what they see of the nation's intellectual theory and commercial entertainment, but they choose not to make distinctions between the various facets of the mass media, and they assign to the wrong people the powers of fiends and demons. The misidentification is both cynical and deliberate. As even Vice President Quayle must know by now, the manufacture and sale of America's cultural product is the work of very large, very profitable and very timid corporations—Time Warner, the Washington Post Company, Harvard University, Fox Broadcasting, Condé Nast, the Public Broadcasting System, Columbia Pictures. Such corporations define culture as anything that turns a profit—no matter how indecent the photograph or how tasteless the joke—and they seldom take chances with any book, movie, situation comedy, revisionist history, hairspray commercial or rap song that fails to drum up a crowd. Nor do they care very much which lies pass for truth. If in one season Richard Nixon can be promoted and sold as a crouching villain—a secondhand car salesman, enemy of the people, and so on—in another season he can be promoted and sold as a benign elder statesman—experienced and wise, the soul of probity. Properly marketed, both editions of the man can be processed into headlines, television time and best-selling books.

The artisans who manufacture the nation's cultural product belong to different guilds—the film producers being bound by different rules and conventions than television anchorpersons or academic literary critics—but at all points on the assembly line they learn to tell their respective audiences what those audiences want and expect to hear. They have no choice in the matter if they wish to make the syndication deal, sell the paperback rights or achieve tenure. Better understood as nervous careerists than as dissident anarchists, they could as easily be making sausage or Christmas toys. Very few of them can afford the luxury of an idea of their own. They follow a market or a trend, and culture is something that they mean to get around to next summer when they have time to read Proust or listen to one of Beethoven's last quartets.

Of the 200 highest-grossing movies that Hollywood releases every year, at least 150 must pass prior review by audiences deemed demographically correct. The film studios run test screenings in suburban shopping malls and then ask the people rounded up for the occasion to fill out printed forms: Was the ending good for you? Which characters were too distasteful? Did any scenes offend? Would you recommend the film to a friend? As described by Paula Silver, president of marketing for Columbia Pictures, the procedures would be well understood by the speechwriters who assemble the public image of Vice President Quayle. "It's the same thing you do with a product," she said. "You sample it: Is it too sweet? Is it too hot?"

Similar terms and conditions govern the manufacture of the nation's news and leading academic opinion. Together with the teaching in the schools, the national media preserve the myths that the society deems precious, reassuring their patrons that all is well, that the American truths remain securely in place, that the banks are safe, our generals competent, our presidents interested in the common welfare, our artists capable of masterpieces, our weapons invincible and our democratic institutions the wonder of an admiring world.

By telling their audiences what they assume they already know, the news media reflect what the society at the moment wants to believe about itself. Believing everything and nothing, the media compose the advertisements for a preferred reality. Yes, say the media, the Vietnam War was a holy crusade (no, say the media, the Vietnam War was a cruel imperialist hoax); yes, say the media, homosexuality is a lifestyle (no, say the media, homosexuality is a disease); yes, say the media, the Kennedys were demigods (no, say the media, the Kennedys were beasts); yes, say the media, America is indestructible (no, say the media, America has lost its resolve).

Yes, Virginia, there is a world out there, and it not only can be vividly described but also looks just the way you always wanted it to look.

Given the commercial premise of the American dream, truth is anything that pays the rent and the stockholders, but the predictably feeble-minded result always strikes me as especially poignant at the country's better universities. Traveling to Yale or Stanford or the University of Michigan to give a speech or conduct a seminar, I expect to meet people who can still afford to say what they think. I find instead a faculty preoccupied with the great questions of tenure and preference. Everybody is studying the art of writing grant proposals or worrying about the proper forms of courteous address appropriate to the magnificence of the department chairman. The market in tenure enforces submission to the doctrines of political correctness, and freedom of expression proves to be contingent upon the circumstances—permissible in some company, not in others.

On a train to New Haven several years ago I remember the late A. Bartlett Giamatti remarking that as president of Yale University he was obliged to speak and write a language that he classified as "the higher institutional." Once he had been a Renaissance scholar and an occasional contributor to *Harper's Magazine*, but he no longer could risk plain statement or strong opinion on any subject likely to rouse even the faintest murmur of controversy. I do not recall his exact words, but the gist of his melancholy was to the effect that it was the task of a university president to raise money from the alumni—or from the government or the charitable foundations or anybody with the money for a gymnasium—and so he was forever bending the courtier's knee to the ruling prejudices of the age. He had thought that a university president was supposed to cut a more dignified figure in the world, maybe even that of a man to whom others might look for wisdom or moral example. Instead, and much to his embarrassment and regret, he found himself constantly performing the part of the court fool, grinning at every rich man's joke, putting on whatever funny hat of a political cliché the donor of a new library wished him to put on. The thought moved him to bitter and mocking laughter. I can still see his gaunt face wreathed in cigarette smoke and the sardonic expression in his eyes as he stared out the window at the rain drifting through the hollow tenements of the South Bronx. "The university president as song and dance man," he said, "stepping lightly through the paces of a beggar's pantomime." His mordant humor spoke not only to the subservience of the university but also to the servility of the movie studio, the publishing house, the network news division.

Quite a few of Vice President Quayle's presumed conspirators would rather be doing something else—performing plays by Shakespeare instead of those by Neil Simon, writing essays for *The New York Review of Books* instead of celebrity profiles for *Vanity Fair* or *Parade*, teaching the novels of Ralph Ellison or Edith Wharton instead of novels by Toni Morrison or Jay McInerney. Many of them feel ashamed of the work made to the specifications of a market survey or a Nielsen rating—ashamed of the perfume commercials brushed with the scent of prurience, ashamed of the books they edit and the music assembled from scraps of prerecorded sound.

But what choice do they have if they hope to advance the token of their career around the Monopoly board of the standard American success? How else can they write themselves into the script of the romantic comedy that Vice President Quayle imagines to be synonymous with the story of a wholesome American life? Assuming that they lack the vice president's comfortably inherited fortune, the lovely white house in the suburbs—the one with the lawn and the picnic and the children coming home on bicycles from church or Little League baseball—trades at the price of aligning their thought with the test results in Midland or Tulsa, of spelling the word "potato" with a final "e" if that is the way it is written on a cue card, or saying whatever it is that the managing editor or the advertising director or the company chairman wishes them to say.

The Republican propaganda about the loss of American innocence blames the servant for the fault of the master and substitutes a fictitious cultural elite for the corporate elite that owns and manages the country's news and entertainment. Unlike the anonymous and wraithlike figures dreamed of in the bombast of Messrs Bush and Quayle, the gentlemen in question are plainly visible and easily named. The United States makes of business its culture, and of its culture a business, and at any fund-raising breakfast or White House dinner, the president and vice president need merely look around the room or across the table to discover the princes of darkness about whom they have heard and told so many mysterious tales. Who would have guessed that they would prove to be so pleasant, or so generous with their campaign contributions, or so knowledgeable about the golf courses in Palm Springs? What an extraordinary surprise. Who would have thought that the little bald man wearing the red bow tie—the one behind the flowers, buttering his toast and talking to Arnold Schwarzenegger and Senator Rudman—just yesterday morning signed a distribution deal for Madonna's next four movies?

The corporate elite makes no secret of its presence, and one or more of its ranking members can be seen every month in the admiring pages of *Forbes* or *Fortune*. As vain as actors, and grinning like amateur sportsmen among deer antlers and ornamental trout, the captains of the country's entertainment industry pose for their portraits against the backdrops of the lawns and horses that prove the worth of cultural products geared to the lowest possible standards of intelligence and taste.

Nor does the corporate elite make any secret of its commercial reading of the text of human nature, or what it means by the store of American moral value. What is moral is what returns a profit and satisfies the judgement of the bottom line. The definition of money as the sublime good leads to the depreciation of all values—family or otherwise—that do not pay. Every now and then one of the Republican voices of conscience—William Bennett or Charlton Heston or George Will—makes public moan in the newspapers about the decay of manners and the loss of virtue, but in private conversation, no matter what crimes a man may have committed or how cynically he may have debased his talent or his friends, variations on the answer "Yes, but I did it for the money" satisfy all but the most tiresome objections. The desire for wealth might not be an attractive or ennobling passion, but as an explanation it answers for most modes of conduct that otherwise might be construed as stupid, cruel or self-defeating.

On more than one occasion over the last thirty years, I have petitioned the corporate elite on behalf of an idea not easily translated into the vocabulary of profit and loss, dancing a "beggar's pantomime" in front of eminences as grand as the chairmen of CBS and Mobil Oil. The gentlemen listen with the same degree of polite attention that they bring to performances of *Rigoletto*. I bow and smile and advance an argument for literacy or school libraries or the teaching of history, but before I reach the peroration I know that I might as well be talking to stones. The gentlemen define education as a commodity and culture as merchandise. The terms of manufacture, distribution and sale meet the same minimal standards of virtue that Vice President Quayle's Council on Competitiveness sets for the manufacture and sale of chemical compounds and automobile engines.

But if the iron laws of profit and loss pertain to the market for goods, then why not to the market for images and ideas? The question makes nonsense of the Republican campaign rhetoric about home-grown family values pitted against metropolitan cultural elites. The hypocrisy is so patently false and so sweet with the air of sanctimony that I am surprised it plays to any audiences other than the ones hired to fill out the printed forms telling the producers whether in the last reel Vice President Quayle wins the golf tournament and loses the election, or wins the election and loses the golf tournament.

September 1992

UPSTAIRS, DOWNSTAIRS

He . . . met every kind of person except the ordinary person.
He knew everybody, so to speak, except everybody.
— G. K. CHESTERTON

A few weeks ago in the *New York Times* I noticed the headline "Increasingly, British Editors Are Setting Tone in the U.S.," and as I read the story about the imported sensibility said to be setting the standards of American taste, I remembered a debutante dance on Long Island in the 1950s and a Texas oil millionaire offering to hire a young Englishman, an officer in one of the Queen's own regiments, as a party favor or a pool ornament. The oilman's daughter had expressed an interest in the gentleman after dancing with him twice and listening to him explain fox hunting and the Battle of Hastings. Her father, newly rich and as loud as he was crass, informed the rest of us at the table that nothing was too good for his little girl. She was an attractive but sullen blonde who looked ten years older than her age, and while her father put the proposition to the British officer, she sat silently, withdrawn into the recesses of a white mink coat, watching the conversation as if it were a tennis match. She was wearing diamonds and dark glasses, and it was impossible to know whether she was embarrassed or amused. The Englishman knew the right sort of people at both Oxford and Buckingham Palace, and he had come to America that summer with the thought of traveling through the Rocky Mountains and the Great Plains. When the debutante's father understood that the Englishman was low on funds, he suggested that he forget the trip and come instead to Texas where he would learn more about the real American West than he would in a year of wandering through a lot of nowhere places that weren't big enough to water a herd of rabbits. The oilman proposed a consideration of $50 a day, the use of a small guesthouse on his ranch in Dallas and a troop of Mexican horsemen to show him the trails through the juniper and sage.

"Yes," said the Englishman, "I see, but what, if you don't mind my asking, would I have to do?"

"Show up for cocktail parties," the oilman said. "Walk around the pool. Lend tone."

The story in the *Times* named the prominent American magazines recently given over to the direction of British editors—among them *The New Yorker, Vogue, National Review, Details, Condé Nast Traveler, The New Republic, TV Guide* and *Harper's Bazaar*—and then went on to rely on an American journalist named Roger Rosenblatt to explain the significance of tone. Like the young lady from Texas, Rosenblatt apparently was deeply impressed by old silver and polished wood: "It may be that the English are so well trained in language and that we are experiencing a reinvigorated appreciation of language," he said. " . . . The English have certain historical skills, such as the skill of argument with grace. Maybe bringing in these English editors shows that we are feeling a little more comfortable with ourselves in allowing ourselves to embrace self-mockery."

In the mauve sectors of American opinion, the faith in British syntax is as traditional as the trust in London tailors. Prior to the Civil War the sensibility was confined to the quasiaristocratic South, but during the 1870s the Northern merchant interests borrowed large sums of British money to finance the building of the transcontinental railroads, and the bankers who arranged the loans returned to the United States deeply impressed by the English manner that they associated with the wonder of wealth, ease, privilege and social rank. As proof of their gratitude they brought with them several ornaments of civilization previously unknown on the western shore of the Atlantic lawns—yacht racing, blazers, the boarding school, the country house. By the 1890s the daughters of large American fortunes were marrying British peers, and if it was sometimes difficult to acquire a duke, it was nearly always possible to acquire an English butler, an English riding habit or the bound volumes of an English author. The works of Rudyard Kipling introduced three generations of American schoolboys to the sport of overseas empire, and throughout the rest of the twentieth century a long procession of British literary missionaries—among them authors as different from one another as H. G. Wells, Virginia Woolf, P. G. Wodehouse and Agatha Christie—pitched the tents of English grammar in the wilderness of American prose. The Anglo-American alliances in the two world wars confirmed the British claim to cultural supremacy. The British might not know how to manage an invasion of Europe, but a British raincoat was always preferable to an American raincoat, and a British poet was by definition more profound than an American poet.

The decorative value of all things English has steadily improved over the last thirty years, but the different generations of American wealth have collected different objects in the catalogue. The railroad and mining fortunes of the 1890s were attracted to noble names, the oil fortunes of the 1950s to the remnants of the nineteenth-century British empire. The present-day media fortunes delight in editors, a passion carried to its most extravagant effect by S. I. Newhouse, who owns no fewer than four of the magazines listed in the *Times*. Editors might not make as much of a show in the world as dukes and racehorses, but they are less expensive to main-tain (less expensive and often better informed) and among the kind of people who speculate in the markets in tone they are another exquisite proof of the owner's refinement, taste and net worth.

The presence of so many British editors in New York at the moment testifies not only to the wealth of their proprietors but also to the social insecurity of the emergent American *rentier* class. As the United States over the last ten years increasingly has divided into the nation of the rich and the nation of the poor, it is only the citizens of the former and more favored nation who can still afford both the opinions and the clothes advertised in the fragrant fashion magazines. It is an opening-night crowd, astonished by celebrity and opulent spectacle, reluctant to read anything that cannot be reduced to five lines of gossip, preferring to display its literary sensibility by being seen at the opera or collecting the Duchess of Windsor's jewels or Andy Warhol's cookie jars. The depart-ment stores trade in a line of goods cut from the same historical pageant, and if the showrooms of Ralph Lauren's "Polo" resemble a set from *Brideshead Revisited*, it is because the customers like to know themselves properly dressed for the cricket at Lords or the racing at Ascot.

In 1990, as in 1950 and 1890, the new money is a nervous and tentative audience, terrified of being made to look ridiculous, constantly in need of reassurance and instruction—where to sit and when to stand, what to say and when to applaud, where to go in the Dry Tortugas and which fish to order at Le Cirque.

The British find it easier than the Americans to make the lists of grace and favor. The spirit of liberty is the spirit that is not too sure that it is right, and the rules of egalitarian protocol prevent the Americans from making invidious distinctions between novelists and hats. We assume that the other fellow might have something valuable to say, even if he doesn't live in Palm Beach, and we like to believe that everybody is as good as everybody else. Heirs to the arrogance of empire and born to the divisions of social class, the British don't suffer from what the Earl of Rochester undoubtedly once referred to as "the democratic vapors," and they feel no compunction about ushering the gentry into the coach and packing the rabble off to debtor's prison. British editors perform the service of British butlers, smiling at some of the guests and frowning at others, arranging the celebrities instead of the forks.

At the present rates of cultural transfer and exchange, it is entirely possible that by the end of the century all the editors in New York will be British and all the topics of polite conversation imported, like all the best croquet mallets, from England. Not, as the doting Mr Rosenblatt would have it, because the editors bring with them a "reinvigorated appreciation" of English prose but because they are fluent in the language of image, status and celebrity. For the most part, it is a language of pictures and signs, not unlike Egyptian hieroglyphs or the rebuses with which children sometimes learn to read. Among its readers in London, the British press is better known for its vicious appetite than for its refined accent, and it is no accident that British editors at the moment also direct the affairs of the supermarket tabloids, lending tone to the freaks and wonders that decorate the pages of *The Globe*, *The Star* and *The National Enquirer*. About ten days after the *Times* published Rosenblatt's homage to the English "skill of argument with grace," the same paper quoted a letter from John le Carré to Tina Brown, the British editor of *The New Yorker*, taking her to task for debasing the magazine with "English standards of malice and English standards of inaccuracy."

If the first of the two newspaper stories reminded me of the Texas oil millionaire, the second reminded me of the late Joseph E. Levine, a Hollywood movie mogul who once bought, for $100,000, an option on what he thought was an original story. The seller was a British screenwriter who contrived to sit next to Levine on a flight between London and New York. Somewhere over Greenland the screenwriter produced seven pages of typescript setting forth the main outlines of a drama to which, so he said, he alone held the copyright. Levine was so excited that he wrote a check before the passengers cleared customs at Kennedy Airport, and when he reached his office in Manhattan, displaying the manuscript as if it were a trophy or a prize, he announced to the assembled company that he had found the work of a genius. One of his vice presidents read the first two pages, and then, after a brief but sardonic silence, he said, "Congratulations, Joe. You bought *Macbeth*."

December 1992

TOWER OF BABEL

The better the technology, the less efficient the
human use of it.
—AUGUST FRUGÉ

For the last seven or eight months, I've been listening to people complain about the lack of anything to watch on television, and I notice that as their options multiply—from ten cable channels to thirty, from thirty channels to seventy-five—so also does the degree of their nervousness and discontent. A few days before President Clinton's inauguration, I spoke to a man who had wired what he called his "situation room" with no fewer than one hundred channels, but the wealth of possibility had tailed to give him joy, and he was bewildered by the emptiness of the view.

"I don't expect you to believe me," he said, "but at ten o'clock last night, there was nothing on."

He was alarmed as well as confused, and I wondered what would become of him when the cable operators deliver, as they have promised to do over the next two or three years, as many as 750 channels. I could imagine him in a state of near panic, pushing frantically at the buttons of his remote-control device, rushing through the channels in search of he knew not what.

The good old days of the network monopolies begin to look like the good old days of the Cold War. Everybody knew who was who and what was what, and the truths told by Walter Cronkite or Johnny Carson were as certain as the border crossings between the capitalist paradise and the communist inferno. But now that the world has slipped the bonds of military empire, it is besieged by the fevers of nationalism—in what was once Yugoslavia and colonial Africa as well as in what was once the Soviet Union. Transposed into the idiom of American television, the parallel expressions of anarchy and irredentism take the form of Rush Limbaugh or Howard Stern, and the façade of cultural imperialism crumbles into the separatist states of moral feeling elected to office by a hand-held camera, a 900 telephone number and a rented studio on Santa Monica Boulevard. The season's political candidates travel the pilgrim road of the tabloid talk shows, making confession to Larry or Barbara or Phil, and in the distant reaches of the cable system, once-upon-a-time celebrities drift like dead moons. On one channel or another, twenty-four hours a day, if not in New York, then in Los Angeles or Chicago or Miami, Gary Cooper and Clint Eastwood teach antithetical lessons in the theory of American justice.

The networks do what they can to sustain the illusion of a common store of value or a unified field of emotion, but their news programs have begun to look like the dioramas at Gettysburg or Epcot Center. I watch Dan Rather interview President Clinton at the White House, and I think of two actors on loan from the Smithsonian, replicating the language of democratic union for the benefit of an audience steadily diminishing in coherence and size.

The incessant division of the American public into the subsections of special interest (cultural and intellectual as well as racial and commercial) spawns the invention of a thousand jargons in which the parties of like-minded sentiment speak chiefly to themselves—lawyer to lawyer, weapons analyst to weapons analyst, literary critic to literary critic, economist to economist.

Four weeks before the release of last year's movie *Malcolm X*, Spike Lee, the director, said that he would prefer to grant interviews only to journalists who were black. Two years ago in New York, while I was taking part in a public discussion of American policy toward Israel, I was informed by a member of the audience that because I was not a Jew my opinions on the subject were worthless. At several of the nation's leading universities the novels of Jane Austen and George Eliot have been remanded to the department of women's studies, the texts subject to explication only by female professors of literature.

The separate audiences recede from one another literally at the speed of light, and the binding curve of technology (satellite transmissions, simultaneous translations into Spanish or Greek, television sets that can choose their own camera angles, and so on) cannot hold together what Sir Richard Livingstone, a former vice-chancellor of Oxford, once described as a "civilization of means without ends." The poor souls searching desperately through the cable channels find themselves lost in the land of the perpetual present, hounded by the desire to grasp or consume, simultaneously, every scrap of vicarious feeling or experience—the glimpse of the half-naked girl on a beach in Rio de Janeiro, the news of next year's financial calamity as foretold by a politician seen briefly on C-Span, the last days of the Third Reich as portrayed in an old newsreel, the dawn rising over the Matterhorn and the sun dropping below the horizon at Java Head. Why compound their anxiety? Why burden them with another 650 proofs of their failure to keep up with the times?

When confronted with this line of objection, the would-be impresarios of channels 101 through 749 speak of the inexhaustible need for information and personal services. I don't envy them the task of filling in the empty space and time, but I have no doubt of their ingenuity, and over the next few years I expect them to astonish the world with the marvels of post-modern aesthetics. The more obvious possibilities consist of repetitions or variations of the current programming—another forty or fifty channels given over to narrowly defined categories of sexual experience, the home shopping networks transformed into illustrated catalogues (for L. L. Bean, Horchow, J. Crew, Bloomingdale's) and maybe a hundred channels following obscure sporting events (badminton tournaments, prep-school soccer)—but even these will not be enough to blot out the horizons of thought, and as further extensions of the present trend I can imagine several lines of likely development:

1. *Medical Cinema Verité.* A variation on the theme of courtroom television. Four cameras in an operating room (one of them overhead) make a continuous record of the work-in-progress. Two or three retired doctors provide commentary in the manner of the retired athletes doing sports broadcasts. They describe the nature of the operation, remark on the surgeon's technique, guess at the patient's chance of survival.

2. *Elvis.* Hourly reports from people who have just run across him in Paris or El Segundo, California.

3. *Tours of Inspection.* Unedited footage of surveillance cameras posted in banks, office buildings, movie theaters, hotels, parking lots and department stores. The primary audience presumably would consist of conspiracy theorists and latter-day Puritans, the kind of people who believe the nation's property and morals must always be closely watched. The show might attract as a secondary audience the merely curious, gossips hoping to see somebody they know checking into a hotel in Dallas when he was supposed to be visiting a relative in St Louis.

4. *Ramtha and Friends.* Conversations with various spirits, druids, Cro-Magnon men, Egyptian queens, departed saints. Sometimes the guests speak in their own voices and languages, sometimes through their mediums or channels. On gala occasions they speak to one another, but they do so only on days that coincide with a solstice, an equinox or a lunar eclipse.

5. *Time Past.* Several channels (376 through 382, or 523 through 535) broadcasting from the historical coordinates of a prior century or era. On one channel the year is always 1846 in America, on another it is 1791 in Georgian London or 1938 in Nazi Germany. Everything is of the period—

the clothes, the furniture, the food, the topics of conversation. People come and go, talking about public events as well as their own domestic affairs. The plots and subplots matter less than the costumes and the sets.

6. *Clouds.* Continuous weather reports from distant deserts and seas. A correspondent posted at the Strait of Magellan reports on wave heights and wind velocities as well as sightings of obscure birds. The show could serve as the sentence of exile for older personnel whom the networks have declared superfluous: a woman makes a mistake with the news from Washington, and she's next seen in the Falkland Islands; an anchorman forgets to dye his hair and he goes directly to the Sea of Azov.

7. *The Last of Their Kind.* Encounters with endangered species. The host, an eminent naturalist, sits across the table from the Florida black bear or the notorious spotted owl and accepts telephone calls from people who wish to express their opinions of the environment. Sometimes the bear nods or the owl frowns. Most of the guests would be plants.

8. *Me.* The life and times of ordinary individuals presented as works of performance art. Chosen at random, from lists of names or because the producer happened to see the person in an elevator or on the street, the newfound celebrities go about the habitual routine of their daily lives. The camera follows them as they do their laundry or their hair, go to their exercise class, eat breakfast, look into a book or newspaper, swat flies, sharpen a pencil, form an occasional sentence.

Sooner or later the technology will make it possible to divide the American public into audiences of one. The camera shot is that of the distracted viewer in the chair, surrounded by the splendor of consumer electronics and armed with the remote-control device that becomes a queen's scepter or a wand with which wizards summon images from a mirror or a pool of standing water. In the brief instant when the viewer changes one channel for another, obliterating the face of the rival celebrity and replacing it with his own, he can imagine that an audience of one is also the government of Ruritania or the will of God.

March 1993

MIXED MEDIA

A work in which there are theories is like an object
which still has its price-tag on it.
—MARCEL PROUST

Although I long ago learned to approach exhibitions of contemporary American art with the same wariness that I bring to government press briefings and Protestant boarding schools, I went to the Whitney Museum in early March with the faint hope that the passing of the Cold War might have tempered the native impulse to correct and improve the conscience of the age. I had no good reason to entertain such a hope, but in reading the work of some of the younger American writers I had noticed less of an emphasis on ideological statement and more of an interest in historical narrative, and I thought it possible that something of the same sensibility might have made its way into gelatin silver print or acrylic paint. The Whitney every two years assembles a biennial exhibition meant to welcome the emerging trends in American art, and any shift of aesthetic mood or intention was likely to show up on one or another of the walls at Madison Avenue and East 75th Street. The exhibition filled the museum's five floors with the work of eighty-two artists, most of them in their thirties and many of them from California, but by the time I had passed through six or seven galleries, I knew that I was doomed to look at slogans and listen to speeches.

The button that served as proof of paid admission was stamped with the message "I can't imagine ever wanting to be white," and the preamble posted on the wall adjacent to the preferred point of entry on the fourth floor spoke of "critical issues and important questions," of "the function of art as socio-political critique," of "the boundaries between art and pornography." The didactic tone of voice reverberated through the whole of the exhibition like the scolding of an angry governess, and even before I reached *Fist of Light* or *Jack F; Forced to Eat His Own Excrement*, I understood that the curators of the nation's conscience had compiled a syllabus of moral attitudes deemed worthy of patient study and dutiful admiration. The attitudes took the form of art objects—compositions in mixed and electronic media as well as sculpture and painting—but they could as easily have been made manifest as political leaflets or religious tracts. Most of the objects required a close reading of the footnotes posted on a nearby wall. It was not enough to merely look at the battered rubber woman or the home movies of homosexual coupling, or the gold-plated tennis sneakers. It was also important to know that the artist "had come to think about history as a dysfunctional idea" or that "these are the people I live with; these are my friends; these are my family; this is my self." The words that recurred in the wall notes—"identity," "imperialism," "difference," "otherness," "void," "oppression"—were borrowed from the dictionary of academic literary criticism, and they all pointed as garishly as road signs to the injustices of gender, race, wealth and social class. By the time I came across *Lard Gnaw* (a shambles of chewed lard mounted on a marble base), I knew that I was expected to read all the homework assignments and refrain from talking in class. The catalogue identified the lard as a "performative gesture" intended as a commentary on the "patriarchal community" that forces women into the "candy boxes" of "consumer fetishism."

None of the lectures in progress everywhere in the museum could be said to flatter or embrace all the assembled grievances, but an untitled fourth-floor installation made mostly of branding irons offered a fairly complete summary of the ruling sentiment. The installation occupied an entire room, and at first sight it was incomprehensible. Arranged in two long and ominous rows, the branding irons dangled from the ceiling in the center of the room, suggesting some sort of fence or jail, and the walls were decorated with what looked like a series of abstract drawings. The effect was both ugly and meaningless until I read the instructions and discovered that each of the branding irons had been forged in the typeface of Gregg shorthand. The two artists, both of them women educated at Brown University, had burned the stenographic symbols onto sheets of muslin, and it was these sheets, mounted on homosote and hung in bed frames, that were to be seen on the walls. Translated into English, the symbols formed single words ("kissing," "licking," "drugs," "intercourse") meant to be read as a communiqué from the frontiers of sexual violence.

After deciphering the riddle of the branding irons, I looked briefly at a collection of pornographic cartoons, read a few more wall messages (about "the psycho-technological mapping of the body" and "the neglected history of lesbian cinema"), and withdrew to the café on the ground floor of the museum to consider the text of the afternoon's lesson. At another table I heard a sophisticated blonde woman in a fur coat tell two German tourists that American magazines and newspapers employ the wrong kind of people to write art criticism. Always, she said, the editors think they owe a debt to a dead muse, and so they send people who have read Goethe and know where to look for Dresden on a map. "An awful mistake," she said. "They should send quacks. Art criticism is like movie criticism—a business for charlatans and frauds. Who else could bear to look at the pictures or read the catalogue?" By some accident of nature, she apparently had escaped the humiliations of branding irons and candy boxes, and the more somber of the two Germans took careful notes, interrupting her antic remarks to ask, please, for the meaning of "elitist crapola."

I take it for granted that most American art, like the bulk of American literature, aspires to the condition of a sermon or a social-science seminar, and so I didn't quarrel with the humorlessness of the exhibition. People dependent on foundation grants and government arts subsidies cannot afford to make jokes. Their talent is the talent for writing funding proposals, and their patrons demand high seriousness and statements of solemn purpose. They illustrate theories of moral and political reform, and they are as suspicious as college deans of unauthorized expressions of sensual or intellectual pleasure. Love is subversive and so is beauty, and joy is a word in Italian. Nor did I expect the exhibition to offer many hints or proofs of genius. In a commercial society people blessed with the gifts of the artistic imagination prefer to work for money, and I had seen all the techniques present on the four floors of the museum deployed to more dramatic effect as fashion design, as MTV film collage, as television advertisement, as Guns 'n' Roses concerts.

What was surprising about the exhibition was its oddly provincial character, as if it had been brought to New York by a committee of very earnest assistant professors amazed by the discovery that politicians sometimes tell lies. The rows of books displayed on the fourth floor (recommended reading for any bourgeois philistines who happened to be passing by) were the kind of texts apt to be seen in a window of a university bookstore during Women's Literature Week or Black History Month. The artists were young, but the doctrine was old. Wandering among the acrylic and the video screens, I noticed so many political tropes on loan from the attic of the late 1950s—the dehumanization of art, the individual lost in the lonely crowd, the imperial white man carried to and fro across the equator on the backs of noble black men, women in tears and the soul in chains—that I wondered where everybody had been for thirty years. Had anybody ever seen anything of the world except its representation in an art gallery in Cincinnati or Omaha? The canon of racial and sexual diversity was the stuff of department-store show windows and primetime television, and over the same weekend that the Whitney opened its exhibition, the

Clinton administration indicated its intention to appoint several hundred new judges—many of them women or minorities—to the federal courts. To the artists making statements on the walls of the Whitney Museum, the news presumably was no more or less interesting than the news from medieval France or ancient Egypt.

As a course of political indoctrination, the biennial exhibition was not only well behind the times but also scornful of the uses of persuasion. If the artists meant to enlighten the audience, why then did they shout so many insults? To whom did they think they were addressing their remarks, and what dream of heaven did they have in mind? The reading room on the fourth floor provided a guest book in which patrons of the exhibition could express their opinions of what they had seen, and on the day that I saw the exhibition, the reviews were mostly bad:

> "The wasted energy on the first floor is an eco-crime."
> "Baudelaire had a phrase for mediocre artists—Les enfants gatés, spoiled children."
> "GWM—35—blond/blue eyes—looking for a sincere relationship."
> "So this is what happens to all the grad students who manage to get through college without learning how to paint."

Favorable reviews were few and brief, but toward the end of the guest book, neatly centered on the page in a handwriting that I took to be that of a professor accustomed to grading exams, I found a rebuttal that defied the mocking critics and set forth the premise of the exhibition:

> "Ninety-nine percent of this audience needs this exhibit. Good going."

Here at last, possibly, was the point. The company of the spiritually elect had arrived from the innocent wilderness (at College Park, Maryland, or under the elm trees at Brown University) to denounce the wickedness of Sodom. It didn't matter that their art was hideous or their polemic as threadbare as the upholstery in a junkyard car. Ugliness was a proof of virtue, and so was the lack of talent. What was important was the scream of righteous fury. I doubt that many of the artists in the exhibition could have said what it was that they were angry about, but clearly something was very wrong with a world that didn't know their names, and maybe if they made some truly offensive "performative gesture," then Senator Jesse Helms might declare them enemies of the state and so rescue them from the pit of anonymity. The dream of heaven was a house in Bel-Air and a gospel of Hallmark cards as simple as the metaphysics of *Dances With Wolves*. Had they been asked to fill out a form indicating their theory of good and evil, I suspect that they would have reached a consensus along the following lines:

Good	*Evil*
The self	The world
Feeling	Thought
Simplicity	Complexity
Equality	Liberty
Expression	Art
Adolescence	Maturity
Nature	Machinery
Innocence	Experience
The country	The city

If only a very rich society can afford to sponsor so naive an aesthetic, only a still-puritan society confuses art with home- and self-improvement. By the end of the century maybe we will learn to do away with institutions as repressive as galleries and museums. Maybe the national endowments will simply let performance artists loose in the streets with pots of red paint, commissioning them to daub scarlet letters (S for Sexist, R for Racist, H for Heterosexual) on the foreheads of citizens suspected of harboring impure thoughts and incorrect opinions.

May 1993

ROBBER BARONS REDUX

> There is more poetry in the rush of a single railroad
> train across the continent than in all the gory story
> of the burning of Troy.
> —JOAQUIN MILLER, 1884

At least twice a week for the last several months, the newspapers have been bringing word of yet another massive deal in progress among the gargantuan media syndicates, and always the breathless tenor of the prose implies exclamation points—Murdoch Acquires

Rights to Asia! Viacom Bids $10 billion for Paramount! Pygmies Flee! Giants Walk the Earth! The stories invariably extol the wonders of the nation's new "information superhighway," and on reading the dispatches from New York and Los Angeles, I think of the furious building of railroads that excited the American imagination during the last decades of the nineteenth century.

The *New York Times* on 21 October published a front-page photograph of eight prominent media executives (among them John C. Malone, president of Tele-Communications Inc.; John L. Clendenin, chairman of Bell-South Corporation; and Raymond W. Smith, chairman of Bell Atlantic) seated side by side behind a row of microphones in Washington, whither they had come, a week after Mr Smith's Bell Atlantic announced its intention to buy Mr Malone's TCI for the sum of $33 billion, to assure the American people that the maneuver was in no way harmful to the public interest. But even as I admired their upright posture and the modesty of their dark and unassuming suits, I wondered how the political cartoonist Thomas Nast would have drawn their caricatures in the old *Harper's Weekly*. Certainly he would have furnished them with top hats and broad grins, also watch chains, florid jowls, brocaded waistcoats bulging with greenbacks, cigars, pet politicians and a general likeness to dressed pork. If the editors had been generous in their allotment of space (a full page and some color in the engraving instead of the customary quarter page for a drawing in ink), Nast undoubtedly would have placed the ragged figure of Liberty under the conference table, a soiled but once-beautiful woman dressed in a tattered American flag on whom the fine gentlemen rested their dainty hog feet.

But Nast has gone off into the mist with Teddy Roosevelt and the buffalo, and "monopoly" is a word no longer extant in the language except when applied to the board game. The *Times* preferred the word "synergy" and stressed the feats of miraculous deliverance certain to take place in the clean, well-lighted rooms of technological advancement. It was an impression encouraged by the gentlemen seated at the microphones, who presented themselves as agents of benevolent dynamism and wholesome change. Not unexpectedly, they were unanimous in their judgement that any interference from the government (that is, any spoilsport nonsense about the antitrust laws) merely would impede progress and delay the arrival of that happy day when all America would travel together along the new superhighway in the sky to the land of the brave and the home of the free. John Sculley, until last October the chairman of Apple Computer and a close adviser to President Bill Clinton, announced the theme of the proceedings in two sentences: "It's impossible for regulators to move as quickly and effectively as the private sector. Government needs to give the private sector a green light to go ahead with investment and innovation."

All present at the conference table seconded the motion, none more loudly than Bert C. Roberts, the chairman of MCI Communications. "All too often," he said, "what we have seen is the government thwart progress." Elsewhere in the room Ronald H. Brown, the secretary of commerce, glistened with the smile of an obliging headwaiter, always happy to be of service, glad to bring the important guests from the media syndicates another pheasant or tax exemption. "I feel like I'm at the Academy Awards," Brown said. " . . . The issue in my mind is not whether companies are big, but whether they are agile, competitive and forward-looking."

Given the unqualified dependence of the communications industries on government subsidy and patronage—in the form of broadcast licenses and cable franchises assigning public property to private use—the ringing endorsements of free trade and free enterprise sounded the customary false note, but, again as customary, nobody in the room made a tasteless joke about the pretensions to good citizenship. Nor did anybody remind the audience that the subject under discussion was monopoly—present, past and future—or that despite the very large sums of money in transit, the combination and recombination of companies served the interests of a very small number of individuals, none of them known for their love of free speech. John C. Malone, president of TCI (the gentleman seated at the extreme left of the photograph, and the one whom Nast undoubtedly would have drawn with the heaviest paunch and the biggest cigar), best exemplified the presiding spirit of implacable and well-organized greed.

As the largest cable television company in the world, TCI owns 1,200 delivery systems in 49 states (roughly 20 percent of the American market) as well as substantial interests in Turner Broadcasting, Teleport Communications, TeleWest (A combined television and telephone company in England) and the Discovery Channel. An ancillary company, Liberty Media, also tendered by Mr Malone to Mr Smith, holds lesser but still extensive interests in Black Entertainment Television, QVC, Home Shopping Network, Courtroom Television Network, Family Channel, Encore and Jukebox. Bell Atlantic presently provides telephone service (land line and cellular) to 13 million customers in 6 states. Consolidated under the same rubric, Bell Atlantic, TCI and Liberty Media combine the carrying capacities of cable television with the switching capacities of a telephone company. Sending its signals through a single wire, the new company must necessarily occupy the attention of 22 million subscribers in all of the country's one hundred principal markets, providing them with television programs, telephone conversations, old movies, sexual fantasies, bank statements, interactive games, doctors' prescriptions and merchandising orders.

At the same time that Malone was arranging the deal with Bell Atlantic last summer, he also was seeking a substantial interest in Paramount Communications—the media conglomerate that owns, in addition to a major movie studio, a large film library, the studio's network television programming, a portfolio of syndicated situation comedies (among them *Cheers, Roseanne* and *The Cosby Show*), a large publishing apparatus (chiefly Simon & Schuster and Prentice Hall), Madison Square Garden, the New York Rangers and the New York Knicks. In this second theater of merger and acquisition, Malone joined his interest with Barry Diller's QVC, with BellSouth (the richest of the country's regional telephone companies), with Comcast (the nation's fourth-largest cable company), with Cox Enterprises (owner of the *Atlanta Constitution* and miscellaneous cable and publishing operations), and with Advance Publications (owner of Random House Books and the Condé Nast magazines).

The attractions of Paramount already had become apparent to Viacom, another of the country's large media combinations (owning, among other assets, nineteen broadcast stations, 1.1 million cable boxes, MTV, Nickelodeon and Showtime), and throughout the late summer and early autumn Viacom and QVC offered increasingly extravagant bids for what the newspapers liked to call "the last studio in play." As Diller assembled allies for QVC, Sumner Redstone, the chairman of Viacom, did likewise, replenishing his own cash reserves with those of Nynex, a regional telephone company, and the Blockbuster Entertainment Corporation. By 7 November the increasingly acrimonious auction put the price of Paramount at \$10.1 billion (offered by Viacom) or \$9.5 billion (offered by QVC).

The financial press made no attempt to quiet its emotions, and always the stories were touched with the bloom of awe. Behold, dear reader, men of genius and resolve—Billionaires! Visionaries! Entrepreneurs!—trading cable systems for telephone lines, and telephone lines for movie studios, and movie studios for cable systems—buying and selling the fonts of celebrity like furlongs of railroad track, risking the hazard of new fortunes for the good of the nation. Most of the same tributes and many of the same adjectives decorated the public effigies of Commodore Vanderbilt, J. P. Morgan and John D. Rockefeller at the zenith of the Gilded Age. The newspapers of the day published ribbons and streamers of praise, and respectful crowds gathered in Grand Central Terminal to watch the lords of industrial creation depart in their private railroad cars for Chicago and Cheyenne. The historian Page Smith summed up the prevalent enthusiasms in a fine paragraph: "The locomotive aroused the deepest emotions of which Americans were capable—awe at its power, at the thrust of its great wheels, the clouds of trailing smoke, the tolling bell, the eerie whistle borne mournfully on the wind (the most haunting music of the new age); greed at the wealth it promised; rage at its dictatorial and unpredictable ways and at the corruption that followed it everywhere like a dark cloud. All that was best and worst in America seemed caught up in the railroad dementia."

The nineteenth-century passion for railroads promoted an outlay of money that Henry Adams thought sufficient "to bankrupt the world," and during the decade of the 1980s American business invested $1 trillion in the myriad forms of information technology, chasing the myriad dreams of limitless freedom and infinite wealth. As was true of nineteenth-century imperialism, some of the dreams were more vicious than others, and not all of them were about the promise of the soul's oasis lying just over the horizon and beyond the next line of cottonwood trees. Malone expressed the familiar hope of commercial dominion on the afternoon that he announced the deal joining the interests of TCI with those of Bell Atlantic. Projecting the vision of a single box on top of every television set in America, a box attached to one wire directing the flow of every conceivable form of information, Malone said, "It will allow us to control all the communications needs of a household with one device."

The words "us" and "control" allied Malone with Commodore Vanderbilt and John D. Rockefeller, both of whom knew that the rules of finance capitalism decreed remorseless combat between the triumphant few (us) and the hapless many (them), and that the amassing of great wealth presupposed absolute command of the means of transportation. Malone apparently replicates their talent for despotism. When the Federal Trade Commission on 11 November obliged Liberty Media to withdraw from the QVC offer for Paramount—because its explicit contempt for the antitrust laws was too flagrant even for the Clinton Administration—the newspapers reported Malone in preliminary discussions with Matsushita Electric (in the hope of buying an interest in MCA) as well as with the Sony Corporation (in the hope of buying an interest in Columbia Pictures). People who know him speak of his arrogance and impatience, of "a bully boy," "an unscrupulous monopolist," and "a guy who knows how to run over people." On being pressed by *Time* magazine for a reply to the characterization, Malone said, "When you're driving plate tectonics, you're going to squeeze people's tails."

The remark bears comparison to John D. Rockefeller's answers to Congress in 1911 about the Standard Oil Company's practice of blowing up freight trains operated by its competitors. Scowling at the politicians whom he held in contempt (for the good reason that he owned quite a few of them), Rockefeller said, "God gave me my money."

A majority of Malone's peers in the big media syndicates exhibit similar traits of character and habits of mind, and as recently as last August the representatives of twelve large cable companies appeared before a Senate subcommittee to read all but identical testimony explaining how and why each of them had decided (independently and without prior agreement) to discontinue payment to the television networks for the right to broadcast their programs. Surprised by the similarity of the statements, several senators inquired if it were possible—just possible, gentlemen, and meaning no offense—that the companies were practicing collusion and restraint of trade. The witnesses professed to be astonished and somewhat hurt by so base a suggestion.

The politicians didn't press the point, and if the Clinton administration holds firm to its social contract with the nation's monied interests (a contract thus far as secure as the ones that defined the administrations of Rutherford B. Hayes and Grover Cleveland), I don't expect the government to raise the antitrust laws as a barrier to monopoly. Asked for an opinion of the Bell Atlantic deal, Vice President Al Gore, in phrases genially opaque, said, "The administration supports any development in the communications marketplace that is pro-competitive and fosters the development of an open, interactive information infrastructure." That same week, Congressman Frederick Boucher (D., Va.) urged passage of a bill granting antitrust exemptions to telephone companies wishing to own cable lines and television programming, and Jim Quello, chairman of the Federal Communications Commission, voiced his belief in "the constructive potential to make real the promise of competitive super electronic highways with multi-channel, multifaceted service to the public."

The language of bureaucratic euphemism is as traditional as the government's willingness to protect the interests of monopoly, even if, alas and woe-a-day, the beneficiaries prove to be, in Teddy Roosevelt's phrase, "malefactors of great wealth." The historical antecedent is unambiguous.

By 1845 everybody traveling west of the Mississippi understood that the new country was rich in five primary resources—land, minerals, furs, timber and government money—and that of these, the last was by far the most abundant. The federal treasury supplied funds for almost any project that anybody could name (railroads, dams, forts, irrigation canals), and the trick was to know the right people in Washington or the nearest courthouse. As a reward for building the first transcontinental railroad, the Central Pacific and the Union Pacific received government land grants in the amount of almost 21 million acres (an estate slightly larger than the combined area of Vermont, Massachusetts and Connecticut), and Collis Huntington, a partner in the Central Pacific (known to both his friends and his enemies as "the crocodile"), made a careful record of the bribes paid to Congress. Meticulous in his bookkeeping, Huntington divided the members into three classes—the Clean, who did as they were asked without payment, the Commercial, who sold their votes at the going rate and the Communists, who disagreed with the railroad and voted their own opinions.

As with the building of the railroads, the building of what the Clinton administration calls "the National Information Infrastructure" requires political as well as logistical decisions. Do the system specifications favor the public or the private interest? Who pays for the laying of the fiber-optic cables, and if the telephone and cable television companies advance the money (estimated at $300 billion over the next fifteen years), then who or what prevents them from charging excessive rates? Why would they not also reserve the right to approve the origin and character of the information moving through their checkpoints? Do the subscribers retain the freedom to send their own messages, ask their own questions, and broadcast their own dissenting opinions, or do they become grateful consumers of the authorized texts manufactured by six or seven media syndicates (Time Warner, Murdoch's News Corporation, Capital Cities/ABC, the Walt Disney Co., Bell Atlantic, Bertelsmann) that own both the means of production and the systems of distribution? In brief and in sum, does the new information order become an open or a closed society?

All the questions touch on the democratic character of the joint American enterprise, but none of them is likely to engender a public debate. Allied with the commercial ambitions that it supposedly restrains, the government will do what is necessary to muffle the political argument, and the press, dazed by the wonders of technology and the splendor of money, will provide the cues for sustained applause. Among the relatively few people apt to make an objection, nobody speaks more eloquently in favor of an open system than Mitchell Kapor, who resigned the chairmanship of Lotus to set up the Electronic Frontier Foundation. The foundation promotes the hope of cheap, easy and equal access to a data highway constructed along the lines of the Internet, the impromptu network of 1.3 million computers in forty countries that allows roughly 30 million people to talk to one another, read E-mail, post messages, download texts (from the Library of Congress as well as from most university libraries), play chess, conduct symposia, organize political rallies, tell jokes—all without having to pay tolls, receive authorization, submit a financial statement or prove that they don't smoke.

Kapor construes the argument at hand as a variant of the early nineteenth-century argument between Thomas Jefferson and the Federalists about the disposition of the western frontier, and in an essay published last summer in *Wired*, he proposed the Internet as a model of the democratic Eden, a public space held in common between two or more linked computers in which individuals might communicate with one another without fear of embarrassment or censure. Just as Jefferson defined the ownership of land as "a natural right" that guaranteed the prosperity and self-reliance of the American farmer, Kapor defines access to information as a natural right conferring the same boons on any American citizen possessed of a computer, a modem and a password. Proposing the image and analogy of a bountiful wilderness, Kapor wrote, "Life in Cyberspace is often conducted in primitive, frontier conditions. But at its best, it is more egalitarian than elitist, more decentralized than hierarchical. It serves individuals and communities, not mass audiences."

By temperament nonconformist and anticorporate, Kapor worked briefly as a disc jockey and stand-up comic before stumbling across the computer trades, and on reading his essay I thought of the fur trappers in the Rocky Mountains in the late 1830s already beginning to notice that the high country was becoming as crowded as Ohio and looking with suspicion at the first wagon trains toiling west across the Great Plains. Like the early hackers in Cyberspace, the mountain men delighted in the beauty and strangeness of a new land, and they were loath to see it sold in sections convenient to the grazing of sheep.

The history of American finance doesn't follow the course of their romanticism and courage. When Jefferson signed the Louisiana Purchase he thought that it would need at least five hundred years to settle the frontier, and through the first half of the nineteenth century the adventurous spirit of the new American nation showed itself most characteristically in the deeds and exploits of the wayward individual—the fur trader, the prospector, the pioneer, the man or woman looking to take a chance on a play of the light or a scent in the wind. By 1850 the mountain men had been reduced to serving as scouts for the immigrant caravans (not unlike the hackers now yoked to the harness of MicroSoft and IBM), and in the latter half of the century the triumphs were those of the corporation— the mining company, the railroad monopoly, the land trust, the stockholders looking for a safe bet and a sure thing.

The story of the great American fortunes is largely the story of well-arranged monopolies—in commodities as various as sugar and tin and football players, and over lines of communication as various as steamboats and pipelines. Jefferson died bankrupt, and the fur trade succumbed to the monopoly operating on the upper reaches of the Missouri River under the direction of John Jacob Astor. At Fort Laramie in 1846 the traders selling goods to the westbound pilgrims pegged the prices of coffee and nails at twenty times their cost in St Louis or Santa Fe. By 1880 most of the land opened for settlement under the Homestead Act had been acquired by speculators or distant corporations (many of them owned by British capital), and the railroad builders at work in the later years of the century measured the value of wayward individuals at the prices paid for the shipment of their coffins.

Although I can share Kapor's hope for a sweeter, greener world, I don't find much reason to believe that the latter-day princes of the fourth estate will act any differently from their nineteenth-century forebears. They dream of cornering a market, of the mass audiences available to cable, not of free individuals speaking to one another on the Internet. Nor do I expect the government to advance the hopes of democracy over the interests of oligarchy. Despite the rebuke offered to Malone and Liberty Media for attempting an interest in both Bell Atlantic and Paramount, the trend in Washington supports the principle of enriching the few at the expense of the many. Representative Boucher already has proposed legislation transferring the management of the Internet to corporate interests, and the Clinton administration has proposed selling to private owners frequencies in the public-radio spectrum. What, after all, would the government want with a forum in which a significant number of literate citizens might organize their politics in a manner unflattering to the status quo?

Toward the end of his essay, Kapor hedged his fear of monopolies with the reassuring thought that even the most dim-witted businessmen surely must see the advantages of an open system, must see how the freedom of mind leads, inevitably, to bigger markets and greater prosperity. His faith in the good sense, much less the humanist compassion, of the prototypical American capitalist seems to me farfetched, if for no other reason than it ignores the lessons taught at every football stadium and baseball park in which the beer and souvenir concessions plunder the fans like scythes moving through wheat. He would be better advised to place his trust in bankruptcy and the press of events.

On this point the historical record is reassuring. Most of the nineteenth-century railroad ventures collapsed under the weight of their own watered stock, and the promoters of the current media speculations don't even enjoy the advantage of an indentured audience. The farmers who relied on the railroads to ship their freight had no choice but to pay what the traffic would bear or watch their produce rot on a siding ten miles west of the nearest middleman, but the market in images isn't as certain as the market in apricots or hogs. Even if the customers live in the same town, their proximity doesn't guarantee a community of intellectual or spiritual interest. Who can guess what they'll pay to watch? The question is one that cable operators tend to obscure, answering it whenever possible with a good deal of talk about the wonders of their new technology and the heartiness of their connections to the necessary politicians. What also was true of the nineteenth century was the breakneck speed of technological change. It took only twelve years to exhaust the fur trade; the heyday of the Mississippi steamboat lasted fewer than ten years; the moment of the overland stagecoach between St Louis and San Francisco, fewer than five. The pony express came and went in the space of eleven months.

Everything was over so soon, almost before anybody knew what to look for or why they had come so far. By the end of the century it was understood that the capture of the American West had ended in both victory and defeat. Victory for the public parade of bustling commerce that so efficiently turned so many things into property. Defeat for the private expeditions that went in search of the soul's oasis. What remained is what still remains—the dreaming optimism of the American mind, its delight in metaphor, and its wish to believe in what isn't there.

January 1994

SPRING LIST

> She was not quite what you would call refined. She was
> not quite what you would call unrefined. She was the
> kind of person that keeps a parrot.
> —MARK TWAIN

As an editor subject to the whim of intellectual fashion, I make occasional lists of the words and phrases that describe the arc of enlightened opinion and maintain their currency as the bearers of the season's received wisdom. The task is sometimes drudging and often frivolous, but it is not one that I can afford to neglect. If I fail to notice that last year's priceless truth has been transformed into this year's imbecile cliché, I run the risk of commissioning manuscripts from authors no longer infallible on topics that have ceased to exist.

The device of an alphabetical list I borrowed from Gustave Flaubert, who appreciated the difficulties as long ago as 1862 and defended himself against the newspapers by compiling a dictionary of accepted ideas. Some of his definitions remain in force ("WINDMILL: Looks well in a landscape;" "FLAG: The sight of it makes the heart beat faster"), but he addressed his remarks to a French instead of an American audience, and within the more advanced circles of opinion in New York, Los Angeles and Washington they might convey an impression of being slightly behind the time. Flaubert never was given the chance to admire the political thought of Rush Limbaugh or applaud Norman Mailer's after-dinner speeches, and I doubt that he could have guessed at the simplicity of the language made for television or foreseen the capture of the universities by the forces of social conscience.

Even so, and much to his credit, Flaubert sought to allay the intellectual nervousness of the age, and he understood that no self-respecting editor or perfume merchant could attend the emperor Louis Napoleon on one of his hunting weekends at Compiègne without a wardrobe of proper opinions —preferably augmented with indications of appropriate inflection, stance and tone of voice. It simply wouldn't do to stand around on the terrace and wonder about the provenance of the wine or the sexual orientation of the huntsmen. To arrive without a correct set of attitudes was almost as bad as to come dressed in last year's clothes. But how was one to know what was expected, and on whom could one rely for advice? Times change, and words once possessed of a plain meaning disappear behind the screens of political correctness. The deconstructions in progress at the universities loose the academic wrecking ball against the plaster façade of what was once known (erroneously) as Western Civilization, and on the scaffolding of a revised cultural history, critics recently arrived from points east and south raise the brightly colored flags of multiculturalism.

Fortunately for all concerned, we are a conservative people, preferring the semblance of social change to any serious interruption of the status quo, and our polite conversation, like our politics and manner of dress, retains over long periods of time the character of inoffensive and reassuring generality proper to *The MacNeil/Lehrer NewsHour* or a well-run military academy. When I first began arranging the definitions in alphabetical order, I didn't expect many of them to hold their value for more than a few weeks, let alone for an entire publishing season or political campaign. What surprised me was the remarkable stability of the opinions welcome in all classrooms and suitable for an appearance in the pages of both the *Wall Street Journal* and the *Washington Post*. Over the last twenty-odd years a small number of phrases have become obsolete ("arc of crisis," "age of scarcity," "Consciousness III"), and a few words have lost their point or shifted their connotations to the historical past ("Soviets," "Watergate," "Cold War," "George Bush"), but for the most part the wisdom in office has remained as impervious to the changes in political or literary fashion as the image of Elizabeth Taylor.

In some instances, of course, proper usage depends upon prior recognition of the dominant prejudice already assembled in the ballroom or at the conference table. In blatantly conservative company (at a yacht club in Orange County, California, say, or at a fund-raising dinner sponsored by The Heritage Foundation) the words "sexist" and "racist" always must be presented with a heavily sarcastic intonation, implying contempt for people who think that either word means anything; among avowed liberals gathered on West Seventy-ninth Street in Manhattan to celebrate a new book by Gloria Steinem or Susan Sontag, the same words should carry the weight of divine revelation, as if they accurately described the entire white male populations of West Virginia, Arizona and Tennessee.

Assuming that any questions of tone and inflection can be answered by glancing at the jewelry of the other people in the room, I like to think that no matter what the topic of conversation—an outbreak of war or semiotics, the sighting of a political prophet in the deserts of California, the splendor of pheasants—the interested reader can offer or advance any opinion on the following list in the certain knowledge that it is both tasteful and safe.

ART: Ennobling. Never enough of it.

BOSNIA: Tragic story.

BUREAUCRACY: Enemy of free enterprise. No bureaucrat knows what it means to take a risk.

CALIFORNIA: Paradise lost—fallen victim to fire, race riot and earthquake. Everybody who is anybody in Brentwood is moving to Montana.

CAMPAIGN PROMISES: All empty. Compare them to a rich man's ceaseless revision of his will.

CHARDONNAY: Grape from which all wine is made.

CHINA: Glorious proof of the capitalist miracle. Every two weeks another 4,000 Chinese become millionaires.

COLD WAR: Lament its absence. The world is far more dangerous without it. Say, in a wistful voice, "We'll be lucky to see its like again."

COUPS D'ETAT: Customary in the tropics.

CRIMINALS: Responsible for their crimes.

CRITICS: Egotistical and venomous, but most of them can be appeased with a $200 lunch at the Four Seasons. They speak only to one another.

DEFICIT (THE): Deadlier than famine or war. Time bomb. "In the end it will kill us all."

DISARMAMENT: Well-meaning notion but impractical. "If the rest of the world were as civilized as the United States, then there might be something in it." Say the millennium has not yet arrived.

DISCIPLINE: Essential in investment managers and college students.

DOCTORS: Incompetent. Most operations are unnecessary. You are more likely to be killed in a hospital than in a traffic accident.

EIGHTEENTH CENTURY: All the women were beautifully dressed, but by the age of forty they went bald and lost their teeth. The century was good at music and politics, but it had no sense of hygiene.

ENTREPRENEURS: Heroes of our time. Most of them started their companies in a garage.

ESTABLISHMENT: Doesn't exist. Vicious, canard circulated by envious intellectuals.

FALSTAFF: Fat man with a zest for life. Anything loud is Falstaffian.

FASCISM: Hitler gave it a bad name.

FOREIGNERS: All selfish. They used to come to New York and Washington to borrow money and admire the American president. Now they come to buy office buildings and demand trade concessions.

FREE LUNCH: No such thing. Liberals believe in its existence, which is why they lose so many elections.

FREE TRADE: Engine of progress. Synonym for democracy. The reason we are all standing here in Italian suits and Chinese sneakers.

FREEDOM OF THE PRESS: Sadly abused. "Yes, the safety of the Republic depends upon it, but why must journalists make so much money?"

"GETTING TOUGH": The only mode of conduct that makes an impression on people who have lost all respect for human decency.

GOVERNMENT REGULATIONS: Compare them to serpents or vines. They strangle the sinews of industry.

GREAT BOOKS (THE): On closer inspection they prove to be the work of racial or sexual propagandists. You don't need to read them.

HAITI: Tragic story.

HOMELESS (THE): Always with us. One must learn to look beyond them. If they were serious about their lives, they would go to California and become rich.

IMPERIALISM: Lost art. The British used to be wonderfully good at it.

IRREDENTISM: Meaning unknown. Goes well in a remark about Yugoslavia or Ukraine. (*See* REVANCHIST)

LABOR UNIONS: More corrupt than big business.

LATIN AMERICA: Terra incognita. Nothing ever happens there that anybody needs to know or remember.

LEADERS: Most perfect examples set by baseball managers and football coaches. Ask in a loud and belligerent voice what anybody thinks would happen if Pat Riley were running the country.

LEFTIST: Endangered species of political malcontent. A few of them still can be found in the quadrangles of the nation's older universities.

MARRIAGE: Old-fashioned domestic art, like knitting or preserving jam. Only a very few people have a talent for it.

MEN: More vain than women.

MEN (REAL): Vanishing species. Those few still extant enjoy after-tax incomes in excess of $20 million a year, which is how one knows they're real and not synthetic.

MERCEDES-BENZ: Sign of virility.

MIDDLE AGES: Poetic time. Nobody was interested in money, and most of the women knew how to talk to rabbits and birds. Mourn the passing of the troubadours.

MULTICULTURALISM: Modern form of ancestor worship. Very fashionable.

MUNICH: Must never happen again. Express contempt for Chamberlain's umbrella.

NIXON (RICHARD M.): Unjustly maligned. "Say what you will about Dick Nixon, he knew how to play the game of geopolitics."

NOVELS: All the good ones come from Eastern Europe or Latin America.

OIL: The lifeblood of freedom.

OUTRAGE (MORAL): Noble passion. Obligatory when discussing torturers or slumlords.

PAX AMERICANA: Military march played at White House banquets.

POLITICAL CORRECTNESS: Despise it. Timid jargon that saps the strength of newspaper columnists.

POLITICIANS: A troupe of actors. They make a profession of being seen. Feel sorry for them. "I know what he's running for, but what is he running from?" Only an imbecile looks upon politics as anything but popular entertainment

PRESIDENCY (THE): Awesome office.

REPRESENTATIVE GOVERNMENT: No longer sufficient to the requirements of the modern state. Regret its disappearance.

REVANCHIST: Meaning unknown. Goes well in a remark about Yugoslavia or Ukraine. (*See* IRREDENTISM)

REVOLUTION (SEXUAL): Still in progress. It is terribly hard on men.

ROLEX WATCH: Sign of virility.

ROME (ANCIENT): Corrupt. The important people spent most of their time going to sexual orgies. Refer to it when talking about the degradation of network television.

RUSSIANS: All paranoid. Understandably so. The memory of Napoleon, Genghis Khan and Adolf Hitler remains embedded in the Russian soul.

SAUDI ARABIANS: Hold very austere religious beliefs. They execute women taken in adultery and punish homosexuals by throwing them out of airplanes.

SOMALIA: Tragic story.

THIRD WORLD (THE): It used to be a fun place to visit, if not for its tourist attractions at least for its teaching of moral lessons. We must be sensitive to its needs.

TOCQUEVILLE (ALEXIS DE): Quote him whenever possible. He saw it all more than a hundred years ago.

TREATIES: Scraps of paper.

TWELVE STEPS: Must be taken one at a time.

VIOLENCE: Too much of it. Bad for children.

WASHINGTON DC: City abandoned to sybaritic luxury. The members of Congress are all millionaires.

WESTERN CIVILIZATION: Defunct. Destroyed by television and the English departments at Duke and Stanford universities.

March 1994

BURNT OFFERINGS

If there were a Super Bowl every day, no American
would ever need a sleeping pill.
—RUSSELL BAKER

T he kind of people who like to name a principal cause for all the
country's troubles lately have appointed the scenes of crime and
violence in Hollywood movies to the office held in prior years by
the Soviet empire, sexual permissiveness, godless communism, the cocaine
trade and demon rum. The new proposition is as witless as its predecessors,
but for the last four or five months it has been all but impossible to escape.
Waiting for a table in a New York restaurant last November, I overheard a
woman say that she had seen statistics proving the correlation between the
box-office receipts of *The Last Boy Scout* and the number of murders taking
place on Saturday nights in the South Bronx. Her companion, a smiling
and agreeable man in an expensively tailored suit, assured her that he'd
never met a movie producer who wasn't either a professional criminal or an
amateur psychopath.

Two days later, in the news from Washington, I noticed that both Janet
Reno, the attorney general, and Senator Paul Simon (D., Ill.) once again
were suggesting that some sort of legal constraint be placed on
Hollywood's passion for savage bloodletting and continuous gunfire. Over
the next several weeks a chorus of newspaper columnists inveighed against
what they called "the culture of violence," deploring the casting of toxic
images into the pure streams of American thought, quoting like-minded
sentiments expressed by President Clinton and the American Psycho-
logical Association, citing figures supplied by Senator Ernest F. Hollings
(D., S.C.) to the effect that the nation's television syndicates present the
nation's schoolchildren with 8,000 murders a year. I couldn't follow all the
lines of all the arguments, but I think somebody said that the country
would find its way back to God if only we could rid it of Steven Seagal
and Chuck Norris, and I remember somebody else saying that the
government should impose an excise tax on Hollywood's use of violence—
like the taxes on liquor and cigarettes.

Although I can think of many objections to most of the movies in
question, I never know what the critics expect Hollywood to put in their
place. Within the American scheme of things, the romance of violence is
as traditional as the singing of "The Star-Spangled Banner." The winning

of the American West was largely accomplished by greedy and ignorant men in search of something for nothing, governed by their basest instincts and praised, in the words of John Terrell's *Land Grab*, "for courage that they didn't possess and eulogized for moral principles utterly foreign to them." When the James gang held up the Kansas City fair in 1872, the local newspaper described the robbery as being "so diabolically daring and utterly in contempt of fear that we are bound to admire it and revere its perpetrators." Two days later the paper compared the gang to the knights of King Arthur's Round Table. Michel Chevalier, an astute and observant traveler in late-nineteenth-century America, noticed that American society had the morality of an army on the march, an opinion seconded by Albert J. Nock in his *Memoirs of a Superfluous Man*. Describing his boyhood in the 1870s, Nock remembered that it was the freebooters carrying off the heaviest sacks of spoil who "were held up in the schools, the press, and even in the pulpit, as prototypal of all that was making America great, and hence as *par excellence* the proper examples for well-ordered youth to follow."

Numerous other writers, both domestic and foreign, have made similar observations, noticing also that in most American narratives—whether of Wall Street or the Alamo—it is the violent man who proves to be the hero of the tale. If they're worth the respect of their horses, both the good guys and the bad guys show contempt for an abstraction as bloodless and chicken-hearted as due process of the law. The archetypal man on horse-back (sometimes known as John Wayne or Randolph Scott, at other times taking the alias of John Rambo or Ronald Reagan) rides into the dusty, wooden town (Abilene or Ban Me Thuot or Washington, DC) and discovers evil in even the most rudimentary attempts at civilization. The villains invariably belong to "the system," which, as every cowhand and aspiring politician knows, is corrupt. The hero appears as a god descended from a cloud, come to punish the sin of pride and scourge the wicked with a terrible vengeance. No matter what the sociopolitical map coordinates —*Miami Vice, The Terminator*, the James Bond and Clint Eastwood movies, *Star Wars, State of Siege*, and so on—and no matter what the outward trappings of character (as gunfighter, police detective or renegade CIA agent), the conventional American hero casts himself as both judge and executioner, pursuing his quarry, on foot or on horseback, by helicopter or automobile, across the Siberian steppe or through the streets of downtown Detroit, proclaiming himself the enemy of the society that reared him, shrugging off the obligations to family and state as if they were the rain on his hat or the mud on his boots. All the stories take place in a moral wilderness that resembles the ruin of Sarajevo, and after the requisite number of killings, the hero departs, leaving to mortal men (to women and shopkeepers) the tedious business of burial, marriage and settlement.

The stories haven't changed much since I first began going to the movies fifty years ago, but what has changed is the purpose to which Hollywood directs the scenes of violence. Instead of advancing the plot, the killing serves as set decoration, meant to be admired for nothing other than itself, as if the sight of a knife being driven into the villain's forehead were comparable to a gilded fire screen or an ornamental vase. The producers apparently have abandoned the hope of art or verisimilitude, and when I see Sylvester Stallone setting fire to a town in Oregon, or Mel Gibson decimating a regiment of road warriors, I attribute the dreams of Armageddon to people who have derived their notions of violent death from the study of other movies. By glorifying the acts of violence as expensive sumptuary objects (bigger explosions, uglier wounds, more generous flows of blood), they somehow achieve the paradoxical effect of making them trivial. The killings play like the gag lines on television sitcoms—as novelties meant to lead into the commercial or conceal the fatuousness of the plot—and I suspect that their smirking, undergraduate character follows from the cynicism of the people who write the scripts and dress the sets. I watch Schwarzenegger in *Commando*, setting off explosions on an island in the Santa Barbara Channel, and I think of the screenwriter and the assistant director arranging swatches of red and orange as if they were flowers or throw pillows.

The dialogue strains for a similarly decorative effect. Before remanding their antagonists to oblivion in a swarm of sharks or fusillade of dumdum bullets, James Bond and Harry Callahan pause briefly for a *bon mot* in the manner of Oscar Wilde. They domesticate the acts of violence by changing them into jokes, and the moviegoing public—safe behind popcorn boxes and fortified with Raisinets and M&M's—gladly lets go its fear of the world outside the Cineplex in gusts of grateful laughter.

What Russell Baker said of the midwinter Super Bowl also can be said of the midsummer bloom of action films. The semi-annual festivals of violence serve as soporifics, not as stimulants, and the critics who think otherwise, who mistake a sophomore's fantasy of suburban revenge for an incitement to urban riot, might do well to reread Shakespeare or Homer. Neither author was squeamish about the depiction of violence, but they had it in mind to describe the actual world of human character and event, not the fairy-tale land of wish and dream.

Maybe it's my age, but if I replay in my mind the sequence of brutal images that I remember seeing in the movies over the last twenty-odd years, I'm struck by their increasingly cartoonish character, which makes it difficult for me to take seriously the fretting of people like Senators Simon and Hollings. Were I to do so, I first would have to grant their prior assumption that the movies under review possess the force of art, that they can awaken in the mind of their audiences emotions strong enough to excite action or thought.

But once divorced from the emotional contexts of human suffering, the scenes of violence lose both meaning and power, and it was this weakness of which I was pointedly reminded in late January when I had occasion to read passages of the *Iliad* (assigned as homework to my twelve-year-old son), on the same evening that HBO presented Eastwood in *Pale Rider* —that is, as Achilles on the old American frontier bringing rough but divine justice to the wayward operators of a California mining camp. The distance between the two variations on the theme of vengeance is the distance between newsreel footage of the Normandy invasion and a fashion photograph promoting Bugle Boy jeans.

Here is Homer, in the translation by Robert Fagles, describing the death of the warrior Harpalion:

> But Meriones caught him in full retreat,
>   he let fly
> with a bronzed-tipped arrow, hitting his
>   right buttock
> up under the pelvic bone so the lance
>   pierced the bladder.
> He sank on the spot, hunched in his
>   dear companion's arms,
> gasping out his life as he writhed along
>   the ground
> like an earthworm stretched out in
>   death, blood pooling,
> soaking the earth dark red . . .

Or again, on a different day and in another part of the Trojan plain, Achilles killing Polydorus, Hector's brother:

> [Achilles] speared him square in the
>   back where his war-belt clasped,

golden buckles clinching both halves
   of his breastplate—
straight on through went the point and
   out the navel,
down on his knees he dropped—
screaming shrill as the world went black
   before him—
clutched his bowels to his body, hunched
   and sank.

The lines evoke the emotions of terror and fear because Homer employs the imagination as a means of apprehending reality rather than as a means of escaping it. Or, as Bernard Knox puts it in his fine introduction to Fagles's translation, "Men die in the *Iliad* in agony; they drop, screaming, to their knees, reaching out to beloved companions, gasping their life out, clawing the ground with their hands; they die roaring, like Asius, raging, like the great Sarpedon, bellowing, like Hippodamas, moaning, like Polydorus."

The gunmen in the Eastwood film fall like targets in a shooting gallery. We see blood spurt from their bodies, but because we never understand them as men, never see them as anything other than symbolic manifestations of evil dressed in matching greatcoats that could have been designed by Ralph Lauren, we look at their deaths as clever tropes. I don't think it improbable that Eastwood intended the movie as an epic metaphor. The camera dwells lovingly on the bleak landscape of the high desert, on the deserted street, on the tentative wooden town lost in an immense wilderness under an empty sky, and I imagine that he intended the figure on horseback, identified simply as "the preacher," to stand as an emblem of righteousness. But after all the gunmen have been punished, the town purified, and the preacher gone over the horizon, nothing has been said that might evoke in the audience even the slightest hint of pity or awe.

Homer can vividly imagine the desolation of death, because he so vividly delights in the spring and surge of life. A surprisingly large number of lines in the *Iliad* speak of the joys of peace, of fast ships and wide-ranging flocks, of the generations succeeding one another in a bright and rapturous dance, of young boys in "fine-spun tunics rubbed with a gloss of oil" and young girls "crowned with a bloom of fresh garlands." Meaning to sing not only the wrath of Achilles but also the preciousness of the life that he so wantonly destroys, Homer imparts to his poem the heavy sense of tragic loss, and I read his lines with fear and dread. I come across Thestor, "cowering, crouched in his fine polished chariot, / crazed with fear," and I remember that as a young newspaper reporter in San Francisco I was surprised by the smell of death in furnished rooms, by the victims of automobile accidents and multiple stab wounds losing command of their bowels, sobbing like children, afraid of the dark, never coming up with a smart remark.

But when I look at Bruce Willis or Mel Gibson annihilating gargoyles, nothing remains of the mess and stink of death. The omission is deliberate. Just as the smiling hosts in the NFL broadcast booths turn fastidiously away from the injured players twisted in pain on the forty-yard line, the manufacturers of synthetic murder delete the sight of human beings reduced to earthworms. Their cameras lift lightly into the air, en route to the next automobile chase or pillar of fire, and although I know that Senators Hollings and Simon like to say that the soul of the nation's youth remains trapped in the burning wreckage with the drug money and the Guatemalan hit men, I think that they underestimated the sophistication of an audience that knows the difference between what is real and what is make-believe. Each of my own children, well before they reached the age of nine, understood *Die Hard* and *Lethal Weapon 2* as video games.

If the Hollywood daydreams lately have become louder and more violent, I suspect that it's because the higher quotients of public anxiety and alarm stimulate the need for stronger sedatives. Even during the excitements of the Second World War, the patients standing in line at the box office could be comforted with *Casablanca* or *The Secret Life of Walter Mitty*. It was enough to know that Humphrey Bogart had been to Europe and could tell the difference between a Nazi, a love song and a crooked roulette table. Most members of the audience assumed that if they had been blessed with a similar degree of sophistication, they, too, could outwit Sydney Greenstreet and leave Claude Rains standing in the rain at the airport with his list of usual suspects. Neither they nor Bogart thought it necessary to carry a semi-automatic rifle or practice the art of kick-boxing. By 1950 the United States enjoyed a position of absolute supremacy in the world, and the Americans who sallied bravely forth to the frontiers of the Cold War (in Berlin and Central America and Indochina) traveled on passports stamped with the visas of omnipotence.

I don't know how many readers will remember Danny Kaye as Walter Mitty, but I think of the movie as the preamble to the James Bond films. Frankly presented as daydream (timid milquetoast falls asleep and imagines himself performing heroic feats of derring-do), the movie anticipates the urbane British intelligence agent on the grand tour of the world's leading resorts, collecting beautiful women as if they were baseball cards, knowing how to play with the most dangerous toys in the Soviet and American arsenals, warding off the evil spirit of nuclear war. But although not unacquainted with sinister plots, Bond is still skittish about the sight of blood. He carries a gun, but he seldom has a use for it, preferring instead the hand-to-hand struggles on the edge of a cliff or a knife.

By 1980 the times had changed, and most of the important protagonists in the Hollywood action films had become paramilitary figures, moving furtively through always hostile terrain, heavily armed with 9mm pistols and semi-automatic rifles, sometimes with antitank weapons and grenade launchers. Unlike Bogart, Mitty or Bond, the newly arrived soldiers of fortune were both paranoid and enraged—angry at anybody and everybody to whom they could assign the fault for the world's evil and on whom they could bestow the proofs of their disappointment. Their enemies were so many and so various—Colombian drug lords, Los Angeles street gangs, wardens of North Vietnamese prisons, Irish terrorists, and so on—that it was no longer possible to ascribe the killing to either a patriotic or an ideological motive. Clearly something had gone wrong in the world, and if the American public was becoming increasingly fearful of both its cities and its politicians, then the cinematic palliative needed to be strengthened and reenforced. The theatergoing audience couldn't drift quietly off to sleep unless it could hear the distant sound of gunfire in the forest on the other side of the freeway, reassured as if by a lullaby that John Rambo or Harry Callahan (or Mel Gibson or Charles Bronson or Chuck Norris) was shooting down the shadows in the trees.

The television networks preach a corollary sermon, but not, as the critics would have it, in their entertainment divisions. Over the last several years, the children's hour (a.k.a. primetime) has been largely occupied by sitcoms or by police dramas that prefer the uses of sex to those of violence. It is the news programs that bring the specters from the abyss—the news programs and their "reality-based" imitations set in bas-relief against advertisements for Chanel perfume and Caribbean resorts. Like the illustrations in a fifth-grade reader, the sequence of scenes teaches the late-twentieth century American catechism: first, at the top of the news, the admonitory row of body bags being loaded into ambulances in Brooklyn or south Miami; second, the inferno of tenement fires and burning warehouses; third, a sullen procession of criminals arraigned for robbery or murder and led away in chains. The text of the day's lesson having been thus established, the camera makes its happy return to the always smiling anchorwoman, and so—with her gracious permission—to the preview of heaven in the airline and travel advertisements. The homily is as plain as a medieval morality play or the bloodstains on Don Johnson's Armani suit—obey the law, pay your taxes, speak politely to the police officer and you go to the Virgin Islands on the American Express card. Disobey the law, neglect your insurance payments, speak rudely to the police and you go to Kings County Hospital in a body bag.

It is the business of the mass media to sell products—their own as well as those of their clients and sponsors—and the critics who complain about the ceaseless shows of violence miss the comparison to the cocaine trade. Whether staged as news or entertainment, synthetic violence is a drug, which, happily for its suppliers, returns a handsome rate of profit in all the major markets. Among the urban poor (that is, people who might be inclined to take up arms against the state), the bloody anodynes check the fever of nonspecific rage. Draw off the pestilent air of perceived injustice through the vents of wish and dream, and it is less likely to seek expression on a commuter train or in an election. Among the American suburban middle classes (people increasingly hard-pressed to maintain their status as residents of the increasingly precarious American Eden, who believe themselves surrounded by enemies of infinite number), the dreadful images confirm the impression of a world beyond the shopping mall that resembles a pitiless desert or a malevolent wilderness. Instill in such people the habit of fear, and it is more likely that their generous and charitable impulses will turn to stone.

Both states of paralysis serve the interests of a corporate media that hopes for nothing better than passive compliance on the part of people shopping for the intimations of immortality. Any doubts that I may have entertained on the point were dispelled some years ago by a well-placed executive at CBS. I had asked him why the networks make so little attempt to broadcast anything other than fairy tales, and he in turn asked me if I ever looked at television.

"Not very often," I said.

"Of course not," he said. "Neither do I. I would hope that we have something better to do."

The mass audience, he said, consisted mostly of people who didn't have anything better to do, who lacked either the will or the travel money to walk out their own front door. Why deprive them of their only means of escape? Why trouble them with the pain of doubt or the labor of thought? Let them feed on wishes and dreams, and they will repay the kindness by looking at more television, swelling the sum of the Nielsen ratings, contributing their pauper's mite to the general state of commercial prosperity and sociopolitical well-being.

April 1994

TERMS OF ENDEARMENT

I too love the great pagan world, its bloodshed,
its slaves, its injustices, its loathing of all
that is feeble.
—GEORGE MOORE

Over the course of the summer I had occasion to reread Marshall McLuhan's *Understanding Media*, and although the argument of the book made a good deal more sense to me in 1994 than it did in 1964, it wasn't until I saw the white Ford Bronco proceeding majestically north on the San Diego Freeway under a royal umbrella of helicopters that I knew why. McLuhan had announced mankind's happy return to the Elysian fields of primitive consciousness, and here was his word being made flesh in the Southern California twilight. Well before the procession moved through the Santa Monica Interchange, the news of O. J. Simpson's whereabouts had reached Tokyo and Rome (the villagers in the distant precincts of McLuhan's global village), and the reverent crowds gathering under the eucalyptus trees on Sunset Boulevard had come to pay homage to what passes in late twentieth-century America for the presence of divinity. The question of Simpson's guilt or innocence wasn't as important as his descent from the starry heavens of network television—a demigod on the order of the doomed Orestes in flight from the pursuing Furies, his aura of celebrity raised to the power of myth by the nature of his imagined crime. The Greek chorus standing by the side of the road held up signs saying FREE THE JUICE while at the same time waiting expectantly for Simpson to shoot himself in the head. The result didn't matter as much as the hushed promise of a miraculous event. As McLuhan had gone to no small trouble to explain, it was the medium that was the message, not the thing that was done or said.

Anticipating the rejuvenation of the cults of personality—the images of Michael Jordan and Madonna replacing those of Apollo and Aphrodite, Nancy Reagan arranging the affairs of state to coincide with her husband's astrological signs—McLuhan's argument infers the transposition of news into entertainment, history into legend and fable. He begins with the proposition that "we become what we behold," that "we shape our tools and afterwards our tools shape us," and then elaborates the premise by examining the diktats of two epistemological revolutions that overthrew a settled political and aesthetic order. First, in the fifteenth century, the invention of moveable type, which encouraged people to arrange their perceptions of the world in forms convenient to the visual order of the printed page. Second, in the late nineteenth century, the discovery of electricity and its subsequent applications (telegraph, telephone, television, computers, and so on), which taught people to rearrange their perceptions of the world in ways convenient to the electronic media.

Once having stated his proposition, McLuhan ascribes to the visual order of print the corollary structures of thought dependent upon sequence and straight lines—on roads, laws, empires, hierarchy, classification, the novels of George Eliot or Jane Austen. The electronic forms of communication eliminate the predominance of straight lines as well as the presumption of cause and effect, and by dissolving the dimensions of space and time, they invite ways of thinking that McLuhan describes as nonlineal, repetitive, discontinuous, intuitive, proceeding by analogy instead of sequential argument. The two sets of circumstances generate different systems of meaning that, translated very loosely from what I take to be McLuhan's dialectic, can be expressed as a series of antonyms. As follows:

Print	*Electronic Media*
authority	power
happiness	pleasure
literature	journalism
civilization	barbarism
will	wish
truth as passion	passion as truth
achievement	celebrity
science	magic
doubt	certainty

(continued)

drama	pornography
history	legend
argument	violence
art	dream
politics	prophecy

The words in the right-hand column more or less correspond to the sensibility implicit in the weightless and self-referential world of the mass media—a world of icons engaging the viewer's participation in what McLuhan understood as a collective surge of intense consciousness ("a process that makes the content of the item seem quite secondary"), a world in which the stars of daytime soap opera receive 10,000 letters a week from fans who confess secrets of the heart that they dare not tell their husbands, their mothers or their wives.

Better described as pre-Christian than postmodern, the pagan character of the electronic dispensation invests authority in persons instead of institutions. Names take precedence over things, the actor over the act, and within the enclosed and mediated spaces governed by the rule of images, the distinctions between fiction and fact melt, thaw and resolve themselves into the malleable substance of docudrama.

When *Understanding Media* was first published in May 1964, McLuhan was an obscure professor of English at the University of Toronto, a gaunt and rumpled figure blessed with a talent for oracular statement—"The electric light is pure information." "We are the television screen . . . we wear all mankind as our skin." Although informed opinion at the time was happy to briefly award him the rank of prophet and sage, not one critic in five hundred was entirely sure what it was that he was trying to say. The explicators of his text guessed that he had come upon something important, but for the most part they interpreted him as a dealer in trendy communications theory who beguiled his audiences with a persona that joined, in Tom Wolfe's phrase, "the charisma of a haruspex with the irresistible certitude of the monomaniac."

The excitements associated with McLuhan's general theory didn't survive his death on New Year's Eve 1980 at the age of sixty-nine; informed opinion had moved on to other things, and the adjective "McLuhanesque" was sent to the attic with the rest of the sensibility (go-go boots, Sergeant Pepper, Woodstock, the Vietnam War) that embodied the failed hopes of a discredited decade. The judgement was poorly timed. Even as McLuhan's hypothesis was being remanded to oblivion, its less

340

obvious implications were beginning to show up on MTV and the other cable networks, on the Internet and in the cellular-phone trade—all of them derived from technologies that McLuhan had presupposed but didn't live to see shaped in silicon or glass.

The guardians of the established literary order in New York read *Understanding Media* as a portent of their own doom, and they were quick to find fault with what the more scornful among them called McLuhan's "incantation." They dismissed with contempt the author's weird and hybrid dabbling in "scientific mysticism"; not having had the chance to behold the folly of the Strategic Defense Initiative (a.k.a. "Star Wars"), or count the crowd at a Michael Jackson concert, or read Bob Woodward's journalism, they disdained his superficial understanding of popular culture, his naive faith in technology and his too primitive belief in "merely physical sensation." A number of the objections were well taken, but for the most part the insulted critics contrived to miss the point, refusing to accept McLuhan's approach to his topic and reducing the sum of his hypothesis to the trivial observation that *The Ed Sullivan Show* was easier to read than the collected works of Immanuel Kant.

But McLuhan was talking about the media as "make-happen agents," not as "make-aware agents," as systems similar to roads and canals, not as precious art objects or uplifting models of behavior, and he compared his critics to the medieval schoolmen who railed against Johann Gutenberg's typefaces as the precursors of intellectual anarchy and "the end of civilization as we know it." Against the more pompous members of the academy (those who insisted that all would be well if only the television networks would improve and correct the vulgar tone of their programming), McLuhan brought to bear a sardonic sense of humor, suggesting that in the twentieth century, as in the fifteenth, the literary man prefers "to view with alarm and point with pride, while scrupulously ignoring what's going on."

The remark could as easily have been addressed to some of the more self-important representatives of the news media who thought it well beneath their dignity to gossip about the progress of a Ford Bronco as if it were an emperor's carriage. As early as 7:00P.M. Eastern Standard Time, the networks had framed the procession with the significance of the Persian Gulf War, and they had hastily assembled the college of oracles to talk to the correspondents hovering over Brentwood. The correspondents knew that they were looking at very, very big news, but they didn't know what it was supposed to mean, and they were badly in need of guidance from New York. No script had been supplied to the studio TelePrompTers, and the oracles were as much at a loss for words as everybody else in the country. Here they all were—Rather and Brokaw and Jennings and Walters— settling on a story of murder and possible suicide like buzzards settling on the carcass of a sheep, but the position was not one that anybody was, as they say at Morton's, "comfortable with." Surely there had to be something more to the story, something important, for God's sake, some civilized message about sports, or the predicament of women, or racial prejudice, or the system of criminal justice—something that could be dressed up in the costume of an issue.

As the last of the natural light faded to black over the walled courtyard in Brentwood that already had become a forest shrine, at least eight channels were showing live footage of a parked car, and the moralists in the broadcasting booths, still uneasy with the proceedings and failing to find anyone else on whom to blame their embarrassment, comforted themselves with the mortifications of their own flesh. It was the media that were at fault, the shameless, vulgar, prurient news media hawking the trinkets of cheap sensation. The anguished rending of garments simulated the effect of a roundtable discussion taking place in a college lecture hall under the rubric "Toward a Responsible News Media," and by the time Simpson showed up in court for his arraignment on the following Monday, the journalistic acts of contrition had become as much a part of the story as the whereabouts of the missing knife or the exact placement and chemical composition of the bloodstains.

Still appalled by what he had seen in the slums of tabloid journalism, Peter Jennings that same afternoon admitted to one of his peers at the *Washington Post* that he had been badly unnerved by the experience. "At moments like that," he said, "we are reduced to roughly the same level as that of the audience." *Time* magazine felt compelled to apologize for the cover photograph that transformed Simpson into a thug, and A. M. Rosenthal, the *New York Times* columnist accustomed to the company of statesmen, asked himself in print, "Are we journalists or garbage collectors?"

The question was as superfluous as most of the criticism directed against the electronic media over the last thirty years, but on reading through the week's catalogue of sermons, I was reminded of some of my own irrelevant pronouncements about the idiocy of network television, and I all too easily could recognize the attempt to reassert the authority of the word, to defend the construct of laws, cause and effect, of straight lines and a political discourse made of something other than the Nielsen ratings. The voices of the anchor persons and the newspaper columnists were the voices of an *ancien régime* as irretrievably doomed as Marie Antoinette. Even as they declared their faith in syllogisms and wondered whether a celebrity of Simpson's magnitude could be sentenced to death, the chorus of bystanders outside the Los Angeles County Jail was holding up signs saying GUILTY OR NOT, WE LOVE YOU, O.J. The house in Brentwood had become a tourist attraction, the networks were interrupting their daytime soap-opera schedules with reports from California trial lawyers, and Simpson's agent presumably was talking book deals with every publisher in New York.

The pious expressions of Christian alarm mistook the pagan terms of endearment under which the news media bestow the gift of immortal celebrity. The bargain is a Faustian one that demands the offering of blood sacrifices on the altar of publicity. In return for the favors of wealth and applause, the celebrity presents the carcass of his or her humanity to the rituals of the public feast. What was once a subject becomes an object—a corporate logo or a T-shirt, a lump of wax suitable to the souvenir molds of primetime docudrama, a brand name awakening with its "personal touch" the spirit dormant in a basketball sneaker or a bottle of perfume, a trace element of the world soul, a delicacy served to an audience accustomed to consuming its heroes and demigods as if they were cheeseburgers or sun-dried tomatoes.

Similar terms of endearment were well known to the very ancient Greeks who allowed their sacred kings to rule in Thebes or Lycia for a single triumphant year before putting them to death in order that their blood might fructify the crops and fields. Enumerating the several forms of the customary sacrifice in *The Greek Myths*, Robert Graves could have been summarizing the headlines in *The National Enquirer* or the promotional tag lines for *Hard Copy*: "His ritual death varied greatly in circumstance; he might be torn to pieces by wild women, transfixed with a stingray spear, felled with an axe, pricked in the heel with a poisoned arrow, flung over a cliff, burned to death on a pyre, drowned in a pool, or killed in a pre-arranged chariot crash. But die he must."

As McLuhan noticed thirty years ago, the technologies of the electronic future carry us backward into the firelight flickering in the caves of a Neolithic past. The habits of mind derived from our use of the mass media—"we become what we behold . . . we shape our tools and afterwards our tools shape us"—deconstruct the texts of a civilization founded on the premise of the printed page. To the extent that we revise the visual order of print, we substitute for the idea of the townsman or the citizen the sensibilities characteristic of preliterate peoples. If all the world can be seen simultaneously, and if all mankind's joy and suffering is always and everywhere present (on CNN or with Sally Jessy Raphael, on the Sunday Night Movie or MTV), nothing necessarily follows from anything else. Sequence becomes merely additive instead of causative, and the inhabitants of the global village, imagining themselves living in the enchanted garden of the eternal now, swear fealty to the sovereignty of the moment. Why then would they require an explanation of O. J. Simpson's appearance in the sacred grove of eucalyptus trees? Or of anything else that anybody cared to mention? Under the rule of images and the dispensation of the electronic media, ritual becomes a form of applied knowledge, and the presence of celebrity signifies nothing other than itself.

September 1994

REACTIONARY CHIC

Men are not sufficiently perfect to exercise justice
in the name of virtue: the rule of life should be
indulgence and kindness of heart.
—ANATOLE FRANCE

The 104th Congress assembled in Washington on 4 January amid a dark murmur of sworn oaths about rescuing the captive spirit of American success from the dungeons of big government, and as I listened to the Right-wing radio broadcasters sending their furious signals from their newly installed transmitters in the basement of the Capitol, I was struck by the resemblance between this season's Republican revolution and the old countercultural rebellion of thirty years ago. Once again the partisans of a romantic antipolitics intended a guerrilla raid on the wicked cities of death and time. Although nobody described the mission in precisely those words, the exuberant cheers welcoming Newt Gingrich to the Speaker's chair in the House of Representatives (loud cries of 'Newt!" "Newt!" "Newt!") swelled with high purpose and zealous intent, the applause rising to the pitch of enthusiasm appropriate to the arrival of a hero or a saint. Here at last was the purifying wind from the South, the politician who had been touring the country both before and after the November election preaching the gospel of revolt, sacker of shibboleths and government spending programs come to lead the American people out of the deserts of the welfare state.

Under the circumstances and given the fierce expectations gathered on the Republican side of the aisle, Gingrich's inaugural address as Speaker of the House was surprisingly and uncharacteristically mild. Pronouncing the occasion "historic," he put aside for the moment his familiar persona as arrogant bully and humbly introduced himself as an adopted child and a common man. He expressed his approval of Franklin D. Roosevelt's social conscience and Benjamin Franklin's faith in God, and generously distributed the alms of his compassion to people who were poor and black as well as to people who were white and rich. The "most painful problems" abroad in the land he identified as "moral problems," and toward the end of his speech he began to talk about bringing the United States more nearly in line with the kingdom of Heaven.

The speech was at once pious and sly, and although I suspect that some of the talk-show hosts in the basement were disappointed by its non-combative tone and because nobody was handing out weapons as well as platitudes, the Republican majority received it with gusts of tumultuous applause (more cries of "Newt!" "Newt!" "Newt!") and quite a few of the members looked as if they stood ready to carry the Speaker on their shoulders to the White House or the Air and Space Museum.[1]

Like so much else about the Republican risorgimento, the political passion was attached to a preferred image rather than a plain or ambiguous fact, not to the Gingrich who had just delivered a conciliatory speech but to the Gingrich renowned for being nasty and brutish and short—the militant Gingrich blessed with a boll weevil's appetite for destruction who had ordered a skull of *Tyrannosaurus rex* as an ornament for his new office in the Longworth building.

It was the scornful Gingrich who had come to stand during his sixteen years in Congress as the shared symbol of resentment binding together the several parties of the disaffected Right—the Catholic conservatives with the Jewish neoconseratives, the libertarians with the authoritarians, Pat Robertson's Christian Coalition with the disciples of David Duke.

---

[1] Peggy Noonan both captured and embodied the fervent spirit of the occasion in an editorial published in the *Wall Street Journal* under the headline "Bliss to Be Alive." Saying that she had been present at the glorious moment when Representative Gingrich "became a great man," she observed that "now and then history turns electric. Last week it was wonderful to see the current light up this town." She heard in Gingrich's speech the trumpet of deliverance—"the authentic sound of post-Reagan conservatism . . . the authentic sound of the next ten years."

Clearly a man for all grievances, Gingrich summed up (in his person as well as in his lectures on the decline and fall of American civilization) the whole of the conservative objection that since the dawn of the Reagan revolution in the early 1980s has comprised the course of required reading at the Heritage Foundation and the American Enterprise Institute. Over the last fifteen years I probably have read two or three thousand variations of the complaint—editorials in the *Wall Street Journal*, articles in *Commentary* and *The New Criterion*, the speeches of William Bennett and the columns of George Will, the soliloquies of Rush Limbaugh, the books in the line of frowning succession, from Allan Bloom's *The Closing of the American Mind* through George Glider's *Wealth and Poverty*, Dinesh D'Souza's *Illiberal Education* and Charles Murray's *Losing Ground*, and so on—but when I delete the repetitions and piece together what remains of a coherent narrative, the entire sum of the great suburban remonstrance fits within the span of a short fairy tale. As follows:

Once upon a time, before the awful misfortunes of the 1960s, America was a theme park constructed by nonunion labor along the lines of the Garden of Eden. But then something terrible happened, and a plague of guitarists descended upon the land. Spawned by the sexual confusions of the amoral news media, spores of Marxist ideology blew around in the wind, multiplied the powers of government and impregnated the English departments at the Ivy League universities, which then gave birth to the monster of deconstruction that devoured the arts of learning. Pretty soon the trout began to die in Wyoming, and the next thing that anybody knew the nation's elementary schools had been debased, too many favors were being granted to women and blacks, federal bureaucrats were smothering capitalist entrepreneurs with the pillows of government regulation, prime-time television was broadcasting continuous footage from Sodom and Gomorrah and the noble edifice of Western civilization had collapsed into the rubble of feminist prose.

The story somehow made more sense when set against the operatic backdrop of the Cold War, possibly because the familiar stage design recalled to mind the first act of *The Nutcracker Suite* when the toy soldier does battle with the army of horrific mice. The evil Soviet empire furnished the book and lyrics for the election campaigns of both Presidents Reagan and Bush, and for a few years it was possible to imagine that the fungus blighting the apple trees in the American orchard had something to do with the weather on the totalitarian steppe. The sudden tearing down of the Berlin Wall took everybody by surprise—the director of the CIA as well as the editors at *National Review*—and the tellers of the tale found themselves in pressing need of other antagonists to take the place of the grim but harmless ogre. The departure of the Russian trolls prompted a casting call for prospective bogeymen and likely villains. The Japanese couldn't play the part because they were lending the United States too much money, the Colombian drug lords were too few and too well connected in Miami; Manuel Noriega and Saddam Hussein failed the audition; the Arab oil cartel was broke; and the Chinese were busy making shirts for Ralph Lauren.

In the absence of enemies abroad, the protectors of the American dream began looking for inward signs of moral weakness rather than outward shows of military force; instead of examining the dossiers of foreign tyrants, they searched the local newspapers for flaws in the American character, and the surveillance satellites overhead Leipzig and Sevastopol were reassigned stations over metropolitan Detroit and the back lots of Hollywood studios. Within a matter of months the authorities rounded up as suspects a motley crowd of specific individuals and general categories of subversive behavior and opinion—black male adolescents as well as Leftist English professors, multiculturalists of all descriptions, the liberal news media, the 1960s, the government in Washington, welfare mothers, homosexuals, drug criminals, performance artists, illegal immigrants. Some enemies of the state were easier to identify than others, but in all instances the tellers of the tale relied on images seen in dreams or on the network news rather than on the lessons of their own experience.

Believing themselves under assault from what they took to be the hostile forces of history, their heirs and servants of American oligarchy chose to cast themselves as rebels against "the system," as revolutionary idealists at odds with a world they never made. The pose was as ludicrous as it was familiar. Here were the people who owned most of what was worth owning in the country (the banks and business corporations as well as the television networks and most of the members of Congress) pretending that they were victims of a conspiracy raised against them by the institutions that they themselves had controlled. What was even more extraordinary was the general likeness between their own revolutionary pretensions and the posturing of the 1960s counterculture that they so often and so loudly denounced. Although I had made occasional notes over a number of years about the similarities between the two camps of *soi-disant* revolutionaries, it wasn't until last 19 October, during the course of a publisher's lunch at the Harvard Club in New York, that I fully appreciated the extent to which the reactionary chic of the 1990s mimics the set of 1960s attitudes memorialized by Tom Wolfe in the phrase "radical chic."

Sponsored by the Manhattan Institute (a think tank that funds Rightist political theory) and meant to welcome the arrival of a new work of neo-conservative doctrine (*Dictatorship of Virtue*, by Richard Bernstein), the lunch attracted a crowd of fifty individuals who for the most part were affiliated with publications and charitable foundations (among them *Forbes, Commentary* and the John M. Olin Foundation) known for their allegiance to the miracle of finance capitalism. The intellectual tide last fall was running strongly in favor of more prisons and higher interest rates, and the mood in the dining room was smiling and complacent. The Democrats clearly were on their way to defeat in the November elections; President Clinton had been brought up on charges of sexual harassment by Paula Jones; Newt Gingrich was marching through Georgia with "The Battle Hymn of the Republic" and the terrible swift swords of Christian vengeance. Even more to the point, two other works allied with Bernstein's tract (Charles Murray and the late Richard Herrnstein's *The Bell Curve* and William Henry's *In Defense of Elitism*) already had reached the season's best-seller lists, which was good news because the authors of both works, like Bernstein, affirmed the great truth so dear to the hearts of almost everybody in the room—that the American upper middle class was a dwindling minority besieged by enemies at all points of the moral and intellectual compass and thus deserving (like other aggrieved citizens) of protection and special privilege.[2]

Introduced as "the John Keats of the *New York Times*," Bernstein, earnest and ingratiating and safe, set forth the thesis of his book as an ominous comparison between the present moment in late twentieth-century America and the moment of the *dérapage* in late eighteenth-century France when the enlightened idealism that had inspired the immortal "Declaration of the Rights of Man" began to degenerate into the Terror forced upon a hapless people by the guillotine and the Committee of Public Safety. He was addressing his remarks to people as little threatened

---

[2] Before coming to lunch I had taken the precaution of reading the book. Bernstein's complete list of enemies appears on page 230. "The penetration of the new sensibility into the elite institutions, in the universities, the press, the liberal churches, the foundations, the schools, and show business, on PBS and 'Murphy Brown,' at Harvard and Dallas Baptist University, on editorial boards and op-ed pages, at the Ford Foundation and the Rockefeller Brothers Fund, the National Education Association, the American Society of Newspaper Editors, the National Council of Churches, and the Pew Charitable Trusts."

by the circumstances he described as the Wednesday matinee audience at *Les Misérables*, but all present were thrilled beyond words to know that they too were living in stirring times, that the barbarians once again were at the gates and that, when one really got to thinking about it, Sam Donaldson and David Geffen were just as awful as Danton and Robespierre.

Listening to Bernstein talk about "the tyranny of the left" crushing the universities under the iron heel of "moralistic liberalism," I understood that I was revisiting a make-believe time and place not unlike the one that used to be known as the Age of Aquarius. The wording of the manifestos might have changed (William Bennett's "Empower America" in place of Huey Newton's "Power to the people"), and so might have the age and social standing of the malcontents (Howard Stern and Rush Limbaugh sitting in for Lenny Bruce and Abbie Hoffman at the drums of a politically incorrect comedy), but the habits of mind remained all but identical, and so did the air of self-righteousness and the settled conviction that virtue is a trait inherited at birth. Thirty years ago it was "the conservative establishment" that was at fault, a conspiracy largely composed of university professors, government bureaucrats and network television executives who couldn't play guitar and trembled at the sound of Dylan's harmonica. Now it is "the liberal establishment" that is at fault, a conspiracy largely composed of university professors, government bureaucrats and network television executives who can't quote freely from *The Federalist* and tremble before the wisdom of Alvin Toffler and Arianna Huffington.[3]

Like the 1960s radical Left, the 1990s reactionary Right declares its principled opposition to the passage of time (the manifestos written by children who never wanted to grow up revised by parents who never want to grow old), but despite everybody's best efforts and the wonders of modern cosmetics, days pass and things change. After the age of forty,

---

[3] Arianna Huffington's New Age meditations, *The Fourth Instinct*, appear on Representative Gingrich's unofficial list of recommended reading; the official list, the one he hands out to stray visitors wandering through the halls of the Capitol, comprises the following texts: the *Declaration of Independence*, 1776; *The Federalist*, 1788; *Democracy in America*, by Alexis de Tocqueville, 1835–40; *The Effective Executive*, by Peter F. Drucker (Harper & Row 1966; reissued by Harper Business 1993); *Washington: The Indispensable Man*, by James T. Flexner (Little, Brown 1974; reissued 1994); *Leadership and the Computer*, by Mary E. Boone (Prima Publishing 1991; reissued 1994); *Creating a New Civilization: The Politics of the Third Wave*, by Alvin and Heidi Toffler (with a foreword by Gingrich and published by the Progress and Freedom Foundation 1994), *Working Without a Net: How to Survive & Thrive in Today's High Risk Business World*, by Morris R. Shechtman (Prentice Hall 1994).

clean shirts and station wagons seem more in line with what America is all about than long hair and motorcycles. The rebellious impulse might remain as strong as it once was, and so might the anarchic turn of phrase, but the terms of what in the 1960s were known as "nonnegotiable demands" now tend to express the certainties of the established order and the doctrines of the bottom line. The partisans of the conservative cause retain their faith in the romance of natural man, but having learned to appreciate the wisdom of Adam Smith, they recant their loyalty to Rousseau and announce a program of liberating capitalism instead of liberating consciousness. In the Republican remake of Jack Kerouac's *On the Road*, the rebellious pilgrims travel west as an embassy of computer salesmen, and instead of looking for Judy Collins in the hotel bar, they order up *Romancing Sarah* from the hotel library of adult films.

But to whom do they then direct their protests, and what names do they put on their placards and cast like stones into the teeth of time? How do they organize the sullen draft of their hastily recruited enemies into coherent legions and simple slogans?

As so often in moments of rhetorical crisis, it was the belligerent Gingrich who answered the questions with the phrase "discredited liberal establishment," which connoted both the absence of virtue and the presence of a monolith not unlike the old Soviet Union. Understood as a conspiracy of dunces, the "discredited liberal establishment" could be held responsible for all the mistakes that had been made with the planning of the American Eden. It was the "discredited liberal establishment" that opened the Pandora's box out of which sprang the three evil spirits that wrecked the economic and spiritual environment. As follows:

The Welfare State

To hear the story told on the fairways of the nation's better golf courses, the American welfare state is a foreign country that resembles Rwanda or Chiapas. Although administered as a protectorate by the US government and supplied with an ungodly sum of money, the metaphysical terrain is so harsh, and the moral climate so poor, that we can never rescue the place, and we would all be better off if we just withdrew our army of Harvard sociologists and let the local rulers sign a treaty with the Baptist Church. If the line of argument is familiar, it is because it so closely parallels the argument advanced by the radical sixties Left in opposition to the Vietnam War. Why continue to underwrite an expensive and futile expedition doomed to certain failure?

The blurring of the distinctions between crime and race and moral behavior plays to the prejudice of an audience eager to believe the worst that can be said of people whom they would rather not know, and to the extent that the word "poor" can be made to serve as a synonym for "black," the big-city slums become alien nations on the wrong side of the cultural and economic frontiers. Gingrich is especially skillful at conveying his point in the unspoken subtext, and during last year's election campaign he often summarized the nation's troubles in a single sentence made to the measure of the six o'clock news: "It is impossible to maintain civilization with twelve-year-olds having babies, fifteen-year-olds killing each other, seventeen-year-olds dying of AIDS, and eighteen-year-olds receiving diplomas they cannot read."

What he had in mind (and what his audiences knew he had in mind) was the desolation of Harlem or East Los Angeles. Taking a similar approach in his inaugural remarks as Speaker of the House, Gingrich only once used the word "black"—in reference to the Black Caucus. He talked about little children found in Dumpsters, or thrown off the roofs of Chicago housing projects, or buried at the age of eleven with their teddy bears, but he avoided mentioning the race of the deceased. Instead of saying that their suffering might be alleviated by the acts of government (or that maybe the mechanics of finance capitalism had something to do with the buried teddy bears), he remanded the obligation to Christian charity and appealed to his fellow politicians to take heed of the parable of the good Samaritan.

The referral is standard procedure among the apologists for the Republican Right. William Bennett, author of the best-selling compendium of uplifting anecdote *The Book of Virtues*, seldom misses an opportunity to suggest that the moral pestilence in the society rises like fog in the urban slums: "During the last three decades a lot has gone wrong in America. Our society is far more violent and vulgar than it used to be. We have experienced enormous increases in violent crime, out-of-wedlock births, abortions, divorces, suicides, child abuse and welfare dependency. The answer to much of what ails us is spiritual and moral regeneration."

Applying the same kind of sophism to the questions of intelligence, Murray and Herrnstein's book *The Bell Curve* argues that the excessive number of crimes committed by black people, as well as their poverty and lack of employment, can be attributed, more or less directly, to their low I.Q. ratings. The pseudoscientific speculation adds a few more brush strokes to the standard portrait of black people as synonyms for catastrophe. The image deletes the greater part of the black presence in the country—the rise of the black middle class over the last thirty years, the success achieved under the rules of affirmative action, the real ratios between impoverished white and black people (two white to one black), the dramatis personae appearing in television situation comedies, the complexion of the United States Army—but it is an image that serves the plotlines of a bedtime story about the wages of sin.[4] As conditions in the slums deteriorate, which they inevitably must as a consequence of their designation as enemy countries, the slums come to look just the way they are supposed to look in the suburban imagination. The burned-out buildings and the number of dead in the streets support the notion that crimes allied with poverty can be classified as individual moral problems rather than a common political problem. At long last and with a clear conscience, the governing and possessing classes can comfort themselves with the thought that poor people deserve what they get, that their misery is nobody's fault but their own. The bleak prospect confirms the Republican faith in prisons and serves as an excuse for imposing de facto martial law on a citizenry construed as a dangerous rabble. Even the sunniest neoconservative optimisms carry the threat of stern punishment, and the tone of the intolerant scold that appears in the speeches of Gingrich and Bennett (as well as those of Irving Kristol, Charles Krauthammer and Michael Novak) has been most succinctly expressed by *Washington Times* columnist Cal Thomas: "If we will not be constrained from within by the power of God, we must be constrained from without by the power of the State, acting as God's agent."

The Liberal News Media

Among the partisans of the populist and suburban Right, no article of faith is more devoutly held than the one about the feral cynicism of the metropolitan news media. Although nobody at the mall ever can remember seeing a journalist who didn't look like the boy or girl next door, the crowd sitting around the tables in the food court likes to think that the news comes to them from sallow-faced Leftists who cut up the wholesome American moral fabric into patches of socialist propaganda and strips of pornographic film.

---

[4] In the proposal submitted to prospective publishers of *The Bell Curve*, Murray didn't mince words about the bigotry that he meant to confirm and sustain. "[There are] a huge number of well-meaning whites who fear that they are closet racists, and this book tells them they are not. It's going to make them feel better about things they already think but do not know how to say."

The supposition bears comparison to Jane Fonda's belief in the innocence of Ho Chi Minh. The manufacture and sale of the nation's news is the work of very large, very rich and very timid corporations—the Washington Post Co., Fox Broadcasting and Turner Network Television. The managers of the commercial television networks, like the publishers of large and prosperous newspapers, define news as anything that turns a profit, no matter how indecent the photograph or how inane the speeches and they seldom take chances with any line of thought that fails to agree with what their audiences wish to see and hear.

The *Wall Street Journal*, probably the most widely read newspaper in the country, heavily favors the conservative side on any and all questions of public policy, and both the *Washington Post* and the *New York Times* fortify their op-ed pages with columnists who strongly defend the established order—William Safire and A. M. Rosenthal in the *Times*, Charles Krauthammer, George Will and Richard Harwood in the *Post*. The vast bulk of the nation's talk-radio shows (commanding roughly 80 percent of the audience) reflect a conservative bias, and so do all but one or two of the television talk shows that deal with political topics on PBS, CNN and CNBC.

Among the smaller journals of opinion, the presiding sentiment is even more bluntly conservative, a state of affairs that didn't come to pass by accident. As long ago as 1972, the corporations began to worry about the number of longhaired hippies attending Grateful Dead concerts and George McGovern rallies, and a cadre of Rightist philanthropic foundations (among them Olin, Smith Richardson, Lilly and Scaife) set about the task of cornering the market in ideas. The allegiance to their preferred worldview as well as to their financial patronage shapes the socio-economic debate presented in the pages of *National Review, Commentary, Chronicles of Culture, The American Spectator, National Interest, The New Criterion, The Public Interest, Policy Review*, and so on. On the nation's lecture circuit the voices of conscience that attract the biggest crowds and command the highest fees (George Will, Gordon Liddy, Safire, et al.) all speak for one or another of the parties of the Right. Augmenting the instruments of the nominally secular media, the chorus of religious broadcasts and pamphlets (among them Pat Robertson's *700 Club* and the publications under the direction of the Reverent Sun Myung Moon), as well as the direct-mail propaganda mills run by Right-wing polemicists on the order of Richard Viguerie, envelops the country in a continuous din of stereophonic conservative sound.

As proof of the absurdity implicit in the complaint about the liberal news media, I can think of no better demonstration than the one offered by Rush Limbaugh to the C-Span cameras in mid December of last year at the Radisson Hotel in Baltimore. Ripe with self-congratulation and glistening under the lights like a Las Vegas lounge comic, Limbaugh appeared as the principal banquet speaker before an audience of newly elected Republican congressmen attending a three day conference organized by the Heritage Foundation and meant to acquaint them with their tasks as saviors of the Republic. Eager and young and as freshly scrubbed as a cohort of college fraternity pledges, they laughed on cue at Limbaugh's sniggering jokes about President Clinton, condoms and mushy-headed liberals. Limbaugh told them that in Washington they would find themselves surrounded on all sides by enemies, by newspaper columnists and anchor persons as treacherous as Cokie Roberts, who would cajole them with flattery and then betray them for the price of a cheap headline. "You are going to be hated," Limbaugh said. "Remember that you are targets. Remain hostile."

After twelve years of the administration of Presidents Reagan and Bush, and two years of the neo-Republican presidency of Bill Clinton, the notion of Washington as a city somehow hostile to political conservatives of any kind was as preposterous as Limbaugh's posing as a victim of liberal tyranny and persecution. The spectacle of his overstuffed pretension brought to mind the sight of Norman Mailer on various occasions in the late 1960s in New York and Washington presenting himself as a victim of fascist censorship and repression before a crowd of self-proclaimed freedom fighters wearing stylish ammunition belts from Saks Fifth Avenue. Like Mailer, Limbaugh was a best-selling author who knew how to provide copy to the credulous news media—two toy revolutionaries playing the part of Caliban, adjusting the grimace of their fright masks to reflect the seasonal fear of the prosperous middle class. During the same week that Limbaugh exhorted the faithful in Baltimore to defy the foul friend of the liberal press, he was appearing as celebrity shill in television advertisements for the *New York Times*.

The Marble Ruin of American Civilization

The last of the dearly beloved tales told around the campfires of the reactionary Right is the one about the once sacred temples of American art and political philosophy turned into pornographic movie theaters by the same crew of guitarists and literary critics that poisoned the pure stream of Republican economic thought. The story has so many variants and inflections that it is hard to fix the precise tone of indignation (sometimes choleric, sometimes wistful or smug), but it invariably entails the assigning of subversive motives to the universities, the Hollywood movie companies, the popular-music business, the publishing industry, the Broadway stage and the aforesaid liberal news media. Although the bad news sometimes takes grandiose forms—Irving Kristol informing the guests at conservative banquets that rock and roll music presents a greater threat to Western civilization than world communism—for the most part it comes down to a complaint about a cheapened sense of aesthetics and school curricula debased by trendy (that is Leftist) political alloys. Instead of reading Chaucer, students read the works of minor African poets; instead of going to see Shakespeare's plays, they gape at the sins of the flesh paraded through the courtyard of *Melrose Place*.

Again, as with so many of the other excited announcements emanating from the press offices of the Right, the facts of the matter have been suborned by the preferred image. The mournful defenders of classical learning and Renaissance humanism ignore the point that the United States makes business its culture and its culture a business. Art is what sells, and education is what draws a paying crowd. Americans go to school to improve their lot, to study the arts of getting ahead in the world, to acquire the keys to the commercial kingdom stocked with the material blessings that constitute our society's highest and most heavenly rewards. The objectives conform to the popular as opposed to the privileged understanding of democracy. As Americans, we make the heroic attempt to educate all our citizens, to provide as many people with as many opportunities as possible, to do for our children what we couldn't do for ourselves. Because the schools serve a political idea (as opposed to an intellectual idea), they cannot afford to make invidious comparisons between the smart kids and the dumb kids, between the kids who read Montaigne's essays and those who read Spider-Man comics, and contrary to the failing report cards issued by people like Allan Bloom, it isn't necessary to know much about the liberal arts to make a success of an American life. Children learn by example as well as by precept, and they have only to look at Times Square and Disneyland, or consider the triumphs of Roseanne or Ronald Perlman, to know that society bestows is rewards on the talent for figuring a market, not on a knowledge of Thucydides.

Nor is the popular culture by any means as immoral as it is dreamed of in the philosophy of the academic deans on the neoconservative and

Christian Right. As measured by its lists of best-selling books and long-running Broadway plays, as well as by its successful television comedies, sporting events and popular songs, the American cultural enterprise (in 1995 as in 1895) is as irremediably conservative as it is relentlessly sentimental. During any Sunday's playing of the Top 40, the rap songs and heavy-metal rhythms show up at the bottom of the list, but as the countdown proceeds upward toward a kindly and forgiving providence, the music turns increasingly sweet and melodic. The lyrics almost always affirm the wisdom of a Rod McKuen poem or a speech by Peggy Noonan: love will last forever; our love will never die; you are the only one; my love for you is like a thousand points of light. The same moral teaching informs ninety-eight of every hundred situation comedies that last more than three weeks on primetime television. To watch *Home Improvement* or *The Simpsons* is to know that virtue triumphs, that love conquers all and that in this best-of-all-possible American worlds, victory is always close at hand and children never starve.

In which of the country's leading newspapers does the editorial page defend adultery as a civil liberty or advance the social program of the Marquis de Sade? A study published last October by the National Opinion Research Center at the University of Chicago showed the American people to be astonishingly monogamous, and the moral attitudes governing the rules of sexual conduct at most of the nation's universities more nearly resemble the ones in effect in Victorian England than those on display in ancient Babylon or late eighteenth-century France. Notwithstanding the proliferation of peep shows made for cable television, we remain a deeply conservative, almost prudish, people, and sex, like art, most fetchingly presents itself as commercial advertisement (to hustle the business or move the product), not as an invitation to a waltz.[5]

When listening to people describe the marble ruin of American civilization (as if it were something seen in a Piranesi drawing or a Louisiana mangrove swamp), I'm always struck by the lack of a historical sense on the part of the tellers of the tale. Lately, I've been gathering research material for a book that touches upon the American condition in the eighteenth and nineteenth centuries, and it's fair to say that the university curricula were always debased and the natives always restless. The

---

[5] The BBC produces two variants of the television drawing-room comedies that venture upon sexual subjects—an unexpurgated version for the British audience and a bowdlerized version for export to the more easily offended American market.

incidence of crime in New York City in the 1870s or on the Texas frontier in the 1840s defined itself as a statistical ratio surpassing the percentages now being reported by the FBI. The divorce rates in colonial America exceeded those of the present day, and in 1905 the immigrant swarm on Manhattan's Lower East Side measured its density at 1,000 people per acre, a ratio that dwarfed the crowding in the slums of Bombay. On no less of an authority than that of Jonathan Edwards, God abandoned the American forest in the winter of 1719, and throughout most of the nineteenth century, prior to the advent of the media circus and Clint Eastwood movies, Americans attended public hangings and the freak shows mounted by impresarios on the order of P. T. Barnum.

At the presumably higher elevations of culture, the air was always thick with Christian piety and bourgeois sentiment. Herman Melville was condemned to obscurity, Mark Twain was obliged to present himself as an amiable clown and Edith Wharton, together with Henry James and Ezra Pound, left for Europe. The joke about the marble ruin is that American civilization never was much of a match for Periclean Greece. When the tellers of the sad Republican tale agree to take questions on the subject (reluctantly and usually in a hurry to leave the lecture hall), it turns out that the lost culture for which they grieve is the culture best expressed by the sensibility of the 1950s, the musical comedies of Rodgers and Hammerstein, the history of the world as told by Disney and Time Life, the list of great books that everybody owns but nobody has read.

Hoisted up by the cranes of populist bombast to the platforms of great expectation, the newly enskied 104th Congress confronts an ancient problem in socioeconomics—how does a wealthy and increasingly nervous plutocracy preserve its privileges while at the same time maintaining its reputation as an oppressed minority and a noble cause? The answer is never easy, but the *soi-disant* anarchists of the 1990s reactionary Right come poorly equipped for the task of making good on their promises. Just as the mock insurgents of the 1960s staged their masques and dances against a backdrop of cardboard scenery, the rebels of the 1990s shape their morality play from images they have seen on television and abstractions they have discovered in books written by their friends and former economics professors. Their delight in theory and ignorance of history saps them of the strength to answer their own call to arms.

What they have in hand is a dissenting rhetoric best suited to cries from the wilderness, a feeling for nostalgia, a faith in the claptrap futurism of

Alvin and Heidi Toffler, the dubious economic theory inherited from the early days of the Reagan revolution and an instinct for repression. Although convenient to pop quizzes and the nightly television news, the syllabus of glib answers bears comparison to the secrets of the universe packaged for sale in the supermarket press, and it isn't likely to prepare the class for the midterm examination. The electorate last fall was saying something about its fear and uneasiness, about jobs being sent overseas and the future (their own and that of their children) beginning to look like the receding objects seen through the wrong end of a telescope. For the last ten or fifteen years, the parties of the Right have managed to convert the emotions rooted in economic anxiety into the politics of cultural anxiety, substituting the questions of moral conduct and deportment (the marble ruin, the heathen poor) for the more intractable ones about the division of the national spoils.

But the act is getting harder to perform, and the audience in the first ten rows has begun to figure out the trick with the coins and the scarves. Let the interest rate continue to rise, and who will applaud the futurist cant ("Parallel Transformations!" "Paradigms!" "Quality Management!") so dear to the heart of Speaker Gingrich? Let the chimera of a balanced budget drift off into the haze of what Washington calls "the out years," and people might begin to notice the difference between the big print and the small print in the Contract With America.

The paragraphs in large print postulate a return to an imaginary time and place in which the work of government could be performed by a volunteer fire department—a few hardy fellows cleaning up the village green after a winter storm, a benign judge adjudicating the occasional land dispute or divorce proceeding, a friendly county official awarding the rights of way for five hundred miles of railroad track in Kansas. The provisions in small print grant the propertied classes the freedom to acquire more property—a freedom expressed, among other ways, in the form of capital-gains tax breaks in the amount of $25 billion a year—and for everybody else, more police and more sermons.

Whether dressed up as a radical or reactionary chic, the striking of revolutionary poses doesn't fit very well with necessarily bureaucratic forms of government. Norman Mailer once ran for the office of mayor of New York City, and I expect that he was glad to lose the election. Maybe I underestimate the talents of the 104th Congress, and maybe the new season's band of guerrillas will figure out a way to play at revolution without the slightest risk of damage to their automobiles or their bond portfolios. But I admit that I am curious to see Speaker Gingrich presenting his formulation of "New Hope!" "New Dialogue!" "New Access!" to a crowd of bankrupt farmers, or expounding for the benefit of five hundred unemployed textile-machine operators the theory of limitless wealth revealed to Adam Smith and Pitt the Younger in the workshop of the Napoleonic Wars. And if for some reason the mood in the hall should turn ugly, I can imagine the Speaker losing his temper and reverting to type as Gingrich the belligerent, sacker of shibboleths, and I like to think of him defying the storm of insults, shouting into the microphones, calling down on the heads of his enemies the terrible maxims of Voltaire, reminding them that the comfort of the rich rests upon an abundant supply of the poor.

March 1995

Index